CULTURAL HISTORIES OF CINEMA

This new book series examines the relationship between cinema and culture. It will feature interdisciplinary scholarship that focuses on the national and transnational trajectories of cinema as a network of institutions, representations, practices and technologies. Of primary concern is analysing cinema's expansive role in the complex social, economic and political dynamics of the twentieth and twenty-first centuries.

SERIES EDITORS
Lee Grieveson and Haidee Wasson

ALSO PUBLISHED
Cinema Beyond Territory: Inflight Entertainment and
Atmospheres of Globalisation, *Stephen Groening*
Empire and Film, *edited by Lee Grieveson and Colin MacCabe*
Film and the End of Empire, *edited by Lee Grieveson and Colin MacCabe*
George Kleine and American Cinema: The Movie Business and Film Culture
in the Silent Era, *Joel Frykholm*
Global Mexican Cinema: Its Golden Age, *Robert McKee Irwin and Maricruz Castro
Ricalde (with Mónica Szurmuk, Inmaculada Álvarez and Dubravka Sužnjević)*
The Grierson Effect: Tracing Documentary's International Movement,
edited by Zoë Druick and Deane Williams
Making Movies into Art: Picture Craft from the Magic Lantern to Early Hollywood,
Kaveh Askari
Shadow Economies of Cinema: Mapping Informal Film Distribution, *Ramon Lobato*

Arab Cinema Travels

Transnational Syria, Palestine, Dubai and Beyond

Kay Dickinson

●

A BFI book published by Palgrave

First published in 2016 by
PALGRAVE

on behalf of the

BRITISH FILM INSTITUTE
21 Stephen Street, London W1T 1LN
www.bfi.org.uk

There's more to discover about film and television through the BFI. Our world-renowned archive, cinemas, festivals, films, publications and learning resources are here to inspire you.

PALGRAVE in the UK is an imprint of Macmillan Publishers Limited, registered in England, company number 785998, of 4 Crinan Street, London N1 9XW. Palgrave Macmillan in the US is a division of St Martin's Press LLC, 175 Fifth Avenue, New York, NY 10010. Palgrave is a global imprint of the above companies and is represented throughout the world. Palgrave® and Macmillan® are registered trademarks in the United States, the United Kingdom, Europe and other countries.

Cover image © Michele Occelli

Set by Cambrian Typesetters, Camberley, Surrey
Printed in China

This book is printed on paper suitable for recycling and made from fully managed and sustained forest sources. Logging, pulping and manufacturing processes are expected to conform to the environmental regulations of the country of origin.
British Library Cataloguing-in-Publication Data
A catalogue record for this book is available from the British Library
A catalog record for this book is available from the Library of Congress

ISBN 978-1–84457–784–2 (pb)
ISBN 978-1–84457–785–9 (hb)

Contents

Acknowledgments

The long journey towards *Arab Cinema Travels'* completion was sadly marked at each end by the loss of very dear people without whom this book could not exist. Gillian Robb passed away as I set off into this project. She was the first person to open my eyes to Arab cinema and a role model for how to think through and act on the privilege and distance of typical ex-patriot life. My father, Bill Dickinson, left us just before I finished the manuscript. If his compulsory schooling ended aged fourteen, playing hooky to read and sneak into the cinema was his real education. I would not be here without him, not physically, nor intellectually. These personal losses join the catastrophic tragedies that have befallen the Arab region as I laboured to write about it. This book honours, as best it can, all those who have lost their lives, families, friends and homes in the struggle for freedom: those who helped me write it; the countless more whom I have never met.

Three chapters of this book turn on research conducted in the countries that are their subjects. My studies would not have been possible without the guidance and support of various individuals, especially the film-makers and festival personnel who kindly consented to lengthy interviews. As the years have passed, these friends may no longer live in the countries to which I now attribute them. I will nonetheless wishfully group them there in contravention of current geopolitics and obstructed return. For help in Syria, my thanks go to Ammar Alani, Nidal al-Debs, Nabil al-Maleh, Mohammad Attar, Donatella Della Ratta, Rania Joha, Mohammad Malas, Joud Said, Riad Shaya and Salim Turkomani, along with (outside Syria's borders) Rasha Salti and everyone at ArteEast, Ashkal Alwan and Beirut DC for augmenting the corpus of rare films to which Chapter 2 is devoted. My research into Palestinian cinema is indebted to Nahed Awwad, Nick Denes, Reem Fadda, Sandi Hilal, Annemarie Jacir, Rashid Masharawi, Enas Muthaffar, Alessandro Petti, Nida Sinnokrot, Mohanad Yaqubi and Khalid Ziada. And the chapter discussing film culture in Dubai benefited enormously from the input of Julie Archer, Antonia Carver, Ayesha Chagla, Rima Nazer, Shivani Pandya, Majid Wasi, Jane Williams and Ziad Yaghi. Financial assistance for these trips came courtesy of the Council for British Research in the Levant and the University of London Central Research Fund.

I test ran elements of this book at various academic fora and gained substantially from insightful comments and questions proffered after presentations at the universities of Concordia, Cornell, East Anglia, Edinburgh, Manchester, Michigan State, NYU, Pennsylvania, SOAS, St Andrews, UC Santa Cruz, Wayne State and

Westminster, as well as the British Institute in Amman. A year-long fellowship at the Cornell University's Society for the Humanities afforded this project rich interdisciplinary input and appraisal, along with treasured new friendships. Thanks to the entire Global Aesthetics group for their engagement with my work, and particularly Joshua Clover, James McHugh and Shawkat Toorawa for reading and contributing further while I was in Ithaca. The most comprehensive trialling of these ideas has taken place, however, in classrooms. The students enrolled in Concordia's 'Arab Cinemas' and 'Arab Revolutions' courses, as well as my consistently motivating doctoral students, past and present, have shaped this endeavour in no small part.

The profoundly collaborative process that is writing a book (especially a book on travel) provokes me to acknowledge a host of co-authors who have guided and sustained me along the way. Gratitude I cannot begin to properly ascribe goes here to Mark Betz, Jodi Brooks, Elizabeth Cowie, Michelle Cho, Therese Davis, Christine Dickinson, Denis Echard, Sabine El Chamaa, Yuriko Furuhata, Terri Ginsberg, Elena Gorfinkel, Iman Hamam, Laleh Khalili, Lina Khatib, Donna Landry, Michael Lawrence, Peter Limbrick, Jo Littler, Gerald Maclean, Aoife Mac Namara, David Martin-Jones, Laura Mulvey, Joshua Neves, Michele Occelli (not least for his central contribution to another cover), Kamran Rastegar, John David Rhodes, Adrian Rifkin, Tarik Sabry, Viviane Saglier, Marc Steinberg, Hanan Toukan, Anastasia Valassopoulos, Belén Vidal, Leon Wainwright and Haidee Wasson. I am also exceedingly grateful to everyone who has ever tried to teach me Arabic, particularly Ahmad Alkhashem, Lucy Collard, Luay Mohammed, Paul Robertson and Wassim Wagdy. Petra Abousleiman and Abdulhadi Ayyad I thank for their help with some thornier elements of translation. Sophie Contento, Lucy Knight, Jenna Steventon and Joy Tucker at BFI Publishing/Palgrave (as well as many other people involved in the production process whom I do not know) expertly shepherded this manuscript from word document to printed form.

Hashem Alshaer I met as a Palestinian in Damascus, thought I had lost in the aftermath of 2011 until we reacquainted as I waited for a Heathrow flight to Dubai, where he had since settled. He is the trajectory of this book in more than a geographical sense. Adam Laschinger I have to thank for accompanying me through far too many Syrian lateral tracking shots (spectatorial, topographical and academic) and for imparting his daily experience of the film industry. Hospitality remains a constant theme within this book and a near-daily delight of my friendship with Luca Caminati and Masha Salazkina. Their ready and constant involvement with this project is one small, but meaningful way in which they have made me feel so at home in Montreal. Glyn Davis, again, came through like the true friend he is, the first person to read this whole book in order. I hope I have done justice to his perceptive suggestions. I do not know what I would have done without Lee Grieveson's incisiveness, rigour and stamina throughout, for all the conversations which disassembled that into absurdity. My sofa misses him.

And, finally, this book's completion was urgently and joyfully disrupted by actions shared as a member of the Precarious Workers Brigade and the library and Whitehead Building occupations at Goldsmiths. I cannot thank you individually; it is from our anonymity and collectivity that I draw the most strength.

Elements of Chapters 2 and 3 were first developed in the following articles, and I am very much obliged to their publishers for permitting me to reproduce sections here:

'The Palestinian Road (Block) Movie: Everyday Geographies of Second Intifada Filmmaking', in Dina Iordanova, David Martin-Jones and Belén Vidal (eds), *Cinema at the Periphery* (Detroit: Wayne State University Press, 2010), pp. 201–27.
'The State of Labor and Labor for the State: Syrian and Egyptian Cinema beyond the 2011 Uprisings', *Framework* vol. 53 no. 1 (2012), pp. 99–116.
'Syrian Cinema: Out of Time?', *Screening the Past* vol. 31 (September 2012).

Setting Off

Stark, searing shots of the Iraqi desert open *The Dupes* (Tawfiq Saleh, 1972).[1] As credits emerge and fade, it becomes more and more apparent that the once-indistinguishable bumps in the foreground are, in fact, a human skeleton. To understand these remains, the film flashes back to the journey (or an equivalent) that has left them there. Three Palestinian refugees make their way to Basra in Iraq in order to place themselves at the mercy of people traffickers. Desperate to stave off the poverty wreaked by expulsion from their homeland by incoming Israeli settlers, they come seeking a share of the Gulf's then new-found oil wealth. Without official work permits, they must be smuggled over the border into Kuwait, a route that has counted significant casualties, frequently fatal, given the blistering heat that these hopefuls must endure on foot, or, in the case of these three protagonists, hidden within a baking, suffocating water truck.

Off-screen, comparable journeys have brought *The Dupes* to fruition. The film was based on Ghassan Kanafani's 1962 novella, *Men in the Sun*, the author born in and then exiled from Palestine to, first, Lebanon, then Syria. By the early 1950s, as a student at Damascus University, his pan-Arabist political affiliations saw him driven out of Syria to Kuwait. In 1960, he relocated back to Beirut, where he died the victim of a car bomb

The Dupes (1972): opening credits

(presumed to be planted by the Israeli secret police, Mossad) in 1972, the same year *The Dupes* was released. Similarly, and necessarily, itinerant was the film's director. Born of a Palestinian mother and Egyptian father, Tawfiq Saleh spent his early years on the road in Egypt, his father a doctor in charge of quarantining within the country. After a period in France on an educational scholarship, Saleh made a name for himself as one of the most talented and politicised movie directors of Nasser (Gamal 'Abd al-Nasr)'s postcolonial Egypt. Buffeted by prejudicial in-fighting within Egypt's newly nationalised cinema sector, Saleh eagerly accepted an invitation to shoot *The Dupes* in Syria and Iraq, under the aegis of Syria's National Film Organization, the subject of this book's second chapter. Although the movie suffered a limited, censorial release in Syria, and none at all in Egypt, it fared well in Tunisia, where it won the Tanit d'Or at the Carthage Festival, moving on to the Moscow Film Festival, here receiving the Lenin Peace Award. Before eventually returning to Egypt, where he died, Saleh spent a period working in the Iraqi film industry.[2]

Given this pedigree, Nadia Yaqub, a scholar of Arab visual culture, does not surprise when she pronounces, 'It is difficult to place *The Dupes* within the national film industries of Arab cinema.'[3] Viola Shafik gives a more historically grounded rationale, naming the film, 'a Pan-Arab production par excellence ... one of the first to give Pan-Arab slogans a more solid base and to state the common responsibility of the Arab states for the disastrous situation of the Palestinians'.[4] The journey *The Dupes* embarks upon to do so sets the pattern for a third, undertaken more than forty years later, the one which provides this book's structure: production is organised through Syria; Palestine becomes an object of representation, often symbolic of something much greater; and the Gulf lures in through its promises of wealth. These coordinates are set by and help establish a particular, central and often seemingly static geopolitical configuration ('the Arab world'), ballasted by accountability, financing and solidarity, fundamentally shaped by the movement of people, goods, ideas and cultures (including those of cinema) across the region. Outside it as well. Just as Saleh fetched up in France for his education, so the population of this monograph make any number of international journeys, for all sorts of reasons, out of free will or otherwise. It is only through movements between these intricate, ever-shifting coordinates that something called Arab cinema comes into being. Registering the consistencies and changes of each of these voyages through time and space proffers a different, more comprehensive perspective on cinema than any based on a staid nation-state-based modelling. My arguments pivot on 'Syria', 'Palestine' and 'the Gulf' being understood as international constructs established through travel.

I could have headed down pathways like 'the global' or 'the transnational' to figure contexts like these, and most certainly do draw on those theoretical paradigms in what follows. However, focusing on travel offers something further. It opens us out to the actual experience of moving through, as well as perceiving and reconfiguring, space: the deadly expeditions across a desert in search of livelihood, the image thereof shunned in Syria, but lauded in Tunisia and the USSR. Travel is typically purposeful, as the examples above attest, thus bringing questions of motive into the frame too. The impact of these rationales is more readily noticed if we group together a broad range of travel practices – not just migration – those undertaken by the whole gamut of social classes and commodities, including academic researchers. With the imperative to register this complexity at the helm, my conceptualisation of travel for this book is as inclusive as possible. It has an eye to understanding the associations triggered by, yes, forced exile, population transferral, indeterminate statelessness and transit, as well as labour migration (from highly skilled and legal to those of shadow economies). But it also takes in the implications of adventuring and exploration, travel for expertise acquisition and politico-cultural exchange, pilgrimage, everyday travel to work, to visit one's family and the like (and its impossibility in certain situations), and trips made by tourists. Within all this human movement, I consider the concomitant circulation of goods, particularly films, regulated by national and transnational legislation, as well as by taste brokers such as festival programmers, buyers, critics and audiences.[5] All of these types of movement, I argue, are much more closely linked than they initially appear to be and it is therefore politically vital that we acknowledge their inter-dependency.

In 'The Cinematic Tourist: Perception and Subjectivity', one of the surprisingly few (and brief) articles to consider cinema in relation to travel, Bronwyn Morkham and Russell Staiff observe that:

> travel is configured into the very heart of (Western) representation ... to read a book, see a film, look at a painting or follow a map is to travel somewhere ... By assuming a shared visual culture for cinema and tourism – both activities, for example, involve spectatorship – it is possible to consider cinema and tourism as inter-related contemporary experiences that share crucial dynamics and processes in the subject's quest for meaning making.[6]

I would like to add that displacement, distance and proximity are also all spring-loaded with their own geopolitical charges in books, cinema and travel alike. Yet shared ground between the experience of travel, its literary accounts and its shaping of cinema is the least of it. Cultural cachet, ambience and implication hover over and implant themselves into physical locations, endowing actual space with represen-tation's magnetism. For sociologist Chris Rojek, 'Cinematic events are dragged on to the physical landscape and the physical landscape is then reinterpreted in terms of the cinematic events.'[7] The somewheres and elsewheres are historically complicated and not necessarily entirely spatial, although definitely that too. And the traffic is clearly two way, allowing cinema to pose vital questions about how the politics and economics of travel shape human subjectivity, its environment and, therefore, cultural expression.

Moving on from Morkham and Staiff's proposition about the mutual imprint upon books and films, *Arab Cinema Travels* aims to invite these modes into prolonged, sometimes dialectical, conversation. Literary adaptation is a particularly convenient departure point. *The Dupes* faithfully overlaps with *Men in the Sun*; it cannot capture the sum total of the novella, obviously, but does, simultaneously, add pertinent commentary all its own. Although the film, quite uncommonly for cinema, choses to rearticulate the bulk of the novella's internal monologues and inward emotions through voiceover, one significant sentiment is left out. As the green teenaged Marwan, the youngest of the lead characters, walks away from a smuggler he perceives to be hoodwinking him and out into the alien streets of Basra, a strange feeling overtakes him:

He wanted to know the reason for that remote sensation that gave him contentment and rest; a sensation like the one he used to have when he had finished watching a film, and felt that life was grand and vast, and that in the future he would be one of those men who spend every hour and day of their lives in exciting fulfilment and variety. But what was the reason for his having such a feeling now, when he had not seen a film like that for a long time, and only a few minutes before the threads of hope that had woven fine dreams in his heart had been broken in the fat man's shop?[8]

Kanafani leaves the reason for Marwan's bewilderment hanging for over a page. In my narrative, I will preserve the same revelation for this book's very last ones. As we wait for resolution, the logical conclusion is that, through transplanting himself far from familiar surroundings, becoming master of his own destiny, travel has fulfilled the same potential that cinema offers.

As valuable studies like Ellen Strain's *Public Places, Private Journeys: Ethnography, Entertainment, and the Tourist Gaze* and Dimitris Eleftheriotis' *Cinematic Journeys: Film and Movement* elaborate in greater detail, movies frequently aim to transport us, to depart from daily life, to take us on a narrative journey. Both travel and cinema encourage a delicate teetering between 'here' and 'there'. How close do we get, and to what? Cinema can certainly replicate a more touristic 'scenic overlook' (Lucy Lippard's term): a ready-made image of the world, set at a convenient remove, which confirms what we had expected to see all along.[9] We might demand strangeness, familiarity or a comfortable balance of both, but at whose expense? Cinema also vigorously activates us. Note the language Tawfiq Saleh uses to state his objectives: 'I consider *The Dupes* an eminently mobilizing film ... My method consists of trying to touch people, trying to move them so as to lead them towards reflection.'[10] Whatever a film-maker's compulsion, cinema's immersive vortex typically pulls us 'out of the ordinary' and into a world that is both hegemonically allegorical and (at least for some) forthrightly real.

This balance between fiction and fact is urgently tackled by *The Dupes*, achieved through techniques impossible to *Men in the Sun*. To add verisimilitude to the story it narrates, to propel its urgent messages about the perils of criminalised migration into the concrete realities of the spectatorial experience, the film weaves in documentary registers. As Abu Qais, the oldest of the protagonists, ruminates on the hardships and humiliations of exile, scenes from his former life on his farm are interposed with news footage showing barbed wire, army checkpoints, queues for food handouts, the refugee camps. Live action later makes way, instead, for static photojournalistic images of failed international negotiations for Palestinians to return to their homeland. Leaders meet and debates ensue at the United Nations while Abu Qais makes his decision to risk all in a migration to the Gulf. Still imagery underscores a stasis in politics and refugee repatriation.

The compulsion to deal in fact necessarily binds us to the unjust realities of a world in motion. To respond with a parallel gesture that will hopefully add weight to my contention that travel is a crucial topic to consider in any cultural arena, I turn to Nikos Papastergiadis' claim that, at the beginning of this millennium, there were:

over 100 million international migrants and 27 million stateless refugees. This means that there are more people living in places that are outside their homeland than at any previous

The Dupes (1972): one of a volley of still journalistic images depicting refugee life

point in history. The turbulence of migration is not only evident in the sheer volume of migrants, but also by the emergence of new subjects, communication networks and forms of economic dependency.[11]

The sphere of travel where statistics are most reliable is inevitably its most lucrative: tourism, considered the planet's largest and fastest-growing economic sector.[12] For 2013, the United Nations World Tourism Organization reckoned that this type of travel accounted for $1.4 trillion in export earnings, 9 per cent of our collective GDP, one in eleven direct and indirect jobs, and 1,087 million international tourists (up from 25 million in 1950).[13] Tourism, quite clearly, absorbs nowhere near the sum total of expenditure on movement globally, it just happens to be one of its most financially documented manifestations. If we add to tourism the experiences and revenues afforded by other types of mobility such as labour migrations (legal, trafficked, forced) or ethnic cleansing, we can stretch Dean MacCannell's claims that '[tourism] is not just an aggregate of merely commercial activities; it is also an ideological framing of history, nature, and tradition; a framing that has the power to reshape culture and nature to its own needs' outwards to fit travel in the broader sense.[14] Given the numbers, travel surely institutes and supports how we might interact and learn about each other, based on specific, contextualised expectations that this book hopes to scrutinise and critique.

The Dupes has given us a taste of how such movements flavour (Arab) cinema and the following chapter will add historical scope through reference to travelogues stretching back centuries. Even the smallest and poorest of Arab villages, as detailed, for instance, in books like Tayeb Salih's *Season of Migration to the North* and Amitav Ghosh's *In an Antique Land: History in the Guise of a Traveler's Tale*, are populated by a cosmopolitan community that is forever leaving and returning. Just as *The Dupes* establishes a 'Palestine' fundamentally on the move through its narrative theme and the activities of its makers, the political lineages and aspirations of 'Arab' or 'Arab cinema' categorically announce an efficacious homogeneity, but one that is ultimately shaped by transnational networks and flows. This will prove the case time and time again in the examples to which this book is drawn. It is no fresh scholarly endeavour to acknowledge what a mishmash identity is. What I hope to add to this essential project is a feel for how identity is marshalled by the regimes of global capital, more particularly by its transport and communications infrastructures. Indeed, for Karl Marx, capital itself is chiefly distinguished by its facility to travel, 'distinct from direct exchange value and from money' because it *'preserves and perpetuates itself in and through circulation* [emphasis in the original]'.[15] The distances that capital spans, that it also creates, between workers, the owners of the means of production and consumers permits all kinds of alienation and exploitation that will be detailed more fully in the chapters to come.

The very same transport and communications networks created by capital and peopled by its subjects also allow films to circulate (or not) around the globe. How do film plots, film-makers and films-as-commodities move on this terrain that they also shape? With what freedom and with whose help or hindrance? If we look to the early history of global cinema, we find the Arab world populated by 'intrepid' traveloguers, exhibitors following hot on their heels, wielding film's majesty and mystique to imagine heroic mastery. Tom Gunning describes the resulting productions as 'explicit hymns to the colonial expansions of the industrialized nations. They provide searing illustrations of spectacle as appropriation, as the traditions and inhabitants of the unindustrialized world were posed for the contemplation of citizens of the modern world.'[16] How on earth, *where* on earth, are we to place and analyse 'Arab cinema' in light of this legacy of flows of manpower, mythmaking and merchandise? One primary consideration that has scarring implications for mobility: there exists an absolute paucity of Arab films available to us in everyday screening spaces across the world or with subtitles in any other language, making it highly likely that many of this book's readers will have never seen a film from, say, Kuwait or Jordan. More than half of the material I shall examine will be inaccessible to those who cannot travel to certain archives to view it or who do not understand Arabic, making accounts of travel (this time for scholarship) all the more crucial.

When Arab films do get to travel, do they subsequently become ambassadors, under-priced merchandise, rallying cries from refugees or tourist board advertisements? Their journeys become a multidimensional and complex paradigm to consider from within the power relations that dictate not only how Arab cinema is made and reaches us, but also how 'strangers' or newcomers might watch it. In turn, how do Arab films process the spaces of their displacement and to what extent might those involved in their manufacture, their funding and their promotion anticipate the repercussions? If Arab films and their makers are usually packaged up and herded round in groups – as exclusive guests when they win festival prizes or as migrant workers, say – then what terms of encounter delineate these experiences for all of us? So often, the meetings seem as ritualistic, as morally and socially ordered, as in need of prescribed 'authenticities' or 'exoticisms', symbolic and emotional markers, as the tourist event is. Just as full of prejudice, aspirations and frustrations.

Chapter 1 involves itself more painstakingly with all these questions of perspective, position, interaction and influence. Here, I shall endeavour to cross streams with and spend time learning about Arab cinema's journeys amid the broader global movements of people, objects and ideas. When travel dictates, and is so dictated by, economic factors, I cannot remain aloof within it, cannot circumscribe a bounded situation or view it from on high. Such standpoints have frequently been procured and guaranteed through imperial domination and its legacies. In *The Age of the World Target: Self-Referentiality in War, Theory, and Comparative Work*, Rey Chow goes as far as to convincingly argue how the aerial perspective provides and supports, while also replicating, the field of vision of the bomber pilot so essential to (neo-)colonial foreign policy.[17]

As an alternative, I aim to interact with Arab cinema as a particular and *classed* type of visitor moving among the elaborate and manifold transactions taking place across this 'terrain': between travelling cinema cultures, travelling scholars, travelling film-makers who perhaps also find it impossible to pin down any of the 'starting points' that allow for staid forms of academic security. Expertise via sustained geographical stability, I argue, cannot do justice to the restless movement of peoples through and across the region we might call – I have already called – 'the Arab world' (and its cinema), across the nebulous regions we might call 'here' or 'home', which may or may not be the same place. Literary explorations of the writer-as-traveller – and here there is quite some tradition of thoughtful philosophising about subjecthood and knowledge acquisition – are a gift to such analyses.

As such, Chapter 1 sets up a theoretical framework for the entire book: using travel as method and travel writing as theory. I draw particular inspiration here from Arabic travelogues (the *rihla* narrative). So much so that their priorities shape the structure of this monograph. Paramount among the reasons prompting travel within this literary canon have been the search for knowledge (explored in Chapter 2) and pilgrimage (Chapter 3).[18] I add to this an investigation of how travel has been conducted for trade (Chapter 4), a major impetus for building the transport infrastructures and diasporic communities on land and at sea that support the other two motives for travelling. Just as these voyages aim towards destinations, so too does this book. Its itinerary transposes from Syria, to Palestine, and then to Dubai. While the journey is chronological, it abides more with the *rihla*'s thematic aspirations than it aspires to be comprehensive of national or even regional developments in cinema. My reasons why will be elaborated in the very next chapter.

After that, Chapter 2 moves on to investigate Syria's state-funded, not-for-profit cinema from the 1960s until 2011. Here I find myself a scholar among scholars, taking as my point of departure the training, films and labour practices resulting from the dispatch of a group of would-be directors to institutes of learning in the Warsaw Pact states (mainly the All-Union State Institute of Cinematography [VGIK] in Moscow). The ensuing investigation draws upon a longer tradition of Arabs travelling for the purpose of study, many of whom wrote memoirs and treatises. These works stand as invaluable models for negotiating terms of encounter, difference, learning and translation that often contributed, as was also the case for Syrian study missions of the twentieth century, to a rhetoric of anticolonial national liberation. Given the geopolitical alignment that these journeys to the Eastern Bloc helped actuate, Chapter 2 investigates how travel establishes or questions influence, and how that relationship might be fostered outside capitalist definitions of property and ownership. One way was through traffic in labour rights, embodied within both how the Syrian state treated its film-maker employees and how workers were represented on screen.

Chapter 3 turns its attentions to how travel defines Palestine, its diaspora and its cinema. As a place of pilgrimage, the 'Holy Land' has resonated globally from trips, sojourns and colonisation over the millennia. During the period examined by Chapter 3, the Second Intifada (2000–c. 2005), Palestinians not only endured ongoing exile and prevention of the right of return for refugees, but the occupation of their territory was also increasingly manifest through Israel's comprehensive curtailment of movement through curfews, checkpoints, roadblocks and the erection in the West Bank of the Wall. We witness a noticeable and understandable obsession in Second Intifada cinema with road (block) movies, which chart the injustices of a foreign force inhibiting movement within their homeland, as well as the various tactics deployed to circumvent such infringements on basic liberties. Chapter 3 studies the ironic complication of this popular film genre, particularly its support of 'freedom' and 'the open road'. How are these ideas to be understood with an eye to the centrality of fuel to such adventures, to conflict in the Middle East and to western foreign policy? In what ways are overseas audiences addressed by these largely activist films and can viewers be drawn in, through the languages of popular global cinema, as fellow travellers within an international solidarity movement? In order to comprehend these associations, Chapter 3 draws, as the films themselves do, on the long history of movement in and out of the powerful 'place-myth' of Israel-Palestine: crusades and pilgrimages, certainly, but also the theoretical propositions of exiles such as Edward Said, a proponent of 'travelling theory'.

If Palestine is perennially constituted through a globally atypical ratio of residents to refugees, Dubai, the constantly traversed and reworked site of Chapter 4, is similarly characterised by migration, with an estimated 73 per cent of the United Arab Emirates' population and 89.8 per cent of its workforce hailing from overseas.[19] In its drive to establish a post-oil economy, Dubai has expanded in new directions towards the creative and knowledge sectors, while augmenting stalwarts from the pre-oil days: activities connected to sea travel, shipping and hosting itinerant merchants. If the Dubai International Film Festival, Chapter 4's focal point, seems to sit exclusively within the former, its support and organisation derive extensively from the latter. As such, this final chapter draws on a diverse body of literature dedicated to travel for trade in order to better understand how the festival interfaces with tourism, re-exporting and port logistics, all foundational to the Emirate's economy. Dubai's position as a port has also inclined it towards the establishment of multiple free zones, a number now dedicated to media output. One of these is Studio City, a film production real estate development that takes offshoring to new levels, courtesy of local legislation and policy honed to encourage and exploit migrant (now cinematic) labour.

By attending even cursorily to these kinds of queries it emerges that travel is an uneven affair riven with its own complex pecking orders. The streams of migrants, exiles, scholars, holidaymakers and media goods flow, evidently and unevenly, according to the whims of global capital, as well as in reaction to or defiance of them. From his position of imagination or privilege, the Syrian-born, Lebanon-dwelling literary theorist and poet Adonis revels in the conceptual malleability of concrete space in his poem entitled 'The Traveller': 'my map – a world I've yet to make'.[20] Yet borders and transport networks definitely stream our travels differently and, for the most part, with a diminished sense of freedom to Adonis'. Hierarchies of travel wave through my own access to various funds, and my British citizenship affords me entry to the West Bank to conduct interviews when Lebanese, Syrian or Palestinian exiles would be blocked by the Israeli authorities that control its borders. I am sanctioned to leave for the Middle East without much prior bureaucracy, often without an advance visa, journeys that are, if not impossible, then extremely arduous to arrange for most citizens of that region – of the world, in fact. At the other end of the spectrum lies the brutality of coerced exile or capture, removal and detainment, some of which has been detailed by *The Dupes*. Movements like these duck and dive the onslaught of international humanitarianism, a dexterity that any trafficker or multinational corporation will also know full well.

Social values are attributed to all the different forms of travel delineated above. Pilgrimage is a duty and blessing to many, exile a condition holding intellectual stature in certain modernist enclaves, while package tourism is abhorrent to the back-packer and labour migration a threat to the xenophobe.[21] What these divergences also open up to us, however, is a plethora of theorising on travel, much of it brand new to film scholarship, that can stimulate the critical study of these very injustices.

As I have earlier stressed, this situation necessitates us getting to grips with the subjectivities of travelling – the topic of the following chapter. In doing so, we can then properly acknowledge the instability and dislocation at the very heart of epistemology. The impossibility of the 'authentic' in touristic, scholarly and exilic-nostalgic encounters alike may offer us a more honest starting point for our journeys into Arab cinema. Working out how to negotiate all this is a serious matter if Arab cinema, or any other cultural product for that matter, is to gain a greater prominence in cultural life 'elsewhere' as nourished by a curiosity from that 'elsewhere'. We need to understand how knowledge about all this is highly tempered by what we bring as we travel, where our existential limits might lie and how they are shaken or reinforced by our journeys. Onwards …

Fellow Travellers: Approaches To and Through the Journey

Here is where we left off: cinema, as an institution and set of commodities, comes into being through movement, as part of its processes of exchange and exploitation. Cinema can also focus a critical gaze upon how supremacy is exerted through the management of these flows. More specifically, travel has vigorously shaped the film cultures of the 'Arab world'. Like anything else deemed to be a 'regional cinema', its make-up crystallises overseas training, input from Arab migrants and diverse non-Arab personnel; it also bears the pockmarks of transnational trade. My title, *Arab Cinema Travels*, foregrounding travels-as-a-noun, frames this book as one dedicated to chronicling these various journeys, remaining vigilant about their political stimuli. Travels-as-a-verb alerts us to how these movements happen, inviting also a figuring of our own tracking processes into a methodo-logy for their study. In this chapter, I endeavour to concoct ways to cross paths with and spend some time learning about and from Arab cinema's concurrent journeys among the more comprehensive global passages of people, objects and ideas. Not simply to analyse experiences and literatures of travel, but to mobilise them *as a means of analysis*. If I stray far from a narrowly constrained conception of Arab cinema, this is because it also does so. Its sense of 'home' (and ours also) may be too cross-fertilised to tolerate such insecure insistences, as has been the case for the region more broadly since well before cinema entered it.

To wit, writing in the fourteenth century, Arab travel literature's most colourful figure, Morocco's Ibn Battuta, catalogued Chinese porcelain in Damascus, Syrian rose water in Mogadishu, Maldivian cord in Yemen, an Egyptian sheikh in Afghanistan and foreign communities and diplomats everywhere to be found.[1] Trade, pilgrimage and conquest routes were so clearly established across the Muslim-majority world by the fourteenth century as to enable these thirty-odd-year rovings of Ibn Battuta around the region and beyond, a journey that covered three times the distance of Marco Polo's voyages. The exchanges that Ibn Battuta documents and benefits from put paid to any erroneous image of the Arab world as a quiet backwater untouched by foreign influence, lacking in curiosity, trade ambitions, or expansionist aspirations.

More than 600 years ago, global flux prompted Tunisian proto-sociologist Ibn Khaldun's celebrated thesis that:

> the conditions of the world, and of the nations, with their customs and modes of occupation, do not persist in one unchanging state or stable pattern, but are transformed with the passage of time and move from one condition to another ... Differences between groups are cultural, not innate.[2]

Community and faith groups still register for Ibn Khaldun, he simply attributes their composition to social mixing rather than isolated development. Moreover, he sets his detailed historical analysis of his region in motion through a dynamic comparison between sedentary and nomadic societies.[3] We thus find nothing particularly new in the much more recent claims of people like Trinh T. Minh-ha, who welcome how travel narratives 'speak to the problem of the impossibility of packaging a culture, or of defining an authentic cultural identity'.[4] For Ibn Khaldun and Trinh, 'self' and 'other' categories persist in transit, but they also mutate along the way, meeting, merging or deflecting, regrouping or finding themselves rehabilitated as implausible holistic ciphers. The material encountered within the following three chapters, like *The Dupes*, has been indelibly shaped by these currents. Such mutability also arbitrates who and what can be or is studied, sold, owned or shared globally.

And so travel, I wish to stress, is not merely the silent conveyor of the matter of life, but indivisible from its very composition. In his influential book *Routes: Travel and Translation in the Late Twentieth Century*, the anthropologist James Clifford underscores how travel must be thought of as '*constitutive* of cultural meanings rather than as their simple transfer or extension [emphasis in the original]'.[5] Moving beyond Clifford's observations, I will also contend that the ways in which travel has been recounted, experienced, profited from, controlled and hosted (sections on each of which follow below) can greatly stimulate and politicise academic enquiry. There is much to be gained from warming to the various positions, attitudes and metaphors that travel can summon culturally. Speaking from elsewhere, Roxanne L. Euben and Georges Van Den Abbeele corroborate the catalysis of European philosophy by perspectives on travel, from Herodotus' witness-claims to Descartes' metaphors of mobilisation. As Janet Wolff remarked some time ago, contemporary theory has greatly expanded its repertoire through recourse to travel: 'nomadic criticism, traveling theory, critic-as-tourist (and vice versa), maps, billboards, hotels and motels'.[6] And film theory has shared this fascination too.

However, as postcolonial thinker Walter D. Mignolo warns us, 'traveling theories may be perceived as new forms of colonisation, rather than as new tools to enlighten ... what is the ratio between geohistorical location and knowledge production?'[7] In sum, travel helps establish the places to visit, to learn from and about, to send things to, to buy from, to conquer, and all this, in turn, establishes patterns of domination. Consequently, theorising through travel will always clearly voice imbalances, their forcefulness less evident in concepts such as 'diaspora' or 'hybridity'. Like James Clifford, then, I do not wish to erase the harm that travel has done, or neutralise the overtones of how it has typically been narrated, 'precisely because of [travel's] historical taintedness, its associations with gendered, racial bodies, class privilege, specific means of conveyance, beaten paths, agents, frontiers, documents, and the like'.[8] The types of travel I discuss are not always pleasant. Travel has been, and so often still is, opportunist, exoticising, accumulative, greedily selfish, survivalist, at the end of a gun. There are a host of alternative categories through which I could have fed this study, ones bearing similar histories, but which render their impacts less visible. The often violent actions of tourism, expatriation and exile surge through how cinema and travel align, but the dubious politics at work within global movements are less readily acknowledged, less historically implicated, when scholars huddle under framing terms like 'diaspora' or 'hybridity'. Keeping an eye on the diverse machinations and interchanges of travel animates an invigorated understanding of how power flows, including through cinema.

This fact that travel and its literatures carry a sullied pedigree, riven with colonial intent, is old news to be revisited soon enough by this chapter. Yet other accounts and experiences still have much to offer and not all of them are so flagrantly conquistadorial. For instance, journeys of and for the mind traverse the Arab literary canon and therefore inform Chapter 2's enquiries into the journeys of aspirant directors to Eastern European film schools. Historically, these accounts have often been inspired by the spiritual illumination promised after completing the rituals in Mecca (*hajj* and, out of season, *'umra*): a return to source, rather than a ravenous expansion. Before the epochs of steam and air travel, this trip could take up to nine months, its fusions, transpositions and convenings spurring intellectual debate en route and at destination point. The spread of Arabic rides the coattails of Islam's growth, a religion for which *hijra* (migration) holds considerable weight. Not simply on account of the Prophet Muhammad's own relocation from Mecca to Medina, but also because Islam beseeches its followers to up sticks if they find themselves in places intolerant of their practices. Petitions to venture forth pepper the religious texts. The hadith 'He who follows a road seeking knowledge, God will make the path to heaven easy for him'[9] underscores the impulsion towards *talab al-'ilm* (the search for [religious] knowledge) which Arab-Islamic travelogue scholar Roxanne L. Euben stresses 'is more than merely a recurrent theme in Islam or an occasional practice of Muslims. It is, rather, an ethos.'[10]

I do not raise these particularities of Islamic tradition in order to wrong-headedly essentialise the study of Arab cinema, a largely secular industry with contributors of many creeds. Instead, I wish simply to coax English-language Film Studies towards dimensions like these (particularly in Chapter 3, which converses with literatures of pilgrimage to the 'Holy Land') to see how they might usefully stretch our purviews. What would it mean to refigure some of the journeys from the Global North (including my own for this book) according to what Ian Richard Netton terms the 'pilgrim paradigm', premised upon the commonality of a voyage shared by people coming from many different directions and converging on one geographical point (in this instance, as a spiritual duty)?[11] Anything but travel for escapism or as an expression of individualised freedom. As a non-Muslim (and there are plenty of other pilgrim types too, as Palestine will surely attest), I wonder what it would be like to think of travel without an implied estrangement, be that the excitement of ogling exotic sights or the critical distance that academic enquiry so often demands. Something closer to the pilgrim paradigm allows scholarship to strive for shared goals over and above competitiveness, the types of unity also encouraged by the barbed critique of self-serving Arab leadership allegorised within *The Dupes* and further discussed in Chapter 3's involvement with collective Palestinian struggle through cinema. After all, when one sets oneself at a remove, it is easier to accept the global division of labour in travel, cultural production and academia alike and to situate its exploitation out of sight.

WANDERING AND WONDERING

There is no denying that travelogues indulge a fill of heroic posturing and that publishing is something of an exclusive privilege. We shall arrive at their critique in good time. But, amid its more objectionable politics, travel writing also tenders a sustained examination into how to fabricate, sell, describe, compare, engage with, learn from, be inspired by, or annul formulations of 'foreignness' conducted by travellers coming from all corners. The interconnectedness-amid-difference that fuels the genre, that drew Ibn Battuta out of Morocco – offering up enough social oddity and exoticism to warrant the effort of recording – is one of the hinges upon which this book swings. For this reason, such writing provides valuable exemplars for the study of cinemas that are not 'our own', as Arab film history isn't (and also is) to me. As most cinema (if not all of it), I need to stress, will be to every one of us.

Travel writing can engorge our Film Studies vocabularies, registers and scopes of imagination. It is this belief that drives *Arab Cinema Travels* and why travel writing deliberately features more prominently in how I analyse than any other type of 'theory'. Central for me here is the pre-eminent Arabic travelogue genre, the *rihla* (or journey narrative), which merges what we might, from here and now, call autobiography, social ethnography, geography, poetry, history and sheer lies, spinning fantastical yarns, some borrowed from mythology, in order to entertain the readership. Cinema shares so many of these dimensions, meaning the *rihla* genre can contribute much to its study, if we first stop to think beyond any initial incompatibilities we perceive, routinised by the persistence of other investigatory models.

Let us see ... What of Ibn Battuta, who spices up his descriptions of foreign lands with rumours, portents and details from his dreams, bursting out of the regimes of truth that might elsewhere box in recorded travel? Can we really gain something from this approach? Among other conceits, Muhammad al-Muwaylihi's *A Period of Time* advances a fictitious dialogue about Egypt between an attentive early twentieth-century recorder ('Isa) and a local informant (a Pasha from the Muhammad 'Ali period in the nineteenth century), who has risen from the grave to guide 'Isa while he is dreaming. Framing the book as a travelogue, its Egyptian author depicts his own country as if it were a foreign land. At the simplest level, these caprices of delivery might discourage shyness about digressing from scholarly discourse's limited stylistic palette.

Wheedling out a delightful diversification of writerly aesthetics is one thing, and a venture that might just stretch the limits of current thinking. But the *rihla*'s dissolution of genre-as-we-know-it can also offer up, for contemporary scholarship, a political challenge to the way information is commandingly dispatched in academic writing. In those realms, subject areas are guarded, unequally funded, pitched against each other, asked to justify themselves via the incapacitating terms of managerial economics, as anyone struggling to research Arab rather than, say, Hollywood cinema will testify.

The *rihla*'s disciplinary combinations, in themselves, question strict epistemological delineations, just as the interjection of documentary material in *The Dupes*' narrative did. Both ask us to probe how knowledge is structured, what is proclaimed to *belong* together and what is invested (quite literally) in keeping ideas apart. As Mignolo remonstrates with respect to the imperative for interdisciplinary intellectual labour and with central reference to the geopolitics of learning:

Remapping new world order implies remapping cultures of scholarship and the scholarly loci of enunciation from where the world has been mapped. The crisis of 'area studies' is the crisis of old borders, be they national borders or civilization borders. It is also the crisis of the distinction between hegemonic (discipline-based knowledges) and subaltern (area-based knowledges), as if discipline-based knowledges are geographically disincorporated. Border thinking allows us to remap cultures of scholarship in terms of 'area-based disciplinary knowledge,' bringing together and erasing the borders between knowing *about* and knowing *from*. Border gnosis will help in imagining a world without rigid frontiers (national or civilizational) or a world in which *civilizations* will have to defend *their unity and their purity*; that knowledge, in the last analysis, did not begin with the Greeks but simply with life.[12]

As is perhaps obvious, but will be substantiated later in relation to Arab cinema and travel, ideas are grouped, disseminated, or marginalised in ways that further specific patterns of economic domination. Eager not to colonise or segregate parts of the world from each other in order to study them, Mignolo pushes onwards to nominate travel, or border crossing, as a means of thwarting this tendency.

Above all, though, Mignolo is troubled by what it means to assert scholarly authority, claims that can be excitingly fuddled by the customs of Arabic *rihla* production. As much as Ibn Battuta appeals to us through declarations of direct experience ('I saw it there with my own eyes'), he is just as likely to qualify his pronouncements with a 'which are said to be', an 'I was told' or 'When I heard this I refused to believe it, but a number of people told me the same thing.'[13] The relinquishment of sole agency in these asides will rematerialise later. The pivotal issue, for the moment, is Ibn Battuta's uncertainty and, more generally, travel writing's acceptance (or, conversely, obfuscation) of just how shaky its mandate to speak is.[14] The undulations in credibility are paramount here because one cannot settle into expectations. Even less so when modern generic conventions are applied: the cut-off point between harmless storytelling and deception varies appreciably across, say, the ground rules of history and autobiography, both of which feature in the coming analyses.

Certainly, there is an aspired-for verisimilitude to many travel accounts. Here dwell figures like Ibn Jubayr, whose travels between 1183 and 1185 carefully assume all the objectivity generated by an effaced self, no reported speech and a fastidious recounting of events and physical features empty of ostentatious flourishes.[15] At the other end of the spectrum, the twelfth-century Moroccan-Andalusian traveller and cartographer Muhammad al-Idrisi clearly relies on second-hand accounts, but passes them off as things he has explicitly experienced himself.[16] Ibn Battuta's work, just like Gustave Flaubert's accounts of nineteenth-century Egypt, delivers similarly dubious 'facts'. It is this *range* of options within modes of contention that matters here and which can unleash new forms of investigation and critiques of old ones. Tawfiq Saleh appreciates the political force of these elisions. He claims:

> I borrowed from reality facts of a documentary persuasion and introduced them into a fictional narrative in order to explain the profound nature of the situation. I do not think one can find in *The Dupes* a single image which does not express the reality of the political situation: at times through a metaphorical style, at others through a documentary one.[17]

The *rihla*'s capacities allow such meaningful dialectics to be honoured.

On the one hand, readers do not expect all-encompassing expertise from foreigners; we query sources more readily or delight in partiality. Right now, I am highly dependent on the research of Kamran Rastegar, Ian Richard Netton and Roxanne L. Euben: admissions like these being the one-track route to an ethical academic plausibility. Travel writing, on the other hand, savours the vaporous comingling of what we might term abuses of trust and poetic licence, more roundly and with less paranoia acknowledging how hard it is to actually *know*, using exactly this as a trajectory for exploration. Wherever a readership is unlikely to visit – and especially before the invention of more realist recording devices – we hear tales of unlikely creatures such as dog-headed humans (found in Europe by Arabs and the Andaman Islands by Marco Polo).[18] These are moments when travel writing discloses awe-inspiring disparity, some since proven to be fact, others heavy clusters of hearsay, still more, flights from fidelity. The threat of investigation is largely absent, be that through practical difficulties or a lack of desire to disprove any of these fantasies. This situation has been re-enacted by the unavailability of most of this book's filmic examples too, particularly Chapter 2's, some of which were only available (and then closely guarded) within archives in Damascus while I was conducting primary research prior to the current conflict. I would not be able to guess at their status now. I have never borne the capacity to release this material onwards (with or without subtitles) because it has been kept deliberately exclusive by its guardians for reasons the following chapter will catalogue, and which are in no way exclusive to this particular film archive. Yet nor do I wish my conjectures on them to be taken as doctrine. These are some of the pronounced pitfalls of hermeneutics, at the mercy of powerful strictures on global accessibility and circulation that mould our knowledge of cinema well beyond this region. But maybe travel literature, with its long history of acknowledging what is unavailable (or prompting critics to do so), not only exposes this, but has also found ways of productively thinking around and through it.

In medieval Arab literature, unsubstantiated statements were termed *'aja'ib* (wonders or miracles) (*'ajiba* in the singular) and became part of the conventions and expectations of the genre. This term will crop up in every subsequent chapter. I would like to treat many of the films detailed in this book, along with their histories of manufacture, as *'aja'ib*, starting presently with a brief return to *The Dupes*. C. F. Beckingham, a scholar of these literatures, is clearly irked by the presence of *'aja'ib*:

> A historian trying to establish the reliability of travel narratives and geographical descriptions written in classical Islamic times often encounters stories of miraculous phenomena and events, *'ajā'ib*, which are plainly impossible and which he can dismiss without qualms, except for the suspicion they may arouse concerning more plausible parts of the work with which he is concerned.[19]

All the more reason, then, to use *'aja'ib* to launch an enquiry into the plausibility of all sorts of (travel) representation and to deliberate over why Beckingham so agitatedly needs to settle into circumscribed interpretation that accords with the binding regulations of one disciplinary stream, namely contemporary history writing. Instead, *'aja'ib* encourage us to think about what we believe and what we want to believe in, opening us out onto all the possibilities, good and bad, that epistemological insecurity can stimulate. This is no mere philosophical game. To situate *The Dupes* historically, even though its style figures predominantly as realist, the movie would have been something of an *'ajiba* at the time of its release. Up until that point, there had been precious few treatments of the Palestinian *nakba* (catastrophe; the Arabic term for the invasion of Palestine and the ensuing dispersal of many of the settled Palestinian populations). *The Dupes* becomes an *'ajiba* through finally handling this topic, bringing into the light something that had, before, been considered cinematically 'unrepresentable'. This new type of enunciation then asks: how do we absorb ourselves in contexts where current paradigms of reporting or scientific observation have not become orthodoxy? How, even, do we fabricate certainty in research findings? As an *'ajiba* of the early 1970s, *The Dupes* constitutes a profoundly political act in these respects.

While the impracticability of the *'ajiba* asks us to question confidence and authority, it can also concede the entertainment value of faith and its wilful (rather than simply gullible) suspension. The *rihla*'s mendacity and evasiveness appeal directly to what Travis Zadeh brands 'the pleasure of perplexity'.[20] He continues:

> While such writing was neither conceived of, nor consumed as fiction, in the modern sense of the word, it nonetheless demonstrates a full awareness of the pleasure produced by tales whose veracity cannot be fully verified. Thus it would be misguided to imagine that Arabic and Persian marvel-writings were written and read solely for their scientific merit.[21]

Conversely, for Ian Richard Netton, the *rihla* was frequently classified as a fiction genre, as were later travelogues by 'Ali Mubarak and al-Muwaylihi, which explicitly unleash their discussions and critiques through intermittent make-believe, judging this mode to attract greater audiences.[22] Perhaps for similar reasons, salacious sexual exploits enliven these accounts, including the very title of socialist and long-time resident of Europe Faris al-Shidyaq's *al-Saq 'ala al-saq* (literally: 'leg over leg'), which alludes both to walking (as a traveller) and having sex in order to stress the pleasure-seeking possibilities of the road. It may very well be that we do not wish to hear what happens between an academic's sheets, nor, more pointedly, to admit the elements of invention in their work. Each of those concessions would undermine a lot. However, what rise to the surface in this comparison are the economies of knowledge and cultural production, to be examined more fully below. The *rihla*, like cinema and – to a greater extent than we often let on – scholarship, can be regarded as an enterprise in the commodification of difference for entertainment. Such dynamics are crucial to how we make and watch films, which suspend disbelief through realist habituations, predominantly to amuse.

As a consequence, I am less anxious to grapple here with refutation of truth-claims when motivation and invocation are more useful, more enthralling. Within the *'ajiba* framework, 'elsewhere' becomes something – some place – extremely complex, rather than an entity one either rightly or wrongly describes. And it is known as such by its readership. How distant from the shortcomings of academic investigation, which Gayatri Spivak so witheringly upbraids by exposing its 'produced "transparency" [that] marks the place of "interest" ... maintained by vehement denegation'.[23] The (Global Northern) scholarly propulsion to get to the truth of the matter, to believe in that core authenticity, perilously flattens out layers of forceful inscription that Spivak understands as ideology. By setting documentary, stylised still further by still images, amid a fictional narrative, *The Dupes* queries the political implications and efficacies of each register. Interpreting within an *'ajiba* framework encourages us not simply to doubt plausibility and veracity *per se*, but, rather, to witness ideological tinkering with the material that finds its way onto our very own disciplinary doorstep, especially that which comes from distant times or places.

The *'ajiba* points back to delicate and motivated trust systems, the like of which still questionably power academic forthrightness and which spring from what Euben calls the 'conditions of intelligibility'.[24] What we choose to misrepresent is highly representative. Tawfiq Saleh, for one, wishes to expose the motivated circumscriptions of Palestine within the region:

> One could say that, for a long time, the Palestinian cause was considered by many of the Arab regimes as a ... hook. A hook upon which each hung whatever they wanted according to their interests. In cinema, this served to concoct artificial films, full of bravado, light operatic heroes, electioneering exploits.[25]

These tropes for navigating difference and command bob around, quite noticeably, within the tides of political domination and obfuscation, colonial expansion and mercantilism too; they are not exclusive to the Middle Ages. When we read, say, Ibn Battuta's *'aja'ib*, they positively invite us to unpack believability and comprehension, to see how the limits of what we understand affect us and to ponder what kinds of stories we might tell when we cannot make sense of something. *'Aja'ib* declare 'I am foreign to what confronts me and it is new, also, to you, the readership – how shall we all deal with that?' *'Aja'ib* help manage anxieties over what can and cannot be grasped, said, conquered, thought of as real or different. Theorising the *'aja'ib* construct, I contend, reveals dilemmas over trust and expertise, highly political in contexts such as the historical recounting of Palestinian exile. *'Aja'ib* are similarly effective for untangling the management of the 'foreign' as stimulated by rarity and unfamiliarity. To sit with *'aja'ib* and work through each of the terms under which they accrue their status is not merely an epistemological riddle, but an extremely valuable act of geopolitical consciousness, or consciousness-raising to be extrapolated at length later. We certainly have not stopped spotting or fashioning *'aja'ib*, despite the claims of modern rationality, especially with respect to how we make and watch films (which embody a similarly complicated interplay between fact and fiction) or, as has been underscored, vis-à-vis how we generate thought.

Consequently, I am keen to acknowledge the *'aja'ib* in all our writing, to feed off what is latent within them and the popularity they accrue. Borne, often, by flights of fancy, they conjure a might-have-been and conceivably-could-be that is also wishful and suggestive. Alternatively, they may prove verifiable according to our own 'conditions of intelligibility', astounding phenomena not withstanding. Lucy Lippard evocatively calls upon the term 'rubber-necking' to describe the traveller's sense of awe at phenomena like *'aja'ib*, the 'willingness or desire on the part of the tourist to stretch, literally, past her own experience, to lean forward in anticipation, engagement, amazement, or horror'.[26] The disbelief that Palestinian refugees should suffer so on the road delivered by *The Dupes* stands as one such example. So, while *'aja'ib* underscore their own rhetorical delicacy, they simultaneously tease out and practically dramatise the possibility for social change through their rare, startling and foreign characteristics. They tender something new and potentially hopeful, phantasmagorical or not. The first key upcoming *'ajiba* of this order appears in Chapter 2, which marvels at the near-unparallelled labour practices once enshrined in the Syrian state film industry, wondering whether its ideals can be truly realised elsewhere, or even, ultimately, in a Syrian past itself.

This *'ajiba* comes into being through multiple journeys: the scholarly exchanges between Syria and the Warsaw Pact states which supported this industry and my own 'arrival' (probably yours too) as we confront a bewilderingly different approach to film-making than is typical of the capitalist for-profit model. The impulse towards horizons new and a better life there harnesses critical thinking to travel for writers like Lucy Lippard, Dean MacCannell, Nikos Papastergiadis and Lesley Kuhn.[27] But these associations are evident in simple, much earlier etymological taxonomies. The Arabic root from which 'to travel' comes – *s-f-r* (and from which English borrows 'safari') – encompasses a thought-provoking knot of derivatives: to shine, brighten; to unveil, to embark. Similarly, *k-sh-f* (the root that gives us 'to explore') clusters verbs such as: to throw open, disclose, shed light, scrutinise, investigate, inform, discover, find out and enquire.

Within Europe (which he then exhorts us to move beyond), James Clifford discovers an enabling connection between mobility and theory via the latter's roots in the Ancient Greek word '*theorein*: a practice of travel and observation, a man sent by the polis to another city to witness a religious ceremony. "Theory" is a product of displacement, comparison, a certain distance.'[28] As if heeding Clifford (and travel)'s compulsions, Roxanne L. Euben attributes to the *rihla* what is ordinarily ascribed predominantly to 'theory': the capacity to generalise, but also to link and to imagine a beyond. She discerns:

> as theorizing is ... inherently comparative, and as comparisons entail acts of translation that simultaneously make sense of and distort the unfamiliar, the *rihla* is an occasion to map complex connections among travel, theory, and knowledge ... they trouble the widespread assumption that political theory is and should be around particular Western texts whose canonical status both presupposes and secures the pre-eminence of the philosophical treatise as the genre most appropriate to the discipline.[29]

Her observations ring true. Ibn Battuta's language is heavily comparative; Rifa'a al-Tahtawi, publishing in the nineteenth century, unambiguously aims to revolutionise Egyptian society by reference to the French political thought he encountered on a study mission to Paris. These writers invigorate social life through actual and figurative repositioning. They assume a critical distance or imagine themselves or others as foreign in order to prompt fresh perspectives, often about 'home'. Theory, in this context, is a form of 'travel' and travel writing can offer itself up as a mode of theorising.

But, bearing in mind Euben's concomitant cautions about Global Northern domination, alongside critiques of Eurocentric perceptual models by writers like

Dipesh Chakrabarty, the position of the comparer-traveller requires rigorous scrutiny. Who has made which voyages? With what agendas or support? What are the terms of their evaluations? What are 'aja'ib to them and why? Which economies undergird all these agents? To answer these questions, we need to get more involved ...

PLAYING IN THE TRAFFIC

To document 'aja'ib, to rubber-neck: these are actions of someone undertaking, rather than observing travel. And someone admitting their difference from and perhaps cultural obliviousness to some of what they encounter. Travel writing is frequently autobiographical and narrativises these imbalances overtly. As with the 'ajiba, the traveller voice immediately reminds us of social divisions which we would do well to acknowledge, investigate and challenge, rather than gloss over.

As previously stated, within this book, I do not simply wish to categorise how Arab cinema 'dwells-in-travel' (to use James Clifford's terminology), but, like travelogue authors, to travel in order to write and to write as a traveller. It is crucial to come to terms with how we *get to* (in every sense, including the expensive and preferential pragmatics of physical proximity) what we study. How strange that most scholars discussing travel or Arab cinema in English are themselves, like me, migrants, but are more apt to write *about* migration as a detached object rather than *from* it. I hope, instead, to move *alongside*, to journey back and forth from what I study without fixing it so, in order to relinquish traditional academic conviction as discussed above and understand what mobility itself can offer scholarship. As a guide, the *rihla*'s means of expression dare us to interact with Arab cinema as a visitor moving among some particularly elaborate and manifold transactions. This objective bears serious epistemological implications, ones that, in many a sphere, would undermine requisite claims at expertise (*not* being an outsider – and so being a native-informant?). The benefits and hindrances of feeling a little lost become more apparent when we are buffeted from different geopolitical angles.

Concentrating on travel also exposes the ubiquity of displacement and the turbulent (often usefully so) energies it can arouse. It undoes some of the securities that regionalised know-how presumes, questioning the disciplinarity of 'area studies' that Mignolo condemns. Moreover, travel, when understood as integral to research methodology, is more than an epistemological attitude. It also helps kick up concrete injustices and privileges in the search for knowledge. Let us presume a Palestinian scholar of cinema born within the state of Israel and carrying that passport. Although deft amid matters of cultural specificity, including language, her passage to the Damascene archives mentioned above would be impossible because of her passport (Syria refuses to recognise the existence of an Israeli state to the exclusion of many of those Palestinians subsumed by it). My journeys into the West Bank to conduct interviews for Chapter 3 will have been significantly easier than hers might be as I am considered less of a 'threat to national security' than she is. If we think in terms of stable domains, and without recognising the curtailments and allowances they still exact, we are surely undercutting the unequal distribution of basic human rights. As Chapter 3 will point out, Palestinians in the Occupied Territories are frequently lost on home turf, a forcefully imparted condition that is the consequence of the state of Israel's deliberate blockages of roads, removal of signs and subterfuge at the level of cartography.

Such experiences deny a lord-of-all-I-survey view across a known terrain beneath and impede the acquisitive traditions that have nourished formalised academic study. In response, I do not seek to be completist or smugly explicative of Arab cinema. For starters, my investigation is restrained to three 'areas' along a particular path and does not presume to master the enormity of the topic (for that, Egypt, the most prolific film-producing nation in the region would have to take up a prominent position). Likewise, historical coverage, while chronological, is partial here. I follow the lead from the thematic emphases of the *rihla* genre, rather than a compulsion to 'tell the whole story'. These imperatives to avoid totalising explain why the word 'mapping' is deliberately excluded from this book, because I distrust the urge to cover, and thus somehow lay claim on ground.[30] Instead, authority must be flagged, unravelled and interrogated. An ethical self-placement should be formulated for research about a group of film workers, products and circulation flows which have, without exception, created and been created in response to – as well as during – cross-border mobility.

Countering these tendencies to assume expertise, the *rihla* packs its authors' inadequacies and estrangements into its generic baggage, loading up with direct accounting and squeezing first-person narration into its more documentary and whimsical passages. Less rarely is direct experience or (mobile) positionality undermined, rendered simplistic or swept out of sight in favour of more 'objective' reporting styles. The tenth-century Kurdish-Arab travel writer Ahmad Ibn Fadlan flips between first- and second-person address; Ibn Battuta's *rihlat* (the plural of *rihla*) are teamwork via Ibn Juzayy's annotated transcriptions of Ibn Battuta's spoken accounts upon his return to Fez. Even the scrupulous observations of Ibn Jubayr were dictated to a scribe. From the nineteenth century, Faris al-Shidyaq speaks in the third person about a character called Faryaq (clearly a truncation of his own name), sometimes in second person and, on occasion, the two conduct conversations before the text digresses into poetry or debates about linguistics.[31] In a later section of this chapter, I will mull over the significance of the *rihla*'s dispersed agency and authorship, but, for the moment, I want to emphasise its amalgam of different registers of reportage, including the most personal and immediate. I am at a loss to bring to mind another corpus of enquiry that cross-examines the impact of encounter and the narration of difference, or that scrutinises comparative frameworks through an *embodied* politics of movement in such a sustained fashion as the travel narrative. Add to this its conviction in imagination and speculation, and how these intercourse with the constraints of reality. All such propensities fuel my confidence in travel literature as a theoretical paradigm for this book.

It feels jarring, even abhorrent to impersonate *rihla* conventions by bringing personal details into my academic writing and that strangeness summons examination. Ali Behdad attributes to first-person accounting the beginnings of the potential to undermine inequitable political clout:

> In recent postcolonial discourses there has been a tendency to displace and contain one's own cultural and institutional situation by foregrounding the politics of representation in the

colonial past, evading any discussion of the ways the 'I' is implicated in relations of power. To avoid a new mode of critical transcendentalism, the conjunctural position of the speaking subject has to be figured into his or her discourse.[32]

For Behdad, the self-involvement exuded by first-person writing (and no one is as aggrandising as Ibn Battuta) pales in comparison to the greater epistemological arrogance of a presumed neutrality. Here we are reminded of Spivak's plea to find otherness within the self, incongruity that is relational, familiarity with our suppositions that we have habituated as normality through erasure. Otherness that is manufactured and cast outwards, a self that owes its very existence and privilege to the exploited labour of colonised or neo-colonised subjects. While such reflexivity never guarantees perfect politics, it helps prohibit the hypocritical aloofness of a posited view from on high over an impossibly bounded situation (so often the prized position of European Enlightenment-inspired thought), or of Film Studies when it imagines it can look down from a bird's eye perspective on a 'foreign' cinema. Or even claim it foreign without pointing out some of the countless actions that have rendered it so or querying their motives. The self-recorded self of autobiography draws the fuzzy boundaries of identity into our sightlines. In the process, all travel writers face or fabricate difference for the sake of meaning-making and do so, as *'aja'ib* reveal, at a chasmal remove from their readership.

Here I am in print all the same and what does that mean? I do not intend this book to become overwhelmingly personal. The topics I go on to discuss are incontrovertibly more compelling than I am, and so will deservedly take centre stage. Yet it cannot be disregarded that I am British, not least on my travel documents, and therein lies quite some history. My father once told me, although perhaps this is itself an *'ajiba*, that 'Dickinson' is a name which mushroomed in popularity after Richard the Lionheart's successes in the Third Crusade (literally, 'son of Dickin', a diminutive of Richard). So: a long-established European conscription in conflict with Arabs and also a 'pilgrim paradigm' with colonial intent. If I am honest, this period was first and vividly evoked for me not by Arab voices, but by Walter Scott's 1825 novel, *The Talisman*: fantasy, politicised revivalism and biography of Saladin (Salah al-Din) rolled into one. There have been times, as a researcher working within this very same territory, that remind me of the opening sections of *The Talisman*, when a knight (Kenneth) crosses an unforgiving desert landscape in the 'cumbrous' and 'unwieldy' garb, 'peculiarly unfit for the traveller in such a country'.[33] Kenneth's shortcomings partner well with my own ill-equipped European research training and yet Kenneth, in his own odd way, acclimatises to the environment and contributes to its shaping. With foreigners on the mind, we might remember that the first ever feature film to deal with the plight of Palestine in a nuanced and sympathetic fashion was directed by an Egyptian national of shared Palestinian ancestry and made with Syrian financial support. 'Nation', like 'home', finds (and loses) itself through travel, to which the migrants responsible for the cinemas of Syria (Chapter 2), Palestine (Chapter 3) and Dubai (Chapter 4) will attest. A key concern endures: not that mobility frames much of life, but *why* do particular people, ideas and objects move to and from particular places?

Like many people in the world, I find it hard to give a simple answer to the question: where are you from? Being born outside my country of citizenship and sustaining prolonged stays in four different continents (including parts of the Arab world) has granted me an often luxurious and pleasurable sense of self-as-migrant, funded both as the child of parents on 'overseas development' salaries and as an adult researcher awarded government grants to bring back information about this region. How much of this can any one person discard? Moreover, to imagine oneself as some sort of semi-'gone native' exception is an act of erasure of these neo-colonial presences on the landscape.

On indulgent days, I warm to Edward Said's definition of the migrant intellectual: not as an heroic figure withstanding adversity, nor one riddled with debilitating nostalgia that yearns for an untenable 'home' or the 'good old days', but as an old hand with a worldly appreciation of the porosity of self/other, inside/outside, settled/migrant boundaries and able, hopefully, to think beyond the injustices instilled in such oppositions.[34] I might have certain skills in translation, but they will always affiliate to specific educational systems. Kamran Rastegar picks up on these comings, goings and mergings when he designates travel writing as *transactional* and capable of foregrounding:

> the material links that bind the home societies of their authors to the colonial metropoles they are traveling to. Through travel, these authors are compelled to face a changing set of material relations that are manifest even at an individual level, and to choose how to act within them. This crisis, and its textual representation, creates a text that is fundamentally transactional. In travel writing nothing exemplifies this more clearly than the narration of material relations within these texts. The subjective turn in travel writing is most often centered around a narration of the subject's emergence into a world defined by a new economy of social relations defined by intercultural transactions.[35]

There is also an economy to such peregrinations; they have been an extravagance. A consistently salaried academic cannot glibly claim too much common migrant experience with, for instance, what a forcibly trafficked sex worker or a stateless refugee might have to endure as they similarly cross borders. Travel, whose price tags are routinely clear to behold, promotes a watchfully comparative analysis of the class structures it inculcates.[36] Broad affiliations across such divisions demand caution, even if they do speak of what we share. With a deep mistrust of how migration becomes an energising trope within critical theory, largely by jettisoning debates about social injustice, Graham Huggan points to the money to be made in our own fields from cosmopolitanism:

> To trade in migrant metaphors can ... become a profitable business, with rewards handed out to writers who, self-conscious border-crossers, know how to manipulate the transcultural codes of a postcolonial 'migrant aesthetic' [here he mentions Salman Rushdie] ... it is not just creative writers who have subscribed, consciously or not, to the present 'geopolitical aesthetic' rules of literary cosmopolitanism. A variety of literary critics and cultural theorists have also jumped on the bandwagon, fostering a fraught alliance between the allegedly transgressive manoeuvres of postmodern traveling theory and the putatively oppositional politics of postcolonial cultural practice.[37]

Privilege drops out of the picture in these alliances. The ubiquitous and arduous experience of alienation features prominently in these canons, but the articulate migrant or cosmopolitan, as Ulf Hannerz observes, is often wont to claim mastery of it.[38] Holding the means to combat what others feel to be dislocation can clearly figure as a marker of economic advantage, be it for a film-maker or academic, and we should surely not report upon their output within the rubrics of transnational studies without synchronously betraying our own similarly implicated access to it as producer or consumer.

Language abilities stand as another marker of cosmopolitanism and expertise alike and, as such, demand attention. While travel literature flourishes on knowing more than the reader, it commonly thrives, unlike scholarly argument, on instances when its author lacks linguistic grasp. Ibn Battuta gets into various scrapes in Turkey because he does not speak the language, yet his trials still make for juicy stories that hit new, atypical notes, as I am hoping my own examinations might.[39] Certainly, those of us a long distance from mother-tongue fluency stumble along so painfully slowly that we often benefit from the opportunity to pause for questions and from the inexperience to query the basics that the proficient would skip over. Many are the times first-language Arabic speakers have remarked that I pick up on etymological connections that they themselves have not noticed, that I take different semiotic routes (backwards) to them. This is because I have learnt the language in a more formal context and as an adult with a greater grasp of linguistic structure, rather than via everyday childhood absorption (although some of that too). We work on these matters together, in solidarity, with help, remembering approaches such as the pilgrim paradigm. Vulnerability alongside luxury, bewilderment that I hope not to bury with bravado: these periods of incomprehension both highlight political blockages and open out new perceptual planes. Edward Said reaffirms and supplements the advantages of the inexpert:

> I shall collect under the name of *amateurism*, literally, an activity that is fueled by care and affection rather than by profit and selfish, narrow specialization.
>
> The intellectual today ought to be an amateur, someone who considers that to be a thinking and concerned member of a society one is entitled to raise moral issues at the heart of even the most technical and professionalized activity as it involves one's country, its power, its mode of interacting with its citizens as well as with other societies. In addition, the intellectual's spirit as an amateur can enter and transform the merely professional routine most of us go through into something much more lively and radical; instead of doing what one is supposed to do one can ask why one does it, who benefits from it, how can it reconnect with a personal project and original thought [emphasis in the original].[40]

Said's first paragraph implicitly addresses the commodification of knowledge and the tendency of its producers to sign up as the lackeys of capitalism and individualism. There is more debate of such things in the ensuing section of this chapter. Taking the second paragraph to heart (and who knows whether this is tenable as a letter of passage for someone holding a full-time and foreseeably permanent job within English-language academia), I find it preferable to remain somewhat lackadaisical, just as the traveller so often is. Throughout this book, I shall wander off from my 'proper place' (as, say, a cinema academic or a Middle East researcher) journeying through such territories as tourism or logistics studies (Chapter 4). I will stray across boundaries, but inevitably carrying things with me as I do so.

Guided by similar precepts, the Egyptian nineteenth-century travel writer Rifa'a al-Tahtawi, to whom I will return in Chapter 2, instigated an important title change to his famous account of a study trip to Europe.[41] Once called *The Extraction of Pure Gold in the Summary of Paris*, the 'in' was quickly replaced by 'towards' indicating the impossibility of ever ably abbreviating a city, or of (the act of) description ceasing to move. My shared disavowal of such solidity is not emphasised in order to rob someone of a sturdy conception that improves their lives in some way (Tahtawi never claimed Paris as anything to him but educational); it is to walk for a while alongside ideas within a newly arrived-at vicinity, perhaps to introduce them to elements familiar from previous encounters without trying to dislodge meanings that they embody when they are elsewhere, mindful always that boundaries and legislations are inevitable. So, *The Dupes*, from within this methodology, is no longer a fixed exemplar of Syrian, Palestinian or Egyptian cinema and my delineation of it does not wish to vie against all others to stagnate its semantics as authoritative proof of my intellectual dexterity. Instead, cinema shape-shifts according to not only its own journeys, but also all the wanderings of its producers, international histories and critical engagements. It is owned nonetheless, but communally, and not irrevocably, according to national property claims and their histories.

But, given the evasive slightness of these suggestions of mine, how respectable can any of them seem? The fact remains that I simply will not 'catch' many things in Arabic. The fundamental question is: why can't I speak this language well? The fact that I do at all, and that many of the literatures in which I situate my research were originally written in it, stands as a meagre and unbalanced gesture of willing within a grossly unjust global division of academic labour: one where the Global North might sit regally waiting for native-informants to scuttle around servicing the need for information about 'their culture'. Such demands replicate other stratifications of the effaced service work that greases the wheels of transnational capital. A mere accident of birth into a history of English-language colonial privilege grants me easier, quicker and cheaper access to pervasively internationalised canons and markers of worth. The number of readers who ask me 'Where's the theory?' when I elect to cite Ibn Khaldun over Jacques Rancière is deeply revealing here.

NOT OF THOUGHT, BUT OF TRADE?

Parallels can be drawn here between the paucity of Arab thought translated into English and the unavailability of subtitled movies, which was detailed earlier. By contrast, big-budget movies shot in the region, such as *Lawrence of Arabia* (David Lean, 1962), flourish on comparable hierarchies of access, exploiting cheap local labour and resources while casting Europeans (like Alec Guinness) as Arabs in a fashion that preserves an implicit pecking order of ability which is also mirrored in the film's colonial narrative. Even fantasies like *Star Wars Episode IV: A New Hope* (George Lucas, 1977) happily adopt the local landscape (Tunisia in this instance),

Alec Guinness as Prince Faisal
in *Lawrence of Arabia* (1962)

mass disseminating it as the planet Tatooine, while Tunisia's own movies are squeezed out of the international circuits of film distribution by such fare. Disequilibria pervade the exchange of knowledge and commercial goods, tied, as we shall soon see, to travel's role in struggles over global resources. Let us now examine some of the historical foundations of this situation.

By the time of the 'Abbasid dynasty's ascent to dominance in the mid-eighth century, a fervour for translation from Indian, Persian and Greek sources was transporting a plethora of ideas across West Asia and North Africa. By the later Middle Ages, Arabs dominated trade exchanges along such circuits as the Silk Route, with and between Europe, Central and South Asia and China. Through them, Europe, for instance, gained access not only to commodities, but also to institutions like the university, Baghdad exceeding Padua as the world's oldest.[42] Ultimately, what this teaches us is that knowledge often follows, even forges, the same routes as trade and is not so easy to deracinate from its products and technologies. This interconnection forms the arc of my book, with Chapter 2 dedicated to trips for knowledge acquisition and Chapter 4 investigating the ramifications of travel in the name of trade.

Learning is clearly not only broadened by travel, but also fuelled by the commercial and religious imperatives to do so. David W. Tschanz spots how the:

> desire to assist the pilgrim's orientation, observation and movements spurred Muslim advances in mathematics, optics, astronomy, navigation, transportation, geography, education, medicine, finance, culture and even politics. The constant flow of pilgrims turned the trails into channels of cultural and intellectual ferment.[43]

Without doubt, the preponderance of *talab al-'ilm* (the search for knowledge) in Arab culture, as I suggest above, can serve as a useful prompt for English-language writers on cinema to stretch beyond the pinioned lone traveller, or viewer, subject positions. However, at the same time, *talab al-'ilm* as a collective imperative has, historically, congregated a host of other motivations for posting people overseas as a means of accruing information of enormous value 'back home', the topic of the coming chapter.[44] It stems from geopolitical motivations too, as anyone aware of the development of 'area studies' research institutes can elaborate.[45] These impetuses need to feature in a broader understanding of travel. In the nineteenth century, the state apparati of the Ottoman-controlled Arab lands dispatched civil servants to acquire European expertise in order to rethink and ameliorate their dominions. As Tarek El-Ariss points out, the encounter with overseas modernity also ushered 'in new articulations of literary and political relations' which continue to reverberate through the region's cinema.[46] Ironically, the concepts amassed set a proto-nationalist ball rolling – but more of this in the next chapter, which fleshes out how Syrian state cinema made exactly these moves. The point being that *talab al-'ilm* absorbs and perpetuates developmental models of growth and, as Ian Richard Netton notes of even the Middle Ages, a careful balance of global cooperation and competition has had to be maintained.

Trade in education (along with travel writing, even Arab cinema) evidently falls into the broader historical ambits of not only the expansion of Islam into Asia, Africa and Europe, but also the Middle East's own domination by outside imperialism. Colonial and mercantile accumulation are both impossible without travel, and travel itself, as my introduction pointed out (and Chapter 4's arguments about tourism and logistics services will continue), has been lucratively and exploitatively commodified.

Recalling the very basics of capitalism, novelty, through the discovery or cooking up of otherness, perpetuates and increases the number of products from which one can profit. Literature and movies are not the sole wares being peddled here. The very locales they portray are on sale too, as the money-spinning guidebook industry and the tourism sector it feeds so readily exemplify. Each day, an armada of coaches and minibuses descends upon the Amazigh ('Berber') village of Matmata, known more readily to these visitors as Tatooine. The popular diversions of travel writing or filmography stem, principally, from the unique, out-of-the-ordinary things they describe. These texts relate new horizons, fresh perspectives, the unusual way things 'really are' or beguiling sights to visit. Is this not also the logic that the Dubai Film and TV Commission (featured further in Chapter 4) avails itself of when it bends over backwards to encourage location shooting in the Emirate, hoping to encourage showcasings of its sights as spectacular as Tom Cruise scaling the Burj Khalifa in *Mission: Impossible – Ghost Protocol* (Brad Bird, 2011)?

As this example insinuates, the selling of *space* is vital to any discussion of travel and its literatures. And to sell space, one must largely justify oneself with an ownership claim. These entitlements are hotly contested, and take us forward into debates about territoriality that must necessarily participate in an engagement with travel writing and cinema. Of the countries starring in the ensuing chapters, Syria and Palestine still withstand colonisation of the classic type by Israel. The United Arab Emirates, as Chapter 4 will bring more fully to light, gains territorial influence over six continents,

Tourists visit the location that became Luke Skywalker's house, Matmata, Tunisia

well beyond its borders, through its tenure of port – and therefore transport infrastructure – management that then bleeds over into foreign direct investment in neighbouring free zones, housing and shopping complexes. The hands of travel writing and cinema alike are dirty from acts of territorial acquisition and, ultimately, imperialism. In consumable book form, writing up or filming one's exploits can career towards the type of travel that Dean MacCannell classifies as (note the terminology) *taking place* 'within prescribed paths which not only honor all territorial and property claims, … [but also become] a kind of homage to territoriality'.[47] As Billie Melman points out, most British explorer-writers 'covering' the Arab world prior to very recent times were affiliated to colonial-governmental agencies.[48] So, here we must negotiate the role travel and cinema play in struggles for land and the resources to be expropriated from it.

Historically, both film and travel literature have striven to contain, to inscribe a foreign home on top of what is found, or to drag the latter back to the seat of empire as booty. The structures of cinematic compilation reek of the authority to frame, contain and restrain. Dimitris Eleftheriotis observes that, as a genre,

travel films (either fictional or 'travelogues') absorb in their textual (and indeed industrial) organisation the nineteenth-century figure of the traveller/lecturer as a subject position. In their narratives, spatial exploration is inscribed both in the actions of the mobile protagonists and in the extraordinary ability of the cinematic apparatus to reveal the world.[49]

Through its classification as entertainment, cinema, as well as travelogues, might also try to belie its support of such factions. Literary and cinematic assertions can thus further, in an alternative register, certain militaristic or otherwise coercive aspirations, including also reclamation and affirmation of an independent nation. Both Syrian and Palestinian cinemas have retained very close ties with the state (the Syrian government) or state-aspiring organs (like the Palestine Liberation Organization), so such contentions about ownership still ring true in more recent times. Yet, on the global stage, as has been observed, their declarations are clearly marginalised through their inability to travel far. My idealistic aspiration, as I have stated, would be to explore the lack of English-language writing on Arab cinema not presenting this as a gap in a market or virgin academic *terra incognito* ripe for discovery, but as a problem of blocked distribution in which I am simultaneously implicated.

It is not enough to simply dream of freer passage for Arab cinemas around the world. Frantz Fanon tips us off: 'You will never make colonialism blush for shame by spreading out little-known cultural treasures under its eyes.'[50] As we saw through brief reference to *Star Wars* and *Lawrence of Arabia*, there are more powerful assertions of proprietorship coursing through these cultural circuits. Ones that, if we look at their panoply of stereotypes, settle the Middle East starkly and with over-exposed regularity as a place of fanaticism, warfare and the oppression of women, rather than of art, culture and entertainment. Ones that impede the flows of Arab cinema through prejudicial market forces and programming, almost without exception omitting to subtitle these movies into other languages, setting them at a disadvantage through recourse to dominant, non-Arab aesthetic values and scholarly parameters that are somehow deemed fixed, if not unquestioningly universal.

Thankfully, a well-established body of critical commentary by the likes of Edward Said, Mary Louise Pratt, Caren Kaplan and Reina Lewis exists to interrogate travel (writing)'s and, by extension, cinema's Orientalism, mercantilism, colonialism, expansionism and privileged swagger, largely through the manufacture of otherness. Prior and contemporary colonialism wields this technique of othering to pin down, brutalise and rule, to compare in order to exert supremacy, they all argue. With this prerogative, cinema can echo the assured and acquisitive sense of mastery that Edward Said famously attributes to the Orientalist compulsion, which does its utmost:

> to make out of every observable detail a generalization and out of every generalization an immutable law about the Oriental nature, temperament, mentality, custom, or type; and, above all, to transmute living reality into the stuff of texts, to possess (or think one possesses) actuality mainly because nothing in the Orient seems to resist one's powers.[51]

For James Duncan and Derek Gregory travel literature accordingly functions as a form of *domestication*, the spatial resonances of which are telling.[52]

Arab travel writing's love of the *'ajiba*, though, proffers a useful opportunity for disassembling this impulse. The *'ajiba* knows full well how fanciful, how partial and disputable it is. We see its intentions coming a mile off and attempt to understand what its initiator wants, rather than to naturalise its assertions. Mitsuhiro Yoshimoto, who draws Saidian vocabularies and Spivakian logic into the orbits of Film Studies, helps to extend how *'aja'ib* might be mobilised:

The so-called imperialist misrepresentation or appropriation of the Other is an oxymoron. The Other cannot be misrepresented, since it is always already a misrepresentation. Imperialism starts to show its effect not when it domesticates the Other but the moment it posits the difference of the Other against the identity of the self.[53]

In his first two sentences, Yoshimoto contends that trying to get the better of the structures that other in order to 'de-other' oneself is next to fruitless when these draw-bridges are so implacable. Furthermore, doing so will set off a harmful chain of estrangement and delay the urgent journey into the heart of radical critique. For that, one must rigorously question not only the designations of self and other, but, more so, the terms under which they are proclaimed and the socio-political manufacture of resultant inequalities. In contradistinction to Duncan and Gregory, Yoshimoto thus intuits the moment of self/other comparison to be colonial representation at its most pernicious, not the accomplishment of domestication. He indeed baulks at the very verb (to domesticate) that Duncan and Gregory push to the foreground.

Let us come to rest, for a moment, on this digression of opinion and understand all this *trading* (commercial or otherwise) in historical and economic terms. The puissant simultaneity of domination (or domestication) and distance (Yoshimoto's otherness, say) lies at the crux of travel's value as a term of analysis. Engaging with the dialogue between these spatialised concepts allows for a cross-examination of real, material injustices, if we understand them more thoroughly as mechanisms of trade, its expropriations and territorialisations. A more sweeping exploitation emerges, requiring greater effort than curtailing harmful representations, of which these are mere fragments.

Addressing the first concern (domination), capitalist accumulation – in the guise, here, of colonisation and neo-colonialism (but otherwise too) – proliferates on multiple levels. It requires natural, physical and human resources to sustain itself cheaply and to trade as profitably as possible. Herein lie the benefits of outside ownership via dominion, enabling expanded territory and the potential for growth in resources and markets. Travel is essential to expanding this pool, transporting goods to those at the seats of power, not to mention flooding captured markets. The control of transportation networks on foreign soil is also an act of colonisation, as well as a facilitator of these flows, which Nasser well understood when he assertively re-claimed the Suez Canal for Egypt in 1956. Dubai, as Chapter 4 will reveal, is currently extending its influence globally by becoming a leading player in world shipping, so crucial to the cheap movement of goods.

But morally uninterrupted outflow of expropriated material has been best facilitated, historically, through arm's length policies, including the fabrication of otherness. Exploitation is so much more palatable from within the oblivion of a guarded and exclusive concentration of wealth, and if it can remain unadulterated by the kinds of comparison which question inequitable income distribution. These distances also abet differentials in currency exchange rates, wages and human rights. Travel in its manifold forms absorbs these capitalist principles, replicating and enforcing them through who and what is (or is not) permitted to roam freely, or who is cast out of what they profess to be their own land, as is the case for millions of Syrians and Palestinians. The administration of territory appropriated under these terms, its acts of dispossession and possession, operates most effectively through an interplay of presence and absence to which travel is imperative and of which travel writing might make us much more critically aware.

What are the material and epistemological impacts of these movements upon a designated, colonised terrain? And how might they be repurposed in a politics of equality? The Moroccan philosopher Abdelkebir Khatibi has much to offer amid these tangles of knowledges, investments and their politics. Khatibi discusses neither travel nor cinema explicitly, and yet I would like to draw him into the mix here. For Khatibi, any factor contributing to thought and action – imperialist and liberationist alike – can function as an ingredient within what he calls 'double critique' or 'an other thinking'. In naming a duality in both neologisms, Khatibi dodges separatism without denying the noisome impact of the divisive colonial politics of othering. In his own words, he calls for 'a plural thinking that does not reduce others (societies and individuals) to the sphere of its self-sufficiency. To disappropriate itself from such a reduction is, for all thought, an incalculable prospect.'[54] Neither a mealy-mouthed apologist for French imperial influence within his home country, nor someone who throws the baby out with the bath water, Khatibi proposes plundering all cultures to hand for their revolutionary potency.

Part and parcel of Khatibi's approach are the epistemological longings laid out earlier in this chapter: to dispel the universality of western theory's claims. Within this, he invites us to interrogate the denigration of majority-world critique to particular regionalised applicability against the ubiquitous awarding of a higher status to more supposedly abstracted thought, thought that is almost always European or North American. Concurrently, Khatibi militates against falling into western globalisation projects as the facilitators and terms of enquiry. So far, so Mignolo.

But his coexisting aim is to invigorate the Global North's theoretical canon with ideas that have traditionally been set at a geographical remove from it (like people, so ideas). The Global South's implausibly 'indigenous' knowledge cannot be preserved in aspic, nor sold on as the latest 'authentic' find; history cannot be halted. More crucially, batting self against other, or 'local' against 'foreign' can either serve to dialectically dissolve the opposition through an acknowledgment of shared agendas, or propel an interchange that revitalises the struggle for emancipation. The Egyptian director Youssef Chahine did just this in the artistic plane when, instead of dismissing *The Talisman* outright as Orientalist claptrap, he extensively quarried the novel for ideas for *Saladin the Victorious* (1963), his epic biopic with Nasserite overtones. While *The Talisman*'s European characters can seem anything but noble, Saladin receives a highly sympathetic treatment in this narrative, one that ultimately disbands multiple black-and-white binaries, be they military, ideological, or erotic, to unveil the intimately interdependent histories that foster both biographical takes. These overlapping approaches of Khatibi and Chahine refuse to deny the impact, perhaps even (dare we say it) the sporadic and patchy benefits, of a colonial history. Arab cinema, via this mind-set, cannot be distinguished through singularity, not even to valorise its cultural uniqueness. That, according to the discourse of Lebanese communist intellectual Mahdi 'Amil, falls prey to European Enlightenment organisation, at one and the same time ignoring this system of thought's very inheritance within Arab history.[55] Thinking through travel and Khatibi, then, not only

A poster for *Saladin the Victorious* (1963)

counters the rubrics of area studies, it also reduces the centre–periphery tendency without undermining the power dynamics that this model comprises, and, ideally, without replicating them. Sociologist Khaldoun Subhi Samman asserts that such multitudinous interactions and absorptions disassemble a notion of distinct civilisations to the point where 'nothing short of a paradigm shift in the profession will do' and comparative analysis must be approached with severe scepticism if it presumes to cauterise regions from each other.[56]

It is worth quoting Khatibi at length now because, unfortunately, the bulk of his work is yet to be translated (here from the French) into English:

> What is *necessary* (the duty of an other thinking) is to broaden our freedom to think, to introduce several strategic levers into all our dialogue: to evacuate the absolutes of theology and theocentrism which shackle the time, space and edifice of Maghrebi society. This is not enough. The dialogue with all thinking of difference is monumental. It aims to unhinge everything by which rehashing and reproduction stupefies us. An other thinking is always a conspiracy, a conjuring, an unflagging revolt and a relentless risk. And we are so unarmed in the face of the power of the world. Such is the 'history' with which our bodies have been stricken.
>
> To shake up the order of dominant knowledge (wherever it comes from) through a vigilant critique is to introduce thought into current social and political struggle. But such a struggle now has its forgotten untimeliness, towards which it is right to move with the energy of historical being, in this world held by an irresistible will to power [emphasis in the original].[57]

Certainly, Khatibi speaks in the vocabulary of resistance here, but a resistance that assimilates its oppressor's ideas as not entirely tarnished and, more pressingly, inextricable from the resistor's make-up. Engaging his methods need not fall foul, say, of Frantz Fanon's more famous entreaties to eschew rigid mimicry or pander to the oppressor's means of expression if what this amounts to is an obsequious paraphrasing and reaffirmation of its motivations. The chapter to come enlists Khatibi to devise an

Arab Cinema Travels

alternative notion of reiteration and creative inspiration. Without the slightest doubt about the damaging impact of colonial regimes of knowledge, Khatibi advocates a dynamic interjectional practice that wishes not to *dwell*, let alone align itself to the domestication processes documented above.

Through travel, a Khatibian conjunctive analysis can draw out and play off travel's capacity to unsettle permanence against solid colonial manifestations motivated by accumulation by dispossession, the fetishisation and commodification of place, as well as the distances these forces cleave to retain exploited workers at a convenient remove from imperial centres. If the forces of globalisation deterritorialise, territorialise and reterritorialise according, most prevalently, to the whims of elites, can counter-mobility evacuate their impingements upon less privileged people?[58] Like Khatibi, literary scholar Georges Van Den Abbeele strikes a responsible, yet enabling balance of give and take:

> Be they real or imaginary, voyages seem as often undertaken to restrain movement as to engage in it, to resist change as to produce it, to keep from getting anywhere as to attain a destination. The theory of an economy of travel is an attempt to explain via recourse to an alternative set of metaphors the paradoxical and contradictory ways in which travel is understood and practiced in our culture ... This complex economics of travel rehearses once more the paradoxical play of entrapment and liberation evinced in critical thought.[59]

Can we entertain this possibility without somehow underplaying the damage travel also inflicts? If so, travellers might seem remarkably suited to aiding this project, to which Chapter 3's exilic and migrant Palestinian film-makers will attest. It is in the specificities of these practices that our questions might be answered, not via latching onto of vagueries like 'nomadology'. As I argued earlier, such travellers tussle not only with mythologies of place, deferral and citizenship, schisms of class and education, their resulting conventions of taste and hermeneutics, but also, perhaps most importantly, with what it means, in rapid-fire, haphazard, sometimes unfamiliar fashions, to meet others along the way.

HOSTS AND HOSPITALITY

As such, the next task is to find modes of interacting with other people (as the traveller and the researcher must). Means that are sympathetic to Khatibi's propositions, which concede hierarchy and greater wisdom, yet function without such close bonds to colonial barbarism. The *rihla* might lead the way here because it so frequently foregrounds its indebtedness to others, its uncertainness and humility. *'Aja'ib*, it has been noted, are fabrications of combined effort that rarely remember their source, a valuable status to counter the divisive genealogies of ownership that Khatibi protests. Collective authorship is also a recognised fact of the genre. 'Ibn Battuta''s rihla attributes joint creativity in its 'Ibn Juzayy adds' digressions and its lengthy quotations from the writings of Ibn Jubayr.[60] George F. Hourani divulges how the traveloguers of the ninth and tenth centuries, 'all wrote the same kind of geographical handbook, using each other's work freely'.[61] The contemporary bourgeois-individualist concept of the author-owner is undermined and the unavoidably collective labour of any writing cannot be so easily effaced. We see this too in the teamwork of Syrian national cinematic production and in the politicised and internationalist interruption of the well-established road movie genre by the Palestinian film-makers featuring in the chapters to come. Proprietorship of the text is thus somewhat deflected, but so too is possession of the territory it represents. Physical property and its intellectual counterparts are unsettled. Travel favours a *relational* dynamics of knowledge acquisition and ordering.

These conjunctions derive, so often, from generosity – with knowledge, but other resources too. So much so that this book's research methodology cannot remain detached from its impact. I am very much guided by certain conventions for encounter that have already existed for centuries within the Arab world; what immediately come to mind here are its traditions of hospitality. These bolster certain laws regarding and circumscribing relationships between strangers and non-strangers, principles less noticeable within the imprinted behaviour and analytical ethics that I have come across in the Global North, where an individual's isolation or withdrawal might be more commonly sought out and valued. This is an *'ajiba* alert.

Most foreign visitors to the Middle East return with a tale up their sleeve about how astoundingly generous strangers have been to them – lavishing gifts upon them, inviting them for meals or to come and stay. As a researcher, this means I am rarely allowed to sleep in hotels as opposed to homes, I have been welcomed onto film shoots (all expenses covered behind my back) and have, by sleights of hand and premature payments, been bought more meals and drinks than I can count. Ibn Battuta's whole voyage was facilitated by such acts of hospitality, promulgated by Muslim camaraderie. Hadiths like 'Islam began as a stranger and it will return as it began, as a stranger. Blessed are the strangers' and 'He who loves God and his Messenger [the Prophet Muhammad] should be generous to his guest' have enabled travellers to find ready assistance throughout the Islamic world when far away from other support networks, such as the all-important Arab extended family. Frequently believed to derive from harsh desert locales, where mutual human support is a reciprocal matter of life and death, assistance of this order crosses religion and region. For instance, Ibn Jubayr secured a place on a Spanish ship in the middle of the Third Crusade and Elias Ibn Hanna al-Mawsili managed a similar act of passage to the Americas in the seventeenth century.[62]

To the newcomer, such behaviour can be confounding (what do they *want* from me?) and, indeed, these experiences often throw those people who are straight off the boat into some confusing discrepancies between what 'property' and 'privacy' mean and are worth in either set of geographically designated cultures. These divergences might well relay an alternative to accumulation by dispossession too.

Generosity is not only an obligation and a means of fortifying the noted Arab emphasis on community over individualism, it is also, arguably, a display of status, appropriate conduct and power. Within this paradigm, and generosity extends to almost all social encounters, Arab cinema is 'yours'/'theirs' (depending on subject position) more by heritage and affinity than by guarded and exclusive ownership claims. In my experience, it is furnished to the researcher as freely as is possible because sharing bears more resonant social value than holding back. The giving is a matter of pride, as too is the celebration of localised production, but not without all involved entering a specific, highly coded game.[63]

Influencing another's thoughts or actions bestows power upon a person, with the more needy or dependent recipients (here a researcher) falling much lower down the hierarchy, further still if they should display an ignoble lack of restraint. The guest resides with rights, but also grave responsibilities. An awareness and adoption of these patterns then duly contradicts the implications of authority assumed through intellectual expertise as discussed earlier and can hopefully prompt an exploration of alternatives to the epistemic violence of wholly imposing imported, 'objective' forms of investigation. As I have admitted, such gestures cannot escape being somewhat Pyrrhic, but the economy of hospitality functions according to some illuminating checks and balances. The return gift of this book (over-reached and partial) to those who have unstintingly helped with it is, we should acknowledge, poor recompense that speaks of my status.

It is also important to register what is *kept* through such astounding acts of giving: most markedly a group affiliation, which also runs through a collectivising term such as 'Arab cinema'. Within this, if I am to take my claims about flux-through-movement seriously, 'tradition' is not a coherent or secure entity, although it might well be used as ballast for a similarly mutable construction of 'Arab'. As shall become apparent in future chapters, film style figures in this equation, establishing Arab idioms in order to shore up particular and opportune continuities.

Logically, and with all this talk of hospitality, it is now time to return to the concept of home and its promised securities, the place to which most travel writers retreat to order their notes, to articulate difference and to be understood.[64] 'Roots' (*asal*), 'authenticity' (*asala*) and what we so subjectively call 'fundamentalism' (*usuliya*) are all extremely close relatives in Arabic etymology, establishing consistencies that are at once geographical and cultural. One of these – 'Arab' – has found its way into this book's title for good reason, because politically expedient reasons for collectivity have arisen in its name. In many quarters, the grouping also manufactures an enemy, a target of suspicion and racism. On the home front, the term has mobilised a long expansionist and anticolonial history that enabled, to take one example, the movement of the fourteenth-century progenitor of sociology Ibn Khaldun from court to court without much incumbent loyalty to his birthplace, Tunisia. Claiming so much territory, but spreading outwards initially from the Gulf area, any sense of a homogeneous 'Arab world' – as has hopefully already become clear – is stretched so thin as to become threadbare in certain geographical and identificatory spheres. Ibn Battuta, although writing (or, rather, dictating) in Arabic, does not consider himself an Arab, a term he uses to distinguish the Bedouin.[65] This gives some sense of how much the definition of 'Arab' can mutate. Always diverse, nowadays it comprises many different religious groups (although a Muslim preponderance) and sizable linguistic minorities, thus rendering claims of unity through language somewhat untenable, especially when even its own dialects can seem incomprehensible to speakers of others. The 'west' or the 'Global North' are similarly incoherent notions; strategic, rather than geographically bound.

And yet an Arab sense of self is in everyday currency, including in movie culture, which exploits the tag to package and market certain groups of films for festival programmes and to assign prizes and production funds under all manner of rationales, something the Dubai International Film Festival (the topic of my final chapter) does. If we look at the history of the category 'Arab', we see a definite shift, say, from Nasser's projection of a third-worldist pan-Arabism (with Egypt, it has to be noted, conveniently at its helm) into more religiously inspired anticolonial affiliations, both of which have vied for supremacy in the uprisings of 2011 and beyond. This book's narrative follows the tracks made by the evolution of the designation 'Arab' over the past fifty or so years of cinema history, from the post-independence Arab nationalism of Syria's government-funded output, to Dubai's more recent configuration of it as almost a 'brand', but also a descriptor for a transnationalised linguistically intelligible creative workforce. Despite all these fluctuations, the word 'Arab' maintains a powerful cohesiveness. In fact, this desire for unity has even motivated lives of travel, as Leyla Dakhli observes of Iraqi-born, Syrian-based scholar Muhammad Kurd 'Ali, whose work bridges the nineteenth and twentieth centuries: 'In order to better appropriate this territory of people who speak Arabic, he sets out on long journeys across Arabia, meeting princes and common people, describing marvels and landscapes, and brings back narrations that retrace the tales of important Arab travellers.'[66] 'Arab(ism)' can and does stand for (alongside various nationalisms) a fight against infringements of territory and resources – most notably, oil and gas. There are reasons why we might refer to different revolutions as the 'Arab Spring'. The concept of 'Arab' is strong enough to maintain a heritage yet evidently migrates, often also finding itself locked into the Hollywood stereotypes of the oil-rich sheikh or the vengeful terrorist.

The banner 'Arab' does not simply rally people for ideological and commercial reasons, it also allows for all manner of comparative enquiries, the kind that draw a number of politicised conclusions from placing, say, Dubai and Palestine side-by-side. At the same time, it tugs the bindings of the similarly efficacious liberationist nationalisms of Palestine and Syria's recent histories, often to sanction streams of support, strategy and refugees. *The Dupes*' attack on the regimes of the region's feckless and impotent responses to the Palestinian *nakba* strives accordingly.

Each of the three 'sites' detailed in the following chapters – and I could have chosen from many other forms of organisation – create place-myths just as they weather the porosity of their conceptual and nation-state borders. These locations are, inevitably, also imagined and fluctuating totalities. Palestine and Syria do not, on most maps, look as their citizens would wish them to (namely, do they incorporate Jerusalem or the Golan Heights?). Dubai is expanding with land reclamation and has many zones that exist outside regular state legislation: free zones, for example, one of which houses its film festival's administration. All these countries are 'multi-ethnic'. The machinery of this interplay as it is affected by and affects the politics of travel is what interests me, not invalidating the 'truths' of trans-Arab or national formations. By concentrating on national configurations positioned within regional constellations, I aim, through travel, to unearth how geographical inscriptions are expounded, warped, ripped away and commodified. What is at stake, say, when (as is quite often the case at post-film Q&A sessions with directors at overseas film festivals) a migrant Palestinian audience member reprimands the work of directors like Ali Nassar or Elia Suleiman (who are both Palestinian but hold Israeli citizenship) for not being 'Palestinian' enough? When these movies travel to Ramallah or Beirut, do the questions remain the same? Or are those viewers more 'at home' with Egyptian or Hollywood fare?

Rifts, displacements, a slew of new and ethically challenging encounters, the crossing, questioning and imposition of borders of many types, an investment in difference which often dissolves before our eyes or is violently reinforced – all of this finds its way into travel and cinema. Both can construct a self, an enemy, a foreigner, a space to colonise, a market and a point from which to imagine otherwise. Even when tourism or Arab cinema sometimes hawk staid senses of space, investigating the travel this requires and promotes reveals that the region is anything but culturally detached and that we all have a stake in its movie culture, different to each of us and in need of interrogation. Whether or not you have seen a single one of the Syrian films discussed in the next chapter (and many Syrians will be in this boat), the role you have played in how their course was plotted will become apparent.

Ultimately, travel will always modify the nation-state or region, even challenge its core principles and most guarded boundaries, but it can also reinforce its powers, starting with the very act of naming a departure point or destination, or requiring a travel permit or visa. What I wish to argue is that analysts cannot simply observe or document this set of actions from the sidelines. Instead, we are drawn into the throng of people who not only travel and must account for those dynamics of power, but who also metaphorise travel in order to activate new ways of understanding. It is with all these considerations in mind that I embark upon a journey that tries to find apt, ethical, imaginative and appealing modes of studying film culture in, from and far beyond the Arab world.

2

Red and Green Stars in Broad Daylight: A Socialist *Talab al-'Ilm* for Syrian State Cinema

This chapter involves itself with revolution. Both film's journey amid revolutionary currents and film-makers' rights and declarations therein. The revolution in question, like many others before it, is nomenclature binding what might otherwise be read as a sequence of power struggles and coups that have undulated across Syrian history since the mid-twentieth century. Notwithstanding, consistent aims were sustained throughout, striving for, largely resulting in: state ownership and planned production; limited private land-holding with little scope for turning profit; state provision (free healthcare, education, pensions and the like) that aimed to level out inequities of wealth; unionised and protected labour; equal rights for women; and a pan-Arab nationalism that was strongly anticolonial in flavour (making this fertile ground for a book intrigued by how the construct 'Arab' travels). This revolution's political affiliation has been Ba'athism, which transmogrified considerably along its journey from wishful theoretical writing to lived governmental praxis. Post-2011, the title 'Syrian revolution' exists precisely to topple this regime, dogmatic and obdurate, criminal and bellicose. We are now travelling back to a moment before the massacres and mass immigrations of the 2010s, but it must be stated that many of the film-makers discussed below, while once employees of the state, have since endured imprisonment and exile at its hands. Oussama Mohammad's searing epistle, *Silvered Water, Syria Self-Portrait* (2014), co-directed with Wiam Simav Bedirxan, for instance, compiles some of the most shocking footage to be found online of what has been inflicted on Syria since Mohammad fled the country. These directors' switch in allegiance tells us much about the difference between revolutionary ideals and their corruption under military rule, allowing us, with caution, to proceed in an investigation of what might be salvageable from the former.

To expand upon the list of objectives from above, the Ba'ath Party Constitution explicitly linked revolution to the industrialisation process – including that of film – as a means of establishing a robust regional sovereignty. Moreover, this is one of the few political manifestos to actually mention movie-making, probably the only one that has latterly become a foundational instrument of government.[1] While these were merely abstract political proposals when the Constitution was written (1947), not long after, in 1963, their intentions for interlacing culture and national revolutionary ideals were consolidated into the National Film Organization (responsible for hiring Tawfiq Saleh to direct *The Dupes*), a wing of the Ministry of Culture.[2] Its role was to administer production, distribution and the import and export of film goods. By 1972, Hamid

Merai, then the director of the National Film Organization, explained that Syria had 'at its disposal relative means for different levels of cinematic activity. We have seven directors and five cameramen, an editing suite, a lab for developing black-and-white film, and a sound studio. Syria can self-sufficiently make black and white films.'[3] In the words of Directive 258, which established Syria's National Film Organization (hereafter the NFO), and, ultimately, the country's state-run movie industry:

The Organization must:

a) Be responsible for the provision of the technical needs of the Organization: studios, equipment and technicians.
b) Produce, purchase, rent and invest in short educational and documentary films, particularly those addressing national and social problems.
c) Produce, purchase and invest in feature-length films which help raise the aesthetic, ethical and cultural sophistication of the people.
d) Support research, writing, translation and conferences on the art of cinema and organise training seminars in auxiliary disciplines associated with cinema.
e) Establish institutions for teaching cinema studies in order to produce the necessary cadres, and finance and supervise such institutions.[4]

While private enterprise ran in tandem, the NFO aimed for a vertically integrated, protectionist system. Salah Dehni explains: 'The hope was that Syrian film would replace, at least partially, foreign ones, thereby permitting the conservation of some of the crucial currency in short supply for other productive sectors.'[5] In this way, the NFO could not only stand up to the pressurising tactics of the movie multinationals (and the spatial encroachment of outside markets), and balance its foreign-exchange reserves, it could also foster a brand of cinema dedicated to socialist themes and structures of labour.

Note, also, the educational bent of the NFO's objectives. In the following decade, Hamid Merai was to pronounce:

We know that cinema is not just a means of distraction, it is an instrument of education and culture ... The number of illiterate people is soaring and even the intellectuals do not read any more, or do so less and less. It is cinema which will have to play a fundamental role in the training and education of the masses.[6]

Education, as will become apparent, was pivotal to the objectives of this revolution. Education was to be extended in unprecedented ways throughout the country, but also gained elsewhere, forging geopolitical affiliations with other global power bases. As such, a focus on *talab al-'ilm* (the search for knowledge, outlined in the previous chapter) provides a compatible praxis for understanding the development of Syrian cinema culture.

Talab al-'ilm encourages learning through travel, rather than static contemplation. In his satirical and picaresque fictionalised travelogue of the early twentieth century, *A Period of Time*, Muhammad al-Muwaylihi comically overemphasises the divorce of the two states:

How can they [people at large] establish themselves a place in a learned circle when they never stay in one place, but spend all their time travelling here, there, and everywhere? The one place where they spend the most time sitting down is in vehicles: horse carriages, steamboats, or tramcars. Affluent people spend months of the year travelling abroad and wandering through Western lands in search of pleasure and amusement … When people are doing so much travelling and are so absorbed in new enterprises, they find it tiresome to read. None of them can read a page of a book without being drenched in sweat and feeling utterly exhausted, angry, and bored.[7]

But one of his book's ultimate aims is a ruthless mockery of the cloistered, inward-looking complacency of Cairo's intellectuals. As if in answer, the learning explored within Syrian cinema insists on dynamism and movement. *The Events of the Coming Year* (Samir Zikra, 1985) launches with a quotation from the tenth-century Mesopotamian philosopher and visionary poet Muhammad Ibn al-Hasan al-Niffari: 'stagnant knowledge is the same as stagnant ignorance'. Its plot turns upon a composer, Munir, just home from Europe and eager to synthesise all he has learnt into a revitalised and expressively Syrian musical idiom. The Islamic imperative of *talab al-'ilm* resonates as a means of contradicting the prospect of torpor expressed in the quotation.

Revolutions, especially, also mean to move: they spread and they draw in dispersed protagonists, people who are themselves moved by political compulsion. What's more, they are defined by a break from continuity, by a movement in another direction. Yet a revolution's potency, while determined by its mobility, also requires cohesion. Doctrine, one might say. Questions flare up as to how a revolution can conduct itself through socio-geographical diversity and how it can be inhabited in different spaces. Reading through the practices of travel enables such questions to be roundly addressed.

A RETURN WITH RESOURCES

One of Syria's most lauded film productions, *Dreams of the City* (Mohammad Malas, 1985), starts with a return. Many classic movie narratives do; returns ably inaugurate the disequilibrium so effective for setting diegeses in motion. Yet returns are especially commonplace in Syrian cinema and are distinguished by striking political vectors. In *Dreams of the City*'s opening shot, the camera pans and tilts its way along the foreboding outside wall of Damascus' Old City. Through a window, there are glimpses of doves trapped in a derelict room, batting unrewardingly against the broken panes and grills. Cut to a bus arriving and the strains of a political speech on the radio. Arab independence and unity, military music and, next, Syria's cinematic signature: a lateral tracking shot. In this incarnation, it runs down the side of the bus, by now swathed in darkness, as a mother and her two sons (Dib and Omar) are ejected into the night street, no family member present to collect them as expected.

The overtones of the sequence nod perceptibly to its director Mohammad Malas' own feelings upon his homecoming after graduating from Moscow's All-Union State Institute of Cinematography (VGIK): 'When I returned to Syria, I was free and under no ideological pressure. I was liberated and tried to transform this country, but I was well acquainted with my society ... its old ambience.'[8] Films like his strive tirelessly to discuss, even close, these gaps, using the return as a means of negotiating change understood primarily according to social – even civilisational – terms. In *Algae* (Raymond Butros, 1991), Mokhtar has been working in Saudi Arabia, a familiar temporary migration for Syrians and prompted by GDP differentials. Once back in his hometown of Hama, he finds himself embroiled in a bitter family feud that has motivated other relatives to flee to nearby Cyprus. Human displacement encourages critical cultural comparison, as well as affording economic and intellectual growth. Here, also safety. These and other Syrian film narratives, it will emerge, extemporise upon their directors' exposure to foreign countries, worldliness they then energetically – on the surface, paradoxically – channelled into postcolonial nation-building. Overseas education, from the outset, has proven pivotal to these developments and not by accident. Most of these ventures were planned and paid for by home and host governments.

There were no film schools in Syria in the twentieth century, so its aspiring directors all embarked upon journeys similar to Malas'. A few to Cairo and Paris, but largely to Moscow (Malas, Oussama Mohammad, Abdullattif Abdulhamid, Samir Zikra, Riad Shaya, Nidal al-Debs and Wadi' Yousef), Kiev (Ghassan Shmeit and Raymond Butros) and Prague (Nabil al-Maleh), the majority on state scholarships. Schooling stands in high regard within Syrian Ba'athist ideology. One year past Malas' departure, another returnee, Sorbonne-trained Michel Aflaq, co-founder of the Ba'ath Party (and by then in exile), was to declare:

> Education is the greatest weapon in the hand of the revolution for it transforms the revolution and transforms the revolutionary hopes and objectives from sentiments and vague wishes into a high degree of clear consciousness, and planned and organized consciousness.[9]

The current chapter aims to follow this leap from revolutionary outlook to revolutionary praxis as taken by a group of Syrian film-makers. The work of these artists – their oeuvre, certainly, but also their scholarly activities and their lived professional ethics – actively arbitrated between and helped sustain circuits of international leftist struggle. It did so, in large part, through travel.

Theirs were expeditions from socialist Syria to then-socialist Eastern Europe. The aim was to build a state-run, not-for-profit national movie industry, offering steady income and job security to its employees. This formation presents itself as an *'ajiba* within the current chapter, one comprising many ideals of film worker and spectator rights that stand against the often oppressive structuring of cinematic production and dissemination under global capitalism.

After the acutely impactful about-face prompted by the fall of the Berlin Wall, Syria became both an isolated outpost and one of the last bastions of elsewhere-thwarted political principles, maintained through militarised stranglehold and challenged by the day. The NFO held tight as an almost-lost branch of something that is otherwise largely extinct: non-commercial feature film production. Its motivity abruptly curtailed by the death of its senior relatives in Eastern Europe, rarely reaching an outside viewership to speak of, it all the while embalmed thematic and organisational standards thenceforth largely marginalised elsewhere. For many, the sector then stagnated into an under-funded and lazy bureaucracy, losing out to the transregional success of Syrian television serials, and threatened in the lead-up to 2011 by Syria's tentative steps towards global free market economy.

Even if you do come from or have travelled to Syria, the forces that unremittingly ostracise its cinema from a wider audience have proven intransigent and indifferent to outside curiosity for reasons that will be extrapolated presently. I would rather not hold the typical traveloguer's advantage of exceptional exposure to the material under discussion here, although I will assert the *rihla* genre's precondition of unfamiliarity and subjectivity as my starting point. Access has not been easy. My scholarship for this chapter is battle-scarred from the hostile rhetoric of English-language source literature generated by the opposing armies of the Cold and Arab–Israeli wars. It is sadly ignorant of Russian and Czech archives, was coolly monitored throughout its course in Syria (all my film viewings at the National Library sat in on, all my photocopies reduplicated), plagued by the stop-starts and broken promises of various bureaucratic apparati and, ironically, conducted on tourist visas – an entreaty of a consulate employee not wishing me to arouse suspicion. The consequences of these restrictions include frustrated attempts to view all the films made by the ten directors mentioned above or to see most of those I did more than once, largely because they are not publicly (and by that I mostly mean commercially) available.

Here the reader must enter into the premise of the *'ajiba* with me. My first request would be that you dispel what seems to be a common advance prejudice about this material: that it is repressed and conservative, curbed according to the brutal methods exercised elsewhere throughout the country. On the contrary, Syrian cinema tackles themes, imagery and vocabularies that rarely surface in Hollywood movies, from breast-feeding (*Listeners' Choice* (Abdullatif Abdulhamid, 2003) and *Sacrifices* (Oussamma Mohammad, 2002)), swearing, semi-nudity (*Verbal Letters* (Abdullatif Abdulhamid, 1991)) and discussions of masturbation (*Sacrifices* and *The Events of the Coming Year*) to abortion (*Public Relations* (Samir Zikra, 2005) and *Under the Ceiling* (Nidal al-Debs, 2005)), rape (*Stars in Broad Daylight* (Oussama Mohammad, 1988)), suicide (*The Events of the Coming Year* and *Sacrifices*), refugee life and social injustice (almost all of these films). We may well encounter these topics, on occasion, in commercial movies, but largely with a much more sensationalist and moralistic inflexion than that presented by Syrian cinema. You will have to take this on trust. I come bearing news of sights and sounds you are unlikely ever to experience.

At the same time, such frustrating crosswinds cannot disrupt the clement atmosphere of Arab hospitality and its generosity towards my studies. 'Arabs are very social people,' attests Fahim in *Public Relations*, a character who is eager to capitalise on regional convention by transforming his traditional, centuries-old family home into a tourist hotel. This research was conducted over lengthy interview meals and journeys to movie locations out of town, via random and fortuitously helpful friendships with film personnel struck up on public transport and at various events overseas. I met Mohammad Malas by sheer fluke as he looked over my shoulder in a viewing booth at the Dubai International Film Festival, his face appearing in reflection on my screen like a frame from one of his own movies. Had I not been watching a short he had directed at the time ...

Moments such as these radiate like 'stars in broad daylight', a phrase equivalent to the English 'seeing stars' in the cartoonish post-accident sense, experienced after a shock or blow. *Stars in Broad Daylight* is the name of VGIK-trained director Oussama

Mohammad's most famous film, inspired by his tutor, Igor Talankin's work of the same title. It is also evocative of Václav Havel's reflection that '[t]here are times when we must sink to the bottom of our misery to understand truth, just as we must descend to the bottom of a well to see the stars in broad daylight'.[10] As will become clear, Syrian cinema frequently assumes the perspective of the downtrodden, mirroring Havel's own insistence upon a bottom-up refusal to live unwaveringly according to party dogma, his desire to assert 'the power of the powerless'. With the added detail of Syrian green and Soviet red variants, the redolent expression 'stars in broad daylight' frames the current chapter, giving socialist colour to these particular *'aja'ib*.

Syrian cinema's value, as an industry, a node in a system of education and a set of texts does not, for me, dwell in its rarity. More pressing are its highly apposite assertions about how ideas and skills can (or cannot) circulate, and who is ordained to transmit them. Picking up on the oddity of its status, Hamid Dabashi conjectures that: '[T]he distinct disposition of Syrian cinema demands a particular theoretical attention. What the particulars of that theorization might be is precisely the reason why we need to look at these films and ponder their aesthetic and political disposition.'[11]

Undertaking such analysis demands immediate engagement with comprehensive interchanges of people, beliefs, ways of living, expertise, goods, aid and capital between two regions. Within this matrix nestle three revolutionary practices that intrigue the later sections of the chapter. First, because these movies are situated within a particular stream of influence, they interrogate the semantics of cultural and intellectual ownership, all from within a framework that disavows certain capitalist inscriptions of private property. Next, how are certain shared socialist standards and rubrics of egalitarianism actually realised (or not) in the working methods of these film-makers and in their modes of representing labour on screen? Last, Syria has promoted itself as a nation-state upholding a particular strain of socialism in the face of not only internal dissent, but also hostile neighbours. As such, it has developed a fraught relationship with the 'border', one that has spilt over into these films' narratives and which specifically and repeatedly redefines the mobility of Syria's understanding of revolution. To comprehensively tackle these issues we must first turn to their historical underpinnings.

SOCIALIST CIRCUITS, NATIONALIST HOMELANDS

The Russian road to Damascus was laid well before these directors' scholarly adventures of the late 1960s, 70s and 80s. In the nineteenth century, the Orthodox church spilled out across the Holy Land, building schools, hospitals and, of course, places of worship throughout Greater Syria, a territory which then also encompassed present-day Palestine, Israel, Jordan, Lebanon and parts of Turkey. By the 1920s, the Communist Party was faring well in Syria, winning representation in the Chamber from the mid-1940s onwards.[12] The cosmopolitanism of the Ottoman Empire, with its policies of educating and posting its employees overseas (Tahtawi was one such figure) also helped create the conditions which saw these Syrian directors dispatched northwards. Most departed on government-administered scholarships provided by their destination countries and all returned, in a sharp rejoinder to the practice of 'brain drain', to forge a nationally funded, publically owned, not-for-profit film industry within Syria.

What motives drove the posting of these students to carefully selected locations? What is it to be 'out of place' while studying? In all they were taught while away, what was to be absorbed, carried, copied and morally refused? In the pre-communist age, perhaps the most renowned Arab asker of such questions, a staunch proponent of this sort of travel for scholarship, was Rifa'a al-Tahtawi, familiar from the preceding chapter. Tahtawi's *The Extraction of Pure Gold Towards* [as amended from *in*] *the Summary of Paris* chronicles his government-sponsored mission – this must be stressed to strike some parallels – from Cairo to Paris between 1826 and 1831, a sojourn where he acted as imam for various visiting Arab students. In his writings, Tahtawi explicitly co-mingles learning and geopolitics. His book thus proffers a series of templates and clues for understanding the Syrian forays of more than a century later and, moreover, for seeing ways in which what was learnt could resound still further.

While reaching for scientific, observational veracity and exhaustiveness, *Extraction* is also peppered with poetry (his own and others'), letters and translations of French constitutional documents. Extending well beyond the typical generic perimeters of English-language writers, the text refuses stasis, not just of knowledge, but also of style. Faris al-Shidyaq's more fantastical travelogue, *Leg Over Leg*, goes a few steps further, incorporating bawdy comedy, neo-classical poetry, translations, philosophy, sermons, history writing, aphorism … the list could go on. His heterogeneous influences span from Laurence Sterne to Badi' al-Zaman al-Hamadhani. Tahtawi and Shidyaq's eclecticism forces style to stand out and make itself known. Insistent formal dexterity therefore alerts us to the (often collective) labour of cultural production, which, as will become apparent, is one significant yield from the fervently politicised employment structures that characterise Syrian cinema.

'[A]s intelligence-gathering … with a focus on concerns of perceived importance for diplomatic, military and governing policy … to advocate specific reforms of the ruling system or of social and government institutions'[13] – this could easily be a checklist of objectives for Syrians pursuing studentships overseas, or workers arriving in Syria from socialist Europe. It is, in fact, Kamran Rastegar's summary of how nineteenth-century Arabic and Persian travelogues, including Tahtawi's, primarily situated themselves. Tahtawi, as should be noted from his title, had set his sights on 'the extraction of pure gold', which would facilitate, ultimately, a counterattack on the more concretely exploitative goals of the Arab world's colonisers, turning their own political-philosophical and juridical weapons against them. Journeys such as Tahtawi's sought to make sense of fracturing geopolitical shifts: for them, the transfer from Ottoman to European domination; for the Syrians of the twentieth century, the turn from first to second world influence. Both parties hoped to forge an Arab liberation epistemology via skills acquisition and social comparison conducted away from home.

Their explorations should thus be read against the grain of how foreign contact and policy had otherwise been historically managed by scholars on Arab land, and as riposte to the taxonomic obsessions of Napoleon's 'mission' to/invasion of Egypt, or the colonial Orientalists of whom we hear so much in Edward Said's writings. In his introduction to Abd al Rahman al-Jabarti's *Napoleon in Egypt*, Said calls attention to these activities:

[The Napoleonic forces'] idea of taking along a full-scale academy is very much an aspect of this textual attitude to the Orient. And this attitude in turn was bolstered by specific Revolutionary decrees (particularly the one of 10 Germinal An III – March 30, 1793 – establishing an *école publique* in the Bibliothèque nationale to teach Arabic, Turkish, and Persian) whose object was the rationalist one of dispelling mystery and institutionalizing even the most recondite knowledge.[14]

Tahtawi's hunger for use-value is less acquisitive (of resources other than knowledge, anyway). The Napoleonic ambitions for surveillance and supremacy are here superseded by the need to transport modernity for the betterment of the region, if such attributes can ever be successfully untangled. For all his curiosity about and wonderment at Paris, Tahtawi is, at heart, a nationalist. This outlook remains strong in the independence period too. Nabil al-Maleh confirms that, 'Back then, working in film was not only about making films, it was about laying the foundations for a national cinema.'[15] Nationalism decisively shaped the plots of the NFO's movies, as well as the structures the NFO created to house the returning directors.[16] Tahtawi lays the foundations, hankering for his beloved homeland from France, while seeking to gather up for Egypt just enough of its successful strategies for sovereignty to combat such countries' imperialist designs. Likewise, writing on the bridge between the nineteenth and twentieth centuries, Ahmad Zaki, a delegate to various Orientalist congresses in Europe, critically immersed himself in various western notions of art.[17] His conclusions – that art, just like religion, could embody and motivate a nationalist élan – borrowed Europe's political concepts, localised them and used them defensively against that continent. For Taha Hussein, one of Egypt's leading twentieth-century intellectuals, who trained in Cairo, Montpelier and Paris, self-governance is inconceivable without attention to education. His *The Future of Culture in Egypt*, written on the eve of World War II, weighs up, like Tahtawi and Zaki before him, the give and take of European colonial influence:

We want this [economic] independence not for its own sake, but for the protection of our wealth and resources … We must therefore use the same means that the Europeans and Americans use to defend their national economies. This would entail, among other things, the building of schools to train our youth for the purpose. Again, who wants the end must want the means. It is not enough, nor is it logical, for us to seek independence while we behave like slaves. Further, we want scientific, artistic, and literary independence so that we may be equals, not slaves of the Europeans in these aspects of life too.[18]

We should take stock here of these established strategies when penetrating how Syria moved into a new sphere of influence and education, away from former colonial powers that had proven reluctant to apportion meaningful economic support for local culture, either during occupation or in the post-independence era.[19]

Largely as a consequence of these many years of infrastructural divestment – save the expenditure necessary to the immediate colonial concerns of resource exploitation – there existed no film schools in twentieth-century Syria. To fill the gap, the Warsaw Pact states offered up their facilities to aspiring directors. Nabil al-Maleh was first to leave under his own steam for Prague in the early 1960s, initially for a degree in

Nuclear Physics, before transferring to the Film and TV School of the Academy of the Performing Arts (FAMU) to become a contemporary of some of the main players in the Czech New Wave. Next went Wadi' Yousef, this time to Moscow, although he will not feature significantly in this chapter as he has confined his work to private, rather than public sector commissions. Mohammad Malas and Samir Zikra overlapped at VGIK between 1968 and 1973–4, followed, three years later, by Oussama Mohammad, and then Abdullatif Abdulhamid, who graduated in 1981. Unlike these four scholarship recipients, Riad Shaya arrived in Moscow of his own accord, citing Sergei Eisenstein and communism as his inspiration and justifying the decision as follows: 'my generation was one of dreamers, with very high expectations of the Soviet Union'.[20] He returned in 1982, the same year that Ghassan Shmeit graduated from the High Cinema Institute in Kiev, where Raymond Butros had also enrolled. Nidal al-Debs was the last to set off in the late 1980s, arriving in a Soviet Moscow and graduating from the newly re-created nation of Russia. His loyalties are apparent: 'We felt very close to the Soviet Union, we were fond of communism. Soviet cinema was real cinema and VGIK was one of the most important film schools.'[21] Mohammad Malas sums up the experience:

> It was fantastic, it changed me 100 per cent ... It was an opportunity for all of us, but it was also planned by the government and, when we returned, our interactions with these powers did not stop. We were thinking: they sent us and they have a plan to change our lives, our society.[22]

The film-makers were far from alone; educational traffic on these routes was thick in those days. Riad Shaya observes that his VGIK class 'came from all over the world ... except the USA'.[23] Nidal al-Debs collaborated on projects with people from the USSR, Mexico, Lebanon and 'actors from all over'.[24] By the mid-1960s, there were over 11,000 people from poorer, non-aligned nations benefiting from free higher education in the USSR and another 3,000 plus dispersed across the rest of the Comecon states in the region.[25] At the end of the decade, more than half of those were citizens of Arab countries, 2,535 of them Syrian studying in the Eastern Bloc and Yugoslavia in 1969, numbers rising throughout the 1970s and early 80s (bearing in mind that Syria's population in 1970 was only a little over 6 million).[26]

Unsurprisingly, then, graduates from overseas universities populate these movies, assuming pivotal, often lambasted, roles as they try to bed down what they have learnt abroad, amid the flows of information, skills and politics that concurrently brought the new Syrian state cinema into being. There is Doctor Maarouf from *Stars in Broad Daylight*, resplendent in his Berlin tracksuit, the toast of his Syrian village for returning to marry his cousin. *The Events of the Coming Year* follows Munir, a budding composer and teacher, schooled in Paris, Rome *and* Moscow, no less. These protagonists, along with the other returnees mentioned above, flesh out the various hopes, anxieties and problems occasioned by *talab al-'ilm*.

Tahtawi, again, can be seen to lead the way. His travels are nationalistically affirmative through the act of comparison, less by asserting the superiority of the Arab world in contrast to Europe (or vice versa) and more by recognising in Europe something lost from his country's past that might be regained. For him, 'Paris ... is filled with all the intellectual sciences and arts, as well as astounding justice and remarkable equity that must *once again* find a home in the lands of Islam [my emphasis].'[27] This proclamation requests that we look for reasons for this decline: within this chapter's context those would be imperial legacy and bureaucratic corruption. Munir, as will be demonstrated, stands in as a typical victim of what director Samir Zikra identifies as 'our present cultural crisis', compatible with Mohammad Malas' enthusiasm for transforming the country's 'old ambiance'.[28]

In all these instances, awareness of foreign conventions and strategies, as acquired through travel, is proposed as a stimulant for local amelioration or, more properly, renaissance. After its quotation of Muhammad Ibn al-Hasan al-Niffari, *The Events of the Coming Year*'s opening shot serves as shorthand for this sentiment, its formal linkages prompting discussion of other types of coalescence. The camera tilts down from an ornate, inlaid, painted ceiling, typical of Syrian palaces, in order to acquaint us with Munir, who is conducting a small European-style orchestra. His narrative-driving quest is to create a popular, respected musical fusion of east and west – 'contemporary Arab music', as he labels it, thereby implying a certain line of progress, still avowedly Syrian and historical, produced through international contact. Repeated references to heritage (domestic architectural heritage in particular) call up 'Arabness', functioning as metaphors for the enduring, the homely, the supportive and, above all, something that must be conserved. Favoured characters revere their culture: the ensemble's singer, Haifa, is first met guiding her deaf-mute students around a stunning but crumbling old mansion. The boorish apparatchiks who block Munir's ambitions pay no heed to their exquisite surroundings and one even deliberately tramples over a mosaic under restoration, mockingly asking, 'Is this where the progressive book fair is?'

This Syrian cultural past grapples with how to cook up a 'contemporary' that folds in more geographically diverse ingredients. Scored by the non-sectarian Lebanese patriot, Ziad Rahbani, who is famed for his intelligent, modernist, iconoclastic and broadly appreciated blending of global styles, *The Events of the Coming Year* does its utmost to come good on all the benefits of both home and foreign culture. But not without extreme ambivalence, perhaps most conspicuous in the film's treatment of Munir's rival, Kamil, a hypocritical Lebanese socialist who has spent time in Bulgaria. For every moment of Europhilia in the movie (such as Munir's profound affection for Prokofiev, to whom he listens while gazing at the elegant minarets of Aleppo's mosques), there is a damning evaluation of outside influence. Munir is compelled to earn money offering private piano lessons to children. One pupil's father, a dead-ringer for Stalin, presides over a house cluttered with European tchotchkes and status symbols, not least the piano itself, upon which his son is required to rehearse 'Für Elise'. Westernised music drowns out indigenous variants. When Munir enquires about the career potential of a boy who sings folk music in a restaurant, a gang of regulars laugh, 'Here'. And nowhere else but. A friend's piano performances at a nightclub irritate the clientele who would rather listen to the DJ's western pop, and another government official tells Munir that this is the 'age of the song'. In both cases, tired debates about local authenticity are reframed as investigations of how geopolitics plays its usual unjust games through the economies of culture.

Tahtawi's hope that the Arab world will 'once again' rise consequently emerges from a state of dispossession – colonial and artistic – that leaves Syria unable to fulfil this dream easily. Returnees, the film points out, have been hobbled by insufficient infrastructural provision that might aid them in pursuing the creative careers for which they have been trained. Much of *The Events of the Coming Year* is taken up censuring the resource gap between returnee expectations and on-the-ground realities. At the bureaucratic level, Munir's every application for instruments, salaries and concert space is rebuffed. In one minister's office, a delirious volley of swish pans tails the fruitless altercation, accentuated by a pet parrot's repetition of salient words from the argument: 'music' followed by 'useless'. After one such visit, Munir dreams of an Ottoman sultan beheading his jester. He and his like-minded ensemble respond to the situation by writing a manifesto that draws on their ability to compare across borders. They demand the state funding apportioned by socialist countries with the pay scales of capitalist ones.

But help did come: only often from outside. Technical aid for Syria fetched up in the form of human-power from the USSR, Czechoslovakia, Bulgaria, Romania, the GDR, Hungary and Poland, accelerating after the successful coup by leftist factions of the Ba'ath Party in 1966. Following the blueprint upon which communist Europe was modelled, the stress was on economic development through heavy industry and infrastructure – the Euphrates dam, a railway, plants, refineries, farms and factories – but educators and cultural workers arrived too.[29] A slew of treaties, agreements and five-year plans underpinned these exchanges throughout the 1970s and 80s. Article 9 of the 1980 Treaty of Friendship and Cooperation with the USSR, a document largely dealing with matters military and diplomatic, even expressly mentions cinema as a locale for partnership.[30] The Russian-language journal *Soviet Film* was translated into Arabic; movies from the Eastern Bloc were regularly programmed and acquired by the National Library; Poshko Vochinich (a Yugoslavian director) had already directed the Ministry of Culture's first short film, *The Lorry Driver* (1960); and Soviet–Syrian Friendship Societies sprang up from 1967 onwards.

Certainly, Syria's dealings with the second world were not without their economic advantages. Soviet–Syrian trade rocketed from an annual average of $36.7 million exports and $24.1 million imports between 1966 and 1970, to $137.5 million and $95.6 million respectively in 1975.[31] From 1979 until 1985, 28.3 per cent of Syria's exports and 12.2 per cent of its imports were attributed to the USSR and the other European Comecon members.[32] In 2010, Russia was still Syria's major supplier of goods (at 9.8 per cent), which helps explain, in part, its strong support for the Ba'ath regime (a customer of its arms industry) thereafter.[33]

Nevertheless, the economic opportunities furnished by these alliances should not overshadow other objectives. In establishing not-for-profit film industries, by sending students and technicians around the second and non-aligned worlds at state expense, these countries also formulated trading practices that contradicted the doctrines and undermined the commercial slant of the capitalist-inclined nations of that period. The Syrian state deliberately cultivated attitudes towards cinema and education untrammelled by the demand for profit. Such logics forcefully impacted upon how anti-imperialist struggle was conducted, foregrounding what Milton Kovner interprets as the obligation to create 'the social and material conditions and the cadres deemed essential prerequisites for the transition of developing countries to a "noncapitalist" path of economic development and, ultimately, to socialism'.[34] The films were not expected to make back their outlay costs, although it is crucial to note that many were extremely popular in their day, with *The Leopard* (Nabil al-Maleh, 1972), *The Extras* (Nabil al-Maleh, 1993) and *Stars in Broad Daylight* running for weeks throughout the country. Standing resolute is the idea that films might exist and circulate under terms other than those of consumerism. 'Cinema is culture and culture is not supposed to make monetary gain,' Nidal al-Debs protests.[35] For Nabil al-Maleh, 'in the majority of Arab countries the relations governing cinematic production come into being as a direct result of capitalism. And herein lies our tragedy.'[36] Mohammad Malas then yokes these stances to the material realities of movie-making in Syria – 'we make films without any commercial pressure'[37] – a precondition that powerfully shaped the working lives of those in the sector. How were the returns from the returnees to be computed, or was the objective to diminish any such accounting? Under the most crass terms of economic advantage, the Comecon scholarships did not discernibly repay their foreign donors. Moreover, the value of the VGIK education was specifically crafted to be incalculable, if this enthusiastic claim by Jay Leyda is to be taken seriously: 'It has aim, but no end. It goes on after you leave the Institute.'[38]

MEANS WITHOUT AN END?

What was the nature of that schooling? In what ways did it seek to encourage broad, life-long skills that would prove portable and relevant, even revolutionary, elsewhere? Although VGIK, the world's first ever film school, was regarded as somewhat stale by the second half of the twentieth century, competition for entry was still stiff and the teaching both intensive and rigorous.[39] Like its Prague and Kiev counterparts, VGIK was organised into departments covering the major areas of film production, such as directing or acting, as well as movie criticism and economics. While students were barred from drifting beyond their allocated degree strand, they all learnt each other's skills and contributed to colleagues' examined projects, the graduation films in particular. Underscoring the breadth of their education beyond mere technical instruction, Riad Shaya notes:

> The 'theory' stream was enormously rich: world culture, world literature, the history of photography, philosophy, the history of philosophy, epistemology, a Marxist economic history of the world, as well as Marxist ethics and aesthetics. This was in addition to two years of music theory. Marxist economic theory was taught on its own, not in relation to film.[40]

Narrow, specialist training – that pillar of competitive labour market differentiation, which often leaves us inadequately adapted later down the line – was therefore somewhat eroded. All the institutions provided the necessary film-making facilities and extensive libraries of global cinema. 'We watched films from world cinema daily. So many films …' remembers Nidal al-Debs.[41] The schools scheduled teaching sessions led by professionals in the field and facilitated apprenticeships within the local industry.

The maximum class size of fifteen allowed for thorough participation in discussions and practical exercises that emphasised problem-solving and non-formulaic response – a world away from the rote-learning norm of Syrian education. Students remained with one principal tutor throughout their course of studies, allowing them to develop a comfortable familiarity with their teacher and peer group. To almost anyone who has been through higher education of late, such resources will seem 'aja'ib indeed – not least because they were supplied for free. In addition, as Riad Shaya points out, 'graduation films were subsidised by the school, unlike in western Europe, where the student pays'; Nabil al-Maleh completed thirteen film projects at FAMU, each one funded by the institution.[42]

The following proclamation will ring true for many people in the depressed economy from which *Arab Cinema Travels* has been written:

> we forfeit all the money we've spent on them [our student children]. Those, like my own son, who take the trouble to get a degree hover around the doors of government offices looking for a job. But all the positions are filled, and the government inspectors are not creating any new ones.[43]

This remonstration, you may be surprised to hear, derives from al-Muwaylihi's *rihla A Period of Time* and refers to the unjust, class-regulated restriction of education and jobs that British colonial agencies were then enforcing on Egypt.

The Syrian experience seems an 'ajiba now, in the climate of mounting higher education fees and subsequent debts, and was certainly an 'ajiba then. Just a few decades earlier, under the French Mandate, Syria had withstood an 80 per cent illiteracy rate.[44] *Verbal Letters* lingers on the rolling damage caused by this legacy, even from its opening sequence. When an official approaches Salma's grandparents for permission to build the railway over their land, they blithely consent with a thumbprint signature. It becomes clear that they have not fully understood what they have sanctioned when they are blown up inside their house in the very next scene. Salma's neighbour and love interest, Ghassan, is a slow and unwilling learner of his multiplication tables. When at home, his father bullies him on the matter, his sympathetic mother proves incapable of helping out because she has not been schooled to even this most basic of levels.

While Syria was still under French occupation, the USSR had dedicated a number of symposia to condemning French rule and cheering on Syria's liberation struggle.[45] Such gestures were greatly appreciated within Syria and, as early as 1944, Michel Aflaq laid bare his affiliations:

> We know that the Arabs see no reason to antagonize a great nation like Soviet Russia which has been expressing, since the emergence of her new system, sympathy with the peoples struggling for their freedom and independence. Moreover, the Arabs hope that the intentions of the Soviet state will have a good and practical impact on international politics.[46]

For the Soviet Union's part, this 'good and practical impact' can be witnessed in the provision of film education. In official documents, their line ran as follows: 'The shortage in this field [trained Arab technicians] is one of the consequences of colonialism, and it hampers the nation's effort to consolidate political gains and achieve economic independence.'[47]

On the home front, and unsurprisingly for a document drawn up by two teachers, the 1947 Ba'ath Constitution accommodates a whole section on education, demanding free universal schooling at every level and the abolition of foreign and private institutions. The dispatch of film students to the Eastern Bloc allowed this principle to be imbibed and shared. What is remarkable is that this policy was maintained throughout the shifts in leadership and the eventual banishment of Ba'athism's founding figures. Save for the existence of private schools, mostly religious, which were still obliged to follow the national curriculum, the original Constitution's ideas were fortified and actualised throughout the revisions to and legislative enactments of this manifesto.

Syrian cinema champions the educational agenda well beyond its condemnation of illiteracy. Dib from *Dreams of the City* and Sana from *Stars in Broad Daylight* aspire to high school diplomas, which were well beyond the reach of their working-class parents. The protagonists in both *The Events of the Coming Year* and *A Land for a Stranger* (Samir Zikra, 1988) are inspirational teachers with nationalist proclivities. Although far less affluent than most countries that posit – or are aiming to transfer – higher education out of the public sector, Syria managed to provide university tuition for its citizens without resorting to market, debt, private investment or employee-casualisation models.

In combative mode, Michel Aflaq was quick to condemn these and other values of western education and, consequently, their inability to prepare Arabs for the struggle for self-governance:

> When young people imitate what they have come to know of the advanced world and when they are deluded that the aim of their lives is to devote their life to personal affairs, private success and free abstract thinking, as young people do in those nations, they will be betraying their nation as well as themselves ... Moreover, they will be shirking the greatest and most honourable responsibility, the responsibility of a generation destined to achieve this historic radical change.[48]

True to this call, the ensuing Syrian movies follow a socially committed path. As Mohammad Malas discloses, 'When we started our life in cinema, we had many, many hopes of making something of our society. We dreamt that culture and cinema could bring about change in our society, our lives and our relationships with power.'[49] Issues of social equality drive each and every one of these movies, whether they deal with the rights of the urban poor (*The Extras*), rural citizens (*Al Lajat* (Riad Shaya, 1995)), sufferers from domestic abuse (*Dreams of the City*) or refugees (*Something is Burning* (Ghassan Shmeit, 1993)).

In sum, social priorities overlapped between the two countries and not solely at the level of diegesis. Nidal al-Debs confirms this:

> There is something shared between the two countries, something quite spiritual, but also cultural; similarities in the languages, in their philosophy and psychology. It is very easy to 'get' a Russian person ... Conversations start very quickly ... I was comfortable in Russia, comfortable with the people and communicating with them. There is another reason, of course: it is also because the way of living was very similar. It was a state with a communist regime and public sector, which is the way we are here in Syria.[50]

Without exception, the Syrian directors accentuate the affinity they felt for their places of study. To Riad Shaya's mind, there exists a 'common world view in both languages [Russian being the language of instruction], right down to their grammatical structures ... This leads to a similarity of thought.'[51] Cultural connection was particularly valuable, given the USSR's ideological need to recognise third world independence. The Treaty of Friendship and Cooperation announced that:

> The Union of Soviet Socialist Republics shall respect the policy of nonalignment pursued by the Syrian Arab Republic, which constitutes a major factor contributing to the preservation and consolidation of the international peace and security and to a lessening of international tensions.[52]

Instead, leftist bonds were forming through cross-border artistic encounters. Internationalist-socialist film culture was on the move, facilitating, to draw on a few obvious examples from the region, the Italian contributions to *The Battle of Algiers* (Gillo Pontecorvo, 1966), or the Dziga Vertov Group's collaborations with the Palestinian militia in Lebanon at the beginning of the 1970s. The NFO joined in at this point by supporting Egypt's Tawfiq Saleh in making *The Dupes*. And the Comecon film schools positively fostered dialogue and collaboration between non-aligned nationals. Mohammad Malas, for instance, joined forces with the Egyptian novelist (and, here, actor) Sun'allah Ibrahim for his graduation film *Everybody is in his Place and Everything is Under Control, Sir Officer* (1974).

So, what, precisely, did the Eastern Bloc gain from all this, if one is to assume a usefully critical standpoint and sideline the benefits of international solidarity? The ever-witty Faris al-Shidyaq asks this question with an eye to foreign domination within a world of ameliorating transport networks, talking of:

> railway *tracks* to bring close far-off *tracts* and create new *pacts*, to connect the *disconnected*, and make accessible what was *once protected*. [In the past], one didn't have to learn many languages. It could be said of anyone who knew a few words of Turkish – Welcome, my lord! How nice to see you, my lord! – that he'd make a fine interpreter at the Imperial court [emphases in the original].[53]

At the very least, might we read all the Eastern European interest in the Middle East through the politics of hospitality laid out in the previous chapter, pursuits that are never solely acts of giving?

The Arab region is, without question, strategic as a trading hub and as a marshal of transnational flows. This has consistently been the case from the earliest times, when the towns of Mari and Ugarit (now in Syria) held sway, to the era of the Silk Route (so crucial for the development of Arab travel literature) and, further to the west, the building (and later Egyptian nationalisation) of the Suez Canal. Unsurprisingly, Syria was a regular recipient of Soviet military training and hardware, although there were no foreign bases on its territory, and sympathetic analysts spin these measures as stemming from peacekeeping rather than belligerent intentions.[54]

Oil and gas, it should be stressed, must also have played a weighty role in the Warsaw Pact states' policies towards the Middle East during the period when these

Syrian directors were studying there. The Soviets, as one might expect, favoured the nationalisation of Middle Eastern oil supplies, siding, where pragmatic, with the producers. Most markedly, they endorsed the Arab embargo following the 1967 War with Israel. A comparatively powerful voice in favour of, say, autonomous Iraqi or Iranian control no longer exists within international diplomacy. While there are limited oil reserves on Syrian soil (which Eastern European engineers have helped drill and refine), these are of negligible importance compared to the influence Syria then commanded as one particularly pan-Arabist state within the region. Through a series of intricate acts of assistance, including the training of film personnel, Comecon nations maintained a friendly understanding with the Middle Eastern nations. While openly asserting their belief in non-intervention, their stake is clearly understandable in relation to European NATO's then 80 per cent dependency on oil from this portion of the world.[55]

A GEOPOLITICS OF OWNERSHIP

We might then call this *influence*. And one whose ambition lay more in inspiring a politics of how goods could be funded and circulated, a concentration on movement that travel writing also encourages. The USSR's unswerving denunciation of capitalism and imperialism can be seen recapitulated within Syrian policy on film financing and distribution. Co-production with unsympathetic entities was not an option, as (a deeply critical) Oussama Mohammad explains:

> The National Film Organization regards collaboration with European counterparts as the road map for colonization. The argument goes like this: How could countries that once colonized us, or coveted our riches with colonial designs be attributed good intentions. Europe does not really recognize Israel's occupation of our territory as a crime, and they have absolved Zionism from the occupation of Palestine, the expulsion of its people from their homes. Europe does not see Zionism as an ideology of terrorism. How can we collaborate hand in hand with countries that defend all these crimes?[56]

For long periods, certain companies were not able to peddle their films in Syria because they also did business in Israel.[57] And thus the exhibition orbits of these movies, while they took in Cannes and Venice, circled more frequently through Algiers, Warsaw, Tashkent, Bucharest, Carthage, Moscow and Sofia.[58] The stated aims of the Damascus Film Festival (under the auspices of the National Film Organization) were, along with the typical 'development of national cinema within the Arab homeland', 'the creation of cultural and intellectual bridges which link Arab filmmakers, on the one hand, to filmmakers of the third world *and then* the world at large, on the other [my emphasis]'.[59]

Socialism organised what these films discussed and how they were manufactured (to be discussed presently), but it also dictated how – if at all – they were seen. Hamid Merai, then director of the NFO, rationalised underexposure partially in terms of unabashedly socialist content: 'opportunities remain limited because this type of film tackles problems and situations that the public is not used to encountering'.[60] But audiences could largely not see these films, even if they wanted to. Only two or three are or have ever been commercially available. To put it frankly, these movies did and do not travel. Even in Syria, the DVD stores have not carried them. After perhaps my twentieth enquiry with a pirate, one, confused and eager to placate my curiosity, pulled out a pile of soft-core pornography, most probably not made under the official banner of the NFO. Sometimes even film-makers do not possess copies of their own work and the NFO was cagey about allowing me study screenings. It was easier to source official Ministry of Culture publications about these films than it was to actually watch them.

To put all this in context, back in the twentieth century, film-making was playing its part within broader nationalisation initiatives. From the mid-1960s onwards, a command economy assumed whole or majority control of most of the country's main industries and banks, with three-quarters of the GDP eventually nationalised.[61] Land reform, introduced during Syria's brief union with Egypt in the 1950s, redistributed 1.5 million hectares of land to 55,000 families during the following decade.[62] These changes were collectively called *inqilab* (profound transformation) and extended also to the creation of a welfare system and ambitious educational reforms.

The travel undertaken by these educational migrants helped consolidate and figure out how transfer out of the private sector might be put into practice. Nidal al-Debs lays out the implications of state ownership for cinematic dissemination:

> The National Film Organization owns the films and does not care to make prints or distribute them. It finds no need for that. Why do it? They will simply be screened at festivals and that will be enough. Syrian cinema makes no profit anyway, so why strike more than one print?[63]

A fair few movies could be viewed on video at the National Library, but these were in a shocking state, often demagnetised or missing a reel in the transfer process. While a matrix of spectatorship once existed between various second world and non-aligned nations, this was, at the point of my fieldwork, drastically diminished, meaning that new Syrian films were more likely to air only at the Damascus Film Festival, and then never again resurface in a theatre.

Positioned thus, they unequivocally refused that cornerstone of capitalism: the maximisation of profit. Syrian cinema was drawn, certainly, to the return, but not when it came to money. What, then, was returned? Was the 'means without an end' principle prolonged here? Might hospitality (of a guarded and partial persuasion) suggest better models of comprehension than the reasonings of revenue generation? In practice, the unavailability of these movies demands that we detach from our standard, predictable attributions of value when it comes to cinema, be these commercially or socially focused, and confront the fact that there will always be elements of life that evade such tidy conscriptions.[64] The obsessive utilitarianism prompting Tahtawi's collection of French strategies and the government officials' disapproval of art's 'uselessness' in *The Events of the Coming Year* are undermined when these films are not released into a wider world.

In the last dregs of the period under consideration, Syrian society was playing an anxious waiting game with the capitalist concept of the asset. While counterfeit products and public ownership were both the norm, the World Intellectual Property Organization, which Syria joined in 2004, seemed to be hovering. Decoupling stylistic concurrence from contentions over origins and possession in this climate allows for a more sustained investigation of how both communism and Arab socialism have aimed to schematise culture outside a particular business model and create, as will be elaborated, what they judged to be fair working condition for its labourers. The oeuvre and its inaccessibility therefore provide an object lesson in how impossible circulation can be for material that is not, primarily, commodified, that does not function hand-in-glove with the oligarchical structuring of global film distribution. These movies are 'aja'ib for me in that they are rare or unattainable, yet I certainly do not hanker, as most travel writing does, to fetishise exceptionality for its own sake, for the market's sake, most probably. The atypical character of Syrian cinema instead coaxes us towards urgent questions about the continuity of not-for-profit cinema and the political ideals it might harbour in a post-Soviet age. Bypassing the dominant networks of access in the name of socialism, this material belongs to everyone, yet no one.

A particular concept of property, as one would expect of a country distinguished by nationalisation projects, was also fundamental to the politics of what these movies look and sound like. Echoing the mixed lineage of Arab variants of socialism, there are unique dimensions to this national cinema, as well as the protraction of certain internation-alised values and aesthetics. Seeking to categorise Syrian cinema textually – and geopolitically too, it should be noted – Richard Peña observes, 'All are fine exemplars of the VGIK style, an approach that opts for carefully composed, almost iconographic shots – the opposite perhaps of the more fluid, hand-held style adopted widely after the explosion of the French New Wave.'[65] A hunt for analogy (so much the glistening linchpin that entices a new consumer base) might also have tracked down The Leopard, with its striking Eisensteinian cross-cuts between victory parties to mark the end of World War II and peasants brutalised by Syrian soldiers on French salaries. There is also The Extras, with its affinity for the bleak comedy, the surrealism and the preoccupation with menacing bureaucracies to be found in Kafka and the Czech New Wave. Or Nights of the Jackal's (Abdullatif Abdulhamid, 1989) quotation of the Soviet co-production I Am Cuba (Mikhail Kalatozov, 1964), which sees Abu Kamal setting fire to his wheat crop rather than have it captured by the Israeli forces threatening Syria's borders.

To concentrate primarily on replication when reading these sequences would imply a politics of source and ownership, which severely curtails the political potential of how Syrian films operate. Moving beyond this interpretation, these citations compellingly insist that culture can be thought of, and can function, outside and in opposition to the ambits of private property and its supposed utility. They ask for an interrogation of novelty as a value within marketplace demarcation. Scholarly and technical expertise, aesthetic registers, common aspirations for nationalisation, universal education and social betterment of a particular ideological persuasion all migrate here. The logistics of their development, the casting of various roles in these tasks hold up for scrutiny the investment of influence with dubious notions of cultural or intellectual property. 'Solidarity' might be a better term for all these gestures. Mette Hjort's 'affinitive transnationalism' another.[66] The diffused authorship, and thus agency, of the rihla genre comes to mind here too.

Peña's comment brings to light the particular geography of education examined above, which is surely key to unlocking some of the complexities of anti-capitalist forms of creativity. But one should be cautious here of how a formalist teleology, the forging of a chain of influence, would edge towards a client-state model of innovation and derivativeness, something that could severely restrict how these films might be motivated, interpreted or could function dynamically within present-day analysis.

Perhaps it might be better to read these travelling scholars, like Tahtawi before them, as translators of pertinent political ideals (Tahtawi brought French constitutional and juridical documents into Arabic for the first time), rather than imitators. The act of translation strives to transmit otherwise obscure knowledge, but it is always also the delicate conciliation of the gaps that lie between languages and cultures, just as Arab socialism is. The Moroccan philosopher Abdelkebir Khatibi, familiar from the preceding chapter, offers some sage advice for getting to grips with the mechanics of influence, how ideas move. He forgoes the more linear chugging of developmental history, concentrating, as an alternative, on charged, largely asymmetrical, interaction between geopolitical units that are proclaimed to be distinct. Jacques Derrida, whom we might remember as 'Algerian', proposes something similar when he claims that:

> [E]very language [is] a language of the other: the impossible property of a language. But that must not lead to a kind of neutralisation of differences, to the misrecognition of determinate expropriations against which a war can be waged on quite different fronts. On the contrary, that is what allows the stakes to be repoliticised.[67]

Khatibi's 'double critique' muddles the impossibly divided positions of leader and follower, oppressed and oppressor, coloniser and colonised as they scarify the interpellated subjecthood of the acknowledged latter. To confound and denounce the epistemologies of divorce, signifiers of each can be pushed to their limits, roughly restitched together, ironised even. They then bring about the sorts of revealing geopolitical conjecture evident when, as in *The Extras*, the cinematic cousins of the Czech secret police break into a small Damascene apartment. Or when *Nights of the Jackal*, via citation, quietly compares Israel's invasion of Syria to American aggression towards Cuba.

It makes sense to think of history and knowledge in these terms too, denting a notion that communism spontaneously sprung from Europe then pushed 'eastwards'. Such ideals are never singularly invented or latterly copyrighted. There is a means by which history can be understood and mobilised outside these fixed, one-way evolutions, a method useful for the analysis of, but also, in principle, heartily encouraged within many of the contexts these Syrian journeys undertook. This is dialectics, a praxis of movement.

INTERNATIONALIST DIALECTICS

Even if ownership was disassembled somewhat within these encounters, Syrians still felt dissatisfied with the unequal access to power and resources – international, internal – that are highlighted by Khatibi and Derrida's critiques. Muhammad al-Maghut, primarily a writer of poetry and plays, but also a film scenarist, describes the relationship with the Soviet Union, tartly recasting the Arab voyager within the era of the space race, when a Soviet rocket launched the first Syrian cosmonaut:

Scientists and technicians, Give me a ticket to the sky:
I come on behalf of my grieved country,
Her aged, her widows, her children.
Give me a ticket to the sky
I have no money ... only tears.

No place for me?
Let me stay in the hold
Or on the deck.
I'm a peasant, I'm used to it.
I won't hurt a star
I won't be rude to a cloud.
All I want is to reach
The sky as soon as I can
To put the whip in God's hand:
He may stir us to revolution.[68]

Such expressions demand attention be paid to an ambivalence within Syria towards bilateral arrangements. Not an outright rejection, but a dialectics through encounter, one that honours the intellectual processing of the 'foreign' in *talab al-ʿilm rihlat* along with the Hegelian impetuses of Baʿath rhetoric.

Confrontational engagements with power, Mohammad Malas points out, were encouraged by his and Oussama Mohammad's tutor at VGIK, Igor Talankin:

I remember wanting to compare. From the window of VGIK, we could see the Institute of Marxism-Leninism. He [Talankin] asked us to look over there. 'That is the Institute of Marxism-Leninism and this is the Institute of Cinema.' In the '69–'70 period, that was not easy. It was an important lesson he taught us.[69]

'Many of the professors were rebels,' Riad Shaya points out, 'and the same went for the student body.'[70] Both al-Maghut and Talankin's entreaties highlight difference. Dialectics then refuses to acknowledge the constancy of either side of the divide, encouraging a thorough critique which pits seeming opposites against each other in order to bring about concrete social change.

This technique, central (in theory, anyway) to the Marxist praxis of the Soviet Union, as well as the montage film-making of former VGIK professors like Sergei Eisenstein, structured the learning experience of the Syrian students. At the core of VGIK's curricula was the equal weighting of theory and practice (the former from eight in the morning until two; the latter running well into the evening).

VGIK, in so doing, aimed to promote a vigorous dialectical involvement of the two inseparable concepts of 'theory' and 'practice'.

Such principles also overlap with Baʿath Party founder Michel Aflaq's aspirations not only for education, but also the functioning of the Syrian state. For Aflaq, revolutionary politics should be unending Hegelian-inspired progress achieved through the interplay of proclaimed opposites, a constantly renewed synthesis. Dialectical processing, unimaginable without movement, was, and is, also vital to how

Arabism and socialism work in partnership within Ba'athism, a set of doctrines that endeavour to enable the co-habitation of, at first glance, incompatible local priorities and internationalist leftism. In its early days, Ba'athism made it its mission to achieve workable political solutions by acknowledging the mobility of concepts and beliefs as a means of accomplishing material, revolutionary change. The heart of theoretical Syrian Arab socialism pumps productive dialectics through incongruence. Unlike the on-the-hoof nationalisation Egypt shaped once President Nasser came to power, Ba'athism had been comprehensively thought through in the 1940s by its founding figures, Aflaq and Salah al-Din Bitar, in line with the specific needs and limitations of pan-Arabism and socialism. Quite some challenge. 'Socialism is a branch and a result of our nationalism,' Aflaq proclaimed.[71] The motives for the ascendance of the 'national' are addressed more fully in the Ba'ath Constitution:

> The Pan-Arab national link is the only link that exists in the Arab State. It assures harmony among the citizens, their fusion in the single crucible of one nation and combats all kinds of denominational, sectarian, tribal, ethnic and regional fanaticism.[72]

For the population of Greater Syria and, later, Iraq, there existed an urgency to fight for self-determination by uniting a diffused society, composed not only of a plethora of religious groups, but also Kurdish, Armenian, Palestinian and other migrants. In relation to the Eastern Bloc, Syria, with its defiantly non-communist form of anti-capitalism, had always been much more independent than a textbook client state. Ba'athism thus aimed to serve up a working model of socialist localisation and compromise. It strove hard to establish a socialism that opposed stern and direct communism (claiming that communism's understanding of class was unsuitably Eurocentric), while aiming to affiliate all this to Islam (too tokenistically and clumsily many aver) – and much to the dismay of various atheist-materialist onlookers.[73] Not without reason, Islamist factions within Syria, long suppressed by Ba'athist regimes, have maintained a fraught and discontented relationship with many of socialism's tenets, violently, to this very day. They are not alone here.

The NFO directors have been consistently critical of the eventual ossification of Ba'ath rhetoric into hard-line political doctrine and violent oppression. Soon into the insurgency of 2011, Oussama Mohammad, Nidal al-Debs, Nabil al-Maleh and Mohammad Malas all publicly put their name to a petition that urged 'filmmakers in the world to contribute to stopping the killing [in Syria] by exposing and denouncing it, and by announcing their solidarity with the Syrian people and with their dreams of justice, equality and freedom'.[74] But well before this decisive historical moment, Nabil al-Maleh defined his film-making technique as trying 'to expose the problems inherent in the revolution ... researching the reasons for its failure, its downfall, and how it can succeed by taking its example from the Arab experience and the forward-looking ideas that already exist within it'.[75] *The Ascent of Rain* (Abdullatif Abdulhamid, 1995) ridiculed moribund socialist rituals and discourse: mindless communiqués are dispatched and political speeches do not appreciably differ from the slogans ('Down with Zionism!') dished out by an uncomprehending pet parrot in one scene. Kamil in *The Events of the Coming Year* is a pretty loathsome example of a dogmatic Marxist. *Sacrifices*, *Nights of the Jackal*, *Stars in Broad Daylight* and *Dreams of the City* are all deeply critical of their bullying patriarchal protagonists – stand-ins for the Syrian dictatorship's ruling elite (Khalil in *Stars in Broad Daylight* is the spitting image of then-president Hafiz al-Assad) and their lackeys (Khalil is a wire-tapper by profession). As part of the wedding entertainment in *Stars in Broad Daylight*, Khalil parades out his two boys to recite empty chants and mindless, everyday militarism:

Papa bought me a present
A tank and a rifle
My brother and I are small
We learnt how to join
The army of liberation
In the army of liberation we learnt
How to protect the homeland
Down, down with Israel!
Long live the Arab nation!

Ironically, but true to its intentions, the revolutionary potential with which Ba'athism endowed its cinema, politically and educationally, then made it possible to work productively with particular social currents that were often at odds with one another. In these instances, dialectics is achieved through concurrent and opposing registers of expression. The words and actions on screen manifest in a matter-of-fact and deadly serious fashion, but, and particularly to those familiar with life under the regime, they are also darkly comical and thus satirise it.

In dealing here with artistic style, it makes sense to return to our *rihlat*. More so, even, because the situations and ideals under critique are figured, in part, spatially. Arab travel literature is adept at negotiating palpable concerns brought to light through geopolitical difference. As director Nabil al-Maleh remarks, 'travel is about finding yourself and the world in which you live, but through *conflict*'.[76] The journeys described in *rihlat* bounce between a sense of bonded unity throughout the Muslim diaspora and recurrent exposure to startling disparity (the kind required for literary entertainment, at the very least). Further, writers such as Tahtawi weigh up these consistencies and divergences, the power relations they catalyse within the specific terrains of scholarship, nationalism, socio-economic development and the design of new political systems.

But, returning to the question of multifarious and inter-relational style, it is Faris al-Shidyaq who perhaps offers the most inspiration. *Leg Over Leg* is a work of astounding montage. It would take pages to list the different genres from which his narrative is compiled, the end effect being much less a decorative patchwork than it is confirmation that migration and cross-contamination are the conditions of art and life.[77] No one register holds court, collapse constantly leading to refreshed presence. By speaking the same circumstances in two conflicting tones, these Syrian movies achieve a similar uncertainty that hopes to prompt change. It is through their travels for study, the Syrian directors happily avow, that they felt assured in carrying out praxis that was critical not simply of the communist bloc, but also of their own nation.

Moreover, they do so frequently through the very labour of the film technician, through aesthetic decisions made primarily on set past the moment of script censorship. With this in mind, the time has come to direct attention away from the value of the end product and towards its mode of manufacture. This is, I want to argue, a more promising site for inspiring political change, given the rareness of these films to present-day audiences and, therefore, the possibility viewing them might prompt for any such perceptual shifts or motivated actions.

SYRIAN CINEMA'S STRUCTURES OF LABOUR

The production process established within the National Film Organization was highly dialectical, consolidated by an insistence on collaboration. Instilled within and carried back from the Eastern European film schools, a lateral mobility among the NFO employees promised to guarantee a multiplicity of voices with no single one permanently held up as authoritative. Samir Zikra wrote *Dreams of the City* for Mohammad Malas to direct; Abdullatif Abdulhamid provided the music for Oussama Mohammad's *Step by Step* (1978); while Oussama Mohammad co-authored *The Night* (Mohammad Malas, 1992). Abdullatif Abdulhamid assumes a leading acting role in *Stars in Broad Daylight* and Riad Shaya contributed as an assistant director.

And so the list goes on, fulfilling an objective advocated by former VGIK professor Vsevolod Pudovkin, and one that takes us back to cinema's involvement within broader Syrian industrialisation initiatives:

> A film factory has all the characteristics of industrial production. The leading engineer can do nothing without his experts and workers. Their mutual efforts will come to nothing if each worker were [sic] to limit himself to the mechanical execution of his narrow function. Collective work is what makes every part of the work a living and organic part of the larger goal/task.[78]

In exactly this sense, these film-makers were a solid team, a set of employees of the same institution who had been awarded permanent salaries. An education achieved through travel had set in motion momentous social relations, but the return was where these took on their full meaning. Jobs were assured for all those arriving home from film school in Eastern Europe. Elsewhere within movie culture, guarantees like these, outside the sway of nepotism, are practically unheard of. Most movies outside Syria are made according to the post-Fordist principles of flexible, precarious labour: a new team for each project and no guaranteed income in between jobs. Upholding a completely different logic, the National Film Organization provided stable civil service jobs for all those it hired. It resided in the public sector, which, in 2003, employed 58 per cent of university graduates in urban areas and 75 per cent in the countryside – people attracted by the job security, enhanced retirement benefits and shorter working hours.[79] The salaries at the NFO were not particularly high and definitely lower than one might expect in similar private sector employment, but stood 20 per cent above the average government wage and, most importantly, remained constant, regardless of production schedules.[80] Furthermore, civil servants could expect to retire at sixty and were not supposed to work for more than forty-two hours per week.[81] For freelancers in, say, the British film industry, seventy-two hours is more typical, a norm that sees them waiving their rights to protection under European labour law.[82]

The motivations for folding movie-making into the public sector can be found, again, in the original Ba'ath Constitution, which deems 'intellectual work the most sacred type', insisting that, 'the state must protect and encourage intellectuals'.[83] This declaration finds ballast in Soviet definitions of the intelligentsia: a social group dedicating their labour to the collective good. For Riad Shaya, these convictions were indeed realised by the public sector: 'Work like mine would have been impossible without the existence of the National Film Organization, which provides all filmmakers with the chance to direct intellectually- and technically-distinguished material ... it's very different from [the rest of] the cinema industry.'[84]

Prolonged experience of these ideals overseas helped render them practicable, believable and unalienated back home on Syrian turf. V. Andashev and P. Oglobin explain the Soviet party line from those days, with a stress on the ties between education and labour:

> In giving aid to Arab countries the Soviet Union and other socialist states are aware that it is necessary for young Arab nations to raise labour productivity in order to achieve social progress. And in order to raise labour productivity, Lenin said, it is necessary to improve the people's general educational and cultural level, discipline, ability to work and organization of work. The Soviet Union regards it as its international duty to help the Arab countries train workers in various fields, especially for industry.[85]

Thus the assistance the Eastern Bloc doled out followed and established particular political patterns, ones that were to assertively shape Syrian cinema not so much by their material exchanges, but more through their encouragement of a particular ethos of labour. Yes, aid came in the form of goods, at times as raw capital (loaned at a 2.5 per cent interest rate), but, as has been illustrated by the movement of people for training and work, *services*, including education, dominated.[86] An ungenerous observation of these gestures would highlight the creation of labour markets for the Warsaw Pact countries, but this has never been the case within Syrian cinema, a sector that remains true to the nationalist declarations of Directive 258, which aimed 'to develop the film industry in the Syrian Arab Republic'[87] and almost exclusively employed its own citizens.

The financial support the NFO provided was not profligate: about $1 million per film.[88] What is peculiar to Syrian cinema's chosen *modus operandi* is that the films *look* much more expensive. Although production was resource-poor in many respects, it took true advantage of the fact that the civil service model renders it time- and human-power rich. Tricky crowd scenes, complex tracking and crane shots, arduous chiaroscuro compositions and exacting framing that are in no way 'necessary' to plots – and stretch the time-frame for shooting well beyond those of the average film – make for a very lush body of work.

The Night showcases some particularly challenging set-ups. A nocturnal air raid scene, for example, contrapuntally plays off approaching horses, running children, incendiaries and the general chaos of war, all within lengthy, fluid camera movements.

Stars in Broad Daylight (1988): goods swing across their path as the family crosses the docks

Orchestrating and adequately rehearsing such a sequence, with highly unpredictable contributors, is an impressive achievement that would be incredibly expensive if everyone involved was paid by the hour. Resetting the scene, should anything have gone wrong mid-take, would have consumed considerable time. There are quite a few such moments in *The Night*, made all the more impressive by the fact that the crew were working with a rickety old dolly that only had three, rather than four wheels. *Stars in Broad Daylight* does not go easy on itself either, notably in the scene at the Lattakia docks, where characters wend their way through some elegantly choreographed heavy machinery. The wedding scene ropes in animals, children and a setting sun – staging that, again, demands precision from notoriously uncontrollable participants. *Verbal Letters* encases two dawn incidents and *Sacrifices* weaves in fastidious positioning of chickens, doves, cows, a snake and a donkey. The opening sequence of *A Land for a Stranger* parades the Ottoman elite, scores of costumed extras, a marching band and a children's choir through the streets of Aleppo. This list gives merely a cursory impression; similar ambition blazes forth from practically every NFO endeavour. In a state where full employment was the goal, and where, within the twenty-five to forty-five years of age cohort, male participation was close to 100 per cent, such ambitious ventures become possible for a low-income cinema.[89] As they did across much of the Comecon world.

Temporal and human resources are similarly milked in how cameras were wielded. There are numerous elegant crane shots; helicopters were even deployed, such as in the denouements of *The Leopard* and *The Events of the Coming Year*. The prolonged tracking shot is a staple. The riverbank chase sequence in *Algae*, or the film's many meanderings through the corridors of the courthouse serve as examples. *The Night*'s opening sequence comprises a long, single take that follows Wisal through her derelict house, masonry falling at defined, punctuating moments (something that would have required a significant rebuild had the process gone awry). Frequently, these travelling shots invite an engagement with the politics of movement. Mobile camerawork in *Something is Burning* sweeps across the boundary-lines between neighbours' properties. Proving these borders both enclosing and permeable, the film stylistically confirms the unstable geopolitical status of its refugee protagonists and their relationship to land. I shall continue with these concerns presently. In other movies about migrants, such as *The Events of the Coming Year* and *Algae*, journeys themselves are captured in series of travelling shots, layering perspective over on-screen movement.

As with the highly wrought staging of the set pieces, such camerawork is laborious, especially if one's dolly is missing a wheel. Oussama Mohammad remarks upon the uniqueness of the Syrian situation in this respect:

> Syria might very well be the last place in this world where a filmmaker is given license to re-shoot a sequence until it is deemed right, where time and space for editing or sound mixing of an entire film can be redone, without a reconfiguration of the film's overall budget. Furthermore Syria is perhaps the only place in this world where a young filmmaker without significant prior experience is provided the opportunity to make a feature-length film, regardless of the viability of the film once it is released.[90]

Here, the stylistic imprint of modestly tenured public sector film-making contrasts vividly with the rationalised and pressurised schedules of most other post-Fordist cinematic production. More usually, drawn-out manufacturing is considered the preserve of wealthier projects, yet this was not the case within the working practices of the NFO where the high salaries of the freelance approach, designed to cushion fallow periods, did not intervene with such ambitions. Nidal al-Debs corroborates, 'we make the films slowly and at an easy pace. We don't have a producer or a company harassing us, so we can make the films we want to make.'[91] A pleasant, unrushed working environment was favoured over maximised output, meaningfully re-engaging the questions about thwarted profit expansion posed by the narrowed circulation of these movies.

More sardonically, Mohammad Malas exclaims, 'time ... yes, we have all the time in the world'.[92] At Syria's completion rate of one and a half films per year before 2011, and with half of the men and 80 per cent of the women on public sector contracts clocking up less than forty-hour weeks, people of a certain get-up-and-go temperament were inclined to grow twitchy.[93] Even the films themselves shuffle along at a ponderous pacing, the majority running beyond the hour and a half norm for features. This unhurried attitude is commonplace within Syrian labour. My experience in the viewing booth at the National Library is illustrative in this respect. Other librarians dropped by for protracted chats with their colleague in the audiovisual room; relationship dramas unfolded; tears were shed; I was involved in several conversations about matrimony; one time, loud construction work made it practically impossible to hear the dialogue of the films; and, initially, the young librarian did not even know how to use a VHS player. 'I've never had to switch it on before. Since I've been working on this desk, no one has come in here except you.' Jobs mingled more freely with other regimens of life, and output and efficiency, so much the darlings of exploitative employers elsewhere in the world, held less currency. We must think about stasis as well as – and in contradistinction to – mobility here. While the films may ask their viewers to contemplate a particular kind of temporality, their protraction might well stem from other desires. Samir Zikra entreats audiences 'to be diligent with the

Verbal Letters (1991): Salma waits in the dark, picked out by chiaroscuro lighting

noteworthy length of our films, their perplexity and burden of detail, for every single film was either the first, or second ... and even possibly the last ... every film was made to say everything'.[94]

In no realm is this more palpable than within the *mise en scène*. A lot can happen at the level of style, as Faris al-Shidyaq has allowed us to recognise. The complex sequences described above are testament to this, but conspicuous precision is loaded into practically all other shots too. 'There is significance to every element of the film,' Nidal al-Debs insists. 'Nothing is there purely by coincidence and that is because we actually have the time to work on these details.'[95] *Al Lajat* provides excellent examples here. Light on dialogue, it creates an evocative ambience through its captivation with visual textures and thoughtful, painterly compositions. There is also a surprisingly low quotient of broad daylight in these movies, with film-makers preferring to experiment with nocturnal atmospheres. Again, these are much harder to shoot, and rarely necessitated by plots in any strict sense. The extensive play of light and shadow (often through mashrabiyya window screens), the creation of ornate chiaroscuro rhythms and the enjoyment of saturated colours distinguishes such films as *Dreams of the City*, *A Land for a Stranger*, *Verbal Letters*, *Stars in Broad Daylight* and, naturally, *The Night* and *Nights of the Jackal*. Deep focus (again, hard to achieve in moody lighting) lavishes attention on multiple planes within the frame throughout Malas' and Mohammad's oeuvre.

There is also a profound affection for mirrors and other reflective surfaces in the films of both these directors, as well as in Raymond Butros' work. *Sacrifices* brandishes the mirror motif because it is appropriate to its doubled characters, the three unnamed and often interchangeable sons in particular. Elsewhere, it is more an exuberant aesthetic flourish. One particularly mannerist scene in *Stars in Broad Daylight* is shot through a glass table which flips the image upside down, then boldly fractures the action as the camera subtly shifts its angle. Certainly, all this betrays the hours the film-makers are afforded to experiment and push their equipment, capabilities and Eastern Bloc training to the limit. At the same time, these techniques bring their labour resolutely to the fore, a workerist ethic that gathered its momentum by travelling back and forth across the socialist states.

Sacrifices (2002): deep focus, a mirror and chickens together in one shot

The mirrors (notoriously hard for sound crews to negotiate) become frames-within-frames, as do the various photography sessions in, say, *The Night*, and the video playback loop that is created for the wedding in *Stars in Broad Daylight*. Perhaps a dry comment on Syrian cinema's small audiences worldwide, there are rarely too many people watching the live feed on the television in the corner of the garden. Worse still, the television that emerges from the father's military kit bag in *Sacrifices* not only transmits images of one of the unnamed sons carrying another television that relays imagines of himself amid war-torn landscapes, but the set also strikes him down with blindness. Less damagingly, *Under the Ceiling*'s protagonist, Marwan, earns his living as a film-maker, his footage bleeding across the narrative and prompting many of the movie's flashbacks. Later into the story, Marwan makes a start on a tourist documentary about Syria. His financial pragmatism triggers debates about the social position of the artist (through the economies of travel), ones that are also raised in relation to his friend Ahmad, a politically committed poet who rushes to the front in the Lebanese Civil War, leaving behind, unbeknownst to him, a pregnant Lina who is then obliged by her family to have an unwanted abortion.

These instances overwhelmingly induce, through their content *and* style, a sense of the weight and labour of representation; the intellectual and technical toil involved in producing all this is not allowed to escape the viewer. If the net result of so many films the world over is the effacement of the effort required to create them, all in the name of uninterrupted entertainment, Syrian public sector movies achieve something different: a respect for labour and a contemplation of its politics within Arab (and international) socialism.

The *'aja'ib* erupting out of Syrian cinema for me, as a contemporary viewer, is the refusal of the casualised economy of film-making dominant almost everywhere else, where free labour (such as the internship) is an 'essential' starting point and each year people in the industry die in accidents caused by extreme fatigue. *'Aja'ib* through the startling difference they present, these movies promote comparison, assimilation and the sorts of dialectical engagement that have also fuelled Ba'athism and socialism – if and when their ideals are allowed to travel. Without doubt, *'aja'ib* are rhetorical constructs and dream of particular and discriminating political valences. They are the fruit of labour and what is revealing about Syrian cinema's own *'aja'ib* sightings is that they also regularly seek to reinforce and panegyrise a leftist image of the worker.

THE WORKER ON SCREEN

To home in on one potent example, Abdellatif Abdulhamid's *Our Hands*, completed in 1982, directly after his return from the USSR, consists almost entirely of close-ups of Syrians' hands interweaving social gestures with a panoply of manual tasks, from laboratory work and type-setting to cotton processing and book burning. *Today and Every Day* (Oussama Mohammad, 1986), a twelve-minute, largely dialogue-free document of everyday life in the port city of Lattakia, necessarily dedicates much of its time to the toils of bakers, fishermen and construction workers, punctuated by a ticking clock. Yet perhaps the group of Syrian workers most immortalised within Syrian cinema are those grafting within the rural economy. Migrants from the countryside appear in city tales, such as *Something is Burning*, and the primary location for *Al Lajat, Stars in Broad Daylight, Listeners' Choice, Nights of the Jackal* and *Verbal Letters* is the farm.

During the period when most of these films were shot, Syria's rural economy accounted for 60 per cent of the country's workers and was supplying around half of all its food needs (down from three-quarters in the 1970s).[96] From the beginning, Syrian cinema exalted these contributions, but it also conducted dialectical explorations into the shift from village to city. *The Leopard* set a tone in 1972 with its dignified and individualising close-ups of farmers' faces contending with French colonial persecution. Its eponymous hero, Abu 'Ali, is a singular poster boy for anti-imperial struggle. Refusing the company of helpers, the subject of legend and song, robbing the rich to give to the poor, he is the hero-everyman who breaks into a military police dinner to denounce them with 'this is the lamb and chicken of the peasants', he is captured, tortured and rendered a martyr to the most noble of all causes.

Our Hands (1982)

In *Among the Jasmine Trees*, his study of modernity within Syrian music, Jonathan Holt Shannon argues that Syrian culture's valorisation of 'the peasant' travelled over with this slew of graduates, pollinated by 'Eastern European conceptions of folklore, nationalism, and authenticity'.[97] This could certainly be argued of *The Leopard*, but what of the other movies, which favour the communal or the extended family as their focus? Just as our travel writers have done, our Ba'athist dialectical materialists too, it pays to set each region's depictions of farmers into dynamic interplay.

Both film industries clearly impress an intimacy between rural workers and the land. In *The Leopard*, the farmers compare themselves to seeds and can survive on the run in unforgiving terrain where their French pursuers cannot. Such analogies are not new to the cinema of socialist countries. Soviet classic *The Earth* (Alexander Dovzhenko, 1930) regularly enmeshes its characters with the land and its harvests, so it is worth inviting it to participate in a dialogue with its Syrian counterparts – and probably not for the first time. All these examples deal, in their own ways, with the collectivisation of agricultural land, but the framings favoured by each cinema are at variance. Frequently shot from below, an angle shared by images of the idealised worker across the communist world, *The Earth* looks up to its protagonists, stark against a clear-sky backdrop. By contrast, the Syrian farmers are mostly viewed from a level setting, never abstracted from the land they inhabit. Less eager to lionise, perhaps, Syrian cinema may have had its fill of such iconography during its trips overseas, may have wished to associate farmers more manifestly with labour in the films' frames as well as in their narratives.

This second supposition can be supported through a comparison of editing techniques. *The Earth* insists upon the worker–land bond through juxtaposition: a young girl, then a close-up of apples or sunflowers. Instead, their Syrian comrades find themselves amid the standard long lateral tracking shots. Adroit camera movement and careful composition engross these farmers with the soil they work at one and the same time. *Nights of the Jackal*'s second scene commences with a dexterous four-minute, thiry-five-second single take. As the politics of representation travels, it adapts to its new environments and contradicts its forefathers. First, the camera performs a slow, almost 360 degree pan across the rural vista before wandering through the protagonists' farm, locating each character as they gird themselves for a day in either the fields or the house. This sequence is one of many content simply to leave the workers to get on with everyday tasks. The seemingly humdrum is near-sanctified, just as the persona of the Soviet peasant had been, by the generous screen time apportioned.

Rural work is not just awarded significant attention in this subset of Syrian cinema, its temporalities often dictate also the pacing of the movies. The annual rhythms of different harvests act as chapter markers in *Nights of the Jackal*, while its soundtrack is evenly punctuated by the repetitive noises of agricultural manual labour: grinding corn, churning butter and such like. Quotidian farm activities consume the bulk of *Al Lajat*'s first act, a movie that stresses the cyclical character of rural time and links its protagonists to elemental forces through Salma's repeated voiceover 'wax and wane, wax and wane'.

In counterpoint to these instances of stasis and cyclicality, there are also dramatic departures from the village, ones that must be understood according to not only the politics of mobility, but also the specific interchanges between Soviet and Syrian ideology and economics as negotiated by the returnee directors. Departure for education is, predictably, a prevalent theme, but above and beyond authorial rumination. In a period when the majority of the population worked the land, but only 2–3 per cent were studying agricultural sciences, it is not hard to discern why scholarship should be a preoccupation.[98] Khalil's contempt for Sana's chosen suitor, Sami, in *Stars in Broad Daylight* is aroused by the fact that he is enrolled on an Arabic Literature degree when he was born into a farming family. Kamal, living alone in Lattakia during his studies in *Nights of the Jackal*, becomes dissolute in the eyes of his father and then, worse still, drops out to become a road leveller. The tensions between industry and farming, town and village, reform and tradition are conspicuous and frequently complicate how learning is managed. Young Bassam from *Stars in Broad Daylight* is reprehended at school for falling asleep because he is dividing his time untenably between school and farm work. In a country where, even in the early twenty-first century, 24 per cent of male rural labour was conducted by junior family members for no remuneration, this was a pressing issue for the Ba'athist universal education ideal.[99] *Step By Step* provides further documentary evidence of these failures, dialectically interjecting children's declarations about what they want to be when they grow up (doctors, engineers) against details about child labour interrupting school, long hours for adults (at least ten hours per day) and the sheer numbers who are forced to leave their villages to assume jobs in the military or day-rate construction in order to survive. A May Day speech on the radio saluting workers, so typical across the socialist world, is made to seem hollow in the context of these hardships.

Flight is also often prompted by love. The bulk of these rural narratives incorporate an eloping couple, serving, by and large, as straightforward critiques of arranged marriages. But not quite that alone. In *Stars in Broad Daylight*, the wedding contract acts to consolidate land ownership. Sami's status is diminished in Khalil's eyes because he has had to sell off a portion of his farm to support his sick mother. The tragic narrative thrust of *Algae* is stimulated by Abu Asaad's dispossession from the family farm by his disreputable brother Ghanem. Such land is indulged, as has been noted, by the camera. All these films keep their framing wide to encompass as much rural space as possible, reformatting the typical aesthetics of character-driven storytelling, which tend to prefer medium shots and close-ups. The urgency to debate territory, however, must be read within the specific context of Arab socialism and its international support structures. Private ownership beyond 380 hectares was forbidden in 1959, making family unions a strategic mode of circumventing collectivisation.[100] Most of the nationalised land was redistributed to farm cooperatives, although some state farms were also in operation. The dream of total public land-holding was, conversely, not supported by the majority of the country's rural citizens, making the topics of these movies sticking points in the free flow of ideology (if not on-the-ground citizen desires) between the Eastern Bloc and Syria. Therein, perhaps, lies these films' reluctance to follow through on earlier Soviet cinema's easy glorification of the peasant. Their focus instead falls on land and labour.

And both were changing fast, changing courtesy of Comecon investment. The Soviet model of postcolonial self-sufficiency via the route of heavy industry, transport infrastructures and the exploitation of natural resources subtly permeates village life in these movies. The centrepiece of Eastern Bloc economic assistance arrived in the shape of a massive hydroelectric and irrigation-enabling dam on the Euphrates River, funded (notably, just after the 1966 leftist coup) to the tune of $150 million by the USSR, which also provided 850 specialists to help 10,000 Syrians build it.[101] The dam is powerfully brought to screen in two documentaries directed by French-trained Omar Amiralay: the up-beat progressivist *Film Essay on the Euphrates Dam* (1970) and the much gloomier return to the scene years later with *A Flood in Baath Country* (2005). The construction of new transport networks appears more often in the remaining body of films. *Verbal Letters'* credit sequence culminates with the sound of folk music slathered over a shot of trees and a crumbling old house. Suddenly, there is the noise of a train, and then, as has already been detailed, a massive explosion as an elderly couple's home is blasted into smithereens with them, mistakenly, still inside. While new technologies and industries were the subject of mythification, often musical exaltation, in Eastern Bloc cinema, Syrian films are more reluctant to praise. This scene foreshadows the arrival of bulldozers, just after a wedding, to erect a soaring viaduct for the coming locomotive line. One of the film's core themes is the uprooting of community and loss of land brought about by these 'developments'.

The most striking way in which such movies discuss the impact of new communications systems for rural workers, however, is through their depiction of media technologies. To wit, the use of the television and video recorder in *Stars in Broad Daylight*, but also the presence of radios, particularly in *Listeners' Choice* and *Nights of the Jackal*. In the former, Saleh unstintingly sends off letters to a music request show, the highlight of the village's week, which they tune in to sitting together under a tree. Love is conducted according to the parameters set by the programme's songs – ideas about what it is and when to get married (Wathifeh will only engage herself to Saleh if their song is aired). *Nights of the Jackal* lays out just how complementary national radio is to rural life. The songs deal in shepherding metaphors; crop prices are announced at appointed times. The film's patriarch, Abu Kamal, is endowed with particular reverence because he can fix community members' broken radios. One of the unnamed boys in *Sacrifices* petulantly stomps off with a stolen radio that erratically emits rousing Sovietesque music throughout the remainder of the film, as omnipresent then in Syrian everyday life as the supposition that such sentiments would be aroused.

And it is through the radio that the villagers' bounded existence is punctured. Crucially, their enlistment into a wider world is prompted by threats to national security delivered by the radio. Israeli invasion, rather than any reference to Syrian urban politics, pulls them towards the horizon, towards conscription and even the sacrifice of lives for their country. In *Listeners' Choice*, the first unwelcome interruption to broadcasting replaces a song the community have requested and eagerly awaited with a newsflash announcing the Syrian forces' successful defence of Damascus during an Israeli airstrike. The substitution of the show by prolonged military music further disgruntles the assembled villagers. The film's closing moments layer Jamal and Aziza's song 'Bring Me A Greeting', shared with a long list of others (in Moscow, in Beirut …) over scenes of Jamal's participation in the army, Jamal being shot, Jamal's coffin returned to the village draped in the Syrian flag.

Ghassan's father in *Verbal Letters* also sees active service, as does the patriarch in *Sacrifices*, whose amazement over the presence of female soldiers in the Israeli army induces a family debate on the role of women within Arab nationalist struggle. So, although sometimes resistant to change, and often recalcitrant, the agricultural worker within Syrian culture of that period could, in a flash, be called upon as a dialectical manufacturer of, a travelling participant in and a symbol for nationalism.

THE LIMITS OF NATION, THE LIMITS OF REVOLUTION

When Syrian film characters mobilise for the nationalist cause, they act always in response to a specific encroachment of an unforgivable nature. Similarly, the *talab al-'ilm rihlat*. Tahtawi exasperates that one of the French's 'bad customs is their claim that the intellect of their philosophers and physicists is greater and more perceptive than that of prophets'.[102] Consequently, 'legal judgements are not derived from holy books but from other laws, mostly political and contrary to the universality of legislation'.[103] There certainly are instances when compatibility through comparison fails and a stand must be taken. Tahtawi concludes with two lines of verse, mono-rhymes with a hemistich in the original:

| He who claims he need | Not follow the law |
| Will be friendless | Damaged and useless.[104] |

Muhammad as-Saffar also invokes God, notably as the 'mover of creation', to implore his readership, with the use of a religious metaphor of travel, not to 'lose their way'.[105] For Susan Gilson Miller, in her introduction to as-Saffar's travelogue, this writer, 'tells us that one can go to the land of enchantment, the abode of both good and evil, immerse oneself in it, and return home wiser yet unscathed'.[106]

Historical narratives such as *The Leopard* similarly and just as unequivocally find that they must – ethically – impose limits, here outright refusing French or British colonisers. However, the incursion of Israeli troops looms largest, edging their way into *The Night*, *Verbal Letters*, *Something is Burning* and *Nights of the Jackal*. The productive dialectic arising from *Sacrifices'* juxtaposition of women's rights across this border falters considerably as intolerable frontiers are reached.

Israel's land grab of the resources-rich Golan Heights, condemned by United Nations Security Council Resolution 242 in 1967, has entailed a switch in citizenship for thousands of Syrians with still more transformed into refugees within their own country. On both sides of the line, nationhood is fortified through an 'us' and 'them' that are potently manifest in who is invited to travel across borders, who is not, who will press on regardless and the intent motivating those forays. *The Night* asserts these preoccupations, as one might expect, through an exacting encasement of *mise en scène*. Nowhere in Syrian cinema is the sense of the threshold more apparent. By repeatedly shooting in deep focus through door and window frames, the movie demands a contemplation of the negotiations of inside and out, between Syria, Eastern Europe and neighbouring countries. These journeys to the brink bring a 'beyond' into view, one that simultaneously creates a differentiated space, a sanctum called Syria.

However, as we have seen, citizenship of this nation has also provided, through its affiliation with others, dispersal, educational opportunities and shared aesthetic persuasions that have then regrouped to encourage exactly these types of cinematic and political framing.

The interlacing of steadfastness with itinerancy comes courtesy of a particular history. Over the last hundred years, no sooner has the ink dried on the map (each country has its own ideological cartography) than the lines are redrawn – and never have these adamant territorial assertions proved binding. Syrian films' concentration on the fluctuating threshold aims to launch an examination of how borders function geopolitically, how they shift and how they organise the circulation of people, property and wealth. Acts of contention brace the nationalist spirit, while also pervasively impinging upon everyday liberties. Like it or not, the Syrian sense of self is mutually authored, and not simply by erstwhile comrades in Eastern Europe or sympathetic proximate Arab or Muslim populations. Because of Israel's continued occupation of the Golan, the Syrian government saw fit to ratify its preservation of emergency law for decades (repealed only in 2011 in response to widespread civil unrest). By focusing on militaristic agendas (including compulsory national service), the state subsequently divested from other sectors, including, Oussama Mohammad would strongly contend, cinema.[107]

Ironically, the only film, apart from pornography, I have ever been offered in shops as Syrian – and this has happened regularly – is *The Syrian Bride* (Eran Riklis, 2004). A Roman-script English-language cover obscures its Israeli origins, which would have otherwise rendered its presence anathema to the ubiquitous and heartfelt boycott of Israeli goods in Syria, regardless of whether any pirate profits found their way back to the country of origin. The movie's own evasion of typical trade embargos is, interestingly, foreshadowed in *The Syrian Bride*'s plot, which follows those few people who were, during that period, allowed to cross the border: Druze women with special dispensation to make a one-way trip into matrimony with men sharing their religion.

Instances such as these expose the impossibility of upholding black-and-white divisions between warring factions. Furthermore, 'them'-status is, quite clearly, born out of similarity as well as difference, most striking at moments of competition for the same limited and equally desired resources in a confined area. This struggle underpins *Something is Burning*'s plot, squarely situated within the quotidian economics of exile endured by a family of Golan refugees displaced to Damascus. Abu Ramzi, the family head, is employed to distribute aid among fellow migrants; his wife, Umm Ramzi, metaphorises that 'poverty is expatriation'; they are all amazed at the roominess of the lost Golan houses that they can now only see on television and in old photographs. Their son, Ramzi, has acclimatised more successfully to the logic of capital. Its modes of translating paid (in his case, criminal) labour into cash and, from there, into personal property is a less familiar chain of conversion for his parents' generation, who had previously worked their land. 'There are troops, barbed wire and the United Nations between you and your house,' he argues with his father. 'Until then, we need money to buy one,' and, 'Homeland isn't a house, it's the money in your pocket.' Here discrepancies in wealth promulgated by the redrawing of borders are posed as the primary provocation for regional conflict, as well as the cause of Ramzi's descent into illicit behaviour.

These unwilling migrants from the Golan are not the only figures within Syrian cinema who register territorial turbulence on screen. They regularly join forces with casualties from other local battles, prompting these storylines to lay claim to broader discussions about dominion, independence and colonisation. Take, for example, *The Night*, whose introductory dream sequence set in the evacuated Golan town of Quneitra acts as a springboard to hurtle the narrative back to the 1936 Palestinian Intifada. A squadron of Quneitran guerrillas ready themselves for a pan-Arab struggle against colonial imposition, a rallying they repeat during World War II, the creation of the state of Israel in 1948 and the 1967 Six-Day War, when Quneitra is vanquished by Israel. Mohammad Malas' more recent short for Al Jazeera Children's Channel, *The Tissue Vendor* (2009), also bundles up a cluster of migration stories. Like *Something is Burning*, the father of the family retains an elegiac attitude towards his lost home in the Golan, eventually uprooting his wife and Damascus-born children to move south, closer to their land.

However, their initial domicile in Syria's multicultural capital, alongside neighbours newly arrived from Iraq, allows the film to penetrate how other borders sculpt the nation and refugee existence. Like many of its precursors, *The Tissue Vendor* illuminates a particularity about the country's borders that forcefully prevails upon the materiality of Syrian life. The border with Israel, one of the world's most impenetrable from the north, is an entirely different beast to both nations' other more porous frontiers, which have, historically, granted passage to significant numbers of non-citizens. Syria's national identity has established itself through contact with the two, often contradictory, groupings that its boundaries define – one which it has historically welcomed in and harboured from oppression (Arabs and Muslims, predominantly) and another towards which it flexes its muscles in opposition to (chiefly Zionist) expansion. Gestures of pan-Arabism and anti-imperialism have been vibrantly reinforced through Syria's stance on immigration, which allows most Arabs entry to the country without visas. As far back as the first Ba'ath Constitution, a selective open door policy was mooted: 'Complete rights of citizenship shall be granted to all those living in Arab countries who are loyal to the Arab homeland and who disassociate themselves from all racist affiliations.'[108] True to these ideals, before the 2011 uprisings, Syria hosted one of this planet's largest per capita urban refugee populations, including half a million Palestinians, up to a quarter of a million Iraqis, thousands of Afghans, Sudanese and Somalis and long-established exiled Armenian and Kurdish communities, all housed among a total of only 22.5 million residents.[109] Arab hospitality indeed, sadly reversed by the current Syrian refugee crisis around the world.

On the ground, however, an assessment of these demographics suggests that Ba'athist pan-Arabism, although impressively inclusive, could only extend so far. Communist training, labour and resources from outside the Arab world initially helped set spinning the centripetal force of Syrian nationalism, yet a considerable swing in social attitudes relating to the treatment of each of Syria's borders (on screen and in history) reveals the geographical coverage, to be sure, but also the limits of this revolution. Issues of property (whose revolution?) re-emerge, decreeing that public ownership, the kind that had cultivated Syrian cinema, could not, in actuality, be truly public, or, put another way, *universal*.

INTERNATIONAL BUFFERS AND LIFE WITHOUT THEM

Given Syria's intricate and atypical configuration, the majority of the theoretical writing on borders is inadequate for its analysis. By and large, this literature engrosses itself in bilateral arbitration, the best part of its energies dedicated to boundaries dividing pronounced discrepancies in wealth (the US–Mexico border putting in regular appearances).[110] This emphasis is all well and good for a contemplation of Syria's relationship with Israel, but only up to a point. Border studies rarely indulge the idea of a barrier that protects against and halts imperialist or neo-imperialist designs, something central to how Syria contrives its nationalism.

Second, this border is more blatantly multivalent than others in the world and thereby helps illuminate the transnational machinations of power at all such geopolitical junctures. Seldom is a line on a map as bulbous as this one, which integrates an internationally policed buffer (or United Nations Disengagement Observer Force (UNDOF)) zone that has been active since 1974. This military presence flags the multiplicity of forces that constitute any given country, reinvigorating what Walter Mignolo terms 'border gnosis'. Syrian–Comecon allegiances have already imprinted an internationalist texture on Syria's sense of statehood and the buffer zone further encourages an ongoing examination of the stakes invested in and against the nation globally. Mignolo's theorising is helpful here because it dedicates itself to subaltern thinking, for him especially puissant at the threshold of the colonised and colonising worlds. Border gnosis prises open the politics of knowledge production to unveil how prejudicial its manoeuvrings can be and what the repercussions of epistemic stridency are on either side of the line.[111] Traffic flows in knowledge have cultivated Syrian cinema and they have also, as has become apparent, all but blockaded its dissemination. Mignolo is keen to point out that border gnosis '(geohistorical, sexual, racial, national, diasporic and exile, etc.) is a way of thinking that emerges as a response to the conditions of everyday life created by economic globalization and the new faces of the colonial difference'.[112] Boundaries are traversed as much as they are imposed according to particular world orders and Mignolo is wise to re-emphasise divisional politics within the supposedly less cordoned actualities of transnationalism. One simple instance: some twenty kilometres north of the UNDOF zone, my mobile phone declaratively chirped a 'Welcome to Israel' (in English) as my service provider automatically switched to a franchise of Orange, the French-owned telecommunications multinational.

There are also more patently physical transnational presences within the buffer zone, which encourage contemplation of how nations are collaboratively constructed and how dependent single states are upon others. On a 2007 visit to the destroyed and abandoned town of Quneitra, I witnessed the following graffiti – 'The monster Chechny [sic]. Grozne in our hearts and in our minds' – probably scrawled by a member of the UN army (again, in English) in response to another contested border, another spectre of the global socialist project. This emotional declaration acts now as an unsanctioned reminder of the catastrophic consequences and repeated aftershocks of a transition out of socialism, a socialism that may have brutally crushed dissent to maintain a questionable type of stability, but whose overthrow offered no simple solutions. Syrian cinema's thematic preoccupations and means of production similarly rankle any easy dismissal of everything a denounced, flailing and defensive socialism stands for within the rhetoric of change in the Middle East. The Golan here is no stranger to the incorrectly presumed neutrality of peacekeeping forces. The clash of American and Soviet interests at the end of the Yom Kippur War comes to mind here. In 1973, Brezhnev even deigned to meet with Nixon and Kissinger to try and strong-arm Israel's withdrawal back beyond its 1967 borders. To Syria's deep resentment, the suggestion was countered by America, leading to an unhappy settlement that surfaces in *Something is Burning*. Abu Ramzi's landlord rebuts pleas for leniency over unpaid rent with a dismissive 'Don't talk to me about politics. I'm fed up with your Kissinger. Has he solved this problem yet?'

Indeed, Abu Ramzi's problem endures, decades later; unresolved, the Golan predicament haunted Syrian cinema indefinitely, rising from the dead in the form of flashbacks. Remember *The Night*'s opening, with its ponderous long-take dream sequence that follows Wisal through the ruins of her lost Quneitran home. *Something is Burning* returns repeatedly to the area too, its first scene an *in medias res* invasion by the Israeli army. Between the Six-Day War of 1967 and the institution of the UN demilitarised zone, Quneitra changed hands several times, culminating in much of it being razed as Israeli forces beat their retreat in the 1973 Yom Kippur War. Now sheltered by the UNDOF, it is under Syrian jurisdiction, but a decision was made by the government to preserve the town as a barely populated ruin, rather than to rebuild and resettle. Intriguingly, the Arabic word for revolution (*thawra*) is an etymological sibling of *athar*, which means ruins, trace or legacy, and stems from the root verb *a-th-r* (to influence). The ruins of the revolution memorialise it and they do so, significantly, at its limits, at the point beyond which its influence cannot reach. Yet, the fragmentary nature of Quneitra is at odds with the solidity of totalitarianism offering up, as we shall see, a form of salvation from it.

In other movies, vestiges of the past have insisted upon unbroken civilisational ascendancy within the region. *Public Relations* marvels at the splendours of the Aleppo citadel and Rasafa through helicopter shots, takes in the *objets* at the Aleppo museum. Fahim, one of its protagonists, first appears repairing masonry at St Simeon's, where he boasts to the assembled tourists that Syrians have retained architectural preservation techniques that have otherwise been lost in Europe. *The Events of the Coming Year*, as has been noted, makes a big fuss of Syria's old houses and mosaics, with Munir selecting the amphitheatre at Bosra for the concert that is his crowning display of the potentialities of a nationalist past, present and future. As the music unfolds, we experience a montage of Syria's most captivating historical monuments, such as the ancient desert town of Palmyra.

Contrariwise, with Quneitra, the Syrian revolution is defined by how it has been unjustly curbed by oppositional military might, 'museumified' as a relic of blame at the propagandistic expense of Quneitra's refugees. As with the reluctance to distribute Syrian films, the wilful suspension of Quneitra, the disinclination to exploit its resources for basic and immediate material use-value or profit, poses questions about the suggestive political power of non-productivity. Obstinacy over maximising growth might have successfully celebrated Syria's anti-capitalism, but, from another perspective, it signalled an impasse in the flow of its revolutionary ideals and a stagnation of principles that now seem untenable, hypocritical or violent to many of its citizens. Quneitra can stand in for the revolution as a whole, left destitute by the retreat of a once-supportive international socialist infrastructure. Quneitra-born Mohammad Malas, eager to return to his hometown, opines, 'It's not a problem that it's destroyed, we live with destroyed things,' a statement that tacitly says a great deal about how he viewed the political situation in his country even before the Civil War.[113] Likewise the ensemble of protagonists in *Under the Ceiling* thinks of themselves as refugees, not from a lost territory, but from a social milieu that cannot tolerate their bohemian leftism.

Cinema becomes a substitute for *Under the Ceiling*'s Marwan just as it does for Mohammad Malas. Malas continues: 'I was drawn [to the medium] by a deep feeling of solitude and exile. The movie theatre was a refuge in which I could break this solitude.'[114] As a director, he counters feelings of dislodgement through the firm sense of location he establishes on screen. With *The Night*, he confirms 'I was looking for a lost place, namely, Quneytra, the village destroyed by Israel. I reconstructed it and recovered its life, cinematically.'[115] A good handful of these films' returns-to-the-past dream up the Golan as a rural idyll, unburdened by the more equivocal representations of farmers customary to other narratives. *The Night* and *Something is Burning* gracefully glide backwards and forwards through time and space. The camera movements are fluid and uninterrupted; long pans unify various agricultural activities such as olive harvesting and grape-treading. Cranes are utilised to sweep over, survey and recapture multiple planes of the countryside. Here travel is wishful, using the *'ajiba* potential of cinema to summon lands beyond its makers' and audience's reach.

With the help of the *rihla* genre, we can do something more than interpret these gestures as essentially evasive or maudlin, and the same would hold for any nostalgia we might try to incubate for the generous *'ajiba* working conditions learnt from the NFO's past. We can think of these fantastical returns as audiovisual quotations from the past, thus folding them into the sorts of politics that arose in the discussion of Khatibi, al-Shidyaq and Michel Aflaq's political philosophy of dialectics. Like Malas' films, Tahtawi's *Extraction* is littered with invocations of a Golden Age, for him the poetry of pre- and early Islamic eras. These verses populate his (description of) modern France, insisting on a continuity that unfixes 'past' and 'present', demanding, in the words of Tarek El-Ariss, that this 'series of movements, ruptures, and incidents' be understood instead as the means through which contemporary Arab (here also Syrian) life 'is staged, tried out, rehearsed, fantasized, and imagined'.[116] *The Night* recreates its spaces in pronounced and unbroken ways, the camera carefully exploring, lingering as if to reacquire every inch of lost territory and proudly showcase Quneitran heritage, but also as a means allowing for a provocative dialectic with the present. On the surface, the avoidance of conspicuous fissures seems to momentarily deny how the border and buffer zone otherwise rupture the region. However, as with Tahtawi's reverence for poems of old, one is then requested to digest the memories, their legacies and their geopolitical disavowal, from within the current situation.

Inside the full narrative contexts of these films, Quneitra ultimately emerges as something of a phantom limb, a palpable and intermittent presence within dreams, deliria and reminiscences, materialising in a variety of incarnations. The documentary imperative also makes itself evident in *Something is Burning*, when a family photo of the Golan (a rare, concrete record of ownership) bleeds into a pre-occupation flashback. On another occasion, the movie logs one of the uncommon visits refugees are allowed to make to the border, from where they greet their estranged neighbours across a barbed wire fence. 'A stone's throw separates me from my house. Who'd have thought we'd be away for so long?' muses Abu Ramzi, cuing a flashback scene of his youthful self gambolling through an orchard.

Avery Gordon, author of *Ghostly Matters: Haunting and the Sociological Imagination*, stresses the potential in the ultimate denial of alterity in cases like these (although she is far from Syrian cinema in her subject matter). She refuses to subjugate spectres, which are, for her, 'pregnant with unfulfilled possibility, with the something to be done that the wavering present is demanding ... that structures the domain of the present and the prerogatives of the future'.[117] Unlike a simple commemoration, the ghost incarnates an uncanny liveliness and prompts a visceral response. A haunting is not merely a Benjaminian flash in a moment of danger; with prompts from the *rihla*'s sense of temporality, it can also reveal itself as a methodology in an unfinished struggle for rights.

At other times, schisms *are* more emphatically stylistically invoked. *Something is Burning* does its best to recreate the disorientation of warfare and exile. There are many instances when we do not know exactly where we are, and others that are roughly and discontinuously latched together, jolting us from Quneitra, to the desert, to inner-city Damascus. Here the multi-generic expansiveness of the *rihla* has much to offer through how it meaningfully writes into its very conventions the possibilities of changes in register. Tahtawi, for instance, breaks into verse in the midst of meticulous documentary accounting of Parisian life. For El-Ariss, the about-turn into poetry, like these giddying cinematic zips to an elsewhere, are anything but clunky or meaningless switches in direction. They signal geographical and geopolitical disjunction and, in so doing, produce a 'space' for its impact to be experienced politically and emotionally, for necessarily new and most likely disoriented subjectivities to be formed.[118]

Or, to put it another way – a way that ties us back to communist Europe – these cuts plumb the relational possibilities of editing. Soviet thinker and VGIK founding father Lev Kuleshov (familiar to all these directors) asserts,

> thanks to montage, it is possible to create, so to speak, a new geography, a new place of action. It is possible to create, in this way, new relations between the objects, the nature, the people and the progress of the film.[119]

For Kuleshov and much of the earlier Soviet school, editing is dialectical. Dramatic inter-cutting plunks Abu Hamdi's desert-set murder of his double-crossing nephew, Ramzi, next to scenes of bulldozers pummelling Ramzi's father's new house – the causes, we must recognise, are one and the same.

Keystones of traditional masculinity – decency, respect and provision for one's family – crumble amid a geography of displacement. The borderlands of the Golan are supplanted by the desert-scapes of another Syrian border, where Ramzi has taken up as a smuggler in order to escape the poverty of landless refugee life. Doing so, he transgresses into the spatial and moral fringes of Syrian society. Meanwhile, his law-abiding father can never feel truly at home outside his birthplace, his stunted life in Damascus underscored by a graphic match between a flourishing Golan tree and a flimsier city specimen, forlornly poking up through a concrete surround. Elsewhere, Syrian cinema has made every effort to finesse an unbroken formal continuity between its citizens and the land, if not the nation-state. At the unpredictably shifting peripheries of the country, though, Syrians and other Arab refugees are deracinated, with post-production labouring hard to engender a sense of empathy for their condition.

Solidarity of this order is a fundamental attribute of Syrian cinema, most unswerving and striking when expressed in response to the displacement of Palestinians. We must remember that the NFO funded *The Dupes*, the first rigorous, sympathetic treatment of the *nakba*'s consequences. Filial pan-Arab sentiment shines forth from Mohammad Malas' outward-looking description of Quneitra: '[l]ingering as the gaping wound in the body of our country's imbrication with the tragedy of Palestine'.[120] With around half a million Palestinian refugees resident in Syria during the period under consideration, it is only logical that they should casually appear in films such as *The Events of the Coming Year*, where Munir's downstairs neighbour is only coded as Palestinian by her accent. *Under the Ceiling* features a Palestinian tailor and registers affiliation through Ahmed's Handala t-shirt, the cartoon figure beloved of the popular resistance movement. The Palestinians' flight from their homeland in 1948 also provides major narrative scaffolding in *Exodus* (Raymond Butros, 1997), *The Night* and Nabil al-Maleh's section of the three-part portmanteau film *Men Under the Sun* (1960).

But perhaps the film that dealt in the most head-on fashion with the aftershocks of Palestinian population transfer after 1972's *The Dupes* is Mohammad Malas' *The Dream* (1988), which meanders and chats its way around the camps of Lebanon (housing, by 2011, many of its approximately 425,640 registered refugees, a hefty percentage of Lebanon's 4.224 million total population).[121] As the documentary wends onwards, it becomes near impossible to discern whether the fantastical and often traumatic events that its subjects describe are, as the title claims, dreams, or, as they sometimes turn out to be, a desperate reality. In both states of consciousness, the border divorcing the exiles from their homeland is regularly breached.

The movie's framing and cinematography, as ever, projects into and out of the geopolitics of the region. Malas' precision with camera and character placement

The Dream (1988): the camera's journey through the tight spaces of a refugee camp

exposes the cramped reality of camp life: a small, armed and uniformed boy hemmed in by sandbags, teachers in squished classrooms, inhabitants unable to leave home because of rocket attacks. Mobile camerawork trails the refugees down the narrow streets of the camps and follows the body of a young man as it is removed from a morgue refrigerator. These images are inter-cut with silent graves and martyr posters of this same young man rolling off a printer. The circulation patterns of the living and the dead assume a particular character here as borders of various kinds are both imposed and traversed, and as a Syrian refugee director travels to Lebanon to talk to Palestinians. In years gone by, these were all one country.

Syria's sustained engagement with Palestine, including its own residents of Palestinian origin, brings to life Abdelkebir Khatibi's concept of the 'awakening margin', which he defines as:

> a thinking which is not inspired by its poverty [and that] is always elaborated in order to dominate and humiliate; thinking which could be *minority, fragmentary and unfinished*, is always ethnocidal. This – and I say it with extreme prudence – is a call not for a philosophy of poverty and its exaltation, but for a plural thinking which does not reduce others (societies and individuals) to the sphere of its self-sufficiency. To disappropriate itself from such a reduction is, for all thought, an incalculable prospect. This gesture – immense in its effects – challenges all thought which assumes its specific locale to be universal, which is everywhere perforated from margins, from variations, from silent questions.[122]

Syria's relations with its Arab-majority neighbours accomplish some of Khatibi's aspirations, particularly his non-ghettoised pluralism and his belief in retaining a politics of the margin nonetheless. The same could be said of Syrian film's inclusive matter-of-fact involvement of minority groups, such as the Druze in Ghassan Shmeit's oeuvre, or the Alawites in Abdullatif Abulhamid and Oussama Mohammad's. It has not been worth highlighting these specific details about the films' protagonists because the narratives do not fixate upon ethnic particularities. These characters are, first and foremost, Syrian because, ideally, being Syrian has integrated diversity.

Khatibi's sentiments are recapitulated in a caution from his compatriot, the novelist and historian Abdallah Laroui, this time with a slant towards the awakening margin as a site of scholarship: 'If we have no desire for the fragmentation of research to result in a cultural protectionism where each keeps his patrimony for himself and forbids others to touch it, we must submit to new rules of the *munāzara* [dialectical controversy].'[123] Certainly, as has been illustrated, Syria transposed much of what it has learnt from its cross-border expeditions to communist Europe into a sense of itself that was predominantly nationalistic – nationalistic in defiance of Israeli expansionism and the support it received from other global strongholds. Then again, Syria's nationalism also opened its doors with a regularity that was as enticing as it was partial. Syria's hospitable policies on and cultural enquiries into migration reimagine Khatibi and Laroui's dialectics, which more often than not stall amid a dominating coloniser–colonised binary. Syria's circumstances reached beyond, insisting upon a politics of cooperation and dialogue between similarly pitted nations, most pressingly in relation to the arrival, from 2007–11, of over a quarter of a million registered Iraqi refugees.[124] Although they failed to feature with any regularity in Syria's movies (*The*

Tissue Vendor incorporates a few), both countries do share a fraught, shared history of Ba'athism.

With the inadequacy and eventual collapse of assistance from socialist nations, and the region still frequently enduring the sting of outside political intervention and internal brutality and corruption, Arabs, including film-makers, have sought alternative support and communication systems. Some, as we have seen, have suffused and percolated out of Syria's understanding of nationalism, which can be Syrian, definitely, but also pan-Arab. Others, as we shall see, digress from these models and look to different international communities. The following chapter will head off in that direction, using pilgrimage literature as its guide, paying particular attention to moveable, contentious and informal borders, which can be unrelenting and rigid nonetheless. These boundary-lines block travel, and they also inflict it against the will of many a reluctant traveller.

3

The Road of Most Resistance: Film-making of the Second Palestinian Intifada

[Jerusalem] is as holy to us as it is to you ... It is therefore out of the question for us to abandon it. The Muslims would never accept it. As for territory ... your occupation is only transitory. You were able to settle in it because of the weakness of the Muslims who then peopled it, but so long as there is war, we will not allow you to enjoy your possessions.

Salah al-Din (Saladin), speaking to Richard the Lionheart in 1191[1]

No one is foolish enough to dare enter through the gate of the Temple courtyard, for he would immediately be put to death.

French pilgrim Barbatre in 1480[2]

One durable founding myth of the Second (or al-Aqsa) Intifada would have it blowing up from a *visit*: soon-to-be Israeli Prime Minister Ariel Sharon's contentious trip to the Temple Mount complex on 28 September 2000. While most observant Jews refuse to enter the area, containing their religious duties to the Western, or Wailing, Wall, Sharon marched in under the protection of over 1,000 armed personnel, declaring the site, which houses Islam's third most holy shrine, subject to Israeli control. Around a million bullets were fired in attempts to quell the first two weeks of reactive protests from Palestinians.[3] The uneasy peace of the Oslo Accords had ended. What those 1993 agreements had established was a shared sovereignty of the Haram al-Sharif/Temple Mount – ultimately, an Israeli admission of Palestinian jurisdiction and thus state administration. And what Sharon's visit achieved was a refutation of that decree.[4]

Sharon's tactic was not so dissimilar from that of the Prophet Mohammad centuries earlier. Exiled to Medina, his return to Mecca to claim its holy sites for Islam took the form of a pilgrimage with military escort. Nor are the sites of the Temple Mount unfamiliar to belligerent influx in the name of religion, annexation on the mind. In 1099, 'Izz al-Din Ibn al-Athir chronicles how:

In the Aqsa Mosque the Franks [European Christian crusaders] killed more than 70,000, a large number of them being imams, ulema, righteous men and ascetics, Muslims who had left their native lands and come to live a holy life in this august spot.[5]

Ibn al-Qalanisi picks up: 'Many people were killed. The Jews had gathered in their synagogue and the Franj [again, a term for crusaders] burned them alive. They also destroyed the monuments of saints and the tomb of Abraham, may peace be upon him!'[6] The pilgrim narratives of the Middle Ages, from Sir John Maundeville's to Bertrandon de la Brocquière's, resonate with military-spiritual declarations seeking Jerusalem's conquest as Christendom's capital. The corresponding Arab accounts figure almost exclusively as documents of military campaign or, rather, expulsive *jihad*. Travelogues and *rihlat* do not simply observe such occurrences, they are themselves over and over again zealously participant in the heavy tread of territorial conquest and capture.

How we write about Palestine today, including its cinema, is as imprinted as the landscape itself is with travel's partisan politics and often ruthlessly marshalled privileges and restrictions. Nabil I. Matar observes how, for instance, Renaissance cartography locked the country into an unchanging 'meta-Palestine, a holy land without history, people and, given the inaccuracies of the maps, even geography ... a palimpsest of what the Canaanites and the Toranic scriptures had inscribed.'[7] Equally, the written descriptions of journeys there. It is these literatures of pilgrimage that provide the lines of enquiry for what follows, an investigation of the cinema of the al-Aqsa Intifada, presumed to end around 2004 or 2005, with its films continuing through post-production into exhibition circuits for a further couple of years. I aim not so much to wrongly see pilgrimage in cinema where it does not exist, but rather to position accounts of travel such as these so that they can expand how we understand film. Despite these literatures' plangent tones of religiosity, they can still proffer, within the otherwise largely secular intentions of cinema (including that of Palestine), a critique of Film Studies' core methodologies, approaches which look to finished text for meaning, much more than to the journeys of transformation involved in producing it.

The call of this chapter, then, is to interact with theoretical and methodological models that are not just imported, neutralised and universalised, but which have been transported with declared intent in relation to conflict. Pilgrimage accounts stand as discourses that have impactfully rallied, named and transfigured Palestine. They do not just describe the land, they have created it. As I argue below, these modes of interpellation and their repercussions resonate multifariously and well beyond Palestine's squeezed borders, offering much scope for both comprehension and action. Palestinian movies themselves also exploit these longstanding experiences of travel, drawing in newly invented ones as tactics in the fight for self-determination. This body of cinematic work refuses to hover aloof from military occupation and the compulsion to resist, nor will my own discussions, which similarly seek to find an engaged and ethical means of travel-as-struggle through and with these very inscriptions.

An overarching aim of pilgrimage writing is to explore or qualify a connection to the land, one that may lay claims literally (in situ, although supported from outside) or symbolically (from near or far). As such, the genre's vigour can justify colonisation, but also encourage solidarity from whatever distance. Speaking more recently than our pilgrims, John Collins has devised the term 'Global Palestine' to define 'a Palestine that is globalized and a global that is becoming Palestinized'.[8] This globalisation spans from the various waves of *kufiya* fashion, to weapons and surveillance technologies that are 'road tested' on Gaza's population. My argument is that this 'becoming Palestinized' has been 'taking place' for millennia, detailed and discussed with great bearing and use-value within pilgrimage accounts. Such involvement has been facilitated, in large part, by travel motivated by ever-mutating and conjoining forms of pilgrimage within colonisation and administrative cosmopolitanism, alongside the traumas of expulsion, both Jewish and Palestinian. The *rihlat* of Ibn Jubayr, Ibn Batutta, Muhammad al-Idrisi, not to mention much more recent accounts such as Mark Twain's *The Innocents Abroad* or Herman Melville's *Clarel: A Poem and Pilgrimage to the Holy Land*, are merely some of the remaining testimonies of thousands of journeys by more ordinary, anonymous travellers. Collins continues by pinpointing how the most modern incarnations of 'becoming Palestinized' incorporate 'transnational processes such as militarization, racialization, capital accumulation, "states of exception," biopolitics and a range of power/knowledge structures',[9] all of which can be witnessed in this corpus of writing, as well as the cinema of the Second Intifada. By bringing these diverse elements into dialogue, we can recognise not simply the wide-ranging injustice of representation, but the integral role travel and its discourses have played in achieving and maintaining the occupation/ownership of Palestine for centuries and by different parties. I mean this not simply in how Palestine is told to the world and itself, but also in very concrete terms.

Yet 'becoming Palestinized' also entails a familiarity with Palestine that well exceeds its borders, a sense of shared meaningfulness that is both critiqued and impelled, as we shall see, by invocations of inclusive community within both the cinema of the Second Intifada and pilgrim literature. To become Palestinised in this context is to answer a call to the world to acknowledge our role, wherever we are in settler colonialism, and to understand Palestine as a node in the greater struggle against such injustices. In fighting these invasions, Palestinian cinema makes repeated strategic recourse to globally shared associations with its country as a means of drawing us all in, implicating us, but also, more centrally, forging affinities between us. A parallel tension coheres the many attempts of travellers to write Palestine over the millennia.

At the same time, a concentration on travel allows for a thorough engagement with a politics of circulation, not least of the films under consideration. On the one hand, the Second Intifada period witnessed a shift in the mobility of Palestinian cinema away from the solidarity club screenings or special interest festivals that 'bear witness', usually through documentary, and largely under the aegis of charities or political parties. Back in the 1970s, production had suffered stifled mobility. Executed largely in the conflict zones and refugee camps of neighbouring countries, the film units of groups such as the Palestine Liberation Organization (PLO) and Popular Front for the Liberation of Palestine (PFLP) found distribution within the homeland proper all but impossible. Manifestos by these units underline the importance of foreign distribution through festival circuits, setting a logical precedent for the travels of Palestinian cinema.[10] In the subsequent decades, auteur cinema created by figures like Michel Khleifi reached certain art cinema venues globally, but not in quite the explosive fashion of material from the Second Intifada period. *Divine Intervention* (Elia Suleiman, 2002) broke all records of international success for Palestinian output. Although statistics on its profits are partial, it grossed more than $1 million in French box office alone and ranked as the USA's 257th most profitable film in 2003.[11] Amid this groundswell, Warner Independent bankrolled *Paradise Now* (Hany Abu-Assad, 2005), a move from a Hollywood studio unprecedented in history, and one which was to garner them more than $3.5 million in worldwide box office and an Academy award nomination.[12]

As all this was unfolding, the ensuing uprising and the ongoing, accelerating violence of occupation beyond September 2000 not only viciously impacted the existences of Palestinians and the cinema they made, but also determined how that cinema, its protagonists and products, could *travel*. The occupation curtailed Palestinian exiles' right of return, constrained leadership to guarded compounds and rendered travel within the West Bank and Gaza (and outside them) near impossible through a complex set-up of barriers, checkpoints, roadblocks, curfews, borders and the newly built Wall. Fresh infringements in the name of transport infrastructure vigorously supported Israeli assertions to the land through the building of extraterritorial Israeli-only road networks that furthered the occupation and curbed Palestinian movement on their own land. The tension between travelling and settling remains a fraught one.

Most Palestinians were now barred from visiting, say, the sites of the Haram al-Sharif; one response was to make movies obsessed with roads and travel. *Divine Intervention* waggishly encapsulates this. Released during a period when Yasser Arafat was consistently under siege in his Ramallah compound, the film's main character, E. S., inflates a balloon emblazoned with the leader's image. It drifts across an Israeli checkpoint, past Gethsemane and over to the Dome of the Rock, circling it as one would when conducting *tawaf*, the ritual circumambulation of Islamic holy sites. The balloon distracts the officers on guard, allowing E. S.'s lover to slip through the checkpoint unnoticed.

Do not read this, a typically sardonic comedic gesture from Suleiman, as an uncomplicated religious turn within the cinema of the Second Intifada. Far from it. Rather, Palestinian film-makers tackle the investments made upon and though their land by a host of different histories, faiths and armies. We might, in Arabic, call this *ostoura*, which Fawaz Turki defines as:

Divine Intervention (2002): the Yasser Arafat balloon makes its way to the Dome of the Rock

Arab Cinema Travels

the force in culture that binds the past–present axis in society along which we conduct our lives. The closest approximation to *ostoura* in English is 'active myth,' a living habit of spirit that recognizes no apartness or extra-territoriality for itself in the time continuum of past–present.[13]

The interest accrued by these presences and overlaps, not least in terms of a symbolic repertoire, both sustains and burdens Palestinian cinema. As 1930s travel writer Ameen Rihani quipped: 'You may travel in Arabia with the Critique of Pure Reason in your saddle-bag; but you have to balance it, willy nilly, with the Koran.'[14] *Divine Intervention* repeatedly lures in (with) and ironises the cathected imagery and narratives the Holy Land must host. A gang of children spoiling for a fight and in hot pursuit of Santa Claus. A crown of not thorns but bullets haloing a *jihadia* (jihadist, feminine form) ninja figure in a crucifix pose. As Nurith Gertz and George Khleifi note, a gesture like this:

> looks ridiculous and loses the symbolic meaning it used to have. Yet at the same time, it regains that meaning by being revitalized through the effect of estrangement ... [Such usages] expose the trivializing of Palestinian national symbols, they also grant them a surreal, hallucinatory, imaginary dimension, thus reviving them and enabling their continued use.[15]

Suleiman's earlier *CyberPalestine* (2000) wryly retells the Mary and Joseph story, updated to contain military checkpoints. Not incongruous to either period, we have to acknowledge.

If one of Palestinian cinema's many objectives is to complicate the way Palestine, its people and their struggle have been depicted, then it is in good company with certain strands of pilgrimage literature. Cinema's analysis can therefore benefit greatly from an interaction with it. Mark Twain's *The Innocents Abroad*, for instance, seems most devoted to declaiming the hype of the Holy Land, calling attention to its puny scale in relation to the vastness of the USA. 'Travel and experience', he declares, 'mar the grandest pictures and rob us of the most cherished traditions of our boyhood. Well, let them go. I have already seen the Empire of King Solomon diminish to the size of the State of Pennsylvania.'[16] Twain's debunking reveals the expectations and, ultimately, the ideological interpellations, projected onto the territory. In unstoppably and enduringly global terms, it is within this milieu that Palestinian cinema must sit, with Suleiman and Twain until now unacknowledged companions in the process of urgent demystification. 'And why should it be otherwise? Can the *curse* of the Deity beautify a land?' Twain continues.[17] The commonality of both artists' senses of humour strengthens their postulations through its historical and geographical breadth. Where the two differ is less in their standpoints than in how Twain stops short at tart kvetching, while Suleiman retools with this iconography to create, as all the film-makers featured in this chapter aspire to, a cinema of resistance.

To give such creative gestures their full credit and to be properly inspired by their objectives, this chapter first turns to the modalities of pilgrim inscriptions of the land, looking to see what these priorities offer an understanding of cinema. I then necessarily turn to the specific lay of the land during the Second Intifada, detailing how its cinema engaged with particular restrictions on movement and a long-maintained imperialist history of road-building in Palestine (which has also made pilgrimage more possible). In response, travel within the Intifada was transformed into a means of liberation through a set of road-based tactics that were simultaneously depicted on screen, integral to the very act of film-making, and which stimulated broader socio-political defiance that shaped more than just this cinema. All the while, mobility was halted through expulsion, borders and checkpoints, prompting a rhetoric of resistance through steadfastness that included the very act of keeping cinema in production and circulation even under such desperate circumstances. To grasp how this was maintained, it is beholden on us to understand the particular configuration of transnational commercial and NGO presences that were on the ascent during the al-Aqsa Intifada, and which tried to shepherd a cinema of 'freedom' according to particular privatised and capitalistic agendas. One thing that emerged, perhaps as a consequence, at this point was recourse to the global genre of the road movie. The international comprehensibility of this genre conjures, at one and the same time, a familiarity, even a banality (little is more everyday than a road), along with shocking disparities that are the condition of occupation exacted through transit infrastructure. The road movie genre itself becomes a thoroughfare too, one that might enable smoother passage, through its international(ist) reach, than is afforded on Palestinian ground.

'HERE ADAM REMEMBERS HIS CLAY':[18] HOW TO PROGRESS LIKE A PILGRIM

Eschatological claims on the 'Holy Land' are strong and need no retrodden description here. What this chapter aspires to do is ascertain how the 'right path' becomes something topographical and thus geopolitical with the help of cultural production (travelogues and films both). As Jaś Elsner and Joan-Pau Rubiés outline of accounts from many hundreds of years ago:

> What is striking in the earliest Christian travel accounts … – of pilgrimages made to the Holy Land in the fourth century AD – is that the various ancient traditions of empirical localism, universalist imperialism and allegorical idealism were combined in the new faith's transformation of the pagan topographical terrain into a sanctified Christian realm … Journeys became a metaphor for the spiritual progress of his readers' lives … [and] Palestine became primarily a scriptural territory, in which landscape, buildings and features of an actual topography were mapped out according to the Biblical narratives of Christ and the Prophet. In effect, the Holy Land became an imaginative geography in which pilgrims could roam through the world of scripture in three dimensions, as it were, with every site testifying to the truth of the text and recalling a Biblical tag or quotation. Just as the text justified the interpretation of any one site as worth visiting, so the site provided material proof of the actual setting and context of any scriptural event.[19]

The same is true of the other two religions with demands upon the space. Edith Turner stresses the materialist expressions of faith played out here, the matching of physical presence to religious enlightenment, even physical healing.[20] The *'ajiba* fast approaches. So too do Talal Asad's notions (inspired by John Milbank) of 'complex time' and 'complex space' wherein the crude rigidity of a nation-state or the impossibility of a borderless world are replaced by overlaps between multiple stakes.[21] Feelings of belonging and mourning, for instance, merge and layer on top of each other, from the still strongly affecting Roman expulsion of the Jews to that of the Palestinians in 1948.

Second Intifada films are filled with journeys within these coordinates, particularly secular pilgrimages to now-destroyed or reoccupied villages or homes. *Land of '48* (Barrack Rima, 2003) follows a Palestinian with European identity papers – and thus easier access to the state of Israel – filming a village for its expelled former inhabitants who have no right of return to their homeland under (internationally violating) Israeli law. While such visits often become ritualistic, *Land of '48* also renders itself something of a *relic*, a key feature on pilgrim itineraries. It is not for nothing that Edward Said, one of the most famous Palestinian refugees, quotes the following lines from Mahmoud Darwish's poetry in his 'Reflections on Exile':

Take me as a relic from the mansion of sorrow.
Take me as a verse from my tragedy;
Take me as a toy, a brick from the house
So that our children will remember to return.[22]

One of the important features of relics, and one that this poem picks up, is that they exist not simply to be visited. Depending on their portability, they can also travel and be traded. According to this logic, might certain films function not simply as partial fragments of personal loss, but also as objects, just like the relic, which move and can thus emit powerful resonances around the world? *Waiting* (Rashid Masharawi, 2005), a fiction film rendered in documentary languages, does exactly this. The narrative wends from refugee camp to refugee camp across neighbouring countries' borders, auditioning hopefuls for a chance to act in a production at the Palestinian National Theatre in Gaza. Of the swarms of non-professionals trying out, each eager for the prospect of actual EU-supported travel into Palestine, many use their audition video as a proxy right of return, sending messages to relatives in the homeland whom they cannot ordinarily contact, but also to a general film audience, inviting them into this broadened encounter. In a landscape where movement is thwarted – the physical impediments in the Occupied Territories or the ongoing curtailment of the right of return – the status of objects that can be transported, such as movies, remains strategic as galvanisation in the way the relic does.

Exile prompts a hankering for objects that travel precisely because this homeland and this 'national' cinema come about in large part through faith and affinity in the face of so much solid geographical exclusion. But Edward Said entreats his people to be wary of compensatory stagnancies: 'How ... does one surmount the loneliness of exile without falling into the encompassing and thumping language of national pride?'[23] For this, we might turn, with selective caution, to pilgrim literatures. Headlong within all the bellicose struggles for sovereignty in the 'Holy Land', these writings regularly accentuate how the edges of territoriality should be disturbed, particularly in the name of care for a more universalised site. The crusades were filled with exceptions to the rules of war, with both sides capitulating in order to guarantee safe passage of pilgrims to Jerusalem during the bloodiest of stand-offs.[24] Ayreen Anastas' film *Pasolini Pa* Palestine* (2004) analyses this possibility by retracing the Italian director's scouting mission, as detailed in the documentary *Seeking Locations in Palestine for the Gospel According to St Matthew* (Pier Paolo Pasolini, 1965). Pasolini announces here that he is searching for a story of Christ 'beyond the geographies of political borders'. Like Twain, Pasolini's own vaunted expectations of the country are already challenged within *Seeking Locations*, with Anastas then placing his footage in dialogue with contemporary shots and sound recordings from the Intifada period. While the imagined landscape – so central for cinematic myth – is deflated by the impositions of occupation, there still lingers the sense that Palestine is more than a nation-state of anyone's ownership, that a different configuration might be possible. Without descending into naive and fluffy peacemaking rhetoric here, it is worth taking stock of pilgrimage's potential for fracturing the harms that nationalism and colonialism might exact, the dispossessions that imperialism demands.

The bonding a community pilgrimage advances may not wholly manifest in a destructively prejudicial fashion. Victor Turner and Edith Turner are quick to point out how pilgrimage encourages:

> release from mundane structure; homogenization of status; simplicity of dress and behavior; communitas; ordeal; reflection on the meaning of basic religious and cultural values; ritualized enactment of correspondences between religious paradigms and shared human experiences; emergence of the integral person from multiple personae.[25]

As Chapter 1 testified, pilgrimage proposes a way of being in the world that is profoundly communal (the 'pilgrim paradigm'). What pilgrimage's priorities bring into analysis more fully is an acknowledgment of the group journey, either narrative and spectatorial or depicted on screen. Leaving to one side, for the moment, the act of collective viewing as an obvious form of community-building, Second Intifada cinema just simply presents more people travelling *together* than we might ordinarily see on film. Along the way, these journeys mingle with the legal, the mercantile, the political and the military, but they do so with a deliberate ethos of the group working as one for the betterment of all.

We might acknowledge a lineage here from Idrisi's pilgrim narrative, fairly typical of the Middle Ages, that weds the factual with the shared endeavour, eschewing individual feelings for the delivery of information that would aid future travellers. Idrisi's text strives for community usability, rather than entertainment value. Given the resonance of the land, it is surprising how many pilgrim travelogues, particularly by medieval crusaders, are devoid of emotional outpourings. Sir John Maundeville, writing between 1322 and 1356 – and most probably a *nom de plume* for a compiler of multiple sources (as per the composite authorial tendency discussed in Chapter 1) – concentrates on geographical accuracy, dedicating precious little time to even the military campaigns. The aim appears to be to provide for future generations through accurate information.[26] Similar principles underpin *Road Map* (Multiplicity, 2003: note the producers' name), a split screen depiction of two differently experienced journeys to the same destination, one via an Israeli-only road, the other along the sole (barely) viable route for holders of Palestinian identity papers.[27] As we are dragged through the distinctly more frustrating Palestinian experience, in a fractional fashion we face the injustices imposed according to nationality in this region, as well as a camaraderie that is lacking in the sealed, silent and uninterrupted drive along the more uniform Israeli-only route. As with Idrisi's documentation, we are given the facts by those who have recorded the journeys – never told what to do with that information.

With pilgrimage literature's primary aim as serving community, it cannot, of course, exempt itself from ideological distortion. But the togetherness it musters still has something to offer the aspiration for freedom. In contradistinction to this oeuvre's factual utility and Road Map's real-time insistence on verisimilitude, 'aja'ib, or miracles, are all the while hosted by this (Holy) land. For believers, perhaps like nowhere else in the world, this is a place where wondrous things can happen. The 'ajiba, if you remember, confounds the distinction between actuality and wishfulness, a strong, yet overlooked principle within cinema. Although I do not want to extend the pilgrim metaphor too extensively, given the secular swing of most of these films or the ironic distance from which someone like Suleiman situates himself from religion, the 'ajiba idea can be fruitfully resurrected nonetheless. Suleiman's film, after all, is called Divine Intervention; Palestine remains, for many, a place where miracles have, do and will still happen. Suleiman's dry, ludicrous take on the occupation, along with the work of a good crowd of other Palestinian film-makers like Larissa Sansour and Annemarie Jacir, blurs, as we shall see, fact and fiction in the way that the written invocations of 'aja'ib have done for centuries.[28]

A wishful ambition looms large in al-Aqsa Intifada cinema. One scene in Divine Intervention sees E. S. (played by Suleiman himself) casually hurling a peach stone from his car window. It then detonates an Israeli tank. His girlfriend's sexy strut blows up an army checkpoint, allowing her to cross this artificially imposed border to the beat of Natacha Atlas' 'I Put a Spell on You'. As with all 'aja'ib in history, the mix of possible and improbable is telling. Director Enas Muthaffar articulates the desire to invent 'a new genre ... Occupation Fiction, like Science Fiction: something surreal because it's fiction, but at the same time related to a certain frame'.[29] Through these aesthetic decisions, film-makers comingle the politically vital need to convey the particularities of the everyday with the specific, often unbelievable strangeness of Palestinian life, something, it would appear, that is also a fundamental spark to its film-makers' creativity and methods. As director Hany Abu-Assad points out, 'Whatever you try to stage, reality will be stronger.'[30] Edward Said concurs in relation to the estrangement of the exile, which 'is unnatural and its unreality resembles fiction'.[31] Such inclinations are more broadly noticeable in the wilful refusal to dichotomise fact from fiction in the quasi-documentary, quasi-fantastical proclivities of Hany Abu-Assad's, as well as Annemarie Jacir's, work.

None of these people dwell lightly on the borderline between the real and the improbable. During the Second Intifada period, while the territory was being illegally criss-crossed by Israeli-only thoroughfares, USAID proudly declared its stake in the regeneration of the West Bank road from the southern border to Ramallah, with America all the while funding Israeli armament bent on its destruction and blockage. The near-surrealism of the situation provoked a disordering of fiction's opposition to fact ('Can this possibly be happening?'), a breakdown that is consequently common to many Palestinian movies. Seemingly impossible political narratives are created at the international level and we all assume roles in their realisation. As multiple media artist Larissa Sansour corroborates, 'It's much more honest to talk about Palestine in a surreal way.' Justifying what might, at first listening, be interpreted as mere recognition of the regularly implausible realities of war, she continues, 'The minute you become the subject of documentary, the minute you lose the game.'[32] The mercurial potential of the 'ajiba surfaces here in counterpoint to the fixed victim-status that more literal registers can suppose and then impose. Palestine frequently remonstrates how it is 'doomed to documentary'. Artist-film-maker Jayce Saloum is revealing in his lack of truck with the documentary format: 'I'm not into this knee-jerk game of show and tell PBS (public television) style. I don't think "understanding" is possible, or that the "subject" can ever be "known."'[33] Certainly, Palestinian film-makers do take on the documentary mode as a responsible action in the service of a community and frequently as a way of countering the appeals to pity that an outsider perspective can impart. But the whimsical still looms large. In the Q&A session at the London Palestine Film Festival, after the screening of her fiction-fact docudrama scramble *Like Twenty Impossibles* (2003), Annemarie Jacir expressed surprise that the audience did not laugh.[34] A sympathetic but unfamiliar audience is so conditioned to be shocked and appalled that this response appears outside the bounds of propriety. On occasions like these, the will to be contrary, bizarre or distorting, even if simultaneously truthful, to conjure 'aja'ib on screen and off, is an assertion of human rights against representational strictures.

But 'aja'ib also carry more grounded use-values than the liberties of fantasy. One particular type of 'ajiba that is sought by the pilgrim is the 'protection miracle'. Throughout the interviews I undertook for this project, it transpired that, stripped of the religious connotations of this idea, the camera was functioning in this way for film-makers. Multiplicity group artists such as Sandi Hilal and Alessandro Petti point out how risky it can be to carry a camera.[35] A *servees* (privately owned minibus taxi) passenger, captured on film in *25 Kilometers* (Nahed Awwad, 2004), expresses concern that Awwad's filming will endanger the entire group of them; they might be shot for shooting. Despite this encounter, Awwad still stresses how, 'at the beginning, the camera was a kind of protection. I was hiding behind the camera in a way, or maybe I was trying to deal with things through the camera to forget my real emotions.'[36] Another director, Najwa Najjar agrees:

> Somehow, maybe the lens of the camera kind of gives you the distance, because it's very painful, so how do you distance yourself from pain? Maybe it's, you know, doing something … but I don't want to say distancing you, because I had so many times a gun just turn round and point straight at me, but it's a way maybe to record and you feel that your time is not being wasted.[37]

Here the protection miracle enables the compulsion to record.

Likewise, the documentary potential of the camera can become a shield against unlawful treatment. If safe passage is the concern of pilgrims and pilgrim narratives both, then, in more modern times, the camera is a shaky guarantee of security. Its capacity to register, to act as testimony of the obscured truths of the situation, might ward off the most perilous aspects of travelling under military occupation. Fully cognisant of this power but perhaps unaware of the irony of his statement, an Israeli soldier caught on film in *Palestine Blues* (Nida Sinnokrot, 2006) as the film details an Israeli move to confiscate land in the West Bank village of Jayyous declares to camera, 'You can watch. This is a free country. No pictures.'

What his statement all too clearly confirms is the literal policing of the image of the occupation. The Holy Land is no stranger to the predisposed representation, upon which some of its travel literatures clearly remark. In an earlier era, Mark Twain lays out just how hard it is to generate an unbiased reflection, here more than other places:

> The veneration and the affection which some of these men felt for the scenes they were speaking of, heated their fancies and biased their judgment; but the pleasant falsities they wrote were full of honest sincerity, at any rate. Others wrote as they did, because they feared it would be unpopular to write otherwise. Others were hypocrites and deliberately meant to deceive ... Honest as these men's intentions may have been, they were full of partialities and prejudices, they entered the country with their verdicts already prepared, and they could no more write dispassionately and impartially about it than they could about their own wives and children. Our pilgrims have brought their verdicts with them.[38]

Michel Khleifi relates that numerous roadside interviews conducted for *Route 181* (2003), the film he co-directed with Eyal Sivan, served almost as psychoanalysis for a group of consistently impacted citizens of Palestine-Israel who are almost never listened to on the conflict.[39] Startlingly partisan, sometimes horrifyingly so, though most of these ruminations are, it is easy to see how these ordinary on-the-ground voices are drowned out by louder ideological noise. The way in which the latter supplant the former is, again, no stranger to earlier travellers to the Holy Land. Yehoshua Ben-Arieh reiterates the explorer Edward Robinson's disquiet at the marshalling of information there:

> Whether Catholic or Protestant, the explorers relied for their information on the monks of the monasteries they lodged in, who acted as their guides. Their reports were thus stereotyped, since traditions based on legend and folklore preserved within the churches and the Catholic orders in the Holy Land were transmitted from generation to generation without any scientific re-examination. Most travelers simply embodied them in their writings without bothering, or being able, to check the origins of these traditions.[40]

An attention to this propensity learnt from more critical pilgrim accounts grounds the censorship of imaging in a long history. Any number of movies from the Second Intifada period chart soldiers, like the one in *Palestine Blues*, forbidding filming, closing the scene with a camera shutdown. At another point, this film presents footage shot covertly from inside a bag as Sinnocrot crosses a checkpoint. With astonishing culpability, *A Few Crumbs for the Birds* (Nassim Amaouche and Annemarie Jacir, 2005) registers the damage its filming of Palestinian sex workers and illegal gas vendors on the Jordan–Iraq border may have promulgated. The police become curious, gas stations are closed down and the hotel-brothel is ransacked. Near the end of the movie, a title card reads: 'We filmed them without knowing that our camera would sweep away the last crumbs.' The camera has been the opposite of protective. Elsewhere, those making movies are then rendered vulnerable, despite the tenuous protective magic of the camera's capabilities. In *Ford Transit* (Hany Abu-Assad, 2003), another factual-fictional crossover of sorts, an Israeli soldier asks 'Are you mocking me because of the camera?' before punching the protagonist Rajai and asserting his dominance over the Palestinian-wielded recording device and its limited potential to voice a truth that will result in conviction or more.[41]

Such technologies of security are tenuous indeed, but they are still clung to, and perhaps none more so than in the form of the car or minibus, both a means of travel and a fragile protective casing. Wavering faith therein deeply engraves the aesthetics of Second Intifada film-making. The automobile is often the safest place from which to film. You might provoke suspicion by parking or render yourself more vulnerable if you exit this space in search of traditional, static establishing shots. Practically every film discussed in this chapter contains what has become a staple: a shot through a car window with the vehicle itself in frame. Many, like *Ticket to Jerusalem* (Rashid Masharawi, 2002) and *Hopefully for the Best* (Raed El Helou, 2004) underline the conceit by starting the narrative in this way, and certain films, such as *Pasolini Pa* Palestine*, count the bulk of their non-archive footage as captured from this position. Others, like *Kings and Extras: Digging for a Palestinian Image* (Azza El-Hassan, 2004) and *Going for a Ride?* (Nahed Awwad, 2003), deliberately include the decorative dangling baubles and dashboard ornaments drivers use to adorn their vehicles as a frame. But none obscure what lurks beyond the car: a slew of military outposts, checkpoints and armed Israeli soldiers. Is this not a rewriting of the promotional logics of capitalistic automotive production, with the raw materiality of the commodity splayed before us, faith held within it, but not unrealistically? How secure, then, is the liberal individualist ideal of the car owner, materially or ideologically, within such a scenario? This privatised space offers simple, risible pleasures in *Divine Intervention*, where a car allows a character to politely wave at his community while spewing an unheard torrent of obscenities at them. The eponymous protagonist of *Rana's Wedding* (Hany Abu-Assad, 2002) finally loses her cool in the relative remove of a car. We see her scream, writhe and cover her ears. The hermetic sealing of the vehicle, familiar to all of us, offers her a fragile safe space, while the manipulative, *'ajiba* capacities of

Kings and Extras (2004): through the windscreen with the vehicle (and driver) in frame

cinema cocoon her in wistful non-diegetic piano music. On all levels, the easily understood benefits of these enclosed environments are presented, but then complicated by the dynamics of warfare. We will witness this again later as a factor distinguishing the road (block) movie as a genre.

What I have been edging towards here are the specificities of the Second Intifada context of occupation. If the travelogue is to function adequately as 'theory', then its strategies and 'aja'ib must be drawn into a meaningful dynamic with the particular in order to create a grounded recounting that offers valuable insights to an ongoing struggle. When acts of God, or acts in that name, justify the current situation, then what is the potential for such logics to battle the untrammelled acts of colonisation that beggar belief?

The travelogue's concern for aiding actual mobility provides a useful prop here. While it is difficult to fathom what watching these movies can achieve in terms of confronting the occupation, the very *making* of these films, the very act of enunciation, is maybe more outwardly radical as a gesture that directly flouts ethnic cleansing. These film-makers travel roads that are literally forbidden to them as part and parcel of a colonisation process. As such, it pays to understand more roundly the circumstances in which these films were shot. What a slant towards travel accounts can add here is attention to the ardours of physical movement, as well as the fruitful vacillation between allegory and geopolitical tarmac, dust and grit reality which is the ground that the 'ajiba also covers.

'PREPARE YE THE WAY OF THE PEOPLES; CAST UP THE HIGHWAY, GATHER OUT THE STONES'[42]

Browse any library catalogue for texts on the Israel–Palestine conflict and you will find a significant number containing the word 'road' in their title: Ziva Flamhaft's *Israel on the Road to Peace: Accepting the Unacceptable*, for instance, or Jamal R. Nasser and Roger Heacock's anthology *Intifada: Palestine at the Crossroads*. One Second Intifada period proposal for a two-state solution bore the moniker the 'Road Map to Peace' and when, a few years later, the RAND Corporation think-tank launched an initiative to imagine a post-conflict regeneration of Palestine, a land-based communications network was its key principle for the ignition of national pride and a national economy.[43] Transport networks are crucial to the flows of not just pilgrims, but trade and troops too. Clearly, roads are both symbolic and strategic. They also claim land for their builders.

Unsurprisingly, then, West Bank roads and the contested control thereof are obsessively referenced within the cinema of the al-Aqsa Intifada, which uses the West Bank as its primary *mise en scène*, although not its greater imaginary. I will concentrate my more socio-historical attentions 'there' too. There are long productions about roads and short ones, fictional narratives, documentaries and many more in between. Palestine's two most prominent feature films of this period both wind around road systems. *Divine Intervention* maps out a love affair at a checkpoint and peppers its storyline with arguments about driveway expansions and car licence plates. *Paradise Now* commences on a road to a checkpoint and ends with a potential suicide bomber on a bus. In between, there are all manner of aborted and successful road journeys for the two lead characters, Khaled and Said, who mend cars for a living. More talk than is ever typical of a feature film is dedicated to discussions of how hard it is to get foreign car parts and what the road rules are in other countries. The epic four-and-a-half-hour Israel–Palestine documentary *Route 181* is structured according to a drive along the original and now largely invalidated 1947 border and composed entirely of scenic shots and interviews with people along the way. *Ticket to Jerusalem* charts a difficult journey to Jerusalem parallel to *Divine Intervention's*, this time with a mobile cinema. *Kings and Extras* outright labels itself a 'road movie' on its DVD box, but is just as much a quest narrative for the lost archive of the Palestine Film Unit. In each place the director visits, she converses on screen with a local cab driver and a fair portion of what we see is shot through car windows. The dramatic highpoint of *Be Quiet* (Sameh Zoabi, 2005) unfolds during a roadside toilet stop; *Like Twenty Impossibles* depicts a film shoot that is dangerously interrupted by a 'flying' (temporary) checkpoint; the quasi-fictional *Ford Transit* follows the travails and escapades of a minibus (also known as transit or *servees*) driver; *Crossing Qalandia* (Sobhi al-Zobaidi, 2002) documents the difficulties of doing just that by car; *25 Kilometers* chronicles the lengthy, arduous and hazardous task of trying to reach Bethlehem from Ramallah, once possible along a road whose length the title reveals and which is, since the film's completion, a journey now blocked by the Wall; *Road Map*, more an art installation than a movie, has concerned itself wholly with two very different, segregated roads; the titular subject of *Rana's Wedding* takes place at a checkpoint; *Going for a Ride?* explores car culture in Ramallah via an art installation that positioned vehicles destroyed by Israeli tanks along a 'road to nowhere'; *A Few Crumbs for the Birds*, as was noted, is set within a gas filling station and a brothel employing Palestinian refugees on the road to the Iraqi border. *Hopefully for the Best* and *Palestine Blues* are both distinguished by lengthy shots of the road captured from on board vehicles; *Trafic* [sic] (Mohanad Yaqubi, 2006) satirises the stagnancy and disruption of the Palestinian situation with a road-based metaphor of crossing signals flashing between the red and the green man. Finally, even when roads do not physically feature, such as in *The Fourth Room* (Nahed Awwad, 2004), there is prolonged and nostalgic mention of trips, usually ones that are currently off limits. Many of these films contain raw and covertly captured footage of brutal checkpoint encounters, or the dramatisation thereof.

Historically less popular than the easily navigable coastal and the commercially advantageous internationally bound roads, the core artery thoroughfare of the West Bank (now known as route 60) has been over-determined, since the Israeli occupation of Canaan in the Iron Age, by colonial design. Traversing difficult terrain, its role was primarily to hold ground, rather than to interlock with a regional trade infrastructure. 'Clear the way of the Lord in the Wilderness,' incites Isaiah 40:3, revealing the historical extent of the correlation between roads, a modernising and civilising agenda and, one could argue, religious imperialism. This very same road from the border into the West Bank is regularly damaged by the actions of the Israeli military, which is then, as noted above, repaired through the munificence of USAID.

Routes to Jerusalem, close by to the south, have traditionally served another purpose. Heavy international traffic for millennia has bred trying experiences of this thoroughfare. The twelfth-century pilgrim Saewulf speaks of how, on the road to the holy city, 'not only the poor and weak, but the rich and strong, are surrounded with perils; many are cut off by the Saracens, but more by heat and thirst; many perish by the want of drink, but more by too much drinking'.[44] Moshe Fischer elaborates:

> Roads lead to Jerusalem because people want to go there, not because it is a natural halting place or caravan city … Jerusalem owes its eminence to the fact that King David made it his capital. This was a political decision, the town being conveniently situated between Judaea and Israel and belonging to neither.[45]

Not so from thereon in. As Fischer continues, 'The importance of Jerusalem lies in the fact that people want to reach *and possess it* [my emphasis].'[46] Jerusalem still hangs in the balance today, with these very roads acting as strings connecting it to territories warring over its sovereignty.

The Umayyad rulers of the eighth century were criticised for spending too much on road-building activities, rather than distributing more funds among their subjects.[47] Yet, given Jerusalem's considerable symbolic importance, it is easy to see why. As Hilton Obenzinger points out, road networks to Jerusalem continued to function strategically in imperial struggles throughout the nineteenth century, as they do today:

> When Mark Twain and other Western travelers labored over the donkey paths that served as the only roads, they were not necessarily aware that proposals to rebuild the road from Jaffa to Jerusalem – even to build a railroad – were regularly rejected by the Ottoman authorities partly as feeble attempts to protect themselves from incursion. As Grand Vizier Fuad Pasha is reputed to have said in 1865, 'I shall never concede to these crazy Christians any road improvement in Palestine as they would then transform Jerusalem into a Christian madhouse.' Acting as a catalyst to 'open up' Palestine to European interests, Napoleon Bonaparte's invasion of Egypt and Syria in 1798 and his subsequent defeat of Acre in 1799 with the help of British forces prompted surveys by British and other European explorers and missionaries.[48]

Going for a Ride? (2003) catalogues the IDF's destruction of an artwork that dignified cars they had already destroyed

Concentrating on the more recent past, Eyal Weizman's *Hollow Land: Israel's Architecture of Occupation* charts how roads have become simply one dimension of a supra- and subterranean complex of imperialism, and a central and unique strategy within it. Of the 5,146.9 km of roads existing in the West Bank at the time of the Second Intifada, 764.4 km were built by Israeli authorities beyond its designated borders, without Palestinian permission, to exclusively serve Israeli users and facilitate movement that bypassed Palestinian towns and villages.[49] Hence their name: bypass roads, although that belies their real impact as a system of ethnic discrimination. Most Palestinians are forbidden from travelling by these routes, even if they are the purported owners of the land being crossed, and this schema effectively prohibits Palestinians from visiting the breadth of their own country. In statistical terms covering the 2002–4 period, 124 km of the West Bank's roads were Israeli-only and on 608 km of them Israeli authorities demanded Palestinians carry permits for access.[50] The institution of what was increasingly dubbed an 'apartheid road system' has no firm foundation in Israeli law, making the implementation of this infrastructure extremely opportunistic, arbitrary and unregulated.[51] The roads themselves are not simply networks, it has to be emphasised; they are also land grabs, a contribution to the 60 per cent control of the West Bank and Gaza Strip (including its borders) during this chapter's time-frame.[52]

Although justified as military requirements, one primary function of these thoroughfares is to connect the isolated and resource-dependent illegal settlements in the West Bank with Israel proper.[53] This is the gated community model writ ten-fold, fortresses of suburban design infused with defensive outpost mentality. The commuter incentives for Jerusalem employees to move out to now well-connected West Bank settlements recapitulate a supported independence that also marks a sort of aggressive, start-up entrepreneurialism that pervades many other arenas within the West Bank, including the 'NGOisation' of provision within Palestine. As will be explored later on, the ideal of private liberty aroused here also shaped the possibilities available to Second Intifada film-making.

While all effort was made to support these enclaves, militarily and resource-wise, the stranglehold on roads for Palestinians, according to Yehezkel Lein,

> resulted in a substantial shortage of raw materials and industrial inputs, which paralyzed many businesses and factories throughout the Occupied Territories. These restrictions also hampered the export of goods from the Gaza Strip and the West Bank to Israel and elsewhere, resulting in heavy losses to the Palestinian economy.[54]

At the same time, the flow of workers from Palestine into Israel was abruptly curtailed by restrictions on border crossings during the Intifada. It is hardly coincidental that *Route 181* commences with a conversation with an Israeli construction team about Chinese migrant workers, drafted into this sector because 'you can't rely' on Palestinians to make it through border closures.

Not only did Israel construct its own roads during this period, it also took iron-fisted control of Palestine's own transport infrastructures. Throughout the Intifada (and beyond) Israeli forces meted out a form of collective punishment by rendering the roads that remained for Palestinian passage inefficient, unpredictable and often dangerous through a series of closures, roadblocks (manned or otherwise) and permanent and flying checkpoints: a system that is hard to quantify, but which, at one point in 2003, amounted in the West Bank to 734 such obstacles.[55] Lein continues by quoting a testimony given to the human rights NGO B'Tselem by a reserve soldier talking about closures:

> If there were only males in the car, we took the keys from the driver – which we later gave to the DCO – and sent them on their way by foot. Several times we ordered the driver to get out and then shot and punctured the tires. For no reason, not because they didn't stop or anything like that, only because of the curfew. That was the command ... When we stopped a vehicle that only had males inside, we would ask them: 'Why are you on the road?' No matter what they said, we had them get out and we shot and punctured two of their tires.[56]

Furthermore, the Wall (which, at times, hits long-established roads at a perpendicular and now invalidating angle) more obdurately bars Palestinians access to their land and its resources, ultimately disallowing anyone without specific Israeli-issued identification from, say, moving between the north and the south of the West Bank. Director Sobhi al-Zobaidi lays this out: 'Ten years ago, I could go to the sea, now I cannot. My personal history, I can measure it with diminishing space. Every year, every month, every day, I have lesser geography.'[57] Access into and out of Gaza, even via the border with Egypt, was almost completely halted, creating what many were then beginning to call 'the largest prison in the world'. And how troublingly ironic that the 2002 Israeli Defense Force invasions of the Jenin and Balata refugee camps in the West Bank, with their high death tolls, should have been code-named 'Operation Picturesque Journey'. It is not hard to piece together how these measures contributed to the fact that 85 per cent of West Bank villagers did (or could) not leave their villages between 2000 and 2003 and that the country's per capita GDP slumped by 30 per cent between the start of the Intifada and 2005.[58] Economic desperation did, of course, lead to movements of Palestinians that were welcomingly sanctioned by Zionist expansionism: migrations to other countries in search of a safer life, including economically. The roads depicted in *Route 181* register this sentiment with their various signs and posters along the route declaring 'Jordan is the Palestinian State: Transfer = Peace and Security' and 'Crush Palestinians. End the War'.

Given these conditions, the way roads haunted the film culture of this tiny and potentially easily traversed country during the Second Intifada, as detailed above, is understandable, while roadblocks, curfews and checkpoints rendered cinematic production and dissemination uniquely difficult. No wonder that Nurith Gertz and George Khleifi, in *Palestinian Cinema: Landscape, Trauma, and Memory*, one of the few monographs dedicated to their topic, title a chapter 'A Dead-End: Roadblock Movies'. One of its subjects, the director Rashid Masharawi, claims, 'I am trying to make films that look like us: roads, maps. This colours our cultural behaviour ... I like road movies and I make them without planning to.'[59]

But how different these bodies of work are from the traditional road movie of whose values Palestinian directors can only dream. 'Imagine, you're just travelling on the highway for hours, nobody stops you,' ruminates film-maker Nahed Awwad.[60] As director Enas Muthaffar stresses:

The road becomes a hero in Palestinians' lives … it's freedom … Wow, we never drive for one hour and a half … From Ramallah to Nablus: stop, start, stop, start, it's psychologically there in the back of the mind at all times.[61]

If the road movie frequently champions rebellion against staid social structures, the right to roam and be free, then its aims are upheld, yet cruelly ironised by circumstances in Palestine and the movies that are their offspring. Most road movies resist the notion of 'home', while Palestinians are still fighting for the right to a home(land). When more typical incarnations of this genre might trace their lineage to the frontier ethos of nation-building and the conquest of space, where, then, does Palestine – if it is allowed to – stand?[62] To address these concerns, this chapter will first consider how Palestinian travellers negotiate the road. Later, I will turn to film-makers' engagement with the road movie as a genre.

TRAVELLING (THROUGH) SHOTS

Director (Hany Abu-Assad): You often use detours?
Transit driver (Rajai Khatib): They saved us. We use them more often than asphalt.

Ford Transit

We thought they [the *servees* drivers] were the best Palestinian artists because they were all the time finding new roads, finding new ways, being very creative.[63]

Sandi Hilal, part of the Multiplicity Project, makers of *Road Map*

Throughout the al-Aqsa Intifada, the drivers of *serveeses* ascended to a heroic, iconic, though never static position, not least within films such as *25 Kilometers*, *Road Map* and, in particular, *Ford Transit*, whose protagonist, Rajai, is a *servees* driver. *Servees* drivers were distinguished by their indefatigable opposition to occupation; their quick-fire transmission of information about obstacles to one another; their deliberate violation of routes prohibited by Israeli forces; their vehicles' transformations into politicised and often educational community spaces; and their subversion of the original meanings of their vehicles (these Ford Transits were once Israeli police vans given to collaborators as gifts and herald from a company – Ford – that is the bastion of historical US economic domination that tirelessly lobbied for road infrastructure). 'If they find out one [trick], we'll invent a hundred more,' boasts Rajai in *Ford Transit*. Within a broader shared project of communication networks (including cinema), there are valuable lessons to be learnt from these drivers, which Second Intifada film-makers have duly noted. The *servees* drivers' status as small-scale capitalist enterpreneurs in contravention of the occupation is one that overlaps with film-making of this period too. If the road is often a symbol of modernity, fluency with it can contradict the settler myth of primitive Palestinian peasantry or the 'land without a people' awaiting its 'people without a land', Golda Meir's infamous founding myth for a post-1948 state of Israel. By thinking through travel, Palestinian cinema (as well as this chapter) gains much from taking in and on *servees* drivers' tactics of resistance. Second Intifada cinema does not just document how travel becomes insurgency, it also effectively incorporates these principles as a mode of production.

Transportation is no new node in the battle for this territory, as the pilgrim narratives have attested. The 1970s witnessed a number of daring plane hijackings and oil pipeline attacks by the PFLP. These choices of target were emotional as well as strategic. Fawaz Turki, paraphrasing a conversation with the poet Mahmoud Darwish, points out, 'Where have Palestinians been more wounded at the core than at airports, refused entry, detained, expelled, questioned, humiliated, and so on, because of their travel documents, their national identity, and their revolutionary reputation?'[64] With Palestinian ID holders' access to international travel increasingly ruled out during the al-Aqsa Intifada, the roads within the Occupied Territories, and particularly the West Bank, became an even more crucial site of struggle. As for *servees* drivers, so for cinema.

The impromptu rule breaking of the *servees* drivers is echoed prominently in Second Intifada film aesthetics. At the level of immediate impact, the viewer becomes viscerally party to that experience. *Road Map* is composed of jerky, point-of-view cinematography that not only draws in its viewers through a replication of the motion sickness-inducing ride, but also opens out onto a particular Palestinian sensibility. As was pointed out, films like *25 Kilometers*, *Palestine Blues* and *Route 181*, to name but three, all feature abundant travelling shots from within vehicles that are featured on screen. In *Rana's Wedding* the dust kicked up driving along illegal routes in a desperate attempt to return to Jerusalem for said nuptials is readily evident on the car windscreen, which is regularly the frame in both directions. As counterpoint to these types of travelling shots, films are also punctuated with footage that must be captured while walking. *Land of '48*'s treatment of refugee camps is necessarily so in order to relay their cramped conditions, through which a car could not easily pass. *Palestine Blues* contains, as was previously noted, a long take clandestinely filmed through a hole in a bag. For the majority who even hold the right to cross a checkpoint like the one depicted here, the experience must be undertaken on foot.

Both this documentary and *A World Apart Within 15 Minutes* (Enas Muthaffar, 2008) also particularise the common experience of being lost. Loss impacts on many

Palestine Blues (2006): covertly filming the checkpoint through a hole in a bag

levels, socially and cinematically. In the most immediate senses palpable within
Palestine Blues, loss results from the impact of rapid changes in an occupied landscape,
with migrant director, Nida Sinnokrot, incapable of finding his way in a territory he
also calls home because so many settlements have been built since his last visit. The
land is lost as well as the director – for the moment. *A World Apart Within 15 Minutes* is
a short featuring two drivers asking, with false naiveté, the route to Ramallah from
Jerusalem of its Israeli inhabitants. To these bystanders, it might as well be another
planet, so culturally and politically estranged are they from their neighbouring town.
Loss manifests psycho-geographically on both sides, rendering it yet another site of
conflict. The emotionally invested tenor of pilgrimage narratives similarly demand
that we admit how territory is owned and disowned not just at the level of
representation, but also through how this then bears down on real people. *Kings and
Extras* acknowledges loss in a fashion that benefits from notions of reliquary. Its
narrative is a quest for the archive of the Palestine Film Unit, disappeared under
mysterious circumstances during the Lebanese Civil War. The fact that many of the
PFU's documentaries can now only be found in leftist libraries and storage facilities
around the world, but outside the region, is some measure of the dispersal not just of
refugees, but also the cultural productions of Palestine.

Of the material that has been preserved more successfully within Palestine,
distinct spatial configurations recur. Nurith Gertz and George Khleifi helpfully plot
these out historically and at length:

> Like the historical time of the Palestinian nation, Palestinian geography, too, has oscillated
> between the abstract, mythical idyll and the concrete reality. In films produced in the 1970s,
> actual geography was not shown. In fact, the real events captured in these films were
> delineated in abstract time and space that symbolically represented the Palestinian space of
> 1948 or earlier. Michel Khleifi, alongside other directors, was the first to draw a composed,
> organized map of the real Palestinian expanses, whose borders are on the horizon and whose
> core is the home. Other directors, mostly those following Khleifi, could no longer have
> depicted such a map. Over the years, the borders of the Palestinian space, uncertain to begin
> with, have become increasingly blurred and threatened, violated by the Israeli settlements and
> army, and replaced by roadblocks, controlled checkpoints, and closures which bisected
> Palestinian space and identity, severing and deconstructing them.[65]

Accordingly, films such as Elia Suleiman's and Rashid Masharawi's are fragmented –
more series of vignettes, each cut off from each other, like the enclaves inhabited by
the Palestinians. The Wall is a disruptive and brutal edit which we see in almost every
one of these narratives, either literally or as a more abstracted motivator of film style.
Turning necessity into a virtue, Hany Abu-Assad sardonically observes:

> The Israelis sometimes make life easy for film-makers because in love stories you need
> obstacles and you want to visualise obstacles and the Wall is such a visualised obstacle. You
> don't need five, six scenes to visualise the obstacle, you just shoot the wall and you go 'oh, in
> order to see his love he has to go over the Wall' ... but it's so tragic for all of us, because we
> have to suffer that. And I think this is the most powerful aspect of Palestinian cinema because
> they're using the oppression.[66]

Sobhi al-Zobaidi reiterates: 'Palestinians have emerged as disoriented people not only in the sense that they don't know where they are going but also in the sense that they know where they want to go but can never reach there.'[67] The circuitous journeys and skirtings of so many al-Aqsa Intifada narratives, each reluctant to commit to discourses of solid truth as the only means of 'arrival', acknowledge the reality of such a blocked landscape.

Yet, crucially, most Palestinian film-makers continue in the same vein as Abu-Assad, looking to turn adversity into advantage as a snub to the occupation. Jean Genet's perceptive observations about the Palestinian freedom fighters among whom he dwelt for a while sheds light: 'Even when they're serious, revolutionaries are only playing, hatching schemes to be worked out properly later. It's all a question of style.'[68] Style consequently becomes a terrain of articulated autonomy, unpredictable to be sure, but redolent with a tenacious eagerness to work with, rather than against, the Palestinian situation. 'Working with' in this instance does not mean settling into or for the impoverishment of life inflicted by the occupation. These mobilisations of style refuse to aim for a transparency of reportage, instead laying bare how occupation transfigures the mode of cinematic production, as it does every other aspect of life.

Many Second Intifada movies are deliberately random and freewheeling in their structure; improvisation (as with the *servees* drivers) abounds and 'acting' and 'being' run into each other. How different from outsiders' accounts of the Holy Land, like Melville's *Clarel*, which is, in the author's own words, 'a metrical affair'.[69] Its regularity 'and cloying rhyme scheme', according to the critic Hilton Obenzinger, 'can perhaps be most enjoyed by ranting out loud to the accompaniment of steady thuds on a kettle drum',[70] a security instructively at odds with the fidgety and fractured aesthetic tactics of Palestine's film-makers.

In short, these are never mere artistic whims. 'There's no use fixing down the script because reality will interfere,' noted Rashid Masharawi while working on his feature film, *Laila's Birthday* (2008), notably about a taxi driver.[71] Its original location of Gaza was replaced by Ramallah when the former was rendered out-of-bounds for the crew. Annemarie Jacir points out that, 'You have to choose your crew, choose your cast, based on ID cards.'[72] Nahed Awwad joins in, 'It's part of the process, it adds to the film.'[73] Moreover, in a country without a firm internal system of authority and with multitudinous stateless compatriots, governance – including how a film production is ordered and controlled – must be handled differently. There is little officialdom to hold court either economically or ideologically over Palestinian cinema, prompting director Tawfiq Abu Wael to claim:

> What's good about being a Palestinian director is that you're free, because you don't have a country, you don't have a government, you don't have a 'father'. It's two sides. On one side, you don't have an industry, an audience, any money. But on the other, you have total freedom to make whatever you want, to criticise your society, to be courageous in your stories and I think it's good to be Palestinian in this aspect.[74]

Rashid Masharawi puts it more succinctly: 'We have the best international cinema in the Arab world because we don't have an industry.'[75]

Ultimately, the way Palestinian film-makers choose to wear their situation carries, or continues, the spirit of intifada: 'spontaneous', yet with deep roots and networks, as we have seen, of solidarity, not least in how its film-makers have translated the specific ethos of popular uprising into cinematic form. Referring with conviction and affinity back to the *servees* drivers of the time, al-Zobaidi theorises and imagines a type of film-making, which he dubs Tora Bora cinema, from these conditions. Borrowing from the hideouts of the militias in Afghanistan, he notes that Tora Bora became a nickname for the most treacherous passages between Palestinian towns and villages. They are:

> those kinds of passages that one is not sure whether one can or cannot reach: both possibilities always equally exist. The line *forks* and one never knows which way one will end up – dead, arrested, or free ... Tora Bora is not another name for the roadblock, because Tora Bora starts from beyond the roadblock. Tora Bora assumes movement to start with. It is a passage, a crack, a flight, or a leap. It is anything but death. Cinema provides Palestinians with this place to be. Cinema is Tora Bora *par excellence*. In cinema Palestinians can smuggle themselves anywhere (in and out of Palestine) and they can go everywhere – as in *Divine Intervention*, with the ninja woman defying gravity, and where an apricot seed destroys an Israeli tank.[76]

For certain directors, making these rather anarchic films is a product of freedom of expression, a continuation regardless that insists upon social autonomy within Palestine, rather than aiming primarily to 'convert' an 'outside' audience.[77] The very fact of survival, of a population or a film industry, against these odds is defiance in the face of the occupation. Within these lawless spaces, there is, paradoxically, more scope for proper freedom.

STASIS AND *SUMUD*: STEADFAST STYLE

Let us sit for a while, as these films invite us to, with this first idea: that the very fact of making cinema is itself a riposte to Israel's territorial expansion and its attempted clearance of a Palestinian population. Livia Alexander proposes that, 'For many Palestinian filmmakers, the establishment of a national cinema is a self-evident aspiration that would affirm the existence of the nation.'[78] In this, the film-makers undertake a well-known mode of civil resistance common to the Palestinian struggle called *sumud*, or, in English, steadfastness. *Sumud* amounts to staying put, holding ground. Its stalwart protagonists are, in the words of Sobhi al-Zobaidi, 'those who did not leave, could not leave, do not want to leave, but are made to disappear'.[79] *Sumud* works amid the interplay between, first, the arrested movement within and into the territory itself (the denial of the legal right of return for Palestinian refugees), second, the facilitated movement and parallel resoluteness of the Israeli settlers and, third, as a counter to the rootlessness of the refugee population, many of whom are blocked from acquiring citizenship elsewhere in the world. In all cases, travel remains central, making insights into mobility useful to continued struggle. *Sumud* in its most profound sense is dedicated to reinforcing structures under threat. Jerky, clandestine camerawork in the face of 'please turn off the camera'. A recognisable and functioning national cinema engenders a form of statehood and sovereignty, ironic though its corpus is about (such) fiction and reality.

Sumud, then, staunchly recapitulates conditions of production through choices regarding formal aesthetics. In al-Aqsa Intifada cinema, the restless mobile framing detailed above frequently functions dialectically with static shots. *Ticket to Jerusalem*, for instance, features a number of pans where a cut might have more typically occurred. The journey of the cinematic take passes uninterrupted, less so the actual journey unfolding in its narrative. *Around* (Mohanad Yaqubi, 2006) deliberately presents relaxed, motionless images of the beauty encountered upon actual *arrival* at Palestinian locations, after the monotony of the checkpoints that it also depicts. The land, the territory – what is left of it – is celebrated and recaptured, as it were, in this road trip documentary, a deliberate defiance of one depicted Israeli soldier who seems aghast, through a life-time's evasive spatial-political education, that there is anything to actually visit in Palestine. *Sumud* and reclamation result also from *Going for a Ride?*'s cinematography, which depicts double-exposed phantom images of cars that partially bring back to life, perhaps as relics, what the conflict has destroyed. Thinking of relics as part of *sumud* helps preserve, cinematically, an archive of resistance for present as well as future use, concretising the values and ideas attributable to cultural production in a location where change is rapid and destructive.[80]

On a day-to-day basis, enduring checkpoints, curfews and roadblocks are perhaps the most trying demands for *sumud*. Unsurprisingly, beyond the non-compliant hidden camera renditions of checkpoint crossings, stagnant camerawork features highly in the way this experience is filmed. Rendering the situation statistically, Adam Hanieh reports that:

> From mid-June 2002 to February 2003, the northern West Bank town of Nablus, with a population of 126,000 people, was under curfew for three out of every four hours. Between December 8, 2002 and January 19, 2003, according to the Palestinian Red Crescent, an average of 430,910 people were stuck in their houses each day. More than 320,000 Palestinians living in the West Bank spent more time forcibly locked in their homes than free of curfew for the second half of 2002.[81]

Emma C. Murphy converts such information into percentages:

> According to the World Bank [no citation], between September 2000 and December 2001, the entire West Bank was under total closure 73 percent of the time, and the Gaza Strip for 4 percent. Partial closure was in operation for the remaining 27 percent of the time in the West Bank and 95 percent in Gaza.[82]

No wonder, then, that a number of films, such as *Lions* (Nahed Awwad, 2002) are shot from within a curfew, this one a meditation on what can be seen through the window of a house that its inhabitant-film-maker is not allowed to leave, followed by an exploration of the devastation once the siege is briefly lifted. Or that the titular nuptials in *Rana's Wedding* have to be conducted in a *servees* at a checkpoint because that is the only place the betrothed can both reach. While these impositions on movement clearly struck at the level of individual discomfort, the films reveal how

Rana's Wedding (2002): the couple's first dance ... at the checkpoint

blockages simultaneously functioned as collective punishment, aiming to destroy the fabric of Palestinian life socially and economically, making political organising on a larger scale more difficult and helping facilitate the much easier annexation of land while its owners were locked inside or forbidden from working it.

Elia Suleiman's oeuvre, dealing with Palestinian life in both the West Bank and the state of Israel, explores the fraught tensions that exist between *sumud* and a stagnancy that is in some ways enforced and, in others, unquestioningly inhabited. *Divine Intervention*, like all of Elia Suleiman's work, toys with seemingly boring interactions like arguments between neighbours; the movie relays, through a dark ludicrousness, how habitually invested a Palestinian can become in the minutiae of a shrunken daily repertoire. Characters often sit squarely in a static frame; they do not move and neither does the camera. *Hopefully for the Best* likewise revolves around everyday folk in everyday jobs such as food preparation. Markedly, though, the movie is punctuated, as is all (Palestinian) life, with road encounters: the weariness of unpredictable waits for ID verification exacted by unsympathetic soldiers on a daily basis. Tedium for the occupier should be noted here too, and Hannah Arendt's conception of the 'banality of evil' does not go amiss on any Palestinian who has read her work. Thus everyday life, infused as it is with this humdrum brutality, becomes central to the rhythms of Palestinian cinema, celebrating it as an extraordinary achievement given the conditions under which it must persist.

In sequences of what might now be read as 'slow cinema', *Hopefully for the Best* builds through protracted takes of multiple minutes at a time, including the one that opens the film, shot through a car windscreen. We become party to another side of occupation here, where conflict is not manifestly presented in terms of an occupier in our sight lines. The car's aimless cruising in one sense hooks into practices undertaken the car-owning world over; in another, it carries the specific resonances of people trapped within very small parameters. As we move from nights to days and the seasons change, the journey remains the same, later rendered in fast motion, as if to fulfil an impossible wish to zoom past this tired backdrop. Multiplicity member Alessandro Petti, one of the artists behind *Road Map*, maintains that '"real" violence ... is easy to represent, everybody knows it'.[83] Their project aims to convey the *temporality* of the occupation's manoeuvrings, how tedium wears its subjects down while unexpectedly inflicting moments of danger and high (newsworthy) drama. Ultimately, he continues, '99% of your time is under occupation because of this [restriction on] movement', something more subtle, more pervaded by the wait than the (inevitable) event, the cruder conceptions of violence that consume the media.[84]

A political staying put is one thing, and waiting another, although the two are linked. Waiting at checkpoints for indefinite hours on end; waiting, as a refugee, to return; waiting for a homeland; waiting for international recognition; waiting for the end of conflict. Within his film *Waiting*, Rashid Masharawi knits together all these variations, using the story hinge of a film shoot to explore waiting's cinematic iterations and possibilities. Once again, travel becomes the pivot upon which waiting can be creatively explored. Nadia Yaqub perceptively observes how Masharawi elides the believable to fabricate a more conjectural sense of travel's ebbs and flows:

> Masharawi's use of this international journey as a structuring device for his film is ironic, for such mobility is impossible for most Palestinians. The ease with which these Gazans cross borders is utterly unrealistic, thereby coding the journey as a symbolic rather than mimetic depiction of Palestinian lived reality. In this regard, *Waiting* is not a roadblock movie, a genre that treats the social significance of the political impediments to Palestinian mobility. The distinction is suggested in the opening scene when Ahmad passes through the Eretz crossing. True, his bag is searched, and he does speak later of having been detained for hours, but the scene lacks the crowds, the potential for violence, and abuse of power that one finds in films that thematize impediments to Palestinian mobility.[85]

Like many of the other protagonists of Second Intifada cinema, Masharawi elects to digress from, and thereby implicitly critique, more typical factual rendition of such human rights abuses.

This choice is instructive. Captured on screen in *Kings and Extras*, Azza El-Hassan, its director, is confronted by a bystander who tells her, 'Now is not the time to be thinking about cinema ... If you want drama, go to the checkpoint. Go and watch men being tied up.' In response, El-Hassan avowedly declares the need to escape what she calls 'news time' as much as the curfew. She acknowledges Palestinians as perhaps the most per capita photographed people on earth, while arguing that such spectacles do little but display these subjects for the mercy or outrage of the viewer. In a sense, these conventions further the objectives of more physical blockages. As I have already pointed out, Eyal Weizman's *Hollow Land* sees the occupation as functioning at the level of air control, aquafers, architecture and so forth. These understandings of restriction are easily expanded to news rendition or cinematic expectation, that Palestinian film-makers 'should' capture certain stock imagery. Talking of borders, which cannot be our sticking point, given how frequently they are moved in Palestine, Étienne Balibar still usefully attests,

> *some borders are no longer situated at borders at all*, in the geographico-politico-administrative sense of the term. They are in fact elsewhere, wherever selective controls are to be found, such as, for example, *health* or *security* checks (health checks being part of what Michel Foucault termed bio-power) [emphases in the original].[86]

Let us take his thinking, instead, as a way of recognising forcibly diminished prospects for Palestinians that multiply beyond the actual roadblock.

Scope arose during the Second Intifada to circumnavigate. While earlier productions by, for instance, the Palestine Film Unit, felt the responsibility to provide newsreel-style reportage, the transnational news institutions, particularly Al Jazeera, provided this sort of coverage throughout the al-Aqsa Intifada, allowing the film-makers of that period to work otherwise, particularly, as has been shown, with temporality. Here we confront a refusal for cinema to act solely as a service provider, particularly one that easily assuages guilt about conflict by allowing a compartmen-talised, harrowing vision that is almost as easily abandoned upon exiting the screening space. Yes, we run into a lexicon of heroic or tragic figures within these films, but they are too mercurial to ever remain just that. Rashid Masharawi angrily recounts attending a Q&A in Cairo where audience members cried before his film had even begun. 'They damage Palestinian cinema,' he remarks.[87] Pity of this order is not a preferred endpoint.

Instead, extracting exact meaning from these films is a challenge. This results, on one level, in a call for freedom through the very mechanisms and choices of interpretation and, on another, a disavowal of the justice that has rarely been forthcoming through clear, ethical statements about the 'truth' of the situation. Representations of the conflict are in constant, blurring motion, never allowed (within these spaces at least) to ossify or to become reified (in a capitalistic-fetishistic sense) so that an audience member might take away something supposedly 'valuable' which is, in essence, already dead. If Palestine has long been a 'laboratory' for outsiders to test everything from their religious convictions to their journalistic ethos and most up-to-date weaponry, then Palestinian cinema both opposes the worst of this and assumes its own right to experiment, rather than solely remonstrate. This imperative drives my desired orientation of what lies above: that what I have written might be taken up not as a poor replication of something so vital, but as an active intersectional node in a transportation matrix; like cinema, constructing rather than conveying, making rather than carrying. As with the topics explored in the previous chapter, it may well be in the manufacture of these movies, in this case *the very fact of making them*, that the insurrectionary action lies, rather than in what they depict and what that can achieve. The funding structures, however, differ enormously between the two neighbouring countries. Palestine's was enabled and constrained by a particular conception of 'freedom', influenced by specific economic actors on the scene who defined this notion less collectively than individualistically. Getting to grips with how these meanings were fashioned – culturally, economically and infrastructurally – will greatly aid my subsequent investigations of how Palestine answered back to global inscriptions of the road and the road movie as a means of resistance and liberation that often simultaneously satirised how freedom had been demarcated from outside.

THE PRIVATE AND THE PUBLIC

In a knowingly ironic sense, the freedom explored and the maverick qualities performed across Second Intifada film-making tally well with the mythos of the car.

The flexibility promised to a car driver, and more so the road movie protagonist, creates less a horizontalised vista of possibilities than a set of zones and limitations of freedom, that divide through distance and accessibility.[88] The automobile links just as it divides spaces that are designated as private (the home) and public (work, shops, sites of leisure). The car, like cinema (at least as it is read through much spectatorship theory), is a mass-produced privatisation, experienced simultaneously by any number of others. Certain shifts in film production in Palestine at around this time witness similar overlaps between public and private. Just as the Intifada itself was both ad hoc and also thoroughly supported by less official, grassroots organising, the sense of a joint venture through unitised film-making needs to be understood as a complex interleafing of public and private, collective (even nationalistic) and particularised.

An intifada is a popular, multi-layered revolt that embraces such activities as film-making and viewing. The *servees* journeys too. These movies' refusal to reinscribe the car on the open road as a neo-liberal personal space instead function like the *servees* mode of community transportation creating a public sphere (destroyed by the day by the occupation, although unwittingly re-established through the commonality of checkpoint queues) in surprising and engaging new ways. As noted earlier, pilgrimage compels a sense of sharing, one in harmony with the rubrics of al-Aqsa Intifada production. Note how Victor Turner and Edith Turner's description of pilgrimage practices overlaps with the spirit of intifada. Along each step of this lengthy classification, 'pilgrimage' could just as readily be replaced by 'Palestinian film-making':

> Pilgrimages resemble private devotions ... in their voluntary character, but differ from them in their public effect. The decision to go on pilgrimage takes place within the individual but brings him into fellowship with like-minded souls, both on the way and at the shrine. The social dimension is generated by the individual's choice, multiplied many times. On pilgrimage, social interaction is not governed by the old rules of social structure. When a pilgrimage system becomes established, however, it operates like other social institutions. The social takes precedence over the individual at all levels. Organized parties make the journey; devotions at the shrine are collective and according to the schedule. But pilgrimage is an individual good work, not a social enterprise. Pilgrimage, ideally, is charismatic, in the sense that pilgrim's [sic] decision to make it is a response to a charisma, a grace, while at the same time he receives grace as he makes his devotions. For this reason, orthodoxy in many religions tends to be ambivalent toward pilgrimage. The apparent capriciousness with which people make up their minds to visit a shrine, the rich symbolic and communitas quality of pilgrimage systems, the peripheral character of pilgrimage vis-à-vis the ritual or liturgical system as a whole, all make it suspect.[89]

The oscillation between self and group that the pilgrimage has fostered is more pertinent still to the particularities of Second Intifada film-making, which aims for efficacy according to political terms, but the right to expression through, perhaps, more personal registers.

We should start with the individualisation of the process. Film shoots of late carry more than ever the propensity to be an isolated endeavour, particularly the case during the al-Aqsa Intifada era, when lighter weight equipment enabled almost the outward appearance of 'home video' during location shooting. Editing, similarly, retreated into domestic, personal computer experience. The sorts of freedoms sponsored within the arts, particularly from a western-facing outlook, it should be remarked, also sit well within the lore of the car and the open road.

The cinema of the film units from the 1970s conceived of itself as much more public-spirited than this. It was, most pointedly, the organ of the state-apparent, specific financial provisions made for it on account of these alignments. In contradistinction, the output of the Second Intifada amounted to a cinema in necessary search of private funds, more of a business venture than the party-sponsored output of before. The auteur cinema of the previous two decades, films like *Wedding in Galilee* (Michel Khleifi, 1987), laid the path by securing funding from sources external to Palestine and its diasporas (for this production, Europe's Les Productions Audiovisuelles, Zweites Deutsches Fernsehen and the Centre National de la Cinématographie). Meanwhile, the al-Aqsa Intifada time-frame witnessed an increasingly transnationalised economy that had great bearing on the terms through which the public and private made themselves manifest. At the informal, street level, individual hawkers began selling pirated products from around the world, including bootleg VCDs that surely had an impact on cinema culture (predominantly imbided in the home, especially under curfew).

More significantly, however, the Second Intifada arose in and continued to run alongside a heavy NGOisation of Palestine, set in place by the Oslo Accords some years earlier and governed by multiple interests, often foreign, greatly atomised and atomising. Writing at the end of the al-Aqsa Intifada, Amal Jamal gives a sense of scale:

> [I]t would not be inaccurate to claim that hundreds of new civil organizations were established following the start of peace talks between Israel and the PLO in the early 1990s, and again after the establishment of the PA in 1994 ... the civil sector is active in 450 locations in Palestine and serves some 1.5 million people, employing about 25,000 people.[90]

Foreign investment in aid work, but also in cinema, recalibrated film's meaning as a particular, sometimes charity-inflected, globalised and marketised form. Jamal continues as to the tenor of these NGOs' principles, discourse that:

> formulates a clear link between the resistance against occupation and the demand for national self-determination with the freedom of the individual. This does not mean that all civil organizations call for an individualistic society, but most of them do favour the reconstruction of a modern society composed of equal and free citizens living in a democratic state.[91]

How perfect, then, the priorities of the road movie, with its frequently individualistic notions of liberty, nourished by the more general propensity for artistic culture (including cinema) to proselytise on uniqueness of vision.

By design or accident, the NGOs endorsed the managerial accountancies and accountabilities of liberal democracy. Their rise came at the expense of a divestment from grassroots organising and statist leadership. Rema Hammami labels the changes spurred by the rise of the NGO as a movement 'from mass mobilizers to development centres'.[92] Promoting capitalist models above all else, entrepreneurship and start-ups were encouraged like never before. Cinema bears the marks of this shift too, with small teams or, more often, lone directors, competing for money and often directly within the sectors of aid and humanitarianism. Different, indeed, not only from the film units of a few decades earlier, but also the Syrian Film Organization of the previous chapter. As the NGO model ascended, it disentangled a whole range of sectors, including cinema, from the hold of the PLO and the other revolutionary parties. The sense of competition in the air even led the World Bank to establish a trust fund handled by a Swiss-based NGO to manage how donor money was distributed, thus creating a very particular climate of what was, ultimately, state-building.[93] The organisational principles NGOisation helped install saw each production as a small-scale enterprise, helmed by a director with auteurist aspirations, disconnected from others more fully than was the case for NFO or PFU production. Sobhi al-Zobaidi confirms this state of affairs, that film-making of this period:

> is better understood as individual filmmaking because of the absence of the institutional base such as foundations, film collectives, film schools, groups, and most important censorship. In fact Palestinian filmmakers act competitively, most often incompatible with each other. Very rarely do they work with each other. An increasing number of filmmakers compete for the same resources. With no institutional bases whatsoever, the whole thing is left to individual improvisation.[94]

Improvisation in production, as observed earlier, but also in mining for production funds.

'Financial assistance from the Palestinian Authority, are you kidding me?' jokes Mohammad Bakri, one of Palestine's most lauded actors, turned director during this period.[95] Where to turn instead? NGOs certainly did not finance the majority of the more successful films of the period, but their prominence within cultural circuits settled them into place both as carriers of certain attitudes towards support and freedom and, increasingly, as viable patrons of cinema. As with any other funders, they came with stipulations. Some tried to enforce a partnership with an Israeli cinema institution, something that most Palestinians chose to boycott.[96] Speaking more generally about this period, Sobhi al-Zobaidi astutely notes how a cinema more outwardly 'independent' than it might have been in the 1970s or 80s was withstanding a 'transition into, surely, a dependence on something else'.[97] He should know; his *Light at the End of the Tunnel* (2000) provides the cautionary tale of what can happen under NGO involvement. Tackling the topic of Palestinian prisoners and commissioned by the Red Cross, al-Zobaidi was expressly prohibited from approaching the film in a 'political' fashion, which is, of course, an acutely political ruling given the widespread violations of legal protocol enacted in Israel's incarceration sector.[98] Pilgrimage literature has familiarised us with the preconceived foreign perception. In the case of the charity patron, this is as political as ever in its own presumptions of 'neutrality', blessed, in this new iteration, by access to well-oiled international distribution machinery.

As elsewhere during the Second Intifada, a limited spectrum of resources channelled under specific management conventions amounted to, as Amal Jamal concludes, 'donor countries and organizations therefore play[ing] a major role in setting the Palestinian civil sector's policies and priorities'.[99] In situations like al-Zobaidi's, humanitarianism poses as distinct from direct politics to insist upon particular modes of cinematic address. By enclosing such activities within aid or charity, it effectively chips away at more revolutionary means of struggling to regain sovereignty. The Evens Fondation, which offered support for *A Few Crumbs for the Birds*, for instance, in its own words, 'initiates, develops and supports projects that encourage citizens and states to live together harmoniously ... It promotes respect for diversity, both individual and collective, and seeks to uphold physical, psychological and ethical integrity.'[100] Such language is a far cry from that of national liberation and, moreover, a sense of dependence can haemorrhage over into the actual content of the movies. Rashid Masharawi claims: 'There are two maps of Palestine, the geographical and the humanitarian. *Waiting* is a road movie through a humanitarian map.'[101] As Nadia Yaqub observes of *Waiting*, which is largely funded by European companies and agencies, including Arte, the Ministère Français de la Cinématographie (ADC Sud) and the Centre National de la Cinématographie:

> Palestinian reliance on international support is ubiquitous [within the narrative]; UNRWA feeds Palestinian children. EU documents, not Palestinian passports, get the crew across international borders. Palestinian institutional authority is embodied in Abu Jamil who is not only inaccessible (throughout most of the film he exists only as a voice on Bissan's cell phone) but also bizarrely beholden to the EU. He refers to the EU, its funding, and the constraints it imposes on him whenever he speaks. Thus, Abu Jamil is less a Palestinian authority figure than a conduit for international attempts to manipulate Palestinian behavior.[102]

EU letters of passage facilitate this travelogue from Gaza to Egypt, Jordan, Syria and Lebanon, but the actual funding provided by foreign institutions remains unreliable. Up once more looms a neo-liberal insistence on precariousness, entrepreneurship and competition as a means of survival, the plot turning on the losses and gains of hard cash.

During the al-Aqsa Intifada, NGOs increasingly also partook of how film-makers were trained. They sponsored any number of workshops, whose impact marks a shift, Rema Hammami argues, 'from what had been the radically informed ideologies of a mass movement to discourses more narrowly defined in terms of development'.[103] The NGOs' selection processes for these events tended to target a particular nominated constituency and recruit 'professionals' familiar with NGO command structures, rather than encouraging organic organising from below. In addition, international organisations, both NGO and governmental, continue to provide scholarships to educational institutions overseas. To access these and many other funds, including those awarded by the international film festival circuit, applications must typically be submitted in English. Implicitly, these requirements favour an elite who have usually benefited from expensive private educations, either in local foreign schools or abroad, thus breeding further privileges for these social groups and creating a schism from increasingly poorer populations.[104] At the same time, their application forms inculcate particular artistic subjectivities, demanding fluency in the NGOs' favoured modes of address and conceptualisations of audience expectation.

Globalised aid networks, constituted in part by particular privileges of travel, not only set out who would be most eligible to make films, but also sought to entice a particular outlook for them. Al-Aqsa Intifada cinema needed to negotiate its notions of liberation amid all these petitions for freedom, competition, enterprise and individualism, preferably presented in a globally comprehensible format. Yet, despite the hairpin turns on support structure formation in Palestine, these films have proven particularly linguistically dexterous, all the while creating a transnational cinema that fosters solidarity. They have done so, as shall be demonstrated, by articulating themselves in specific generic terms that squarely address the politics of travel.

GLOBAL GENRE, GLOBAL ADDRESS

The Second Intifada brought to life its road (block) movies amid, in response to and often funded by these globalised economic landscapes, which had been built, of course, over longer periods of international travel. Livia Alexander observes how the grammars and vocabularies of cross-border communion infused this body of films to craft, 'a cinema addressing universal sensibilities, the metropolitan in-vogue issues of identity politics and human rights'.[105] Generic comprehensibility has undoubtedly proven pragmatic here. The hefty capital investment required to make feature films is difficult to whip up, especially given Palestine's small domestic market, subjected as it is to the sorts of travel restrictions that make movie theatre attendance less possible or enjoyable.[106] With the internationalist-socialist 'market' (the kind that had initially made Syrian cinema more mobile) evaporating during the Oslo period, eyes lay more on backers and, as a consequence, audiences from the Global North. *Ticket to Jerusalem*, for example, raised money from Australia and France (the TV channel Arte); *Paradise Now* was unprecedentedly backed by Warner Independent Pictures. The urgency to address a Palestinian audience, as projected by the predominant actuality and regionalised address of, say, some of the Palestine Film Unit's material, gave way to more globally palatable work that could fit snuggly within a 'world cinema' or human rights film festival programme.

Placed next to the fact of millions of refugees dispersed around the globe, there is much scope, however, to consider the readability of the road (block) movie as something far exceeding two-dimensional Global Northern aspirations. When film-makers talk of 'finding a home' for their projects, these realities must be taken into account. Such movies are also a marker of a cosmopolitanism symptomatic of diasporic life, one acknowledged side-effect of ethnic cleansing. With 2,000 actual Palestinian houses in the West Bank and Gaza destroyed by Israelis during the al-Aqsa Intifada alone, the motivation for a some-time migrant director, amid all this international dispersion, to take up (why not?) funding for *Paradise Now* from a wing of a Hollywood major becomes clearer.[107]

And yet, I still render the generic classification that has shaped this chapter with a parenthetical '(block)' to signify the extent to which these Palestinian movies both belong to an internationally readable narrative type and consciously stand up as an exception to the standard road movie. What the road (block) movies achieved was a series of broadly understandable statements on travel, transport and mobility cleverly managed to insist upon the inequities of these systems. Or, as Mahmoud Darwish more eloquently puts it:

> We travel like other people, but we return to nowhere. As if travelling
> Is the way of the clouds. We have buried our loved ones in the
> darkness of the clouds, between the roots of the trees.
> And we said to our wives: go on giving birth to people like us
> for hundreds of years so we can complete this journey
> To the hour of a country, to a metre of the impossible.[108]

'We travel like other people, *but* ...' 'Like other people,' a normality that also encompasses our shared familiarity with the Holy Land, the call of the Nazareth Santa Claus chase scene in *Divine Intervention*. The 'but' is the crucial sticking point, comprising the relentless inconstancy of diaspora life and its ruptured relationship with another Palestinian reality: one of curfew, checkpoint and forbidden access to territories supposedly, although not in practice, protected by international law. Homeland nonetheless. Cinematically, the road (block) movies of this era worked hard to deploy reference and genre so they might interrogate, rather than adopt, the assumed norms and privileges of 'other people'. All such entries into road movie-making expose the geopolitical affiliations and concrete restrictions on movement that globalising forces have simultaneously protracted.

One recurrent tactic to make apparent such crucial distinctions was the simple comparison – 'like other people, but ...' – a device familiar from travelogues. The split screen of *Road Map* has proven an obvious example. We are pummelled by the Palestinian journey and notice the lack of camaraderie in the smooth uninterrupted drive along the Israeli-only route. Comparison also lies at the heart of *Route 181*, whose narrative conceit is a road journey along the two countries' 1947 partition line. 'A divorce before a marriage,' as Eyal Sivan, the Israeli director of the dual directorial team (one from each side of the 'border'), calls it.[109] Composed of encounters with the normal people they meet along the way, the documentary leaves us with the impression that the predominant group in these areas is Israeli, given that the boundary line has extended much further into Palestinian territory over the years. Between the interviews, we witness the anatomy of the travelling car, its dashboard, windows and rear-view mirrors, along with the noises of the vehicle and, early on, the quiet hum of the landscape. Such interludes give pause for thought between some often astonishingly hate-filled interviews, opening up to a landscape of conflict and colonisation: the Wall, barbed wire and settlements. In the middle of a day, we see the empty city of Ramallah under curfew, tanks and other military vehicles, the only people a Palestinian man attempting to convince soldiers to let him take his sick mother to hospital.

Pasolini Pa* Palestine compares by overlaying new footage and dialogue across *Seeking Locations in Palestine for the Gospel According to St Matthew*. The same places have changed immeasurably over time and at the hands of the occupation. In both decades, inadequacies in representing Palestine (on screen) emerge. Like Mark Twain, Pasolini found it increasingly difficult to re-enact the legends prompting his arrival here: 'My conception of the holy sites has changed completely. I must adjust my imagination to reality,' he admits. The 'but' in Darwish's poem enables (mis)conceptions such as Pasolini's to be reconfigured and steers Palestinian film-makers beyond modest genre cinema to the point where stock phrasing touches 'other people' in an activist manner.

Oftentimes resemblances are drawn across geography, underpinned by genre. *Palestine Blues* takes pains to reveal the American suburban design of illegal Israeli settlements. It unmasks, with the help of the road movie formula, the centrality of American-style car-dependent modernity and its understanding of freedom to the narratives of the settlers who purport to liberate 'Judea and Sumaria', otherwise known as the West Bank. *Ford Transit* selects Ennio Morricone's theme from *A Fistful of Dollars* (Sergio Leone, 1964) for its opening shot, not only evoking similarities to the lawless Wild West, but also referring immediately to America's own practices of colonisation and land clearance, and their generic glorification on screen.

While Palestine may seem like a geographically specific crisis zone on one level, issues of expansionism, freedom, democracy and privatisation resonate outwards from within its borders (and vice versa), through foreign policies impinging upon oil-producing nations and the supposed liberties of the 'open road' that are exhorted by road movie mythologies. Palestine's roads (all roads, in fact) also intersect with larger arrangements of geopolitics and, ultimately, oil distribution. Earlier in this chapter, representation was discussed in terms of *investment*, building up what the land can be meant to mean. The films also uncover, through generic reference, other investments that have impinged upon the Arab world in the name of fuel, fuel that we all use. Palestine's part within this features obliquely in *A Few Crumbs for the Birds*. Filmed on the border of war-torn Iraq, the documentary concentrates on supporting players: petrol smugglers, oil tanker drivers, itinerant journalists who have brought money into the town and the Palestinian sex workers in a roadside brothel. The film thereby renders explicit the broader networks binding oil, migration, car culture and Palestinians. As Jean Genet notes of the red-light district in this same country – Jordan – sex workers also 'calmly [link] the shanty town to the rest of the world, and hence to the Palace'.[110] *Palestine Blues*, as we have seen, connects the Israeli West Bank settlements to Californian suburbs, and thus to a mode of petrol-dependent privilege that rests on severely unsavoury foundations.

And, through these globalised infrastructures, ideas, including cinematic genres, have travelled to Palestine. *Divine Intervention* nods to Hong Kong martial arts films, and thus to *The Matrix* (Wachowski Brothers, 1999), to Sergio Leone westerns as well as Jesus and Santa Claus, protagonists more squarely associated with the region, but also international travellers par excellence. The character of E. S., who spans a number of Suleiman's features, is mute, deadpan, seen by the director as a cousin of a Hollywood silent comedy or a Jacques Tati performer, thereby hooking into a particular legacy of silence, but then asking us to question where silences live geopolitically.

There is a sustained history in Arabic literatures of travel of these sorts of appropriations, particularly, as I have discussed, in its educational treatises. To recapitulate: Taha Hussein, who studied in France, at Montpellier and the Sorbonne, similar to Rifa'a al-Tahtawi before him, declares, 'I am pleading for a selective approach to European culture, not wholesale and indiscriminate borrowing ... the preservatives of defense, religion, language, art, and history can be strengthened by the adoption of

Western techniques and ideas.'[111] Travel writers of this ilk deem European modernity not only available, as we might reckon the road movie, but also divisible and utilitarian as a tool for national liberation within the region.

Such authors presume an intermediary role that is so often adopted by Palestinian film-makers, both inside and out. The mobility of both these sets of people, evident in the very structures and themes of their work, prompts a migration of thought too. We have observed how they benefit from dislocated peoples' frequent endowment with the heightened skills of comparison so vital to social change, wedded to a multi-lingual (cinematic) fluency that, despite its regular imperial legacy, can transmit and translate liberationist struggle with enormous effectiveness.[112] Refugees too straddle at least two (often competing) cultural communities at once, regularly dismantling the blocks obstructing movements between. We cannot be guilelessly optimistic about the transferability of all expression (given the checkpoints used to maintain these flows), let alone the appositeness of certain specific emancipation gestures in every given environment, but surely there is scope here. Their agility hints at the potential for both collectivity and insurrection against the unthinking and politically dubious resonances of established genres.

From these points and subjectivities, the idea of the 'road movie' is thereby not 'foreign' to Palestine. Add to this the fact that Palestine's borders are not ever themselves closed or secure (whether or not its people wish them to be so). These contributions to the international road movie genre insist on the impossibility of 'otherness', which is, at the same time, an enforced and very much experienced condition. The insinuation of a Palestinian participation in the traditional preoccupations of the road movie – rebellion and freedom – not only democratises these aspirations, not only exposes how W/western ideals (as embodied in the car and road mythologies) are often founded, as has been noted, on extreme exploitation, but also speaks to us from and about that very topography which is consequently reinscribed and colonised.[113] In so doing, Palestinian road (block) movies work to confuse hierarchies of expression and create a space for involvement.

At this point, it is worth remembering Chapter 2's recourse to Abdelkebir Khatibi, who disabuses any sense that replication is purely belated imitation or that 'origins' can be situated with facile confidence outside the perimeters of such a long-term inspiring place as the Holy Land, rather than in dynamic, often abusive, relationship with it. Here Palestine cannot be denied as a source of so much considered to be 'western'. At the very least, it is the wellspring of much of the religious ethos embedded in everyday secular life in that region and its mind-sets, the 'becoming Palestinized' of which John Collins has spoken. Longstanding histories of pilgrimage help us understand this, given how they foreground the particularities of foreign influence across Palestine. Accounts such as Henry Maundrell's from the late seventeenth century attest to large settled communities of 'foreigners' in Jerusalem and, by the 1870s, around 10,000–20,000 pilgrimages were made per year, many visitors either writing up their experiences or settling in colonies in the Holy Land.[114] At all times, it has to be stressed that Palestine was not always entirely conquered or governed by such forces, but that it was, and is, still very much internationally authored.

From this perspective, while the road movie may seem American, we can come to see that genres are not owned in any such simplistic way either. They are certainly not beholden to intellectual property rights legislation. As an ironic counter to the occupation, which has taken so much from Palestinians, this assumption of genre toys with origins and national inclinations, but deliberately works with an apparatus that cannot be considered 'property' in these most damaging of ways. The road movie genre is something from which Palestinians prove they cannot strictly be dispossessed. Within it, their alignment between the shared (the global everyday; the road) and the exceptional (the specific contraventions of Palestinian human rights; the block) prompts a sense of familiarity and humdrumness eased into place by musical and cinematic affinities that at once demand a joint ownership not only of property, but also of responsibility.

The previous chapter also delineated the political puissance of entering into established cinematic lexicons with the objective of solidarity rather than mimicry – Syrian films speaking the film languages of Eastern Europe as calls to acknowledge a legitimate sharing of concerns. Pilgrim narratives, for all their shocking naiveté to colonial trauma, radiate hopefulness about unity within diversity. They can coax a type of voyage into the cinematic experience and its academic coverage that is not so much a description of what supposedly exists (road cartography, as it were), but an entreaty into mutual *constructions* of thoroughfares as an international endeavour. One such action is the pooling of a diverse variety of seemingly suitable resources. Within the context of this argument, I would like to draw upon a perception of the road movie that does not deny a Global Northern knowledge or placement. It acts, at one and the same time, as small-scale subversion and as a direct invitation to audiences to identify (just as they may have done with the references to everyday life).

In this, Palestinian road (block) movies connect comfortably with more communal and political narratives within the genre, such as *Get on the Bus* (Spike Lee, 1996). The use of African American musical registers in al-Aqsa Intifada soundtracks at one and the same time directly links two violent dispersals of peoples that are not as often compared as they might be, while also highlighting the structures of cultural globalisation that work to transport political music and render it 'everyone's'. In *Land of '48*, a jazz score under the direction of Patrice Hardy accompanies the travelling shots; these are improvised pieces which spontaneously invent in the face of unpredictability that is typical to both life under occupation and al-Aqsa Intifada film production. *Ford Transit*'s soundtrack draws on Dr Dre's 'Big Ego' and scores from westerns precisely to imply a continuation of various territorial and economic inequities so manifest in this music. In so doing, the film links up various resistance movements to freely exchange modes of dignified survival and point out how porous our world (of ideas) actually is. Hamid Dabashi labels this 'cross-metaphorisation'.[115] As Nida Sinnokrot announces at the beginning of his movie, quite naturally, as an exilic Palestinian, 'When I'm in New York, I listen to Palestinian hip hop. But when I'm in Palestine, I listen to the blues.' We hear Muddy Waters and Blind Willie Johnson. By foregrounding a rural American musical idiom, *Palestine Blues*' shots from the back of a tractor thus allow for a resituation of agricultural transport in a place where land confiscation and military hardware disrupt and endanger farming life by the day. A parallel disenfranchisement of farmers is drawn across time and space, while the aggression of such acts is underscored with visual reference to vehicles, juxtaposing tractors with tanks and bulldozers. The credits roll to 'Min Irhabi?'/'Who's the Terrorist?' by Palestinian hip hop act Dam, known for insisting upon their rightful place within this musical genre because of its lineage of civil rights protests and international rallying. Akin to rap, Kamran Rastegar's soundtrack for *Like Twenty Impossibles* incorporates the ambient sounds of conflict, here an army jeep pulling away, walkie-talkie crackles and such like.[116] Similarities in experience are drawn through style, while traces of the 'real' add another layer to the deliberate foxing of the fact–fiction divide discussed earlier, as well as pointing out how analogous realities and fantasies extend around the world. Recourse to global hip hop, as to the road movie, asserts that we cannot purely conceive of 'Palestine' as a localised site, nor can we untangle it from greater transnational currents. Access to the international marketplace and a wider audience can prompt connection and consciousness-raising.

Ultimately, this body of films makes inroads that simultaneously ironise the limitations of the genre and implant imagery missing from the representations of this land. The very different accesses to mobility depicted and experienced ask how the 'road' can work more dialectically, as the split screens and comparisons in these films clearly do in formal terms. The classic road movie typology is placed, displaced and replaced, in the process speaking not only of the effaced labour and colonial expansionism that has enabled such journeying across the land, but also the need for augmented international access to the genre and its capabilities. I would also hope that the overlaps *and* the vehement separations that distinguish my journeys into Palestine and its cinema from those of others insist, through their similarities, a commonality and, through their variations, an urgency to liberate all the ways through. The 'but' in Darwish's poem functions as a fulcrum enabling a supportive and inquisitive observation of road-users who are, in many ways, 'like us' (in simply trying to arrive as promised) and, in others, utterly and unpardonably unique.

Here contemporary Palestinian cinema entices us to reconsider not only, as I have argued, the power dynamics of the coloniser–colonised divide, but also the stamina required for quotidian (versus 'spectacularised') existence under occupation. With Palestinian state structures fragile or non-existent, the revolutionary inscription of everyday life ('like other people') becomes more urgent than ever, and it is crucial to understand how roads, their travellers and the art that interacts and amalgamates with them work accordingly. Mark Twain's withering juxtapositions, while glib, expose a banality 'within' Palestine crucial to undoing some of the damaging myths opportunistically created. What renders Palestine special, and often to its inhabitants' distinct advantage, is the claims we make on it, the implausible things we ask of it. Curmudgeonly though Twain can be as a pilgrim, his sense of underwhelm renders Palestine hopefully mundane when he asks:

it is the neat thing to say you were reluctant [to leave the Holy Land], and then append the profound thoughts that 'struggled for utterance,' in your brain; but it is the true thing to say you were not reluctant, and found it impossible to think at all – though in good sooth it is not respectable to say it, and not poetical, either. We do not think in the holy places; we think in bed, afterwards, when the glare, and the noise, and the confusion are gone, and in fancy we revisit alone.[117]

Palestinians in the thick of it, or unjustly deracinated from home, are rarely afforded the luxury of this abstract contemplation. But a cinematic examination of placement and injustice might allow such work to happen because it is in dialogue with the world, rather than sitting in solitary meditation. As, in the end, is Twain's comparative appraisal.

Within the seismography of all such conflicts, opportunities are afforded at the same time as others are ripped away, and one of the road-building skills that has been constantly maintained – ironically, through Palestine and its diaspora's spatial instability – is a concentration upon dialogical dexterity of which this fluency in cinematic genre is but one incarnation. Certainly there are forces at work attempting, often successfully, to block Palestinian voices, but there are other, partial modes of arriving at articulation, including through film production. As director Raed El Helou points out, 'I don't speak English well; I speak no other language except Arabic and that is one of my weak points. But I speak cinema.'[118] From here, it makes sense to return to the end of Mahmoud Darwish's poem, precisely because it deals with the paradoxical and concomitant fragility and power of expression, the sharing of the territories of metaphor, genre, history and everyday life, and, most pointedly, with the necessity for road-building by precisely these techniques as a means of easing the ardours of travel:

> We have a country of words. Speak speak so I can put my road on the
> stone of a stone.
> We have a country of words. Speak speak so we may know the end of
> This travel.[119]

4

'Travel and Profit from It': Dubai's Forays into Film

Ibn Battuta is alive and well, enjoying extended shore leave in Dubai. Towards the south of the city, a couple of miles from Jebel Ali container port, a shopping mall is named in his honour. Alongside large models of the great traveller, displays showcase the sophisticated civilisation of the Arab Middle Ages, with its advances in astronomy and even human flight, the labelling overwhelmingly pledging itself to peace, tolerance and sharing through travel. The mall unfolds in sections, each an architectural pastiche of the geographical regions Ibn Battuta visited, with the noticeable exception of sub-Saharan Africa. While not yet the case in modern-day Iran, Starbucks can be found in 'Persia' here. The effect is a version of the world parcelled off into discrete zones with unique cultures, a tendency noticeable in many other parts of Dubai. As Waleed Hazbun, a political scientist of tourism, observes, city planning across the Emirate partitions space prohibitively according to wealth differentials. He points out that entry to this once ritzy mall (now somewhat out-dated by more ambitious complexes) would be tricky for the many South Asian labourers who undoubtedly built it.[1]

Here, in the Ibn Battuta Mall, dwell many of this chapter's themes in close quarters. We have fetched up in Dubai to analyse the connection between travel and trade, drawing on interviews and observations I conducted during the 2009 Dubai International Film Festival, topped up by a return visit in 2014. Venerated within a shopping complex, the Arab world's most famous explorer discloses the commercial incentives driving land- and seafaring. He pronounces a history that is sadly understated in how Dubai (shiny and new-seeming) is typically written up; his mall stresses how enduring and multifarious the dependencies between trade and travel are. Shopping draws droves of tourists to Dubai, but, more so, the values and practices of consumerism, service and exchange in goods are central to the Emirate's identity. And cinema? Although distinguished by a thriving VHS then DVD culture, Alia Younis registers how the Arabian/Persian Gulf, 'barely even had cinemas until the late-1990s development of the mall culture and its consequent multiplexes'.[2] The Dubai International Film Festival (hereafter DIFF), which is the pivot point for this chapter, screens the majority of its programme in the Mall of the Emirates, once the world's largest retail complex, famous for its indoor ski slope. Most of the remaining films, as well as the festival's headquarters, scheduled talks and workshops are hosted by the Madinat Jumeirah, a smaller faux-Arabian souq and hotel complex. In both venues, between films and meetings, there is little to do but browse the shops and

DIFF's logo is eased into place at the Madinat Jumeirah; the Burj Al Arab hotel looms behind

restaurants. DIFF therefore makes manifest, I will contend, the fundamental coadjuvancy between cinema, commerce, networks of transportation, people on the move and, as I shall go on to stress, current and historical port economies.

In its attempts to thrive financially, independent of its depleting oil reserves (now accounting for only 1.5 per cent of Dubai's GDP), Dubai has worked hard to generate the bulk of its revenue from rent, its longstanding re-export trade and consumer spending, all of which, as will become apparent, are central to how DIFF functions.[3] The Dubai Shopping Festival attracts more than 4 million visitors per year and, to be more particular about how Dubai maintains a competitive edge, spending in the Dubai Duty Free Zone (a founding sponsor of DIFF) amounts to $700 million annually.[4] DIFF thereby nestles in with consumer culture as part of what Ahmed Kanna defines as Dubai's 'urban landscapes of "bourgeois gratification"', which aim to confect an ambience of neo-liberal cosmopolitanism that renders the Emirate somewhere attractive for foreigners (as well as citizens) to live, work and visit on holiday.[5] With an estimate of over 90 per cent of Dubai's workforce registering as non-nationals, this is no mere tourist board enticement, nor one that stops at the doors of the bourgeoisie.[6]

Above and beyond being a diligent supplier of 'bourgeois gratification', however, DIFF projects itself as a 'film market', dealing in more than just finished products through exhibition. To elaborate its post-oil economy, Dubai has built institutions like DIFF in order to expand into the sectors of service and knowledge, rendering cinema a useful and visible example of how trade in these goods operates. In *Film Festivals From European Geopolitics to Global Cinephilia*, Marijke De Valck lays out how events like these proliferate such commodities, inaugurating something of a cinematic vertical integration:

In recent years, film festivals have become professionalized. They have developed more and more initiatives that involved local companies (sponsorship) and international film industries ('match-making' markets, training and funding) in the festival network. Nowadays, commerce is no longer dogmatically considered the 'evil other' and festivals fully recognize the potential of cultural entrepreneurship for expanding their strategic influence. Most interestingly, they have begun moving into pre-programming activities ... [which] use the festivals' position as established institutions for cultural legitimization to not only add financial resources to film productions, but also cultural value, *before* they are completed, giving them a head start in the festival circuit [emphasis in the original].[7]

DIFF is chock full of these initiatives: development workshops, seed funding, post-production support, schemes for pairing talent with investors, and experiments within distribution, all in consort with a diverse programme of films targeted at a general audience.

To properly fathom the workings of a festival-as-film-market, and of cinema as a form of mobile trade in moving images, I argue that we require a thorough understanding of trading practices that prioritises the travel of goods and merchants. Moreover, travel itself must figure as a service and an industry involved in competitive transaction. As part of this endeavour, I shall soon draw inspiration from travel literatures dedicated to commerce. One aim here is to establish a *longue durée* for Dubai, habitually conceptualised as a spanking new space (it is, as a city and a nation-state, admittedly) to the exclusion of acknowledging its extended history in trade and port expertise. By downplaying this past, highly ideological conclusions that the city-state is a 'clean slate' have been pushed centre stage.

The historical literatures in question digress significantly in style from many of the *rihlat* of earlier chapters. Personal reflection and positioned comparisons through encounter are all but erased from this writing. Details on human relations, although often heartfelt and personable, stress and strive for ease of transaction above and beyond more subjective emotional responses. The emphasis falls instead on factual descriptions of, often statistics concerning, infrastructures, resources, goods and their efficacious movement, even within the most fantastical enclaves of the sub-genre. Accumulation is the order of the day: as with goods and profits, so with practical knowledge. The relationality therefore emerges less through the coordinates of home and away, and more with an eye to how trade routes, sites of production and markets might interact. Calculations abound. You will therefore notice a shift in writing style in what follows as I try out these registers to test their benefits for an understanding of trade. An understanding of trade that aims not to advance it so much as to expose the toll it exacts on many of its subjects. Film scholarship gains significantly from a detailed plotting out of the mechanisms, movements and tactics of commerce, allowing us to take on board some of the roles that our objects of study play within the global economies of culture, knowledge, tourism and transportation.

HISTORICAL ANCHORAGE, LITERARY CHANNELS

The designation of 'middle' in our region's Eurocentric, probably naval nomenclature (the 'Middle East') linguistically pinpoints its strategic position as a trade crossroads between Europe, Africa and Asia: one that can be traced back five millennia.[8] By the time of Pliny's accounts in the first century AD, the region was traversed by carriers of cotton, silk, spices, metals, wine, perfumes, jewels, hides and slaves.[9] Spurred by developments in shipbuilding and the astronomy necessary to navigate oceans and deserts, the sea route from the Gulf to Guangdong, plied by the Umayyad Caliphate of the seventh and eighth centuries, remained the longest in regular use until the European expansion into these realms in the sixteenth century. These journeys enabled the spread not only of Islam (its Prophet a merchant by trade), but also of goods of all kinds.[10] The Red Sea saw wares crossing paths between China, India and Africa to the south, while vessels passing by what is now the United Arab Emirates at the mouth of the Gulf wended their way up the Tigris-Euphrates basin, to Baghdad and Mesopotamia, and thus to Turkey or the Mediterranean.

Over the centuries, the ports of the Gulf have consequently attracted a diverse population of foreign merchants and bankers, at first mainly from (what are now) India and Iran. For Madawi Al-Rasheed, this convergence predisposed the area to be 'a transit station for larger commercial flows in recent times'.[11] The modern nation-state of the United Arab Emirates also arose from these trade configurations. In the nineteenth century, the Asian influence over such a strategic point in the Gulf piqued the British, so desperate to secure safe passage from and to their colonies that they entered exclusive agreements with the ruling families of the region (thereafter termed the Trucial States). Britain soon claimed protectorate status over the territory and, upon independence in 1971, the United Arab Emirates (UAE) as we know them were born. The UAE's formation, then, is one based on strategies and rivalries of intercontinental sea trade and, as then and to this day, these hinge on activities of extraterritorial extraction, expropriation and exploitation.

Where does a film festival sit within this nexus? Most scholarship on festivals, particularly Marijke De Valck's, makes a reliable case for the nation-building objectives of such events. Given the newness of the state in question, this has surely been a priority.[12] However, Dubai's history as a port, read through centuries' worth of writing on travel, allows for an interpretation that diverges from the academic tendency towards defaulting to place branding in festival studies. Interacting with literatures of seafaring instead provides new inspiration for understanding the quick, smooth, safe transportation of cinematic goods around the globe. While port cities feature prominently on the festival map, from Rotterdam to Busan, scholarly attention to this fact is rare, relegated almost exclusively to how cultural economies might revitalise – or 'Bilbao-ise' – a post-industrial city.[13] Given Dubai's hulking status as an international entrepôt port, the ninth busiest in the world and the only one in the top ten outside East Asia, regeneration surveys are clearly not the avenues to pursue.[14] In what follows, I intend to maintain some of this attention to the puissance of the creative and knowledge economies, but expand our scope beyond the borders of nation. The histories and literatures of Arab sea travel enable a more pertinent understanding of how festivals (and film-making more generally) burgeon within modern transnational infrastructures for trade, including, as this chapter will extrapolate, re-exportation, logistics, supply chain building and free zone and just-in-time manufacturing, all of which profit from the strategic manipulation of global flows in labour.

The port is the central node from which all these spokes extend. Situated on the sea edge of a meagre hinterland, with little latitude to develop space-guzzling industries, but in a handy location between Africa, Europe and Asia, Dubai has striven hard to establish itself as one of the twenty-first century's 'superterminals'. The port is supplemented in this capacity by the airport, which, in 2014, registered the most international traffic of any in the world, with a second even larger under construction.[15] The limited land mass thus generates revenue by instead temporarily enticing traffic from around the world in and out, always in motion, rarely staying put for very long.[16] Its port is home to companies from over 130 different nations and, by allowing any airline to use its terminals, Dubai also benefits, as mentioned above, from significant duty free sales.[17]

Dubai has been active as a port for centuries. But one significant date for the Emirate is 1956, which heralded not only the world's first container ship voyage, but also Dubai's commissioning of the British Sir William Halcrow engineering firm to dredge its creek so as to allow for sizable maritime traffic. To position this alongside a more detailed picture of the Emirate's evolution, this was also the very first year a concrete block building was erected in Dubai.[18] More momentously, 1956 witnessed a striking anticolonial move to gain control of shipping routes within the region: the nationalisation of the Suez Canal, otherwise known as the 'Suez Crisis'. Against this backdrop, with its early oil money, Dubai built a newer and much larger port at Jebel Ali and its first airport.

Dubai's port specialises in re-exporting, or transhipment, as it is often also called: the cheap, efficient and reliable redirection of goods received from elsewhere. Very few of these commodities start or stop their lives here, and the same is explicitly true of Dubai's expansion into cinema. The festival, its film rights sales, production financing and, ultimately, studio usage has been eased into place – as will become clear, and as is typical of Dubai – through first building an infrastructure. In both cases, the aim is to speed through, and generate revenue from, the *passage* of commodities by reducing friction on their movement. This matrix of support boasts reliable onward transportation by road or air; minimal bureaucracy; low or no taxation; and a range of quality services, from ship repairs and on-site light manufacturing to freight-forwarding and business networking facilities. Although I may appear to be describing maritime transport here, I hope to reveal how Dubai increasingly does its utmost to profitably avail the global film industry of these amenities too.

This being the case, we need to grasp how a port – and an airport – no longer simply register as a place where goods or passengers are loaded and unloaded. They are competitive global hubs which distinguish themselves by driving down transport costs and adding value. Expertise and ownership now push beyond state borders. Dubai's DP World (part of the larger Dubai World, which manages the government's portfolio of businesses) took over Britain's P&O shipping giant in 2006, and now operates over sixty-five marine terminals across six continents, handling 60 million twenty-foot-equivalent container units in 2014.[19] More than just specific interchange locales, such sites have indelibly altered the character of contemporary capitalism, their tactics now extending, as we shall see, into other sectors, such as cinema. By rolling out this model beyond port management, Dubai is now forging new economies and practices for film distribution and manufacturing that challenge the rubrics by which we understand festivals. Just as Dubai amassed key infrastructural elements like ports, airports and an airline before extending outwards, so too has its entrance into the film industry progressed not with a national body of film works, but a network for dissemination: an international film festival. Production, as will be detailed later, is currently in the offing, commencing now only after, not before, the establishment of the festival.

Such far-sighted planning comes easier to the Emirate's monarchical yet corporatised patterns of ownership, which belong to the state, but are run according to private sector principles of competition, growth and efficiency. An entrepreneurial command economy, if you will. If I sometimes say 'Dubai' in this chapter, it is because it readily serves as a signifier for this broad web of proprietorship and management that simultaneously engenders no minor amount of local loyalty and national pride. To highlight one small corner of this interweave, majority shares in both Dubai World and Dubai Holding are held by the Emirate's ruler, Sheikh Mohammed bin Rashid Al Maktoum. The latter is the parent company of the media free zones through which DIFF is run, while its Jumeirah Group manages the hotels and shopping complex where much of the festival is held and its guests put up.

Yet, despite these concentrations of power, the transnational sensibilities of Dubai's transport interchanges, free zones and even hotels and shopping malls reveal the obvious: that 'film industries' no longer unambiguously cluster under the custodianship of a bounded nation-state. Just like port and shipping management, movie production is globalised. Travel literatures not only add a complexity to understanding movement for and through trade, they also crucially detail how these networks are lived and experienced, if not through explicitly personal declarations of feelings. The *rihla*, to which we attribute that take on the world, in fact rarely tackles commerce in any overt fashion. Its tendency has been to concentrate on travel for either knowledge acquisition (Chapter 2) or religious enlightenment (Chapter 3) without explicitly owning up to how reliant both have been upon trade route construction.

The next section of this chapter thus unites with a less substantial body of writings on travel for trade, particularly by sea, to glean from them insights and priorities absent from the analysis of contemporary cinema. After that, it will prove critical to understand Dubai more generally as a trading post and port, the systems of support and trust it has had to establish over the years in order to flourish in this capacity, how they configure its contemporary international film festival and what film scholarship at large can gain by attending to these realities, including how it might need to retune its methodologies. Situating a free port to the front and centre (as Dubai does) gives birth to a particular political and economic beast. Dubai's top-down liberalised entrepreneurial ethos slipstreams cinema culture into specific commercial, circulatory practices, particularly with regard to what DIFF itself often dubs the 'emerging markets' of the Global South. An understanding of the current orbits of 'global cinema' benefits enormously from reading its stakes according to these economic terms. Here Dubai relies on a much longer history of trade brokering and facilitation that incorporates, these days, its airline, shipping and hotel interests, all of which sponsor

DIFF within a landscape of tight horizontal integration. Dubai's livelihood, it will be stressed, derives less from acting as a direct merchant of (film) goods, but rather as a facilitator of dependable and fleet transactions expedited by its muscle in the spheres of re-exporting and logistics. Too long have these factors been absent in how we probe cinematic distribution.

As a stopping-off point along supply chains, Dubai has keenly ventured into 'value added' provision to often near-complete commodities, these services typically dominating over large-scale from-scratch industrial production. More often than not, this processing is sequestered in Dubai's many free zones, where low taxation, eradicated custom duties on imports or re-exports and the possibility of full foreign ownership ease competitive light manufacturing of many descriptions. Again, cinema lives closer to all this than we might imagine, as I will lay out in this chapter's later sections. If free zones are commonly thought of as areas more where film viewing hardware is made at rock bottom prices, then it may be surprising to learn that DIFF functions out of Dubai's Technology and Media Free Zone Authority, which extends free zone coverage to the creative industries. Its Deputy Director General, Abdulhamid Juma, is also DIFF's chairman. This confederation's newest free zone, Dubai Studio City, is of particular concern to DIFF and my investigations into cinema, given that it promotes itself as a 'one-stop shop' for production companies to avail themselves of backlots, sound stages, offices and even indoor water tanks. The TV titan Discovery has recently moved in and part of Bollywood blockbuster sequel *Welcome Back* (Anees Bazmee, 2015), starring Amitabh Bachchan, was shot in town with support from Studio City. New productions are initiated by the day. As these examples reveal, Studio City now asserts itself as not only a regional base for large companies, but also somewhere seemingly capable of competing with India in terms of production costs. How and why will become clearer within the final section of this chapter, which investigates the labour policies governing these free zones, ones that make use of a flexible, global workforce with few claims to rights within the Emirates and who, as such, present very little financial risk to it. Bringing together literatures on travel for trade and employment migration helps build a surer picture of a new and, in many senses, worrying prospect for how film production is carried out. Dubai's re-exporting expertise does, ultimately, seek to territorialise in particularly mobile ways, aggressively carbon-copying its free zone models to other corners of the world. This chapter's closing section will assess how these expansions quicken the speed of cinema's race to the bottom, price-cutting trampling workers' rights in ever-new ways.

With this as our map for the rest of the chapter, it is now time to come clean with the fact that Dubai features scantly in the history of discourses on travel, cartographic or literary. If Palestine, as the previous chapter testified, both suffers and benefits from an overloading of inscription, the reverse has very much been the case for the UAE. Dubai has only really established itself as a global city in the past few decades (experiencing all the boons and repetitive cautions prompted by rapid expansion and 'carte blanche' innovation). Before that, only brief glimpses materialise within foreigners' travel records. Perhaps its earliest mention comes in 1095, in the Andalusian-Arab geographer Abu Abdullah al-Bakri's *Book of Geography*; we do not hear of it again until the sixteenth century via the Venetian pearl merchant Gaspero Balbi.[20] The lesson from this absence, then, is to look less to the land and more to the *sea*, which receives abundant attention and opens up fruitful new channels for understanding (Arab) cinema.

Writers dedicated to sea travel are particularly commercially minded. The nineteenth-century Moroccan traveller Muhammad as-Saffar remembers the hadith 'travel and profit from it', which here we might take rather more literally than was originally intended.[21] Presenting an overview of who typically took to the seas and why, S. D. Goitein points out, 'a traveler invariably was a carrier of goods, who had to keep an eye on his own merchandise and often also on that of someone else'.[22] Leo Africanus, an Andalusian Berber writing in the sixteenth century, regales with gripping accounts of sea battles and piracy. Yet when he moors, he settles into detailed descriptions, almost ledgers, of the wares on sale and the means by which they may have arrived.[23]

Financial loss at sea weighs heavily upon what was happening on land. In his *Book of Wonders of India*, the tenth-century Persian merchant captain Buzurg Ibn Shahriyar notes, without too much exaggeration, that the sinking of certain 'ships and their cargoes of goods contributed to the decline of Sīrāf [in modern Iran] and Saymūr [Chaul, in India], because of the great quantity of wealth and the number of important shipmasters and captains and merchants in them'.[24] By the same token, Dubai's fortunes have accrued in part through the safe passage of goods, a skill it hopes to exercise within the world of cinema.

None of these writers have been speaking in particular about Dubai. Yet perhaps the most famous seafarer in Arabic literature did set repeated sail around the Gulf and across the waters of what are now the UAE. This is the fictitious Sinbad, both a merchant and a maritime adventurer. Yarns to be sure, but ones that, similarly, impress the desire to reach other places in the name of trade, and whose very narrative impetuses involve embarkation for that purpose. Sinbad's voyages, 'laden with merchandise' to sell abroad, are awash with *'aja'ib*: the roc, the Cyclops, a sea monster, familiar, perhaps, from Ray Harryhausen's stop-motion model animations for *The 7th Voyage of Sinbad* (Nathan H. Juran, 1958), *The Golden Voyage of Sinbad* (Gordon Hessler, 1973) and *Sinbad and the Eye of the Tiger* (Sam Wanamaker, 1977), as well as *A Thousand and One Nights*.[25] As is the case for many *'aja'ib*, Sinbad's fantastical beasts inhabit an otherwise geographically precise world that can only have been drawn from factual accounts. While his astonishing encounters linger longest in the viewer or reader's imagination, it should not be forgotten that the stories always terminate abruptly with the successful sale of the material wealth he has gathered en route: 'I retired to my home, loaded with riches and honours,' the end.[26] His constancy as an adventurer in search of wealth will prove unexpectedly useful for reading travel through capitalist ambition.

At the other end of the literary spectrum, but consistent with Sinbad's inclinations, lies a rare collection of Jewish merchants' epistles from the Middle Ages, compiled and translated by S. D. Goitein as *Letters of Medieval Jewish Traders*. Correspondence of this type, normally ephemeral in the extreme, was safeguarded by the regular practice at the time of burying, and thus preserving from desecration, writings that mention the name of God. Discovered in Cairo, they hail from places as far from Egypt as India and Aden. Neither descriptive nor comparative like their relatives the *rihlat*, these documents give precise and often directive insights (like 'encourage him to buy quickly') into how trade was conducted and how a concern for supply chain efficiency is nothing new.[27] The letters allow us to get some measure of travel's place in trade relations, in the importance of trust, security and middle-manning vital to the rise of Dubai as a free port and its ever-increasing influence within the global circulation of cinema. Flooded markets and scarcity, pirate plunder, lost cargo, miscommunication and the disruptions of war and colonisation all figure within the human relationships, cemented by letter-writing, that keep trade afloat. These are every bit the concerns of contemporary commerce and, as such, this correspondence proves instructive in generating a complex social and economic picture of logistics and exchange.

TRUST, TRAVEL AND TOURISM

Typical of these communications is the entreaty of one twelfth-century merchant, Hilal bin Joseph of Alexandria:

> I have sworn that I shall not enter into any agreement with anyone in the world unless he makes a legally binding declaration that I am *trustworthy* and that I am free from any *responsibility*. I notify you of this. God is my witness that, had I not given such a binding oath, I would not have written you anything of the kind, for between the two of us there is more trust than exists in the whole world, and I know well that you are more trustworthy than I am myself [emphasis in the original].[28]

The mainstay of many of these exchanges is the question of how to establish confidence in someone conducting transactions on another's behalf at a great distance. The letters, in large part, when not dealing with fluctuations in price, help fashion safety nets for goods dispatched afar, both contractually and through associations of distinct warmth and kinship. The persuasively factual bent of commercially minded discourse noted above aspires similarly for credibility.

This body of correspondence therefore encourages an attention to how faith is established within film circulation, a topic not so readily addressed in studies of distribution. DIFF advertises itself in terms of reliability too. For instance, Ziad Yaghi, Director of the Dubai Film Market, makes similar promises of DIFF's Cinetech facility, which furnishes its industry delegates with the opportunity to watch screeners of festival fare through a rank of booths containing unique touchscreen portals. Their habits are tagged and analysed; there are options to directly contact the agent and arrange meetings, as well as to leave messages for the film-maker. Yaghi elucidates how this unprecedented availability is managed in an uncertain environment rife with the illegal movement of film copies as digital files replace physical objects:

> [The industry has] trust in the festival, because a lot of people are scared to hand over a DVD because of pirates, but, because of the trust they gave us in the first year, and in the Dubai film festival itself, people have now given us 120 more titles.[29]

Faith of this order has proven essential to Dubai's larger industry of re-exportation. First, in a competitive port, goods cannot wander, get stolen or clogged up in processing. As Deborah Cowen's compelling study, *The Deadly Life of Logistics: Mapping*

Violence in Global Trade, emphasises throughout, this sense of trustworthiness is exacted biopolitically through the harsh disciplining of workers, whose rights and own safety are repeatedly subordinated to the guarantee of breakneck goods processing. As we shall soon witness, trade route security ranks higher than job security. Second, logistics analysts stress just how decisive broader reliability is to merchants' use of particular ports. After conducting extensive empirical, survey-based research, Chin-Shan Lu *et al.* conclude that 'political stability is the most important incentive'.[30] Dubai doggedly cultivates the necessary image of not only transactional, but also political and economic steadiness, a literal port in the Middle East's political storms. Ultimately guaranteed by its wealthier UAE neighbour, Abu Dhabi, Dubai can assert economic dependability too, particularly in contrast to historic, but often war-torn, regional banking centres like Beirut.

Marketing constantly reinforces this image. 'Brand Dubai' deftly enmeshes the idea of the Emirate as neutral, open, well organised, robust and responsible with outsiders' precious cargo. In a world where we will rarely meet those in charge of transporting our commodities – film or any other – such faith is of the utmost.[31] Alongside multiple partners within Dubai, DIFF enthusiastically sways international public opinion thus. Its logo 'Bridging Cultures, Meeting Minds' speaks the language of political neutrality and cooperation. Similarly, one of its six strategic aims laid out in 2008 was: 'To continue the development of an international cultural bridge using cinema as the medium to promote dialogue between different cultures and nations.'[32] Long gone are the socialist declarations of, say, the Damascus Film Festival in the 1970s. DIFF's publicity material repeatedly spotlights how the event becomes a space for 'dialogue', one fostering an exchange of balanced views, rather than a militant opposition to wealth and geopolitical inequalities. Evidently, DIFF requires trust in order to function effectively, but it also helps build it for Dubai at large. The Emirate's 'openness', as I will go on to point out, figures within the vocabularies of the neo-liberal marketplace where freedom equates with free trade.

Interestingly, 'branding guru' Simon Anholt, who insists that this sort of coordinated, multi-sector consolidation of image must be achieved as 'a *style of policy making* rather than a method [emphasis in the original]', cites tourism as key to the fulfilment of these aims.[33] For him, tourism 'is often the loudest voice in "branding" the nation, as the tourist board usually has the biggest budgets and the most competent marketers'.[34] I see this as a prompt for transporting an understanding of the recreational movement of people into how we conduct studies of cinema, allowing us, as a consequence, to grasp how mobility stratifies the broader leisure economy.

Although tourism in its modern guise might appear a recent entrant into Dubai, its roots find sustenance in the trading communities of yesteryear. Quite logically, as Goitein points out, 'seafarers sought protection [from bad weather or pirates] by taking refuge in ports or roadsteads on their way'.[35] These structures of (profitable) hospitality (explored methodologically in Chapter 1) regularly doubled as sites for regulating commerce. Historically, merchants in transit would stay in what is variously known as a *khan* or *funduq* (or travellers' inn). Interestingly, the contemporary word for a hotel, as used by a tourist, is still *funduq*. In fact, in many towns, foreign salespeople were even obliged to exclusively stay in designated inns, often free of charge, thereby allowing the port or town to monitor movement while proffering

Conjoined enterprises: the Film and TV Commission and Studio City's neighbouring exhibition stands

benevolent provision. The *funduq* was consequently more than a mere resting place. *Funadiq* (plural of *funduq*) safeguarded precious goods and acted as de facto meeting points for these diverse trading populations. *Funadiq* were also where taxes were levied and prices set or controlled.[36] Although such activities have, for the most part, shifted from actual hotels, because tourism and real estate assume prime positions within the Dubai economy, the interconnection foregrounded by this precedent is still deeply relevant to any study of the city.

Sponsors of DIFF over the years have regularly come forward from the UAE's tourism portfolio: the Emirates (its airline), Dubai Airports, the Jumeirah Group (hotels) and Dubai Duty Free. As Shivani Pandya, DIFF's Managing Director, points out, this is a 'coordinated effort … Everyone's aware of the goals we're trying to achieve in the next few years, so we're fairly streamlined.'[37] Note her recourse to the ergonomics of movement here. Given the establishment of the Dubai Film and TV Commission – government-owned, naturally, and taking up a prominent place alongside Studio City within DIFF's exhibitor stalls – she continues, 'If you have films shooting here, films always encourage tourism anywhere and that's why you have film commissions and governments putting in money for that.'[38] For the festival, the Emirates airline assists with flights, hotel chains provide delegates' rooms and, ultimately, DIFF helps to render Dubai a *destination* for both tourism and film work.

This suggests a desire that Dubai no longer be consigned as a transit point between potential beginning and end points. It wishes to increase spending in situ.

DIFF employs more staff in its Guest Relations and Hospitality department than it does in programming and no wonder, given the Emirate's stakes in tourism. It is the Arab world's most visited city and the world's fifth, clocking up 12 million visitors in 2014, a ratio of 4.8 to every resident, who collectively spent $10.95 billion, thus maintaining an important flow of foreign cash into Dubai.[39] Of these arrivals, a fair number will be in town, as they are for DIFF, as part of this millennium's surge in event, conference and business tourism.[40] A rising niche within tourism, the business event (such as DIFF) draws on, populates and shares costs with Dubai's more established infrastructures – its airline and hotels, for instance – in order to diversify and cross-promote newer investments like Studio City. All the while, these events furnish bounteous opportunities to showcase not only the goods that pass through its ports and other portals, but also the transport facilities themselves, from which Dubai predominantly profits. A probing of these dimensions of travel leads us into vistas of industrial synergy, wider than our typical Film or Area Studies parameters. Tourism towers as an economic sector, generating one in twelve of the world's jobs.[41] The way it coordinates with other sectors (from which it can never be so easily disentangled anyway) means that its study, as Carolyn Cartier argues, 'implicates a full range of questions about culture and political economy in an era of globalization'.[42]

Dean MacCannell puts it more emphatically in an argument I cited at the beginning of this book: 'Tourism is not just an aggregate of merely commercial activities; it is also an ideological framing of history, nature, and tradition; a framing that has the power to reshape culture and nature to its own needs.'[43] For starters, tourism inaugurates a moneyed encounter with difference, not unlike Sinbad's 'great desire to see new curiosities' facilitated by his inherited wealth.[44] So too film viewing, especially when programmed, as it is during DIFF, as a panoply of diversity under section headings like 'Cinema of the World' (including Hollywood's) and 'Arabian Nights' (hello, Sinbad). Both tourism and cinema peddle a comfortable, safe and ritualised encounter with the 'foreign'. The 'exotic location' or the 'representative person' (who can be a tourist or viewer from any nation as well as a 'local') meets a particular politics of encounter that seeks to earn revenue.

Extending this impulse, DIFF goes to great lengths to bring its films' directors into town for post-screening Q&As, courtesy of the largesse of the Emirates airline and the hotel sponsors. In one of the few academic considerations of cinema and tourism, Felix Thompson asks a question revivified in so many of these sessions:

> [C]an the presence of a tourist dimension suggest ways in which metropolitan audiences are implicated in what appears to be a distant set of problems or a distant way of life? A film or television programme, once associated with tourism, is readily construed as manifesting diametrically opposite clues to those of radical politics in the Third World.[45]

Situated within a mall multiplex, DIFF's varied, non-specialist audience routinely makes demands on the film-makers to fulfil their consumer desire for documentary images. The festival works responsibly to ease these interactions, most notably, by appealing not to political affiliation, but to the presumed-universal values of artistic skill. In a pamphlet designed to soften the blow of some particularly hard-hitting material coming out of Israel's 2008–9 attacks on Gaza, audiences were invited 'to see these films not only as genuine, courageous documents of war, but also as *cinema*, complete with crafted, gripping narratives, talented direction and editing, original style, warmed by the intimacy of family, friends and colleagues'.[46] Let us meet these films somewhere away from pure politics. Yet, despite establishing such delicate measures, Palestinian directors are regularly chastised in person by their audiences if they stray from hand-wringing depictions of colonial bloodshed or crying orphans.[47] While, at first sight, Thompson's sense of 'radical politics in the Third World' is palpable, the entreaty to service a foreign viewer's expectations of the conflict shares common ground with a touristic impetus.

Individualised encounters like these easily fold into the larger dynamics of contemporary capitalism, if we pay heed to tourism's own global agendas and its particular marshalling of movement and transaction. Ginger Smith points out that:

> trade in tourism services has played a significant role in the progressive liberalization of markets through the reduction and removal of barriers to international trade. Over 120 countries have made commitments to the World Trade Organization to liberalize trade in tourism services, more countries than for any other trade sector.[48]

In this sense, tourism is not freestanding as a leisure activity (as if it or film-going ever could be), nor is it purely economic. It is part of and infused by a broader hegemonic drive. As a primary mobiliser for trade liberalisation, tourism takes charge of the global flows not only of people, but also goods and capital, in specific ways, according to and exacerbating inequities of wealth. Habib Bourguiba, former president of Tunisia, for instance, talked of his country's relationship with Europe as 'the balcony across the way'. By invoking the country's tourist architecture with its western-modernist high-rises and Mediterranean-facing balconies, Tunisia's self-projections of hybridised postcoloniality meet the global economy through an appeal to Europe's holidaying multitudes.[49] Does DIFF's programme project something similar? We certainly rarely confront the nationally funded Third or Second Worldist cinema of old, as exemplified by the Syrian examples in Chapter 2 (which rarely made it to overseas market, even if it wanted to). Nor is DIFF's material entirely left adrift at the sole mercy of private sector competition. Dubai, for one, holds its own national stakes in the project, located though they are within a mall setting. In order to get the measure of this particular comingling of capitalism and culture, it is first incumbent upon us to gauge Dubai's squaring of state and free enterprise.

FREEDOM OF THE CITY-STATE

In many ways, Sinbad provides a template for the Dubai spirit (its 'brand', rather than a city-wide consensus). Always on the look out for new prospects, Sinbad's motivations merge the entrepreneurial with the adventurous, ending at home and in opulence. Sinbad's hunger for expanding his horizons finds its modern-day counterpart in Dubai's still-mounting trade growth (consistently rising, by a particularly striking 13 per cent in 2012).[50] Like its fictional counterpart, the Emirate resourcefully searches out further opportunities in the region, be they the booming markets of Saudi Arabia or Iraq, or on-the-up countries within Africa.

Sinbad's opportunism finds its match in how Dubai has flourished as a free port. At the beginning of the twentieth century, Dubai fortuitously trumped Bandar Lengeh in Persia as the gateway to the Gulf when the Persian leadership opted to raise taxes for the local and South Asian merchant classes. Before long, Dubai was the preferred stopping-off point for steamers in these waters, welcoming an experienced, heterogeneous and well-connected foreign trading community beneficial to its growing culture of re-exportation.[51] With the closure of Aden port in 1967, during the independence struggles of the People's Republic of South Yemen, Dubai was set to become the leading entrepôt in the region. A prevailing commercial philosophy sets it apart. As Antonia Carver, a long-time programming consultant for DIFF affirms, 'Dubai has a very different entrepreneurial spirit in business' from that of its neighbouring countries, and, she continues, this has 'tipped over into culture'.[52] Carver has observed a spurt in small screening and film-making initiatives, often, interestingly, arranged in the warehousing spaces we might traditionally associate with shipping layovers.

Yet it would be misguided to read this as symptomatic of an entirely spontaneous and self-motivated cinema scene. Dubai's unusual concoction of almost a top-down entrepreneurialism renders these developments, including DIFF, somewhat unique, although a relative of other heavily state-sponsored models like those radiating from and into, for example, Korea's Busan International Film Festival. Dubai's industries are tightly integrated, both horizontally and vertically. In essence, the Emirate is run like a corporation reliant on sovereign wealth funds, swollen by early oil money, but carrying a particularly outward-facing bent. Autocracy over bureaucracy, and often in deficit to worker rights and protections. More of that to come. To wit, the Dubai government provides the bulk of the financing for the festival's Enjaaz production and post-production support and pays for the organisation of its Film Connection, which has helped find international backers for film-makers. DIFF's sponsorship, as has been observed, derives predominantly from other parties within the state portfolio. Key Emirate businesses like these are state-owned, or, rather, in the hands of the ruling Maktoum dynasty, but run by fairly meritocratically hired entrepreneurs and according to private sector models of competition, growth and efficiency. Discussing this federation and its social impact, Ahmed Kanna observes that the royal family,

> either founded or consolidated large holding corporations that would, in effect, control Dubai's economic trajectory, public space and public culture. These corporations [including the TECOM free zone cluster, which houses DIFF] ... [represent] today's Dubai as an inevitable outcome of a teleology from which politics have been erased and in which, for example, modernity is equated with consumerism, authoritarian capitalism, and free-trade ideology. These companies have also become the milieus in which Dubai's flexible citizens reframe cultural values in neoliberal terms.[53]

Given these coordinates, diversifications into realms like cinema not only rely on, boost and consolidate established economic concerns such as tourism, they also strengthen a larger management vision and pitch a particular neo-liberal agenda. Paraphrasing an interview with Ahmad Bin Byat, Director General of the media free zones, Executive Chairman of TECOM and Executive Officer of Dubai Holding, Kanna details how the stress falls on:

> the assumption that free market policies will modernize the UAE and its people's mindset; and that for Tecom [sic] and organizations like it to pull the rest of Dubai and the UAE into the modern age, these companies must first carve zones of governmental exception from the larger state. There is also the Tecom self-image of an organization that values individuality and creativity, unlike the surrounding national and regional contexts where states allegedly treat their people like numbers.[54]

This consideration shines forth from the festival's selection policies, which sanction, according to programmer Antonia Carver, a pretty loose rein on what gets screened. To give just one example of how DIFF shores up a sense of Dubai as 'open' in relation to its neighbours, 2009 saw the premiere of *Banana* (Meqdad Al Kout), an experimental short exploring sexual frustration and infidelity, which had been banned in its native Kuwait.

Freedom here travels under the umbrella of freedom of trade. Dubai prides itself on its aloofness towards manifold protectionist measures, tendering to business, local and international, an environment with fewer restrictions, regulations and taxation than elsewhere, especially in its free zones. Its history of managing ebbs and flows of lawlessness sets this precedent. The free port standing that Dubai established at the beginning of the twentieth century and its heavy traffic means that, like many major ports, only an estimated 5 per cent of cargo is ever inspected.[55] Along with all the above board movement of goods, a grey economy (advocating, in its own way, for unfettered freedom of trade) prospers through money laundering and the trafficking of everything from drugs and arms to people. Re-exportation of a different order. With interference from the authorities light, legal boundaries become distinctly porous to transnational flows of capital, people and goods. Known for many years as the 'Pirate's Coast' (well before Cinetech fended off the video pirates), the inhabitants of what is now the UAE were once so much of a threat to transnational shipping that deals were struck between the most powerful families in the area and foreign, mainly British, interests. The former's political ascendancy, still maintained to this day, was shored up in return for protection of foreign ships in its waters and within the ports of its coastline.[56] Dubai's sense of freedom, therefore, looks and opens outwards, but from a solid national base.

Aihwa Ong scrutinises a spectrum of states of this ilk, including Dubai's role model, Singapore. She identifies an all-encompassing coordination at work that seeks 'to shape a new space of governmentality attuned to global competition. Political leaders view their city as a globalized field of intervention, a national space of problem solving that relies on methods both irrepressibly global and resolutely situated.'[57] Dubai operates globally and hosts international business within the parameters of state control and approval, Sheikh al Maktoum, its leader, favouring, upholding and promoting globalised capitalism as paramount (through an encouragement of foreign investment), and running public concerns as if they were a private company.[58] The maritime economy and the international film festival obediently function within this paradigm. To take one easy example of many, in 2009, DIFF partnered with the Alliance of Civilizations Media Fund (AOCMF), fashioning, to quote DIFF chairman, Abdulhamid Juma, 'a dynamic public–private partnership with a mission to promote and support media that can affect greater mutual understanding and respect between polarised cultures'.[59] Again, we hear the language of reconciliation with a sense of a level playing field that does not foster critique or struggle, beyond those residing within the realms of capitalist initiative. More broadly, while national in spirit, DIFF concurrently speaks of and to the world, through its international programming and its goals of supporting and selling on its wares elsewhere. The festival thus helps create an atmosphere and population base where the culturally enterprising can seize the opportunities promised by the global economy.

The very notion of a film festival sits well within and helps advance these objectives, even if, as this book has attested, Arab cinema culture has often historically aimed to be stridently anti-market. Festivals push for an expansion of viewership within a highly unbalanced ratio of cinematic production to distribution and exhibition. Yet, as authors like Marijke De Valck argue, festivals have somewhat cornered these markets with the help of regional subvention, making the launch of different forms of independent film-making and dissemination trickier than ever.[60] The model that festivals embody is one of transience and limited temporality, rather than sustained day-to-day presence. In contradistinction to the Syrian National Film Organization's tenure of salaried directors, DIFF, along with most other film festivals that sponsor production, does not offer stable nationalised support, sheltered from the maelstrom of profit models. Instead, film-makers must compete for one-off awards like those offered by the Enjaaz scheme, or have been encouraged by the Dubai Film Connection to broker co-production deals outside their country of origin. The latter has effectively reinforced long-term state divestment within the region (paradoxically, but not unusually, promoted on instruction by the government) and, ultimately, a global fragmentation of labour provision, which is the topic of this chapter's closing sections.

DIFF, like other festivals, is awash with awards for shorts, features and documentaries. Accolades raise the competitive edge of the winning movies in a flooded market and subsequently advertise the festival when these films move onwards. At the same time, DIFF carries a competitive attitude towards other festivals. In 2008, it set itself the strategic aim of becoming 'the leading film festival in the region and one of the leading film festivals in the world by 2010'.[61] In its earlier years, it distinguished itself with glitzy red carpets and its plush treatment of invited film-makers – famous and novice – numbering stars like Omar Sharif, Shah Rukh Khan, Oliver Stone and Ang Lee in their ranks. The 2009 edition secured the world's second screening of *Avatar* (James Cameron, 2009) within the week of its premiere and prior to its general release. Quite the coup for a newcomer festival. For DIFF, competition rules the day and, it hopes, pays off in the marketplace.

This model encourages the survival of the fittest rather than broad, even support. The high-stakes sector of cinema at large – where more films make a loss at box office than survive, and few even make it to this stage – embodies risk in its most imaginative and glamorous variant, propounding capitalist ethos in a desirable commodity form. In 2009, the hotly touted new Emirati film *City of Life* (Ali F.

Mostafa), heavily plugged by the festival, translated all this into narrative terms, starring Dubai itself (note the title) as the site for the thrilling makes and breaks that capitalism affords. The movie unfolds a tableau of various stereotypes dwelling in the Emirate: spoilt rich-kid locals, a sexually strident Eastern European flight attendant, a British playboy working in advertising, an Indian taxi driver dreaming of Bollywood stardom and a silent, unnamed Filipino rubbish collector, who, as luck would have it, finds a winning million dirham scratch card at the film's denouement. Risk society incarnate, the film stages how 'anyone can make it' in Dubai. And risk-taking has paid off in the Emirate historically, with Sheikh Rashid bin Saeed Al Maktoum quickly and deftly pouring early oil money into far-sighted ventures such as modernising and expanding the ports and investing in the airline and airport. A lottery all their own, these actions associate risk with growth in a quintessentially neo-liberal fashion.

The drive towards expansion and accumulation pervades DIFF's accounts of itself, just as Sinbad's fantastical travels are not undertaken purely for the sights and spectacles and conveniently allow him to amass rare and exotic spoils that will render him rich. In its first five years, DIFF expanded its programme from seventy-six films from twenty-seven countries in 2004 to 168 films from fifty-five countries in 2009, pushing forward with its strategic aim to 'further accelerate the growth of the film industry in the region'.[62] Its self-proclaimed 'formidable showcase of over 300 films from the Arab world, Asia and Africa', feeds the Dubai Film Market, which DIFF's promotional material calls 'a forum for clinching potential trade and distribution deals'.[63]

These intentions stem from macro-economic policy-making driving home Dubai's dedication towards coordinated and comprehensive supply-side domination. The Emirate has been committed to creating opportunities for maximising production in the belief that the greater the output, the stronger the economy. In line with this, the Dubai Film Connection, which helped arrange co-production until it was folded in 2014 (the reasons to be detailed presently), progressively upped regional film-making. By more than doubling the projects it supported throughout this millennium's first decade, DIFF has lent its hallmark to successful regional features like *Amreeka* (Cherien Dabis, 2009) and *Every Day Is a Holiday* (Dima El-Horr, 2009), which premiered at the Cannes and Toronto festivals respectively, as well as directly creating product for its own programme.[64] Later on, this chapter will provide a fuller picture of Dubai's supply-side economy through an examination of its free zones, and how they augment production, particularly by encouraging foreign investment, lowering taxes and taking full advantage of loopholes in the global job market. For the meantime, let us focus on how Dubai realises these ambitions through a diversification into ever-new industries.

The Emirate's hunger to profit from the knowledge economy is clearly articulated in the government's Dubai Vision 2010 policy document. Its very first statement of intent is: '[By 2010] Dubai will have become the symbol of what a knowledge economy can achieve,' with the aim of swelling its proportion of the GDP to 25 per cent.[65] In practice, this included developments such as the Knowledge Village free zone, which huddles together a number of international learning institutions, all run according to the tenets of private capital, with the aim of fostering a globally translatable sense of innovation and idea generation.[66] If I were writing in *rihla* style now, I would be tempted to think laterally towards the free education discussed in Chapter 2. Situating these investments and capitalisations instead within a more local history, Antonia Carver calls attention to how, 'Dubai has always been this trading capital, a place where *ideas* as well as goods get traded.'[67] Within this constellation, the festival becomes not simply a place for dialogue, not even just an environment for honing the necessary critical acumen and diversity of experience for an effective knowledge economy, but also a motor for the generation, commodification and retailing of thought and cultural expression. That all these initiatives should materialise within an (admittedly state-fostered) private sector is a measure of a broader trend spearheaded by the likes of the World Bank and the IMF to reorganise production (including cultural production) outside public management and provision, the kind witnessed in Chapter 2's case study.[68] We should acknowledge how a parallel withdrawal of backing in poorer countries, often coerced by these transnational bodies, spurs the diverse migrant populations working in Dubai today and draws international film-makers to DIFF as a haven for support of a radically different nature than that which was provided by national(ised) industries in the twentieth century.

MERGING AND EMERGING MARKETS

Dubai positively courts these overseas centres of production and consumption. Although DIFF participates in the region's own buttressing against the omnipotence of Hollywood appeal and the UAE has even made inroads into financing US films, the real thrust of the planned expansion aims elsewhere.[69] The language of emerging markets – both labour markets for film production and consumer markets for watching this output – stands strong within DIFF's self-presentation. Nashen Moodley, the director of the AsiaAfrica strand in the 2009 edition described his programme as 'designed to stimulate and expose film-making from emerging markets', while one of the strategic aims hopes DIFF will 'become a centre for discovering and showcasing excellence in cinema from emerging markets defined as Asia & Africa'.[70] Note, also, the vocabulary of exploration, as if these territories were *terra incognita*. While Dubai plays the host, perhaps even the *patron*, geographical specificity permeates what gets labelled an emerging market. The chosen foci blend seamlessly into broader patterns of Gulf ownership and private foreign direct investment (FDI) across exactly those regions, including within their media.[71] Sights fall on definitively cheaper ('competitive') labour markets where paid-for media consumption is simultaneously on the rise, encouraging a current heralding of Africa as 'a new frontier for the development of Dubai' in, moreover, an unquestionably imperialist turn of phrase.[72] With DIFF's fingers in all these pies, Ziad Yaghi is able to claim that, through 'the Film Market we can now say we helped at every phase of pre, production and post-production and sales afterwards in having it in theatres'.[73]

First to actual film-making. For sure, DIFF would never state such a motive amid all its language of dialogue and diversity, but we should, all the same, recognise how much cheaper a supply-side economy looking to boost production statistics will find film-making beyond the richer orbits of the Global North. Instead the talk is of 'making South–South relationships', to quote Antonia Carver, where 'we can find funding for films in the region, and that means we don't have to go to Europe'.[74] The resulting autonomy comes as a welcome relief against a historical backdrop of transnationalised inequity of access, commercial domination, residues of military occupation and, of course, the pressures erupting from regional differences in taste. DIFF Industry Office Director Jane Willliams stresses how, 'As soon as a European funder comes on board, the perspective changes ... most film-makers would really like to see they could find money here.'[75] At the same time, and somewhat contrary to Williams' declaration, the piecemeal funding structures of the decentralised, privatised normalities of film production insist upon a multidimensional provision that challenges these more localised ambitions. One festival-supported film, *Fix Me* (Raed Adoni, 2009), for instance, additionally drew on Swiss and French money, including the Fonds Sud. DIFF has sought financial assistance for training from European Audiovisual Entrepreneurs (EAVE), whose name leaves little space for doubt as to its ethos and whose mission is to answer questions about a project's viability or its maker's desire to penetrate the international (read: European) market.

When all is said and done, however, the festival does its utmost to discern what is needed to, in the words of Shivani Pandya 'develop this [the Arab] market'.[76] Although what this amounts to changes from year to year, the festival's Dubai Film Connection has provided workshops for producers, screenwriters and directors, as well as hosted panels on film journalism, distribution, digital frontiers and market trends. In a country where no formal film education existed until very recently, these are valuable efforts. During a workshop on production and financing, producer Mohamed Hefzy joked that, in the Arab world, 'if you say "development," people think you mean processing the film in the lab'.[77] Reinforcing the value of these initiatives, Alia Younis observes how:

> the students who didn't know who Spike Lee was in 2008 are making their own films today. This is, in significant part, a result of workshops and other educational and funding opportunities by the three major film festivals in the region ... All three have been competing with each other to be the incubators and nurturers of a local film industry.[78]

Beyond educational initiatives, the festival has donated pre-production and post-production funds to competition applicants over the years amounting to hundreds of thousands of dollars, sourced from the media industries themselves, but largely from the festival's own revenue streams (government-sponsored, ultimately). The recipients have been Arabs, a subset of the 'emerging markets'. Khadija Al-Salami, the prize-winning director of *I am Nojoom, Age 10 and Divorced* (2014), is representative of a raft of film-makers who can claim, 'Without DIFF, I wouldn't be here.'[79]

But what is the rationale for such munificence? To develop the regional industry, most certainly, and there are all sorts of commercial motives for that. But also to create fodder for DIFF itself, as well as for the festival circuit more generally. Following a move typical of festivals since the 1990s, DIFF does not simply handpick completed projects it imagines will blossom within its programme, it also determines and shapes some of that content from the outset. For Jane Williams, DIFF's funding schema 'works very well for the festival, it means we get more films or better films and more interest and audiences for those films, so it works out well for us'.[80] This cannot be an end in itself; the outlays of production funding will not be recouped in the box-office receipts from a couple of festival screenings. What we need to discern is the value (financial or otherwise) spawned by these investments. An eye should be turned now to how DIFF positions itself within the greater logistics and re-exportation markets of Dubai, if not by actually further distributing its programme, then through accelerating its onwards movement. South–South alignments feature prominently in this traffic, driven less by nostalgic Bandung hopefulness, and more by exactly the priorities of global capitalist expansion that logistics have eased into place. As part of Dubai businesses' moves into fresh realms like the media economy, they have needed to identify their most profitable markets, which include the Gulf itself.

Shivani Pandya recognises that this necessitates creating a culture of spectatorship: 'We'll build and educate the audiences and that will help with future distribution and future acquisition.'[81] Beyond that, though, DIFF has conducted significant research into how and to where film products might gainfully be transported. If DIFF's early years of opulent international red carpet events seem to have muted, this is because, as Ziad Yaghi explains,

> We noticed that there is no potential to have a market like the one in Cannes, the marché du film ... people do not want to travel to an additional destination to buy content because the booths are too expensive ... and [big companies like Warner Bros.] sell their content five years in advance so they don't need a platform like this one.[82]

Through commissioned *Focus* reports, modelled on Cannes' research into audience trends, but using regional statisticians like THR Intelligence and Nielsen Egypt, it transpires that the 'emerging markets' operate closer to home. The UAE's own box office, for instance, represents more than 65 per cent of the Arab world's (legal) film consumption and the Middle East is currently considered the world's second largest growth region for exhibition.[83] Towards the end of the millennium's first decade, DIFF spotted that Arab media outlets, particularly the large TV corporations like ART and Rotana, were attracted more and more to their market. As Jane Williams describes, 'There's an increasing interest in producing Arabic-language material for an Arab market, broadcasters,' something also registered by the hike in regional film financing too.[84] No wonder, then, that, in 2014, DIFF eventually dropped its AsiaAfrica strand to concentrate instead on its Arab categories.

This move represents significant affinity with Dubai's broader placement within patterns of circulation. Iraq ranks at number three in the Emirate's list of top re-exporting destinations, preceded only by the populous state of India (worth $6.53 billion) and then Iran.[85] Meanwhile, Dubai steams ahead towards its fellow members in the Gulf Cooperation Council (GCC), the region's common market. By 2013, trade had swollen by 28 per cent over two years with $190 billion of Saudi Arabian exports (amounting to 45 per cent of its total) directed through the UAE.[86] From Dubai's position as a barrier-free gateway to the Gulf region, but also to other international markets, DIFF is now positioning itself as not only a guardian of cinematic re-exportation, but also a shaper of actual film content. This chapter's next section will examine its re-exportation strategies, but first we must scrutinise the lay of the land in terms of content.

Make no mistake, Arab films, and not just those analysed in this book, tend towards politics. A survey of what DIFF has screened over the years will unequivocally present an attention to these registers. As such, how the festival frames that politics is telling. A search for the 'personal' sprang up repeatedly in my interviews with DIFF's core selection staff in ways unfamiliar to the group affinities advocated within the contexts of Chapters 2 and 3. Jane Williams edges towards how this emphasis becomes a substitution:

> We've been most successful in finding partners for films with a more personal voice ... there is a real interest to encourage film-makers from the region to develop their work from being very issue-based and politics-based to stories that have emotional relations in the foreground rather than politics ... to do with their characters rather than their politics.[87]

Film-maker Michel Khleifi, one of Palestine's most prominent and familiar from the previous chapter, had just completed his DIFF-funded film *Zindeeq* (2009) when he substantiated this perspective in a panel discussion: 'my movies put the politics in the background and concentrate on the humanitarian'.[88] I have already insinuated the bonds between contemporary humanitarianism and certain imperatives of global capital. The effect here is a parallel muting of direct engagement. Beautifully shot, but keeping its narrative more 'human' and its politics in long shot, *Every Day Is a Holiday*, from the same year, focuses more on the inter-relationship and transformation of a diverse group of women on their way to visit prisoners than on the jail itself or the reason for their relatives' incarceration. Such gestures are handy for marketing a film to an imagined general consumer audience. The languages of the individual and the human(itarian) collude more squarely with western capitalist and NGO standpoints than those of the Arab region's struggles for independence.

Movies like *Budrus* (Julia Bacha, 2009), which screened in the large Madinat Jumeirah theatre in 2009, are emblematic of a trend that was discussed earlier. Set in the West Bank, its focus falls on peaceful demonstration as a successful strategy against Israeli annexation of one Palestinian village's land. Although the documentary does not and would not hope to flatten out the inequalities in the conflict it represents in the way that DIFF's 'cultural bridge' implies, the solid endorsement of a film so dedicated to non-violent protest is indicative of a consumer-friendly outlook. Ayed Morar, a leading figure in the documentary relates, 'All our activities are peaceful ones ... it's in the best interests of the Palestinian people.' We hear both sides of the story, from the lips of Yasmine Levy of the Israeli Border Police. And Ayed is friends with Ahmed Awwad from Hamas, crossing a typical divide between left secularists and political Islam on the West Bank to say, 'We're not against anyone, just the occupation.' Dubai's media business literature continues in this vein. High within the promotional blurb for Studio City, and before we learn about the facilities on offer, the talk is of 'long-standing political stability' and 'more than two million people and 200 nationalities peacefully coexist[ing] within 4,114 square kilometres'.[89]

I have already outlined how Dubai trades hard on its image of safety and security, here through promulgating neutralised diversity. Understandable, considering how the port prospers as a point of interchange for low-weight, high-value goods such as precious stones and metals. We have just spent some time with this freight's cinematic companions and how DIFF deals in workable commodities for and from 'emerging markets'. Now to understand how DIFF channels those products to their destinations.

THROUGH TRAFFIC: DIFF'S LOGISTICS ADVANTAGE

Over the years, DIFF has entered into distribution. For its artistic director, Masoud Amralla Al Ali, 'Film festivals play a key role in creating awareness about powerful movies; however, it is important to take the next step forward, and create a distribution outlet that makes these films accessible for the larger public.'[90] In 2009, DIFF struck arrangements with the Picturehouse chain to curate a run of highlights from its programme, with Front Row coordinating DVD releases.[91] Despite the growing size of the regional market, however, distribution and exhibition are hazardous ventures, given the extent to which multinational chains have stitched up these circuits, the expense of the marketing and releasing patterns needed to attract a contemporary audience, and how much viewer taste leans towards the fare of more established industries like Hollywood. Predictably, such enterprises have folded over the years with Shivani Pandya tellingly declaring, 'We're not calling ourselves distributors ... Our objective is to help, assist and encourage in the process and not have huge ROIs [returns on investment].'[92]

What tack, then, is DIFF taking? I shall argue that, instead of following typical film industry pathways, the festival recapitulates and diversifies Dubai's long-held strengths in port management here. As I have outlined, the majority of Dubai's port activity registers as re-exportation, otherwise known as transhipment, a particular means by which goods (including now cultural ones) travel. Re-exporting warrants special attention because, despite the central role it plays in the global movement of commodities, it scarcely (I cannot think at all) figures in how Film Studies understands the circulation of movies. To reiterate, re-exportation is the act of bouncing an already-existing product onwards to a final consumer destination. During the period of this chapter's primary 'fieldwork' (2009), this amounted to $38 billion's worth for Dubai to Asia alone.[93] The port here takes advantage of various free trade and bilateral agreements. These can lessen costs, as is possible with movement in and out of the GCC single market, home to leaders in regional TV, like Orbit, Rotana and MBC, where no further taxes on goods are deducted after entry to Dubai. Dubai also acts as a crossroads where trade sanctions, such as those upheld between the USA and Iran, can be (covertly) overridden.[94]

These tricks are merely contemporary incarnations of sea-trading practices of old. The correspondence collected in *Letters of Medieval Jewish Traders* presents a picture of dispersed merchants trying to establish systems of exchange and trust at the lowest achievable costs and with as few barriers as possible. Partnerships, like more modern bilateral agreements, guarantee a favourable trading climate. In the current period, a transhipment port like Dubai similarly elicits commodities via its competitive tax and administrative advantage, and then helps them on elsewhere, thanks to the preferential opportunities it can offer through cross-border trade agreements and first-rate transport infrastructures. Dubai generates revenue from services and port fees, obviously, but also 'added value'. A familiar example: DIFF's hallmarking of its chosen films as a sort of 'quality control'. Shivani Pandya's comment about return on investment rings true here: it is not so much that DIFF is sinking hefty sums into creating film commodities from scratch. Rather, they are looking to establish themselves as a service provider in the movement of those goods, one that allows them to steer a wide berth around the financial burdens incumbent on owning them or preserving an end stake in their unpredictable retail. To comprehend this as a profit model with fewer of the financial hazards typical to film production, distribution or exhibition, Dubai's history as a re-exporting hub offers many crucial pointers.

The Gulf ports have long been points where cargoes were moved from one ship to another. From the tenth century, smaller vessels travelling down the Euphrates/Tigris were swapped for larger ones fit for the voyage to India or China.[95] Such transfers, as has been pointed out, worked in conjunction with the web of regional *funadiq* (inns), which levied tariffs, stored goods, lodged merchants and acted as a space for negotiating and fixing prices, as well as buying and selling.[96] Since the 1970s, Dubai has established itself as a strategic stopping-off point to split, manage and redirect the flows of goods globally, from here progressing onwards to over 200 countries, with a recurrent accent each year on India, Iran, Iraq, Hong Kong and Saudi Arabia.[97] It has been witnessed how the South–South flavour of this trade is mirrored by DIFF's programming priorities. Here is some sense of why from a wider angle. Dubai availed itself early to containerisation, fully equipping Jebel Ali port for this now-dominant mode of goods transportation and signing over port management by agreement with then-leading container shipping company Sea-Land, thus making possible its first container routes to India by 1980.[98] In 1991, Dubai resumed port control from these foreign interests, forming its own Dubai Port Authority.[99] At present, Dubai is the world's third largest re-export centre after Hong Kong and Singapore.[100]

Dubai itself has little to export except oil, gas and petroleum-related products. But the stratospheric rise in imports in the Gulf prompted by the oil boom, just after the UAE's establishment as a nation-state, led to heavy traffic. Dubai here affirmed its consummate ability to instead ease trade between more established manufacturing and consuming centres to its east and west, including, as of old, the reallocation of goods to more suitably sized onward-faring ships, planes or trucks that deliver them across an often Dubai-administered network of routes. No wonder, then, that DIFF's logo embraces a bridging metaphor. The festival, like Dubai at large, is a means to various geographical ends.

And yet the port – so too the festival – is not simply a point on a thoroughfare. Capitalising on the booming markets of India and China and trade between Asia, Africa and Europe, the UAE generates over $9 billion a year in revenue from logistics, a sector we might read as reaching out to the film industry via DIFF.[101] Logistics is the art of keeping things in motion, of saving on time or manpower so as not to impede the fast, economical distribution of commodities. It creates systems for coordinating across multiple locations and commercial service sectors. Logistics are as fundamental to film markets as to any other, particularly within a digital landscape of torrenting and piracy. According to John Mangan *et al.*, 'it is now generally accepted that supply chains, and not individual firms or products, are the basis of much marketplace competition'.[102] Dubai, from its fortuitously strategic position along the trade corridor between Europe, Africa and Asia, the largest port between Singapore and Rotterdam, has top-down streamlined an unbeatable combination of transport infrastructure, minimal bureaucracy, political stability, trustworthiness, all the latest technologies and low labour costs, while eradicating many customs duties so as to sky rocket not only traffic, but also the services it requires.

To be more specific, logistics subsumes a raft of services that transport companies now outsource at ports, including storage, fuelling, unloading and loading, adding extra components to half-finished goods, repackaging, splitting and then dispatching goods onwards as quickly, cheaply and as free from time-consuming bureaucracy and inspection as possible.[103] Being able to keep track of goods in transit is as essential today as it was in the time when the Sinbad tales were set. It should be noted that, even when our hero is marooned on what turns out to be a whale's back and separated from his wares, he is later reunited with them at another port, where he distinguishes the lost bales by their unique markings.[104] Dubai logistics would be proud. A keen interest in how to manage these movements reliably finds its way into more general observations within *rihlat*. Muhammad as-Saffar, for instance, dedicates over three pages of his account of a visit to France to how the rail infrastructure is financed, its balance of state and private investment.[105] A key concern is how different transport infrastructures harmoniously coordinate, later a snagging point for early containerisation, before all the necessary elements were standardised and therefore properly synchronised. Dubai's government harmonises these components, unfolded from a master plan. Sea, land and air transport services, plus the port, work together to generate revenue for the Emirate under the aegis of Dubai World and Dubai World Central Logistics City free zone, which legislatively eases, as we will see, transnational involvement.[106]

Given the current centrality of logistics and supply chains to the world's economy, it is surely beholden upon us to involve these considerations in how we theorise film festivals alongside curatorial, national and place branding paradigms. While I shall later propose that supply chain management, particularly through free zones, impacts the techniques through which films come into being (the industry's labour practices), it makes sense to start with how DIFF's assumption of Dubai logistical canniness first brokers the necessary deals for financing and then distribution.

Shivani Pandya makes this intention clear, 'we've become a platform and so many films [from DIFF] have gone overseas, whether to other festivals, whether for distribution ... We've become a destination for that and that's what we hoped to do.'[107] DIFF thus assumes the role of a hub that is also a destination, very much in keeping with how Dubai has promoted itself as a short stopping-off point in all manner of journeys.[108] The hospitality on offer from the hotel sector spreads over into the hosting of business meetings for the film industry – long a staple practice at festivals with film markets – with a lick of logistics expertise spurring it along. As in the *funduq* of old, deals are struck, supplies and demands are managed. Many of the letters from the medieval traders are targeted towards go-betweens, such as the recipient of a letter of direction from Nahra, an eleventh-century merchant from Qayrawan (Tunisia), who must negotiate business in the name of his employers.[109]

These functionaries detail transactions in each stage of their goods' journeys, calculating costs based on the arrivals and departures of competing traders, not necessarily themselves making a steady income.[110] In this vein, Shivani Pandya is eager to point out that DIFF is 'a non-profit and the mandate is to help Arab cinema'.[111] How similar a gesture to that of Ibn 'Awkal, a merchant based in Egypt in the early eleventh century, whose self-presentation is typical of the correspondence in Goitein's collection: 'I am your servant and prepared to deal, for your profit and without advantage for me, with anything you might send me. By God, my lord, this will give me only pleasure.'[112] One wonders at the rewards of such generosity, which leads to a scrutiny of the motivations of contemporary logistics. Here profit is secured within ancillary sectors – the malls, hotels and airport – and goodwill accrues to Dubai as a competitive site for the knowledge and creative industries. Relying on established revenue earners, less volatile than film, the riskier financial transactions are left to the visitors.

For Jane Williams, one key remit for DIFF is to bring talent and money together:

> We've set up a whole series of meetings for film-makers to meet with potential partners ... for people who've got money to come and be involved in and work with us in developing Arab talent. And that's really been our motivating force throughout this. It's been about saying to the international community, but also to the region, there is an enormous source of talent in this part of the world ... We don't need to send these film-makers to Hollywood to make these films and the money that's in this part of the world should be invested to support and develop this talent here.[113]

To speed this along, DIFF hand-picks invitees, insists that film directors are already paired up with a producer capable of handling budgets and keeps a weather eye on growth sectors, be they from TV, as was the case a few years back, or video on demand (VOD) more recently. To access these benefits, Williams argues, one must come 'here', aided, at one level or another, by Dubai's transport infrastructures. Dubai will keep the wheels of production and distribution oiled, with beneficial stopovers in its hinterland, but without too much cost to itself in terms of its own manufacturing or merchandising capabilities. Dina Iordanova and Stefanie Van de Peer read this move as follows:

> Instead of investing in production, the festival in Dubai focuses on distribution via what is quickly developing into a successful film market ... In other words, where Abu Dhabi and Doha invest in production and development initiatives to draw attention to gulf-based and Arab filmmaking talent, Dubai, with its film market, actually exercises the role of a de facto distributor for Middle Eastern films.[114]

While there has been truth to this closing statement, and distribution has been attempted, I am contending that this has not been of the traditional variety, wherein a merchant takes stock of wares. DIFF prefers to have a hand in distribution without the liability of ownership, offering the space for negotiation, or the bridging of (sales) cultures instead.

The role that comes to mind, rather, is *brokerage*. And, when directly asked if DIFF considered itself to be acting in this capacity, Pandya responded, 'we are'.[115] Maintaining Pandya's chosen terminology from earlier, Ziad Yaghi asserts, 'we really try to become a platform for them [the films] to go into Cannes and other festivals which is what happened with *Amreeka* ... We want to become a hub for helping Arab,

Asian and African film-makers have their films shown everywhere.'[116] These days, it can be assumed that a fair quota of the world's films will not receive substantial theatrical or domestic release; their shelf life thus consists of hopping from festival to festival hoping to garner screening rights payments. DIFF offers itself as a nodal point here, availing film-makers, producers and programmers of the chance to hustle at its film market and other (paid-for) networking events.

Electronically, as well as face-to-face. As in the logistics industry, great attention is dedicated to updating technologies so that the movement of goods is ever hastened. The sooner a product arrives, the sooner its merchant makes money, with the transport and logistics industries earning by facilitating this transfer. Within shipping, high-speed cranes have replaced human dockworkers; computer systems track and thus minimise the amount of empty containers in transit.[117] Developments such as these have now reduced the journey of a ship's cargo from Jebel Ali to an aircraft at Dubai airport to four hours.[118] An equivalent was designed by DIFF in the form of Cinetech, proudly launched in 2009, a first-of-its-kind touchscreen interface that linked industry delegates to a bank of over 300 screeners, as well as *each other*. Ziad Yaghi, a trained media lawyer and ex-head of acquisitions for Orbit, comes on as Cinetech's cheerleader: 'Lots of people do acquisitions and sales at the festival, but they do it on the side, in the restaurant or the coffee bar. Why don't we create a professional platform to do so?'[119] By

The Cinetech booths in action

reducing human interaction to a more efficient minimum, Cinetech allows industry representatives to search by categories such as title, genre, country and actor in order to home in on what they are looking for. Each movement on the forum is personalised and tracked, the data returned to the sales agents and film-makers, with the option always available to leave information for them to arrange a face-to-face sales meeting, if this seems advantageous. Yaghi continues through the prerogatives of logistics: 'It is designed to assist buyers, distributors and broadcasters in the screening process while allowing them to maximise their time.'[120] In 2014, DIFF extended this opportunity online to registered delegates, inviting them to continue browsing the catalogue and making sales connections for several months after the event.

By providing a space for these transactions (physical or screen-based), alongside other corresponding services, DIFF operates like another entity that expedites trade: the clearinghouse. I take this comparison from the actual language of festival personnel. Jane Williams again:

> What became clear last year was that we're becoming like a clearinghouse at the DFC [Dubai Film Connection]. There are two things that we've done that are really important. One is that we go through 120, 150 projects every year and select fifteen to twenty and so we're like a clearinghouse; we do the selection and we have an international group of people who do that selection operating in the international marketplace, so they have an idea of what to look for and what might find partnerships on the international market and so people started to recognise that this was a really good place if you were looking for good projects, to come to the DFC and meet with those projects and those film-makers. And when those companies were coming to the DFC they also had the opportunity to see the international interest in those projects, so they could also see if they wanted to take steps towards working in the international market, they had the opportunity to evaluate whether these projects would find partners elsewhere.[121]

A clearinghouse conventionally performs as an intermediary, guaranteeing, through trust and collateral, a safe transaction between two or more trading partners. While typically assessing financial credibility, here DIFF appears to be assuring *cultural* viability, which will then garner its own value in the markets that any film later enters. DIFF thereby shoulders none of the risk or culpability of a real clearinghouse. These actions, again, can trace a long heritage back to the Middle Ages, to the *wakil al-tujjar*, an agent acting on the authority of overseas traders, handling legal matters, storing wares and buying and selling on behalf of absent clients.[122] The goods have changed, but the principles remain similar to those of this twelfth-century merchant, whose letter reads,

> I am asking you now, relying on your favors, when this shipment, God willing, safely arrives, to kindly take delivery of one-half of the aforementioned bales and sell them for me for whatever price God will apportion and grant. After the price is agreed upon, turn everything into gold and silver – nothing else – and distribute it among various merchants, coreligionists, or others, if they are known as reliable, and send it on.[123]

Thus far, I have largely been eager to emphasise a continuity in practices from the Middle Ages to today in order to dissolve any stereotypical notion that places in the Arab world like Dubai are new to this game, thus wrongly stereotyping the region as an 'undeveloped' backwater before the discovery of oil. However, it should be noted at this point that equivalent transactions in the current age veer away from the solely financial, and that spotting such differences through noticing historical change sharpens the eye to new expansions within contemporary capitalism. The 'brokering' now comes in cultural forms, with DIFF, for instance, creating an environment where Palestinian film-makers can raise foreign consciousness by 'exporting' evidence of their colonial condition. The Q&As, the invitations to film-makers and the sometimes-extensive programme notes that DIFF provides help set these values in motion.

Dubai thus builds resourcefully on its position as a global crossroads. It presents itself as a 'contact zone' in Mary Louise Pratt's sense of an actual location for encounters between dispersed people, goods and ideas; a site where, for Antonia Carver, 'we bring people together from around the region and get them to teach each other ... People ... who can then invest in these films.'[124] Carver is convinced that Dubai can do that 'better than anywhere else', and the Emirate's logistics and tourism supremacy would seem to substantiate this, assisted by a centuries-long tradition of hospitality in unfortunate league with the particularities of contemporary regional strife. The extreme difficulty of now travelling to the national contexts of my previous two chapters in search of cinematic commodities, say, weighs heavily in favour of Dubai's purportedly tranquil ambience and ease of access to citizens of the entire Arab world – and beyond. The cultivated and sustained 'neutrality' of Dubai within international opinion renders it an ideal site over most others in the Middle East.

An ideal site for what, exactly? Dubai cuts and runs, in many respects, from the risks of production and traditional distribution. While ports may offer temporary custody prior to customer purchasing, the pace logistics urges lessens this duration and ultimately requires manufacturers to instead keep up-to-speed in these fast-moving tides. As Jasper Bernes emphasises in 'Logistics, Counterlogistics and the Communist Prospect', his wonderfully politicised account of the damage wreaked by logistics, 'one firm's agility is another's volatility, and the more flexible and dynamic a firm becomes the more it "exports" uncertainty to the system as a whole, requiring other firms to become more resilient'.[125] For Deborah Cowen, this amounts to nothing less than:

> the recalibration of international space by globalized market logics, transnational actors (corporate, nonprofit, and state), and a network geography of capital, goods, and human flows ... the reorganization of national economies into transnational systems that stretch the factory across national borders and even around the world.[126]

By subordinating production to circulation, logistics takes its toll in social and economic terms on human workers, as I will presently elaborate. Within the film industry, these dispersed yet significant injustices only fully come to light if we direct our investigations of entities like festivals towards these most recent marshallings of how their goods travel. Given film's typical timeline of years between conception and consumption, movies have, historically, figured as highly unreliable wares, many productions sinking in their efforts to complete this journey, pulling investments down with them and rendering profits difficult to predict and even generate. While logistics hastens the traffic along these supply chains from pre-production, principal photography, post-production, distribution and costly marketing to exhibition or unit sales, this through-line is not without its casualties. To ethically engage with who these are and how they might be squeezed, it is crucial to first grasp the economic modelling that logistics can actualise.

ADDING VALUE, LOWERING RISK: THE FREE ZONE AND A LOGISTICS OF PRODUCTION

Cheaper transportation, more commodities, greater profits. Before the current systems were so technologised, Tunisian political reformist Khayr al-Din al-Tunisi opposed the social inequities resulting from this pattern. Writing within the lifetime of Karl Marx, his travelogue on Paris observed how control of machinery, transport and circulation sanctioned an uneven placement of secondary processing sites and therefore instated an unjust global distribution of wealth. He urges Tunisia:

> to use our country's industries to process the goods we have produced, [as] a major source of gain. Corroboration of this statement is in seeing, for example, our shepherd, or silk farmer or cotton framer, dying of fatigue for the entire year, sell the produce of his labor to the European for a cheap price, and then in a short time buy it back, after it has been processed, at a price several times higher. In sum, we now get only the value of our land's raw materials. We receive none of the increased value resulting from the manufacturing process, the basic means of creating abundance, both for us and for others ... if the value of imports exceeds the exports ruin will unavoidably take place.[127]

Today, thanks to the completion of its Studio City free zone, Dubai is now geared up to carry out all the stages of film production that equate to al-Tunisi's phases of refinement. It is through its highly tuned logistics infrastructure – including DIFF – that Dubai can transfigure film manufacturing in a fashion that allays many of the financial risks of old. If cinema is currently a saturated market, over-production far exceeding the limited spots in the profit-making sites of theatres, pay-per-view, official DVD purchasing and the like, then Studio City aims to attract outside production that will cover its own costs and risks, offering the most efficient, logistics-led opportunities for lean (film) manufacturing.[128] In 2014, journalists and directors alike made much of how DIFF had scaled down its financial support for regional talent. While many interpreted this move as a marker of DIFF's commercial failure, it instead, for me, denotes a calculated move away from an initial need to brand the Emirate as a film-friendly place and a shift towards new, and more profit-generating, spaces of production now that the former has been established.[129]

Studio City provides (mostly foreign) crews with facilities, services and the logistics muscle to pull in a skilled and wage-competitive transnational workforce at very short notice, courtesy of the Emirate's transport industries and its business-favourable foreign labour legislation. The very first sentence of the 'Why Film in Dubai?' section of the *Film Dubai Production Guide 2014* presents this as the greatest incentive to locate to the city: 'Physically situated between Asia and the West, Dubai connects the world as a major transit hub. With direct flights to over 130 global destinations, Dubai offers easy access for both crew and equipment to come into the country when required.'[130] The inauguration of the Dubai Film and TV Commission, in 2012, was expressly designed to promote production in the city and given the sole authority by the government to process, at great speed (three days tops), local shooting permits.

In essence, Studio City promises to metamorphose film production according to just-in-time principles. The model works by drawing in only what and who are explicitly needed for the project in hand. No extra overheads, as little as possible time to completion and the highest potential to meet ever-fluctuating audience demands before fads dissolve. As will become evident, and as Dubai's businesses have proven profitable over the last nearly fifty years, this method comes courtesy of logistics' imperative to cut out 'superfluous' links in production and supply chains, to sublimate resources into capital as quickly as possible. Jasper Bernes warns that:

> [L]ogistics is more than the extension of the world market in space and the acceleration of commodital flows: it is the active power to coordinate and choreograph, the power to conjoin and split flows; to speed up and slow down; to change the type of commodity produced and its origin and destination point; and, finally, to collect and distribute knowledge about the production, movement and sale of commodities as they stream across the grid.[131]

Already highly globally fragmented, film-making these days frequently sees, for instance, scriptwriting undertaken in one corner of the world, shooting in another and post-production somewhere else. The geographical hunt is on to track down wherever provides the necessary quality of any of these given units for the cheapest price. A logistics-led film industry drives these practices to new levels by increasingly squeezing costs across systems of circulation, including, as will become clearer, those regulating capital and worker movement.

First, how does Dubai seek to position itself as a centre for movie-making upon this map? The 'value added' from which the UAE re-exporting sector benefits can be shipped over into this one. Through its highly 'competitive' production free zones – now opened out to media manufacturing – Dubai profits from accommodating the transformation of what are termed 'intermediate goods'. Marc Levinson explains that these are:

> factory inputs that have been partially processed in one place and will be processed further someplace else ... the manufacturer or retailer at the top of the chain will find the most economical place for each part of the process.[132]

As has just been observed, films have proceeded around the world in this fashion for quite some time. If such nimble movement of half-finished goods from one cheap place to another was once obstructed by transport costs or state protectionism, logistics has played a significant part in lessening these barriers and, ultimately, diminishing the typical costs of the border. As an incentive, the Dubai Film and TV Commission offers to 'reduce hefty production costs associated with travel, accommodation, and film making fees by providing lower discounted rates for travel expenses, accommodation, location fees, and fees for production resources. Implementation of such incentives can reduce production costs by 20–30%.'[133] For Dubai, the advantage lies in its ownership of the means of transportation, and, once a crew is in the country, expenditure within hotels and restaurants, not to mention at the rented and staffed film-making sites.

For sure, there have been outlays – and thus gambles – involved in building Studio City. To quote its publicity material, 'Studio City comprises soundstages, pre-built studios, warehouses, dressing rooms, workshops, office spaces, indoor water tanks, a 3 million square feet backlot, the latest in satellite communication facilities, recording studios and a variety of ancillary services.'[134] Backing came from TECOM Investments, which has specialised in knowledge economy business parks. TECOM's parent company is Dubai Holding, owned by the Government of Dubai with the Sheikh holding a 99.67 per cent share. Feeding off the Emirate's mighty real estate sector, everything is on hand to build cheaply, including, most controversially, cut-price migrant construction labour whose demands on its workers (as will become apparent below) can be next to insufferable. These sectorial synergies are foregrounded by the free zones' publicity material: 'Dubai Media City is a managed, real estate-driven cluster designed primarily to attract existing firms to that location.'[135] DIFF's downsizing of production funds here makes way for Dubai's more established strengths. There is no immediate urgency to launch new film companies when ones that are already up-and-running will pay their own costs, renting space within a free zone.

This harmonisation across different areas of tried and tested investment, shored up by the Emirate's centralised business plan, gives birth to a mini-agglomeration economy with a difference. Studio City's brochure continues, 'Companies across the media production value chain are based in Dubai Studio City, including production and post-production houses, animation studios and other service providers in areas such as dubbing, makeup, costume design, stage design and casting.'[136] Bundles of private enterprises can thus converge under one roof when necessary for any given project. This template mirrors, in a sense, the integrated model of the studio systems of old, save that the ownership of the means of production is now available for rent without Dubai's corporations themselves having to ride the vicissitudes of production profitability within this largely unpredictable creative industry. Logistics works in

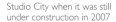
Studio City when it was still under construction in 2007

league with real estate instead, and, furthermore, this is a type of real estate – the free zone – expertly tempered to maximise logistics' potential.

I want to quote Shivani Pandya at length now because, in 2009, before Studio City was open for use, she straightforwardly articulated Dubai's film master plan:

> With the free zone at the back of the mind, [there were] always plans to look at setting up a film industry here ... obviously there's a long way to go because you need the talent and the resources, it has to be organic ... So, in the long-term plan of developing Media City in terms of actually having facilities, we started putting Dubai on the map through the festival as a destination where film people and the film industry were aware of. Then we started with the location services for people coming down and doing location shooting. And, with that, you get more talent developing here or you have access to it and we have the resources coming together. And, in the interim, the government and Studio City invested in setting up big huge sound stages and studios here. So, with that as the long-term objective and side-by-side we're building an infrastructure and that is why the festival is also here, so, apart from our mandate, the big picture for Dubai is to create an industry, a really thriving industry, here. All the elements are coming through in different pieces. Suddenly it'll all come together and you'll wonder how it all happened so suddenly.[137]

Future plans for Studio City include a residential area, hotels and an amphitheatre that will host DIFF.[138]

The model draws inspiration from the already successful Media City, also part of the larger TECOM Investments portfolio. Media City, the world's first free zone dedicated to this sector, offers a similar collection of facilities and up-to-the-minute technological infrastructures. Logistics know-how augments the profitable services on offer, including the arrangement of permits and visas, housing, transportation, technical support, banking, insurance and even schooling for dependants, all largely provided by well-established Dubai companies.[139] Its Deputy Director General, Abdulhamid Juma, as was highlighted earlier, is also DIFF's chairman. With more of a focus on broadcast TV and radio, publishing, marketing and advertising, Media City is now home to regional bases for giants such as CNN, Reuters, the BBC and Al Jazeera. It takes advantage of the large Arab satellite channels' desire to diversify operations, with companies like MBC, ORBIT and ART now based across Egypt and Lebanon (where talent levels are high) and Dubai (where costs are cheap and business-friendly policies ease productivity and profit generation).[140] By asserting its cross-border logistics muscle, Dubai no doubt sees itself as capable of usurping these other production centres by making the mobility of workers to its soil as simple as possible and thereby capturing the offshore market with equivalently low labour costs and complicity, as well as tax breaks. The aim with Studio City was to provide more ambitious production facilities that work in tandem with TECOM's other free zones, enabling larger shoots. Films that have already been shot within Dubai include *Syriana* (Stephen Gaghan, 2005), *Dabangg* (Abhinav Kashyap, 2010), *Mission Impossible: Ghost Protocol*, *Dabangg 2* (Arbaaz Khan, 2012) and *The Bourne Legacy* (Tony Gilroy, 2012). Studio City hopes to entice many more.

But what does the free zone offer, or take away, that distinguishes it from other sites of production? This differs from country to country, but, in Dubai, free zones afford the unimpeded transfer of capital in and out, full foreign ownership, exemption from most taxes and custom duties, minimal set-up paperwork (two to four weeks processing time for any new company) and access to strategic markets through Dubai's indomitable international infrastructure and its many free trade agreements.[141] In essence, enhanced mobility of capital, inputs and goods. Similar in spirit to the free port model of old, foreign business is lured in with fifty years free from personal income or corporate taxes. Moving capital out is eased by Law No. 1 of 2000, which legislates over the media free zones and waives 'any restrictions on repatriation and transfer of capital, profits or wages in any currency to any place outside the Free Zone' for the same time period.[142] As will become apparent later, the slick travel of capital onwards is matched by uncomplicated influxes of the cheapest and/or most skilled labour. The free zones maintain an international portfolio of freelancers, with visas promised for foreign film workers within one day of application.

While many nation-states house peripheral free zones for manufacturing, Dubai surpasses any other country's ratio of free zones to normal territory. Home to twenty-one (and mounting), the Emirate accommodates a portfolio dedicated to an ever-growing set of specialised practices, from Gold and Diamond Park and the Heavy Equipment and Trucks FZ, to Healthcare City and Humanitarian City. There is even a free zone given over to the outsourcing industry and, tellingly, a Logistics City. All these ventures stretch at the rubrics of what was, once, an arena designed largely for heavy manufacturing, hence the prior nomenclature of the *industrial* free zone. Manufacturing of this type is not even allowed in Media City.[143]

Historically, free zones were established around the world in order to kick-start 'developing' economies, to render them competitive enough to join the global market, but largely as a temporary measure. By 2006, 130 countries hosted 3,500 zones employing 66 million people, with Dubai drawing over $5 billion in FDI from its own.[144] As such, free zones clearly demand our urgent attention not simply because of how they accelerate the transnational movement of capital and goods, but also because they treat sizable armies of workers in a largely worrying fashion (the topic of this chapter's next section).

Although free zones typically operate at arm's length from their countries proper (as a state of exception, if you will), Dubai's dance strategically between proximity and remove from the greater city. Their inter-relationship starts at the level of governmental ownership, which enables the smooth flow of ideas, investment and personnel between them and the municipality at points of mutual advantage. Moreover, these zones and the policies of free zoning have been commissioned by the state, as Deborah Cowen reveals, 'not as an element of urban form but as an urban form unto itself ... critical infrastructure is not simply *located in* the contemporary city but *constitutive of* contemporary urbanity [emphases in the original]'.[145] Their design institutionalises the objectives of logistics within the domains of planning and architecture, making space for certain kinds of profit generation, blocking and opening access to the beat of logistics' regimens.

The free zones' autonomous characters modularise the city, intensifying the fragmentary nature of the Emirate's class-stratified housing – the gated community idea gone lucratively non-domestic. Catering to niche specialisation, each operates, as Ahmad Bin Byat, Director General of the three media zones (Internet, Media and Studio Cities) and Executive Chairman of TECOM, puts it, 'like a tiny little country'.[146]

This holds at the legislative level too. Law No. 1 of 2000 allows the chairpersons of any given zone the ability to instigate certain regulations that would not extend elsewhere.[147] For the media operators, this included special exemptions under the heading of 'Freedom of Expression', sanctioning the necessary liberties to report and discuss issues that might otherwise be expurgated in the UAE.[148] Relaxed media censorship, for instance, permits DIFF, Antonia Carver states, 'pretty much free rein on what we show', even though the screening venues are in malls outside the free zones.[149] This sectional structure not only upholds a quintessentially post-Fordist mode of production, it also sets in place strict social hierarchies that subjugate workers, above all else, to the strong currents of logistics-dominated commerce. Membership to these clubs comes with an employment invitation or an investment, yet practically no one is allowed to stay beyond this prerequisite. Weighing up the effects of how this small hinterland is parcelled off means asking important questions about what it means to make, as well as watch and circulate, films through free zones.

I want to start my evaluation by returning to the core theme of this book – mobility – to sketch out how free zones enable the flows of people and capital at the most privileged end of the spectrum. UAE federal law forbids majority foreign ownership. However, this rule does not pertain to the free zones, where there is no obligation to find a local partner. Free zones enable non-natives to hold considerable stakes – in the form of property – in Dubai, yet it has to be stressed that these people will never become citizens. This manoeuvre incarnates a very particular model of transnationalism, wherein their capital will not be repatriated. Unsurprisingly, then, especially as companies are free to hire whom they choose globally (save Israelis), Dubai has become a popular destination for MNCs, such as Halliburton, seeking a regional base.[150] At the same time, smaller businesses are encouraged. At Studio City, Shivani Pandya points out, 'There are various programmes that allow people to come in and set up shop as an individual. Where else can you do that in the world?'[151] The resulting influx, detractors will remonstrate, amounts to a global, rather than more regional, presence, frequently set at a geographical, social and legislative distance from Emirati nationals.[152] The 'global self', to adopt Chad Haines' term, is certainly capitulated across a number of strata, including the global chain stores in the shopping malls, the ubiquitous use of English, not Arabic, for business and the foreign educations on offer in Knowledge Village.[153] And, let us not forget that DIFF operates according to an explicit remit to provide international fare for its diverse population with regular migrant cinema programme strands.[154] Such gestures contribute to and benefit from 'Brand Dubai''s self-image as an open, cosmopolitan place, its most coherent proponent, as we have seen, the Emirate's tourism wings, which create a symbolic currency that translates into actual lifestyles across the city.

These terms of engagement are established for a globalised population by, most centrally, the service and, in particular, the tourism industries. In aiming to attract film production to Dubai during a DIFF workshop, Mohammed Sharif al Baidhaei of Studio City announced, 'Your local production company is like a tour guide.'[155] He continued by listing potential investors from real estate, who would be keen to promote their properties as locations. Across the gamut of free zones, each avails newcomers of a corporate concierge service that undertakes the kinds of tasks necessary for setting up a business there. Non-nationals are thus interpellated as guests, ones whose ventures may flourish, but who are still ultimately subject to UAE control and inspection at any point. This adoption of and invitation through the vocabularies of leisure, as my next section attests, is somewhat misleading, because, despite Dubai's image of touristic opulence, almost anyone involved in cinema is there to work. And work under very specific circumstances.

WORKERS ON THE MOVE

Dubai requires its workers to travel. With the native population so low and economic growth so high, the Emirate is indebted to millions of foreign workers for its very subsistence. Until very recently, the territory was predominantly inhabited by nomads, families who have now become the settled elite. Traders from India and Iran set up shop in the port in larger numbers from the seventeenth century onwards and these communities are still active in the city today, along with the ancestors of settlers and former slaves from all across the Indian Ocean and the Gulf Peninsula.[156] Skilled migrants arrived upon the discovery of oil in 1966 and, as the city has grown, there has been a call for much larger numbers to come and build it, both physically and economically. Dubai does not publish official statistics on imported labour, but estimates suggest that migrants comprise around 80 per cent of the city's population, contributing between 90 per cent and 96 per cent of its labour.[157] No wonder, then, that Dubai must entice people from afar with touristic turns of phrase. In many senses, it wishes its labour force, particularly its creative workers, to be adventurers. Travel literature, as has been apparent since the outset of this book, is fundamentally concerned with the foreign, and its own foreignness, as, among many other things, a commodity. The same often goes for the migrant worker. In its ideal form, work overseas is promoted by the same yearning for heterogeneity (as well as wealth) that whetted Sinbad's appetite. Less fictionally speaking, it is often the tales of returnees, nearly as fantastical, that spur on a pattern of migration somewhere, and this surely holds true of why so many people move to the bright lights of Dubai to better their prospects. Their accounts form contemporary versions of ancient 'aja'ib. More credible, perhaps, than Sinbad's rocs and Cyclops, but maybe never entirely 'real' either. To get a sense of the 'aja'ib within temporary residents' perceptions and experiences of Dubai, we must first penetrate the structure of their conditions in the Emirate.

As has already become evident, Dubai's economy, thanks, in part, to the logistics revolution it helps promote, is as susceptible to global fluctuations in labour concentration as anywhere else. This largely uninhabited desert space with its tiny indigenous population requested outside labour upon the discovery of oil, and now too fights to remain competitive within economies of outsourcing. Close to home, DIFF's brand manager, Zeina Alami, lists herself as an offshoring and outsourcing expert. And the new sectors into which Dubai increasingly aims to situate itself – the so-called knowledge economy – are particularly lightweight and therefore mobile.[158] A film, for instance, in many stages of its (post)production, is digitally transmittable, meaning that contributions to it can be delivered from wherever labour costs are cheapest. A script could be conceived in the UK, shot wherever its narrative dictates, with its post-production completed in Dubai by a team of Lebanese editors.

According to the logic of capital mobility and the 'race to the bottom', such contracts can flourish in one place on one day and dry up the next when another raft of cheaper skilled workers can be secured elsewhere. The once-strong Egyptian and Syrian film industries are now in turmoil, in large part because of the political situations in those two countries. Lebanon trains up many more qualified film personnel than its industries can absorb, rendering its workforce 'competitive' and therefore willing to travel for jobs if needs be. As evidence of Dubai's exploitation of these global economic instabilities, one has only to look at recent demographic shifts. In the early days of oil discovery, around 80 per cent of the foreign workforce hailed from the Arab world.[159] By 1996, they constituted only 10 per cent of the expatriate population, replaced, in large part, by South Asian workers, cheaper and less linguistically (and therefore legally) adept in Arabic than their earlier counterparts.[160] Come 2007, there were at least a million Indians working in the UAE.[161] This shift is but one example of how Dubai configures its workers as expendable according to internal economic and political demands.

Shrewd, then, in its manipulation of these vacillations, the state of Dubai has devised policies on labour that ensure, for the meantime, that production stays put within country, remittance flows healthily out of it, and capital and labour remain mobile and thereby rapidly replaceable. In promoting the capacities of Studio City, Shivani Pandya discloses that 'we will be looking at resources and talents coming from everywhere else ... pulling in resources from South Africa, India, London. People could be flying in from Morocco, Algeria, wherever.'[162] The Dubai Film Connection's selection committee in 2009 comprised nationals of Lebanon, Holland, France and Egypt.[163] Global cinema, of course, has long flourished through migrant involvement, with Hollywood, Bollywood and the Hong Kong industries as testament. Yet, in Dubai, I need to stress, it is next to impossible for a migrant to stay on past their contract, let alone to become a permanent resident. This condition renders its film workers more expendable than is the case in comparable agglomeration economies.

Chris Forrester has observed the ubiquity of the mantra that 'Dubai is going to be the next Bombay.'[164] The onus now falls on the city, with its up-to-the-moment infrastructure for film-making and its synergies with ancillary sectors, to compete with Bollywood in terms of labour costs and skills. In what follows, I argue that a new 'ajiba emerges in the form of working conditions that the film industry has not heretofore imagined. Its birthplace is, in many ways, the free zone. Touted as a 'clean slate' by its proponents on account of its lack of entrenched and entangling bureaucracy, from another perspective the end result is an eradication of worker rights legacies. Bringing these into the fray requires the sorts of insistences upon history I have been making throughout. With each free zone remodelling how its designated concentration can operate within entirely private sector enterprise remits – be that education, humanitarianism or film-making – an upholding of, for example, prior non-profit functioning or egalitarian state provision recedes to a point of invisibility. Long gone are any of the assurances or consistent incomes, benefits or rights detailed in Chapter 2's Syrian National Film Organization case study. Given this comparison, for me the most urgent and salient issue here is how the national cinema production paradigm, with its stabilising affiliations and legislations, is severely challenged by the prospect of Studio City.

The same leaning towards business practice models inflects how migration to the Gulf works, rendering the region perhaps the most in tune globally with neo-liberal paradigms in how it treats foreign workers. Governmental or humanitarian intake quotas fall by the wayside; movement in and out is, instead, dictated by private sector arrangement and sponsorship. Rainbowy cosmopolitanism, as also promoted by DIFF, helps seduce workers, but the potential to hairpin turn on migrant presence mirrors the nimbleness of the logistics industry. Residence is only permitted with a job, often without accompanying family, and staying on beyond a contract is next to impossible. An employee is therefore entirely reliant on her job for the right to remain and in an environment where bosses are known to retain their workers' passports as a guarantee against absconding. Migrants receive none of the lavish state benefits of the small indigenous population; they are not protected by minimum wage legislation, nor are they allowed to join trade unions. While the bulk of the criticisms against logistics point to its decisive facility for moving capital quickly so as to outmanoeuvre rising costs or organised labour, we should also attend to how logistics can preserve these profitable, but rarely just, balances within a single city.

Some of the foundations for this were set in place by a practice widely instituted across the Gulf known as *kafala*. Non-nationals wishing to conduct business in the region are obliged to secure a *kafil*, a guarantor or sponsor. Interestingly, the concept has its roots in Bedouin laws that once obliged outsiders to find such a figure to assure safe passage across an extended family's territory.[165] It is a word thus long associated with an ever-changing dynamic between local land rights and foreign travel. These days, *kafala* is most typically conducted via employers or agencies who then take on the legal responsibility for the people they bring into the country. Human rights abuses of this system are well-documented and, most typically, affect those on the lower end of the pay spectrum, particularly construction and domestic workers, who constitute a large quota of the incoming workforce. Complaints include the withholding of passports and pay (thus instituting a form of indenture), poor housing, little access to healthcare, exhausting hours of work and sexual and physical abuse.[166] Without recourse to the legal standing of citizens, and fearful that grievances will (and largely do) result in termination of contracts (and therefore the opportunity to stay on in the UAE), only a tiny minority raise objections in court, especially given an employer's right to send an employee home before a case gets that far. Even if litigation ensues, it is rare for Emirati nationals to be prosecuted.[167] These problems are stubbornly recapitulated by Dubai's refusal to ratify or implement the UN Convention on the Protection of Rights of Migrant Workers and Their Families, which would afford non-nationals recourse to international law on issues such as job and social security, as well as fair and equal wages.[168]

In Dubai's media free zones, the zone's authority acts, for a fee, as the *kafil* for its companies' employees.[169] Although the zones' builders and other blue-collar workers may be vulnerable to these infractions, most 'creatives' lead a distinctly more luxurious existence. That said, they are still bound, as are all migrants, to the basic principles of *kafala*: they are forbidden from unionising, they are dependent on holding good standing with the free zone authority for their livelihoods and tenure within the UAE, and they may only work there as long as their employer feels the need for their service. Unfair dismissal protections and protocols do not really exist. Without question, this engenders a feeling of tenuousness that provokes compliance and competitiveness.

In a nutshell, migrants are reduced almost solely to economic entities. With no asylum or refugee status granted in the country and little, if any, recourse to state provision, non-nationals hold radically diminished scope to deviate from this social role. Dubai's migration policies align with a neo-liberal casting of subjecthood in this respect, leaving migrants exposed to the inclinations of private enterprise, the flexibility demanded by fluctuations in the global market and a deliberate lack of social welfare provision, save what might be required for securing economic growth. The lives of foreign workers are, therefore, tightly contingent on market demand and its evaluation of the jobs they undertake, which, in turn, engenders a precipitous social hierarchy across the Emirate.

At the sharp end of this lies wage discrimination, qualified not only via experience levels, but also by nationality. The heterogeneous pool of applicants affords Dubai and its foreign businesses the latitude to set their salaries (with no minimum wage in the private sector) according to home-country costs of living and employment desperation. Although TECOM's media properties are bound by Federal Labour Law – which holds to reasonable regulations on breaks and leave, for example – free zones do still operate as mini fiefdoms granted fairly generous allowance in how they devise their employment conditions.[170] Free zones ultimately perform at a remove from state jurisdiction and as they see fit in the search for profit within their sector.[171] Moreover, in all free zones, the relationship between the governing body and the company renting space is legislatively hands-off. Even if a Media or Studio City worker's rights compare with standards in the Global North (in order to attract the best and brightest), the fact remains that access to these benefits is limited to only those employees, thereby enshrining a macro-level structural inequality across the Emirate, where not everyone is so fortunate. Free zones get away with whatever they feel they are capable of, rather than abiding by more universal ethical principles arrived at by legal negotiation. Add to this the fact that a worker is bonded by their work permit to their employer, decreasing the chances of upward mobility that switching jobs, or even applying for new ones to gain leverage, might tender.

International inequities of wealth distribution among communities living in very close geographical proximity are thereby replicated in miniature, compounded by more classic ghettoisation via housing costs. At the top end of the privilege scale sit the native Emiratis. By contrast to their overseas colleagues, they have access to public sector employment (should they wish it), where salaries, contracts and benefits are generous and stable. Policies of 'Emiratisation', which aim to enfranchise locals into the workforce, dictate that all companies must fulfil a quota for hiring nationals. Unlike their colleagues, their jobs are not constantly under threat; they may even hold fewer skills and be paid more. Beyond work, there is free housing for any struggling Emirati, low-cost housing for everyone else, free water, electricity, healthcare, local phone calls and education up to university, along with exemption from community charges.[172] At the same time, citizens can often feel engulfed by the changes that have taken place within their country, including the prominence of leisure activities, like alcohol consumption and gambling, which violate their traditions. Obviously, salary-wise, there are also many well-paid foreign workers who earn more than lower-level citizen government employees.

Next in the pecking order sit the sorts of skilled foreign professionals who populate DIFF's payroll. These internationals will have been allowed to migrate with families and are afforded a greater sense of permanence all round, as well as often generous tax-free incomes. But a class system remains within structures like DIFF and not simply through whom it hires and what they are paid. Like most festivals, DIFF programme strands often classify by country of origin, recapitulating, to some degree, a stratification of audiences. More damagingly, applications for production funds 'should really be made in English', even when the awards are exclusively for Arab film-makers.[173] English has become the *lingua franca* of work across Dubai, not just at the festival. Its normalisation, however, should not allow us to overlook the high prior income levels required by a national of, say, Syria or Algeria, where English does not figure prominently on the public school curriculum, to sufficiently educate themselves, most probably privately, to be able to present their work thus. Basic language facility is the least of it; applicants must also contend with the more complex task of mastering the grant-writing and creative self-presentation norms required by the globalised cultural industries. Prize winners, save for the Gulf competitions, have tended to come from outside the country, whereupon they are sponsored to provide a creative service for those inside and according to the latter's financial stipulations. Gaëlle Le Pottier, talking more generally about the contemporary Arab media industries, presents a local truism: projects 'are mostly financed by Gulf investors, geared to the taste and demands of a Gulf consumer audience and most often operated and controlled creatively by Lebanese and Egyptian professionals'.[174] A similar distribution is true across DIFF, and will possibly be the case for Studio City output. The class system repeats itself.

These differentials of role, wage, lifestyle and job security, although globally ubiquitous, take a new turn as Dubai moves further into film production, and therefore warrant our close attention. The DIFF programme during my fieldwork year of 2009 was, ironically, crammed with movies concerned with labour injustices (child workers alone feature in *Little Wings* (Rashid Masharawi), *Very Humane* (Ossama Fawzi) and *The Tissue Vendor*), or human rights abuses (these are simply the prison movies on offer: *A Prophet* (Jacques Audiard), *12 Angry Lebanese* (Zeina Daccache), *Lola* (Brillante Mendoza) and *Every Day Is a Holiday*). However, a DIFF employee has little scope to stand up to such ills beyond screening material (from other countries, notably) that tackles these issues. Within the bigger picture across the Emirate, high-income migrants commonly remain ignorant, oblivious, apathetic or too dazzled by the comfort of their own economic set-up and the luxurious amenities of this global city to think deeper on the matter. For nationals, their government's targeted benevolence is argued to buy a large measure of collusion. The UAE's social order is immobilised by both policy and the rigid employment landscape it instils, rolled out across the entire city, including DIFF itself.

Of course, privilege still colours our social perception of cinematic labour, making it seem, on the surface, an unlikely place to campaign against workplace exploitation. For many within this sector – and the same will go for film crews shipped in for productions in Studio City, most likely – their job offers have not been clutched at out of economic desperation. Given their training and skills, festival staff and film-makers avail themselves of a range of employment alternatives of one order or another. As such, their migrations reckon more as opportunities for adventure, the like of which propel the tourism industry.

Yet, at the same time, and as I have argued, these foreign workers are still constricted by the insecure, rotational realities of the UAE job market. Gone are many of the traditional safeguards of the middle-class professions – media sector or otherwise. In most parts of the world, migrants, including refugees and asylum seekers, present a constant source of anxiety to order-building, both social and economic, in that it is near impossible to balance broader capitalist with local interests. Less so here, where the Gulf's exceptional migration policies create the potential to easily replace not just individuals, but whole sections of society. Activating the principles of logistics within a home labour market has put paid to these thornier historical issues of population management. Many critics interpreted the immediate impact the 2008 crisis exacted on Dubai's foreign workforce, with luxury cars parked up at the airport, their owners never to return, as glitches or failures in the Emirate's central planning. Chad Haines, however, is more on the money when he interprets these actions as merely a supple and temporary scaling back, such that labour is cut back when, at any given moment, it is not required. Their departures indicate emphatically that these people were never authorised to remain in situ anyway, a 'burden to the state', as the unemployed might be perceived elsewhere in the world. With no such rights, superfluous workers must merely evaporate to elsewhere. In conclusion, Haines argues that, 'Dubai's staying power feeds off the structured chaos of globalization, shifting markets from South Asia, to East Asia, the United Kingdom to the United States.'[175] It achieves this status by keeping a huge majority of its (temporary) population in a state of insecurity that is systemically exercised across all economic strata.

Individuals discipline themselves accordingly. They constantly look over their shoulders, work to their limits, and toe their lines in the full knowledge of their disposability. This has proven the overwhelming norm within post-Fordist project-by-project film production too, the exceptional 'ajiba of governmental employees to be found in places like the Syrian National Film Organization rapidly receding. But the typical contract precariousness of most film, TV and festival work is amplified here, with firing or redundancy escalating to territorial deportation. In line with the efforts of logistics to minimise costs, this workforce is dispensable like no other, with very little ground on which to fight for better conditions or rights. If co-production (the kind that the Dubai Film Connection has also sought to stimulate) might be read, ultimately, as another incarnation of offshoring, then the sorts of multinational just-in-time crews that Studio City can speedily assemble, from wherever is cheapest, further this trend in an already globalised and geographically fragmented production line. The surfeit of qualified film workers around the world makes this a highly viable prospect.

The challenge now remains: how to build communities to fight, rather than cave, to such whims of capital? With the transience of migrants and film crews shared, it becomes exceedingly difficult to achieve long-term and long-lasting political victories. How can a large swathe of exploitation be transfigured, within all this perpetual motion, into a commonality that might serve as a basis for collective struggle? The sheer numbers of migrants holding Dubai together at any given time – whatever their income, paradoxically bonded by insecurity – is perhaps the ultimate weapon here. What could a 90 per cent population achieve?

EVERY PORT IN A STORM

The presumed *tabula rasa* of the free zone model presents itself as the linchpin here, for either side in this opposition between capital and labour. The 'clean slate' that the free zone presumes to embody (although the travel literatures populating this chapter insist upon a much longer history) has certainly taken its toll on those who populate these spaces. At the same time, as Aihwa Ong points out, what scope is there in 'emerging' Asian cities such as Dubai, Shanghai, Hong Kong and Singapore to refuse to follow 'an established pathway or master blueprint' and instead conduct 'a plethora of situated experiments that reinvent what urban norms can count as "global"' in a less harmful fashion?[176] The cities Ong discusses decline to become replicas of the long-held centres of capital; by operating differently, they bear the potential to formulate something 'better' or 'worse' under the banner of global capitalism. They borrow extensively, but with a highly refined strategic eclecticism that could, as was apparent across Chapter 2, group together diversity so that it fosters solidarity. Dubai's unwavering perseverance with logistical efficiency over worker rights makes this a tough battle to win for the latter. Yet the tales of injustice all these travellers into and out of Dubai might relate to each other could help us converge upon a more equitable future. Stories of travel, I have hoped to convey, are important tools for conceiving such possibilities in a particularly embodied, although always usefully peripatetic manner.

These are pressing concerns as Dubai's corporate structures go all-out to export (or re-export) its models of business, housing, free zoning and, one might soon imagine, film production. If the issues raised within this chapter seem like marginal concerns, confined to a small nation a long way from other buoyant film industries, then I must stress how readily Dubai has become an exemplar for the future of the 'global' or the 'cosmopolitan'. While 'Brand Dubai' certainly attracts workers and tourists alike, it is, itself, a simultaneously re-exported concept. Deborah Cowen itemises manifold cases where the USA and Canada have consciously emulated Emirati free zone and logistics policy through spatial design and the handling of workers.[177] Dubai-modelled complexes, from shopping malls to gated communities, abound from Djibouti to Vietnam to Peru.[178] The accent on logistics readily links housing to production schema and thus labour practices. Why not film-making too? Just as Dubai instated its networks and logistics first, its festival and then its media production free zones, territorialisation soon follows infrastructure.

The broad international aspirations concocted, advertised, incarnated and *moved onwards for profit* from within Dubai should not be underestimated by film scholars as the Emirate begins to reconfigure cinematic production. Writers like Chad Haines observe that Dubai advertises a pleasing model of modernity for the Global South that runs counter to western globalisation, of particular appeal to the Muslim citizens of the world, so disenchanted by their treatment at the hands of the Global North.[179] The sense of hope emanating from Dubai was palpable in the bountiful years of DIFF's Enjaaz funding and in the festival's multipronged means of redirecting regional film-making away from, for instance, the dominant European gatekeepers of art cinema circulation. Let it not be forgotten that the cross-border affinities stitched in place by these shared aspirations, be they Arab, Muslim or 'third world', see some of their points of origin in the sorts of world exploration that underpinned the *rihlat*. Islam, its Prophet himself a merchant, spread effectively and predominantly along land- and sea-trading routes, from the Gulf to the North African Atlantic coast to the South China Sea. Jerry H. Bentley explains how, in the Middle Ages, Muslims disseminated their religion through contact along their trade routes and compounded its presence when mercantile diasporas settled. A curiosity was cemented among certain locals who would then travel in the opposite direction, to Mecca. And, finally,

> in many cases, ruling elites recognized political or economic advantages in Islam, and as a result they lent official support that enabled the new faith to establish itself securely in their lands ... Thus rulers, merchants, and others engaged in long-distance trade gravitated naturally towards Islam, which linked them culturally with their counterparts in all areas.[180]

It comes as no surprise, then, that pattern books for a workable Muslim modernity should disperse through these very same lines of old, with Emirati real estate developments, luxury communities, shopping malls and, increasingly, media (including cinema) bedding in everywhere from Egypt to India.

As with the spread of Islam, there are adventurous antecedents. Such standard bearers often function at a financial, but definitely not promotional, loss. In the hotel sector, the famous 'seven star' Burj Al Arab hotel consistently failed to keep its accounts in the black. More importantly, though, it set new benchmarks, became a talking point, and put Dubai on the map, functioning as the herald of things to come as the Jumeirah Group expanded its hotel empire into new realms, from Morocco to China.[181] Likewise, DIFF is fully sanctioned not to generate significant revenue. It has certainly stimulated production through benevolence, which cannot be said of the luxury hotel. This surely does no harm in attracting a global industry to its new film-making facilities and, in fact, might even have helped train up a suitable local and regional contract employee base. DIFF has thus mirrored the Burj Al Arab by successfully projecting an impression of the Emirate as a viable, enticing and trustworthy destination, this time for the movie business. Here DIFF continues a strategy common across the media industries in the Arab region, which, according to Gaëlle Le Pottier, 'are essentially non-profitable' but are kept afloat by wealthy public and private sector investors 'in exchange for greater prestige and influence at the regional level, if not at the international level within the Arab diaspora'.[182] They seek cultural, social and political standing and swing.

But not only. Entrepôt expertise quickens the flow of goods and ideas, religious or capitalist, and, as a result, John Mangan *et al.* note, 'Over the past half-century, most countries have seen an increase in exports as a share of GDP.'[183] By cheapening the costs of transportation, logistics have figured prominently in this economic turn, something that Dubai has used to also extend control beyond its national borders. Dubai interests now manage more than their own UAE-based hubs for imports, exports and re-exports. They have integrated vertically, across into the field of air, sea and road transportation, with DP World (majority-owned by Dubai World, and thus the government) now one of the principal port operators in the world. The Emirate's leadership have taken advantage of global trends in privatising once-nationally owned ports, a practice set in motion by heads of state like Margaret Thatcher in the 1980s.

DP World has voraciously responded to tenders for port management far and wide, to the point where it is now one of the world's largest marine terminal operators, running over sixty ports across six different continents, expanding by the year.[184] With no compulsion to support or protect any given host nation-state's employment or productivity, a foreign port operator is at liberty to function in a fashion that best suits a logistics, rather than a fair employment agenda. In addition, increased ownership across the supply chain authorises the shipping line to dictate the routes goods will take around the world in search of its own interests in cost reduction and labour efficiency. As Marc Levinson points out, 'By deciding where to employ their vessels, the big ship lines [held] the power to determine which ports succeeded and which struggled.'[185] Ultimately, this synergy in how goods are moved around the world amounts to much greater cross-border economic control than is initially apparent.

At this moment, while the Emirate's film industry is still fledgling, it is important to watch out for how Dubai's patterns of translating logistics edge into real territorial control. The free zone is where this expansionist strategy reigns supreme. Stephen J. Ramos catalogues how 'most projects begin with DP World acquiring a local port to manage, and essentially replicating the Jebel Ali Port, Free Trade, and residential/commercial mode *in situ*'.[186] By implementing this plan, the labour conditions detailed above are sown globally to DP World's advantage. It has already been demonstrated how Dubai profits from free zone activity at the expense of its disenfranchised foreign workers. Now that model is being offshored. Within this set-up, we may well see film, along with any other number of industries, losing all sorts of national legal protections for its trade and its workers.

In the long run, then, while the concentration in logistics took advantage of capital's need for mobility, capitalism properly comes home, and makes its home, with an augmented control over resources, beholding them to its whims of how productivity and pricing should function. As with the migrant workers in Dubai, compulsions to support the welfare of any employees involved can be kept to a bare locally legal minimum, their status (as with migrant workers in the UAE) constantly under threat that a contract (for work or marine terminal operation) can move elsewhere. Gulf FDI in the 'emerging markets' of the Middle East and South Asia now exceeds that of any other interest and, in the Mediterranean region alone, this amounts to three times more than that of the European Union and twelve times that of the USA.[187] Having a hand in how cinema is produced is one small component of all this and events like DIFF help to ease along a sense that such liaisons are friendly, supportive and advantageous.

In the end, the travel for trade discussed within this chapter manifests some of the exact same aspirations that the voyages witnessed in the previous one does. Familiarity through travel there bled into colonial acquisitiveness; here the transportation and facilitation propensities of Dubai's infrastructures take root and, in so doing, exert real foreign influence over weakening sovereignty. How DIFF and Studio City's films travel is part of a larger bid for something much more than distribution, and, in this, it is crucial to acknowledge that circulation is also a central factor in how (film) workers are exploited under capitalism.

Here I am beginning to compare across chapters. This has not been the preferred approach of the travel literatures adopted for this chapter. Their protagonists set out into the world merely to accumulate (Sinbad) or to found networks to better that activity (the medieval trader letters). At this point, then, it seems apt to consider once more writing genre as methodology. The historical materials drawn into this chapter have provided inspiration to scrutinise infrastructure, which, in turn, has encouraged me to follow the pathways created by the connective tissue of the festival and film labour. We have thereby learnt how they are attached to tourism, shipping, re-exportation, logistics and free zone conditions, all crucial, I argue, for a rigorous understanding of cinematic trade and circulation. Like these writers, I have amassed facts, ones that my political sensibilities consider 'aja'ib and more often than not in ways that refuse to fill me with joyful wonder. The complicated, rhetorical, constructed nature of the 'ajiba that I delineated in Chapter 1 should, as it did there, expose motive. This chapter is rhetoric, but I want you to believe in it. I have been writing, as merchants do, of facts and figures with a sense that my work will be helpful, but the use-value, to me, should not benefit the sorts of commerce we have witnessed here. These journeys of mine have been more for talab al-'ilm in the modern sense laid out in Chapter 2. For that, we need to compare across time and space like the rihla. In this framework, any registration of difference might make us appreciate other options (as it did for Mark Twain) or encourage a generative project full of new ideas for social amelioration and ethical judgments about what is appropriate for the immediate given context (Tahtawi). Placing Syria's National Film Organization employees in dialogue with Studio City's, a largely fictional move that recalls the imaginary conversations in Faris al-Shidyaq's Leg Over Leg, should bring labour into an urgent dialectic. Such moves would probably be anathema to this chapter's types of travel writing. But a non-comparative mind-set, it should be emphasised, also allows for an ahistorical take on Dubai's legislative tactics, which, in turn, can enable free zones to function unfettered from certain previous protocols for social equality. The distances that are pivotal to travel writing mean that we cannot 'go back' to Syria, nor, seeing where that leads now, is this a place for the present. Certain labour rights then and there, if anything, serve as relics, remains of the dead holding potency for the faithful in the present and elsewhere. Hence the dialectic, rather than the replication. The encounter on the road, rather than the return.

This is all the more critical given the movement outwards of the 'Dubai model'. If we only 'see' the Emirate cinematically as occasional flourishes like Tom Cruise scaling the Burj Khalifa in Mission Impossible: Ghost Protocol, then we are not doing enough to acknowledge that this is just the tip of the 'Brand Dubai' iceberg. Expenditure on our hardware and our DVDs will most probably have swelled the coffers of Dubai's ports, transport lines and logistics companies. Its model of film production may be coming to a port free zone near (or within easy shipping distance of) us soon.

Outgoing Cargo

We finish where we started, in the desert. A desert now transformed into a dazzling metropolis by migrants similar in desperation or aspiration to our protagonists from *The Dupes*, holding different nationalities or legal statuses perhaps. *The Dupes'* journey set the path for this book: a film made under the Syrian National Film Organization, about three Palestinian refugees trying to smuggle themselves into the Gulf for work.

Throughout this book's voyage across these borders (and others), it has asserted the international fabric of cinematic production, content, distribution and consumption familiar from *The Dupes*, woven on the warp of travel's insights and infrastructures. Travel and cinema share global histories and vacillating ethics of exchange, and both benefit from each other's different responses to dis*place*ment. Acknowledging their interdependence, I have argued, allows us broader access to the geopolitics of learning (Chapter 2), the languages effected for collective struggle over mobility and citizenship rights (Chapter 3) and the commodified circulation of workers and what they produce (Chapter 4). In turn, awareness of these manoeuvres stimulates a recognition of cinema as a moving experience, one formed through particular availabilities or blockages to mobility as it has been regimented, sold, undertaken and theorised throughout its history, and before.

By insisting that (Arab) cinema only attains its character through journeys into, across and out of its more bounded territorialities, I have implicitly intended to counter dangerous projections of the region as ethno-religiously isolationist. At the same time, I have never attempted to overturn certain ontological mainstays, such as 'Arab cinema' – indeed my chapters have each been premised on the affirming conceptualisations of nation-states. Effective as political realities, often of an anti-imperial persuasion, their simultaneous porosity all the while compels us to acknowledge the impact of global trade and exchange on us, and to join in the formulation of more egalitarian placements and engrossments within these networks. The international community would do well to sit for a while and own up to our place in the polyvalent make-up of cinema, of the Arab world and of the struggles the region and its film cultures uphold for and against particular liberties. Understanding Syria's cosmopolitan make-up, the traffic of international ideas, ideologies, peoples and arms presented in Chapter 2, has vital bearing for achieving peace in the region. Likewise grasping our own embroilment in the occupation of Palestine and Palestine's appeals to us through international vernaculars. And, lastly, Chapter 4 has implicated us within a worldwide grid of transport infrastructures that delivers our cultural commodities, but also exploits and disenfranchises workers on a global scale.

These are just a few of the urgent concerns that travel far beyond the Arab world has helped us address throughout this study, with cinema as a starting, but, necessarily, not a sole end point. Such issues have been critically explored via disciplinary peregrinations, ones which aimed to downplay the territoriality that often partitions bodies of thought from each other and, as a consequence, unfairly dictates what is appropriate to examine in any given field. I hope those forays, full of travelogue ingenuousness, convey some of the value of transposing our thinking outside its habitual limitations in order to gather up the dispersed ideas we might require to act responsibly in the face of the severity of certain situations. In crossing so many borders, I cannot stand as a specialist (although let's register my privilege of mobility all the same), and I deliberately allege not to be one so that there is room for movement and conversation that escapes narrow academic niche marketing.

I have also refused scholarly comprehensiveness as a marker of ill-claimed mastery and instead followed the exigent path trodden by *The Dupes*. The film exposed us in my opening pages to the deplorable realities of exile and migration, encouraging extrapolation on the conditions migrants might endure (as well as benefit from) throughout what unfolded in subsequent sections. A rare moment where the film departs from *Men in the Sun*'s plot exposes differences, juxtaposed and questioned more adamantly through travel, which should remain at the forefront. In Kanafani's original novella, the three migrants hold their silence while stowed in the water tank, obedient to smuggler-driver Abul Khaizuran's request, suffocating rather than exposing their presence. In *The Dupes*, their dying thumps and screams do penetrate the sides of the tank, but are drowned out by the loud chug of the air-conditioning units artificially cooling the border police's office as the Palestinians succumb to unliveable temperatures within. This illicit journey across a border gone horribly wrong reiterates our serious need to understand how travel marks out, while also preserving, manifold injustices and inequities.

My *Dupes*-inspired structure has also revealed something of the economic history of such conditions of travel by way of cinema's own. The film's coordinates help plot out some major transformations over the last half-century in how exchange has been conducted globally and how rights and incomes, as well as culture and ideas, have been distributed accordingly. Chapter 2 investigated Syria's anti-market praxis, and therefore its relationships with international communism, which, in turn, impelled a distinctive distillation of worker entitlements and disadvantages. Chapter 3 saw how Palestinian Second Intifada cinema read international presence and colonial imposition through the global (film) economy. This oeuvre found less scope or efficacy in outright rejecting the damage caused by global trade, instead wielding its internationally authored concepts ironically in the service of revolution, all the while asking us to assess differences in access to rights and mobility. Most recently, Chapter 4 landed us in the malls of Dubai, contained within the webs of global trade, its commodities sped along their way by logistics' dedication to the swift movement of not only capital, but also its subjects. If the criminalised passage of *The Dupes*' refugees is indicative of this landscape in real terms, it is also a dark metaphor for how cinema culture tries to sustain itself through travel in the face of home front divestment and social disintegration.

The Dupes' journey, then, is one of dire purpose. And an examination of types of travel according to purpose has fired my studies: travel for scholarship, for pilgrimage, for trade. If the motivations for migration of *The Dupes'* three protagonists conclude in bleak tragedy, then that is our warning of how travel often exacts injustice, as well as our incitement to internationalise the struggle for a more equal state of play. While *The Dupes'* denouement unfolds without its characters' arrival at their aspired destination, this runs meaningfully counter to the travel narrative cliché of a return home fundamentally altered by the experience. The film's repudiation of a happy ending ricochets through an environment that has changed more catastrophically than this author during the book's journey to completion. The Arab world has weathered fundamental fluctuations of late, rendering impossible the sorts of research I conducted in Syria between 2007 and 2010, along with most other aspects of normal life.

Such befores and afters, along with travel's switches in location, prompt, as is customary in the *rihla*, comparisons that allow us to recall alternatives: Syrian labour rights, Palestinian notions of liberation. In the words of Jasper Bernes, praxis of this order empowers us 'to place struggles side by side, to render struggles visible to each other and to themselves'.[1] My chosen topic and theme groupings, though seemingly disparate, also underscore continuities and, through them, latitude for solidarity and tactic exchange. All three case studies joined in tussling with the dynamics of global capital in ways from which we have much to learn: from how to resist or deny it (Chapter 2); corrupt or transmogrify it coherently as a rallying call (Chapter 3); or acknowledge its dispersed potency and the way in which it constantly consolidates or updates how it travels (Chapter 4).

Cinema unlocks distinct possibilities amid these overwhelming matrices. Let us revisit a passage from *Men in the Sun* that I detailed at the very beginning of this book. As Marwan exits the corrupt smuggler's office into the unknown streets of Basra, he is unexpectedly pervaded by an experience of openness and prospect, which seems strangely analogous to a trip to the cinema:

> He wanted to know the reason for that remote sensation that gave him contentment and rest; a sensation like the one he used to have when he had finished watching a film, and felt that life was grand and vast, and that in the future he would be one of those men who spend every hour and day of their lives in exciting fulfilment and variety. But what was the reason for his having such a feeling now, when he had not seen a film like that for a long time, and only a few minutes before the threads of hope that had woven fine dreams in his heart had been broken in the fat man's shop?[2]

If you remember, Kanafani leaves the reader to ponder on causes for a couple of pages; I have drawn out the suspense for the entirety of this monograph. In the interim, as was noted back then, a plausible response is to deduce that Marwan's sense of autonomy comes from travel, from making a controlled, apt, adult decision, independent of his home habits and securities.

It so transpires, however, that this serenity and confidence derives from the act of writing. Marwan has just finished a letter to his mother, committing to paper how he truly comprehends his family's troubled relationships. We should take this liberty-through-writing to heart. The potential within this activity comes less from the opportunities writing furnishes us to express ourselves (although that too), and more from the way in which it, like travel, establishes a *distance* between writer and recipient. Distance allows for the important acknowledgment of difference and a space of removal for clear reflection, contemplation and transposition. Simultaneously, there is both a writer with immediate personal conviction and a reader they aim to address under certain conditions, so the detachment marks a gap through association. Their positions vary, but are traversed by correspondence.

In this way, both cinema and writing proffer unique means, through their respective particularities of format, for grasping the issues at stake in travel, be it forced, restricted, leisurely, in search of work or enlightenment. I hope I have engaged film and literature's travels in a dialectic that also extends outwards into other types of movement to provide lessons and possibilities to those greater contexts. By adopting the very conventions of the travelogue into the stylistic delivery of this book, I have aspired to understand writing as a mode of (scholastic) production. It has proven crucial that I myself remain in transit as a researcher (just like a *rihla* author) trying to involve myself with a culture and a subjectivity in inevitable flux, such that I cannot, first and foremost, anchor myself with authoritative presumptions. In all this, I have striven to further the insights of *rihlat*, which unravel how knowledge is imagined, motivated and constructed geopolitically.

Marwan later articulates a similar sense of incomprehension in its most critical form. He means what he says epistemologically, politically and spatially, which is something that travel literature has unstintingly encouraged. In the stretch between the two border posts of Iraq and Kuwait, he states (in the film, but, notably, not the novella): 'We're all lost ... we shouldn't have come. We're moving backwards.' It has been this book's intention to foreground its own much less unfortunate sense of being lost so as to examine the pressing material conditions that provoke Marwan's. To contribute in tiny part to a much greater global imperative to alleviate the reasons why he has embarked on such a dangerous journey and why he feels that he is moving backwards, rather than in the direction he wishes.

The Dupes (1972)

Notes

SETTING OFF

1. The title of this film is also sometimes translated as *The Duped*. Likewise, the director's name is variously transliterated as anything from Tawfik Saleh (see Nadia Yaqub, '*The Dupes*: Three Generations Uprooted from Palestine and Betrayed', in Josef Gugler (ed.), *Film in the Middle East and North Africa: Creative Dissidence* (Austin: University of Texas Press, 2011), pp. 113–33) to Tewfiq Salah (in Guy Hennebelle and Khemaïs Khayati (eds), *La Palestine et le cinéma* (Paris: E100, 1977)).
2. Hesham Taha, 'Tawfiq Saleh (1926–2013)', *Ahram Online*, 29 August 2013, http://english.ahram.org.eg/News/80208.aspx; Yaqub, '*The Dupes*'.
3. Yaqub, '*The Dupes*', p. 113.
4. Viola Shafik, *Arab Cinema: History and Cultural Identity* (Cairo: American University in Cairo Press, 1998), p. 155.
5. Few writers merge these different modes of travel, but one exemplary model here is Milica Z. Bookman, *Tourists, Migrants and Refugees: Population Movements in Third World Development* (London: Lynne Reiner, 2006).
6. Bronwyn Morkham and Russell Staiff, 'The Cinematic Tourist: Perception and Subjectivity', in Graham M. S. Dann (ed.), *The Tourist As a Metaphor of the Social World* (New York: CABI, 2002), p. 298.
7. Chris Rojek, 'Indexing, Dragging and the Social Construction of Tourist Sights', in Chris Rojek and John Urry (eds), *Touring Cultures: Transformation of Travel and Theory* (London: Routledge, 1997), p. 54.
8. Ghassan Kanafani (trans. Hilary Kilpatrick), *Men in the Sun and Other Palestinian Stories* (Boulder, CO: Lynne Rienner, 1999), p. 37.
9. Lucy R. Lippard, *On the Beaten Track: Tourism, Art and Place* (New York: The New Press, 1999), p. 139.
10. Tawfik Saleh, interviewed in Hennebelle and Khayati, *La Palestine et le cinéma*, p. 132 (translated by the author).
11. Nikos Papastergiadis, *The Turbulence of Migration: Globalization, Deterritorialization and Hybridity* (Cambridge: Polity Press, 2000), p. 10.
12. Ginger Smith, 'Tourism Economy: The Global Landscape', in Carolyn Cartier and Alan A. Lew (eds), *Seductions of Place: Geographical Perspectives on Globalization and Touristed Landscapes* (London: Routledge, 2005), p. 72.

13. World Tourism Organization, *UNWTO Tourism Highlights 2014*, http://www.e-unwto.org/doi/pdf/10.18111/9789284416226, p. 2.
14. Dean MacCannell, *Empty Meeting Grounds* (London: Routledge, 1992), p. 1.
15. Karl Marx (trans. Martin Nicolaus), *Grundrisse: Foundations of the Critique of Political Economy* (London: Penguin, 1973), p. 262.
16. Tom Gunning, '"The Whole World within Reach": Travel Images without Borders', in Jeffrey Ruoff (ed.), *Virtual Voyages: Cinema and Travel* (Durham, NC: Duke University Press, 2006), p. 29.
17. Rey Chow, *The Age of the World Target: Self-Referentiality in War, Theory, and Comparative Work* (Durham, NC: Duke University Press, 2006), p. 12.
18. According to Richard van Leeuwen in *The Thousand and One Nights: Space, Travel and Transformation* (London: Routledge, 2007), p. 20: 'These two forms of travelling (for knowledge and pilgrimage) laid the foundation of Islamic geography, which was mainly developed in the 9th and 10th centuries.'
19. These estimates are derived from Robert Govers and Frank Go, *Place Branding: Glocal, Virtual and Physical Identities, Constructed, Imagined and Experienced* (Basingstoke: Palgrave Macmillan, 2009), p. 81, and Nasra M. Shah, 'Arab Migration Patterns in the Gulf', in International Organization of Migration (ed.), *Arab Migration in a Globalized World* (Geneva: International Organization of Migration, 2004), p. 94. However, the United Arab Emirates, as we shall see in Chapter 4, do not themselves release these sorts of statistics.
20. Adonis (Ali Ahmed Said) (trans. Samuel Hazo), *The Blood of Adonis: Transpositions of Selected Poems* (Pittsburgh: University of Pittsburgh Press, 1971), p. 27.
21. See Caren Kaplan, *Questions of Travel: Postmodern Discourses of Displacement* (Durham, NC: Duke University Press, 1998) for a book-length exploration of the use of such tropes within western critical thought.

I FELLOW TRAVELLERS: APPROACHES TO AND THROUGH THE JOURNEY

1. Ibn Battutah (ed. Tim Mackintosh-Smith), *The Travels of Ibn Battutah* (Basingstoke: Picador, 2002), pp. 40, 89, 145, 233. Note here that this volume spells the explorer's name with an 'h' at the end. I have elected not to use this transliteration, although it will necessarily feature in any bibliographic reference to this particular book.
2. Ibn Khaldun (trans. Charles Issawi), *An Arab Philosophy of History: Selections from the Prolegomena of Ibn Khaldun of Tunis (1332–1406)* (Princeton, NJ: Darwin Press, 1987), pp. 30, 50.
3. Ibn Khaldun (trans. Franz Rosenthal, abridged and ed. N. J. Dawood), *The Muqadimmah: An Introduction to History* (London: Routledge and Kegan Paul, 1978), pp. 91 and 296.
4. Trinh T. Minh-ha, 'Other Than Myself/My Other Self', in George Robertson *et al.* (eds), *Travellers' Tales: Narratives of Home and Displacement* (London: Routledge, 1994), p. 22.
5. James Clifford, *Routes: Travel and Translation in the Late Twentieth Century* (Cambridge: Harvard University Press, 1997), p. 3.
6. Janet Wolff, 'On the Road Again: Metaphors of Travel in Cultural Criticism', *Cultural Studies* vol. 7 no. 2 (1993), p. 224; see also Kaplan, *Questions of Travel*.
7. Walter D. Mignolo, *Local Histories/Global Designs: Coloniality, Subaltern Knowledges, and Border Thinking* (Princeton, NJ: Princeton University Press, 2000), p. 173.

8. Clifford, *Routes*, p. 39.

9. Hadith 223 of Abu al-Darda'.

10. Roxanne L. Euben, *Journeys to the Other Shore: Muslim and Western Travelers in Search of Knowledge* (Princeton, NJ: Princeton University Press, 2006), p. 38.

11. Ian Richard Netton, 'Arabia and the Pilgrim Paradigm of Ibn Baṭṭūṭa', in Ian Richard Netton (ed.), *Islamic and Middle Eastern Geographers and Travellers: Volume III, The Travels of Ibn Battuta* (London: Routledge, 2008), p. 156.

12. Mignolo, *Local Histories/Global Designs*, p. 310.

13. Ibn Battutah, *The Travels of Ibn Battutah*, pp. 22, 38, 99, 208.

14. The same is also true of European Orientalist modes of writing. Edward Said observes how this corpus is composed of, 'a set of references, a congeries of characteristics, that seems to have its origin in a quotation, or a fragment of a text, or a citation from someone's work on the Orient, or some bit of previous imagining, or an amalgam of all these' (Edward W. Said, *Orientalism* (London: Penguin, 2003b), pp. 176–7).

15. See Ian Richard Netton (ed.), *Islamic and Middle Eastern Geographers and Travellers: Volume II, The Travels of Ibn Jubayr* (London: Routledge, 2008).

16. As documented in A. F. L. Beeston, 'Idrisi's Account of the British Isles', in Ian Richard Netton (ed.) *Islamic and Middle Eastern Geographers and Travellers: Volume I, Medieval Geographers and Travellers* (London: Routledge, 2008), pp. 311–27.

17. Tawfik Saleh, interviewed in Hennebelle and Khayati, *La Palestine et le cinéma*, p. 138 (translated by the author).

18. See Alauddin Samarrai, 'Beyond Belief and Reverence: Medieval Mythological Ethnography in the Near East and Europe', in Netton, *Islamic and Middle Eastern Geographers and Travellers: Volume I*, pp. 366–87.

19. C. F. Beckingham, 'The *Rihla*: Fact or Fiction?', in Ian Richard Netton (ed.), *Golden Roads: Migration, Pilgrimage and Travel in Mediaeval and Modern Islam* (Richmond: Curzon Press, 1993), p. 86.

20. Travis Zadeh, 'The Wiles of Creation: Philosophy Fiction, and the '*Ajā'ib* Tradition', *Middle Eastern Literatures* vol. 13 no. 1 (April 2010), p. 41.

21. Ibid., p. 24.

22. Ian Richard Netton, 'Basic Structures and Signs of Alienation in the *Rihla* of Ibn Jubayr', in Netton, *Golden Roads*, p. 60; for more on Al-Muwaylihi's framework, see Roger Allen's introduction to Allen (ed.), *A Period of Time: A Study and Translation of Hadith 'Isa ibn Hisham by Muhammad Al-Muwaylihi* (Reading: Ithaca Press, 1992).

23. Gayatri Chakravorty Spivak, 'Can the Subaltern Speak?', in Cary Nelson and Lawrence Grossberg (eds), *Marxism and the Interpretation of Culture* (Urbana: University of Illinois Press, 1988), pp. 279–80.

24. Euben, *Journeys to the Other Shore*, p. 89.

25. Tawfik Saleh, interviewed in Hennebelle and Khayati, *La Palestine et le cinéma*, p. 134 (translated by the author).

26. Lippard, *On the Beaten Track*, p. 2.

27. MacCannell, *Empty Meeting Grounds*, frontispiece; Lippard, *On the Beaten Track*, p. 2; Papastergiadis, *The Turbulence of Migration*, p. 11; Lesley Kuhn, 'Trusting Tourists: An Investigation into Tourism, Trust and Social Order', in Dann, *The Tourist As a Metaphor of the Social World*, p. 109.

28. James Clifford, 'Notes on Travel and Theory', *Traveling Theories, Traveling Theorists, Inscriptions* vol. 5, p. 198, http://www2.ucsc.edu/culturalstudies/PUBS/Inscriptions/vol_5/preface.html (website no longer live).

29. Euben, *Journeys to the Other Shore*, pp. 13–14.

30. At the same time, I have the greatest of respect for the more expansive volumes dedicated to relaying the diversity, skill and value of Arab cinema to an English-language readership, such as Shafik's *Arab Cinema* and Lina Khatib's *Filming the Modern Middle East: Politics in the Cinemas of Hollywood and the Arab World* (London: I.B.Tauris, 2006).

31. Kamran Rastegar, *Literary Modernity Between the Middle East and Europe: Textual Transactions in Nineteenth Century Arabic, English and Persian Literatures* (London: Routledge, 2007), pp. 101, 103–4.

32. Ali Behdad, *Belated Travelers: Orientalism in the Age of Colonial Dissolution* (Cork: Cork University Press, 1994), p. 138.

33. Walter Scott, *The Talisman* (London: Collins Clear-Type Press, 1825/n.d.), pp. 11 and 10.

34. Edward Said, *Culture and Imperialism* (New York: Knopf, 1994), pp. 326–36.

35. Rastegar, *Literary Modernity Between the Middle East and Europe*, p. 80.

36. John D. H. Downing (ed.), *Film and Politics in the Third World* (Brooklyn: Autonomedia, 1987), p. 69, provides a strong polemic on these dilemmas.

37. Graham Huggan, 'Unsettled Settlers: Postcolonialism, Travelling Theory and the New Migrant Aesthetics', in Sam Durrant and Catherine M. Lord (eds), *Essays on Migratory Aesthetics: Cultural Practices Between Migration and Art-making* (Amsterdam: Rodopi, 2007), p. 133.

38. Ulf Hannerz, *Transnational Connections: Culture, People, Places* (London: Routledge, 1996), p. 103.

39. Ibn Battutah, *The Travels of Ibn Battutah*, pp. 115–18.

40. Edward W. Said, *Representations of the Intellectual* (New York: Vintage, 1996), pp. 82–3.

41. As pointed out by Daniel Newman in his introduction to Rifa'a Rafi' Al-Tahtawi (trans. Daniel L. Newman), *An Imam in Paris: Al-Tahtawi's Visit to France (1826–1831)* (London: Saqi, 2004), p. 85.

42. See Janet L. Abu-Lughod, *Before European Hegemony: The World System AD 1250–1350* (Oxford: Oxford University Press, 1989) for a full exposition of the functioning and control of these 'world systems'.

43. David W. Tschanz, 'Journeys of Faith, Roads of Civilization', in Netton, *Islamic and Middle Eastern Geographers and Travellers: Volume I*, p. 87.

44. S. Maqbul Ahmad and Fr. Taeschner, 'Djughrāfiyā', in Netton, *Islamic and Middle Eastern Geographers and Travellers: Volume I*, p. 53. These authors list the following travelogue writers of the twelfth to fourteenth centuries by way of example: al Māzinī (d. 564/1169); the *rihla* of Ibn Djubayr (d. 614/1217); *Ta'rikh al-Mustansir* (written in c. 627/1230) by Ibn Mudjāwir; the *rihlat* of al-Nabātī (d. 636/1239), al-'Abdārī (d. 688/1289), al Tayyibī (698/1299) and al-Tidjānī (708/1308).

45. For a superlative, in-depth analysis of this tendency, see Chow's *The Age of the World Target*.

46. Tarek El-Ariss, *Trials of Arab Modernity: Literary Affects and the New Political* (New York: Fordham University Press, 2013), p. 10.

47. MacCannell, *Empty Meeting Grounds*, p. 4.

48. Billie Melman, 'The Middle East/Arabia: "The Cradle of Islam"', in Peter Hulme and Tim Youngs (eds), *The Cambridge Companion to Travel Writing* (Cambridge: Cambridge University Press, 2002), pp. 113–14.

49. Dimitris Eleftheriotis, *Cinematic Journeys: Film and Movement* (Edinburgh: Edinburgh University Press, 2010), p. 76.

50. Frantz Fanon (trans. Constance Farringdon), *Wretched of the Earth* (London: Penguin, 2001), p. 221.

51. Edward W. Said, 'Orientalism: The Cultural Consequences of the French Preoccupation with Egypt', in Abd al Rahman al-Jabarti (trans. Shmuel Moreh), *Napoleon in Egypt: Al-Jabarti's Chronicle of the French Occupation, 1798* (Princeton, NJ: Markus Wiener, 2004), p. 175.

52. James Duncan and Derek Gregory, 'Introduction', in Duncan and Gregory (eds), *Writes of Passage: Reading Travel Writing* (London: Routledge, 1999), pp. 4–5.

53. Mitsuhiro Yoshimoto, 'The Difficulty of being Radical: The Discipline of Film Studies and the Postcolonial World Order', *boundary* 2 vol. 18 no. 3 (1991), p. 257.

54. Abdelkebir Khatibi, *Maghreb Pluriel* (Paris: Denoël, 1983), pp. 17–18 (author's translation).

55. Ibrahim Abu-Rabi', *Contemporary Arab Thought: Studies in Post-1967 Arab Intellectual History* (London: Pluto Press, 2004), p. 341.

56. Khaldoun Subhi Samman, 'The Convergence of World-Historical Social Science: "Border Thinking" as an Alternative to the Classical Comparative Method', in Ramón Grosfoguel and Ana Margarita Cervantes-Rodríguez (eds), *The Modern/Colonial/Capitalist World-System in the Twentieth Century* (Westport, CT: Praeger, 2002), p. 275.

57. Khatibi, *Maghreb Pluriel*, pp. 33–4 (unpublished translation by Andrew Goffey).

58. For an excellent explication of de- and reterritorialisation within the tourism industry, see Waleed Hazbun, *Beaches, Ruins, Resorts: The Politics of Tourism in the Arab World* (Minneapolis: University of Minnesota Press, 2008), p. xvi.

59. Georges Van Den Abbeele, *Travel as Metaphor: From Montaigne to Rousseau* (Minneapolis: University of Minnesota Press, 1992), pp. xix–xx.

60. Ibn Battutah, *The Travels of Ibn Battutah*, pp. 31, 32.

61. George F. Hourani, *Arab Seafaring in the Indian Ocean in Ancient and Early Medieval Times* (Princeton, NJ: Princeton University Press, 1995), p. 67.

62. Ian Richard Netton, 'Ibn Jubayr: Penitent Pilgrim and Observant Traveller', in Netton, *Islamic and Middle Eastern Geographers and Travellers: Volume II*, p. 84; Paul Lunde, 'The New World Through Arab Eyes', in Ian Richard Netton (ed.), *Islamic and Middle Eastern Geographers and Travellers: Volume IV, The Post-Medieval and Early Modern Period* (London: Routledge, 2008), p. 290.

63. For a fuller definition of the gift economy in other cultures (where the gift turns into the asset), see Marcel Mauss, *The Gift: The Form and Reason for Exchange in Archaic Societies* (London: Routledge Classics, 2002) and Georges Bataille, *The Accursed Share: An Essay on General Economy, Volume One* (New York: Zone Books, 1991), p. 69. Even more relevantly, Teshome Gabriel provides a poignant understanding of how gifts function for migrants, interlacing his narrative with his experiences as a film-maker-academic in 'The Intolerable Gift', in Hamid Naficy (ed.), *Home, Exile, Homeland: Film, Media, and the Politics of Place* (London: Routledge, 1999), pp. 75–84.

64. Patrick Holland and Graham Huggan, *Tourists with Typewriters: Critical Reflections on Contemporary Travel Writing* (Ann Arbor: University of Michigan Press, 2003), p. 5, offers a fine examination of this narrative implication.

65. Ibn Battutah, *The Travels of Ibn Battutah*, p. 101.

66. Leyla Dakhli, 'The *Mahjar* as Literary and Political Territory in the First Decades of the Twentieth Century: The Example of Amin Rihani (1976–1940)', in Dyala Hamzah (ed.), *The Making of the Arab Intellectual: Empire, Public Sphere and the Colonial Coordinates of Selfhood* (London: Routledge, 2013), p. 166.

2 RED AND GREEN STARS IN BROAD DAYLIGHT: A SOCIALIST *TALAB AL-'ILM* FOR SYRIAN STATE CINEMA

1. Ba'ath Party, 'The Social Policy of the Party (Article 41, 'The Culture of the Society', Number Two)', in *The Ba'ath Party Constitution*, http://www.baath-party.org/old/constitution6.htm (website no longer live).

2. Rasha Salti, 'Critical Nationals: The Paradoxes of Syrian Cinema', in Rasha Salti (ed.), *Insights into Syrian Cinema: Essays and Conversations with Contemporary Filmmakers* (New York: AIC Film Editions/Rattapallax Press, 2006), p. 4.

3. Dj. E. Merdaci, 'Syrian Cinema: An Instrument of Education and Culture. Interview with Hamid Merai', reprint from *El Moudjahid* (27 October 1972), n.p., in Various, *Cinémas des Pays Arabes* (Paris: Cinémathèque française/Cinémathèque algérienne, n.d.), n.p. (translation by author).

4. Directive 258, uncited quotation in Jan Alaksan, *Tarikh al-Sinima al-Suria 1928–1988* (*The History of Syrian Cinema 1928–1988*) (Damascus: Publications of the Ministry of Culture, 1987), p. 53 (translation by author).

5. Salah Dehni, 'Le Cinéma Syrien en 1963', in Various, *Cinémas des Pays Arabes*, n.p. (translation by author).

6. Merdaci, 'Syrian Cinema', n.p. (translation by author).

7. Allen, *A Period of Time*, pp. 229–30.

8. Mohammad Malas, interview with author, 16 December 2009.

9. Michel Aflaq, 'The New Stage is a Stage of Foundation' (1969), excerpted and translated, http://albaath.online.fr/English/Aflaq-15-Students%20and%20youth.htm

10. Václav Haval (trans. and ed. Paul Wilson), *Open Letters: Selected Writings 1965–90* (New York: Vintage, 1992), p. 180.

11. Hamid Dabashi, 'Foreword', in Salti, *Insights into Syrian Cinema*, p. 18.

12. Mohamed Heikal, *The Sphinx and the Commissar: The Rise and Fall of Soviet Influence in the Arab World* (New York: Harper Row, 1979), p. 86.

13. Rastegar, *Literary Modernity Between the Middle East and Europe*, pp. 80–1.

14. Said, 'Orientalism', p. 171.

15. Nabil al-Maleh, 'Scenes from Life and Cinema', in Salti, *Insights into Syrian Cinema*, p. 89.

16. See, for example, R. D. McLaurin, *The Middle East in Soviet Policy* (Lanham, MD: Lexington Books, 1975), pp. 132–3.

17. See Nazik Saba Yared, *Arab Travellers and Western Civilization* (London: Saqi, 1996), pp. 112–13.

18. Taha Hussein (trans. Sidney Glazer), *The Future of Culture in Egypt* (Washington, DC: American Council of Learned Societies, 1954), p. 16.

19. Elizabeth Picard, 'The USSR as Seen by the Ba'thists of Iraq and Syria: Ally or Threat', in Zaki Laïdi (ed.), *The Third World and the Soviet Union* (London: Zed Books, 1988), p. 42.

20. Riad Shaya, interview with author, 11 April 2009.
21. Nidal al-Debs, interview with author, 17 April 2010.
22. Mohammad Malas, interview with author, 16 December 2009.
23. Riad Shaya, interview with author, 11 April 2009.
24. Nidal al-Debs, interview with author, 17 April 2010.
25. Karel Holbik, *The United States, The Soviet Union and the Third World* (Hamburg: Verlag Weltarchiv, 1968), p. 56.
26. V. Andashev and P. Oglobin, *Soviet–Arab Friendship: What It Means in Practice* (Moscow: Progress, 1972), p. 70; Pedro Ramet, *The Soviet–Syrian Relationship Since 1955* (Boulder, CO: Westview Press, 1990), p. 237; World Bank, 'Public Data', http://www.google.ca/publicdata/explore?ds=d5bncppjof8f9_&met_y=sp_pop_totl&idim=country:SYR:IRQ:SAU&hl=en&dl=en
27. Al-Tahtawi, *An Imam in Paris*, p. 130.
28. Samir Zikra, uncited quotation in Mahmud Qasim, *al-Film al-Riwa'i al-Suri* (*Syrian Fiction Films*) (Damascus: Publications of the Ministry of Culture, 2003), p. 171.
29. Ramet, *The Soviet–Syrian Relationship Since 1955*, pp. 219–20.
30. 'The Treaty of Friendship and Cooperation Between the Union of Soviet Socialist Republics and the Syrian Arab Republic' (1980), reprinted in Azzedine Souyad, 'The Soviet Union in Syria's Foreign Policy 1970–1980: Ideology Versus Regime Interest' (PhD thesis, Exeter University, 1999), p. 262.
31. Efraim Karsh, *Soviet Policy Towards Syria Since 1970* (London: Macmillan, 1991), p. 54.
32. Ramet, *The Soviet–Syrian Relationship Since 1955*, p. 218.
33. Emporiki Bank, 'Country Trading Profiles: Syria – Economic Indicators', 2010a, http://www.emporikitrade.com/uk/countries-trading-profiles/syria/economic-indicators
34. Milton Kovner, 'Soviet Aid to Developing Counties: A Look at the Record', in John W. Strong (ed.), *The Soviet Union Under Brezhnev and Kosygin* (New York: Van Nostrand Reinhold, 1971), p. 72.
35. Nidal al-Debs, interview with author, 17 April 2010.
36. Nabil al-Maleh, interviewed in M. Amghar, 'Nabil Maleh: Réalisateur Syrien, "Un Cinéma qui reflète le moi collectif"', reprint from *El Moudjahid Culturel* (17 January 1975), n.p., in Various, *Cinémas des Pays Arabes*, p. 28 (translation by author).
37. Mohammad Malas, interview with author, 16 December 2009.
38. Jay Leyda, 'Advanced Training for Film Workers: Russia', *Hollywood Quarterly* vol. 1 no. 3 (April 1946), p. 285.
39. Maria Vizitei, 'From Film School to Film Studio: Women and Cinematography in the Era of *Perestroika*', in Lynne Attwood (ed.), *Red Women on the Silver Screen: Soviet Women and Cinema from the Beginning to the End of the Communist Era* (London: Pandora Press, 1993), pp. 215–16.
40. Riad Shaya, interview with author, 11 April 2009.
41. Nidal al-Debs, interview with author, 17 April 2010.
42. Riad Shaya, interview with author, 11 April 2009; Nabil al-Maleh, speaking at the 'Unfixed Itineraries' symposium, University of California, Santa Cruz, 26 October 2013.
43. Allen, *A Period of Time*, p. 85.
44. Derek Hopwood, *Syria 1945–1986: Politics and Society* (London: Unwin Hyman, 1988), p. 121.

45. As is pointed out in A. R. C. Bolton, *Soviet Middle East Studies: An Analysis and Bibliography, Part VIII Syria and Lebanon* (Oxford: Oxford University Press for the Royal Institute of International Affairs, 1959).

46. Michel Aflaq, 'Arab Nationalism and Its Attitude Towards Communism' (1944), excerpted and translated, http://albaath.online.fr/English/Aflaq-17-Foreign%20Policy.htm

47. Andashev and Oglobin, *Soviet–Arab Friendship*, p. 68.

48. Michel Aflaq, 'The Duty of Nationalist Action' (1943), excerpted and translated, http://albaath.online.fr/English/Aflaq-15-Students%20and%20youth.htm

49. Mohammad Malas, interview with author, 16 December 2009.

50. Nidal al-Debs, interview with author, 17 April 2010.

51. Riad Shaya, interview with author, 11 April 2009.

52. 'The Treaty of Friendship and Cooperation Between the Union of Soviet Socialist Republics and the Syrian Arab Republic' (1980), reprinted in Souyad, 'The Soviet Union in Syria's Foreign Policy 1970–1980', p. 261.

53. Faris al-Shidyāq (ed. and trans. Humphrey Davis), *Leg Over Leg, or The Turtle in the Tree, Concerning the Fariyāq: What Manner of Creature Might He Be Volume 1* (New York: New York University Press, 2013), p. xi.

54. Karsh, *Soviet Policy Towards Syria Since 1970*, pp. 34, 47; Heikal, *The Sphinx and the Commissar*, p. 77. This claim is, it must be stressed, a matter of semantics. From 1971, the USSR (later Russia) leased a naval installation at Tartus in Syria, which it calls a 'material-technical support point', rather than a base.

55. McLaurin, *The Middle East in Soviet Policy*, p. 30.

56. Oussama Mohammad, 'Tea is Coffee, Coffee is Tea: Freedom in a Closed Room', in Salti, *Insights into Syrian Cinema*, p. 157.

57. Abd al-Karim al-Hassan, 'Al-Sinima al-Suria: al-Bidaya al-Thaniya' ('Syrian Cinema: The Second Beginning') (BA dissertation, Algiers University, 1988), p. 68.

58. Ibid.

59. 'Aims of the Damascus Film Festival', uncited quotation in ibid., p. 57.

60. Merdaci, 'Syrian Cinema', n.p. (translation by author).

61. Hopwood, *Syria 1945–1986*, pp. 110–11; Karsh, *Soviet Policy Towards Syria Since 1970*, p. 54.

62. David Roberts, *The Ba'th and the Creation of Modern Syria* (London: Croom Helm, 1987), p. 97.

63. Nidal al-Debs, interview with author, 17 April 2010.

64. For a full examination of this idea and the repercussions of 'waste' of this order, please see Bataille, *The Accursed Share*.

65. Richard Peňa, 'Foreword', in Salti, *Insights into Syrian Cinema*, p. 15.

66. Mette Hjort, 'On the Plurality of Cinematic Transnationalism', in Nataša Ďurovičová and Kathleen Newman (eds), *World Cinemas, Transnational Perspectives* (London: Routledge, 2010), p. 17.

67. Jacques Derrida (trans. Patrick Mensah), *Monolingualism of the Other, or The Prosthesis of Origin* (Stanford, CA: Stanford University Press, 1996), p. 63.

68. Muhammad al-Maghut, 'An Arab Traveller in a Space Station', in Abdullah Al-Udhari (trans. and ed.), *Modern Poetry of the Arab World* (London: Penguin, 1986), pp. 88–9.

69. Mohammad Malas, interview with author, 16 December 2009.

70. Riad Shaya, interview with author, 11 April 2009.

71. Michel Aflaq, uncited quotation in Souyad, 'The Soviet Union in Syria's Foreign Policy 1970–1980', p. 15.

72. Ba'ath Party, 'The Internal Policy of the Party (Article 15)', in *The Ba'ath Party Constitution*, http://www.baath-party.org/old/constitution3.htm (website no longer live).

73. See Robin Buss, *Wary Partners: The Soviet Union and Arab Socialism* (London: Institute for Strategic Studies, 1970), p. 21; Ilana Kass, *Soviet Involvement in the Middle East: Policy Formulation, 1966–1973* (Boulder, CO: Westview Press, 1978), pp. 20–1; and Heikal, *The Sphinx and the Commissar*, p. 88, for further discussions of these digressions from a socialist 'norm'.

74. 'A Call from Syrian Filmmakers to Filmmakers Everywhere', *Facebook*, 29 April 2011, www.facebook.com/notes/syrian-filmmakers-call/a-call-from-syrian-filmmakers-to-filmmakers-everywhere-%D9%86%D8%AF%D8%A7%D8%A1-%D9%85%D9%86-%D8%B3%D9%8A%D9%86%D9%85%D8%A7%D8%A6%D9%8A%D9%8A%D9%86-%D8%B3%D9%88%D8%B1%D9%8A%D9%8A%D9%86/126777020733985 (accessed 25 July 2011).

75. Nabil al-Maleh, interviewed in Amghar, 'Nabil Maleh', p. 24 (translation by author).

76. Nabil al-Maleh, interview with author, 12 April 2007.

77. For further elaboration on this argument, see Rebecca C. Johnson, 'Forward', in al-Shidyāq, *Leg Over Leg*, p. xxx.

78. Vsevolod Pudovkin, 'Kollektivizm – baza kinoraboty ('Collectivism is the Foundation of Cinematic Work')', in *Sobranie sochinenii v trekh tomakh*, vol. 1 (1974), p. 129, translated by Masha Salazkina in 'Moscow–Rome–Havana: A Film-Theory Road Map', *October* no. 139 (Winter 2011), pp. 9–10.

79. Geri Øvensen and Pål Sletten, *The Syrian Labour Market: Findings from the 2003 Unemployment Survey* (Oslo: FAFO, 2007), pp. 30–1.

80. Lawrence Wright, 'Disillusioned', in Salti, *Insights into Syrian Cinema*, p. 46.

81. Emporiki Bank, 'Country Trading Profiles: Syria – Labour Market', 2010b, http://www.emporikitrade.com/uk/countries-trading-profiles/syria/labour-market

82. BECTU, 'How Many Hours Are You Doing Today?' http://www.bectu.org.uk/news/gen/ng0217.html (website no longer live).

83. Ba'ath Party, 'The Social Policy of the Party (Article 41, 'The Culture of the Society', Number Three)', in *The Ba'ath Party Constitution*, http://www.baath-party.org/old/constitution6.htm (website no longer live).

84. Riad Shaya, uncited quotation in Qasim, *al-Film al-Riwa'i al-Suri (Syrian Fiction Films)*, p. 250.

85. Andashev and Oglobin, *Soviet–Arab Friendship*, pp. 68–9.

86. Karsh, *Soviet Policy Towards Syria Since 1970*, p. 52; Kovner, 'Soviet Aid to Developing Counties', p. 68; McLaurin, *The Middle East in Soviet Policy*, p. 9.

87. Dehni, 'Le Cinéma Syrien en 1963', n.p. (translation by author).

88. Marché du Film, *Focus 2009: World Film Market Trends* (Cannes: Festival de Cannes, 2009), p. 67.

89. Øvensen and Sletten, *The Syrian Labour Market*, p. 94.

90. Mohammad, 'Tea is Coffee, Coffee is Tea', p. 157.

91. Nidal al-Debs, interview with author, 17 April 2010.

92. Mohammad Malas, interview with author, 16 December 2009.

93. Øvensen and Sletten, *The Syrian Labour Market*, p. 47.

94. Samir Zikra, 'A Cinema of Dreams and ... Bequest', in Salti, *Insights into Syrian Cinema*, pp. 147–8.
95. Nidal al-Debs, interview with author, 17 April 2010.
96. Hopwood, *Syria 1945–1986*, pp. 105, 122.
97. Jonathan Holt Shannon, *Among the Jasmine Trees: Music and Modernity in Contemporary Syria* (Middletown, CT: Wesleyan University Press, 2006), p. 16.
98. Hopwood, *Syria 1945–1986*, p. 122.
99. Øvensen and Sletten, *The Syrian Labour Market*, p. 37.
100. Hopwood, *Syria 1945–1986*, p. 106.
101. Marshall I. Goldman, *Soviet Foreign Aid* (New York: Frederick A. Praeger, 1967), pp. 151–2; Ramet, *The Soviet–Syrian Relationship Since 1955*, pp. 39, 219–20.
102. Al-Tahtawi, *An Imam in Paris*, p. 180.
103. Rifa'a Rafi' al-Tahtawi, *Takhlis al-Abris fi Talkhis Baris* (*The Extraction of Pure Gold in the Summary of Paris*) (n.p.: Hijazi edition, n.d.), uncited quotation in Adonis, *Al-Thabit w al-Mutahawil* (*The Permanent and the Changeable*) *Book Three* (Beirut: Dar al-Saqi, 2006), p. 37 (translation by author).
104. Tahtawi, *Takhlis al-Abris fi Talkhis Baris*, p. 243, cited in Adonis, *Al-Thabit w al-Mutahawil*, p. 37 (translation by author). To convey a sense of Tahtawi's taught rhyming and metrical scheme here, I have transliterated the couplet as follows:
Man ad'a an lahu hajatan   takhrijahu 'an manhaj a-shar'a
Fala tukunnana lahu sahiban   fa inahu darun bila naf'an
105. Muhammad as-Saffar (trans. and ed. by Susan Gilson Miller), *Disorienting Encounters: Travels of a Moroccan Scholar in France 1845–1846* (Berkeley: University of California Press, 1992), p. 73.
106. Susan Gilson Miller, 'Introduction', in ibid., p. 69.
107. See a lengthy and articulate argument to this end in Mohammad, 'Tea is Coffee, Coffee is Tea', pp. 152–3.
108. Ba'ath Party, 'The Internal Policy of the Party (Article 20)', in *The Ba'ath Party Constitution*, http://www.baath-party.org/old/constitution3.htm (website no longer live).
109. United Nations High Commission for Refugees, *2011 UNHCR Country Operations Profile – Syrian Arab Republic*, http://www.unhcr.org/cgi-bin/texis/vtx/page?page=49e486a76
110. For a full account of this literature and its focus, see David E. Johnson and Scott Michaelsen, 'Border Secrets: An Introduction', in Michaelsen and Johnson (eds), *Border Theory: The Limits of Cultural Politics* (Minneapolis: Minnesota University Press, 1997), pp. 1–42.
111. Mignolo, *Local Histories/Global Designs*, p. 9.
112. Ibid., p. 304.
113. Mohammad Malas, interview with author, 16 December 2009.
114. Mohammad Malas, interviewed in Tahar Chikhaoui, 'A Conversation with Mohammad Malas', in Salti, *Insights into Syrian Cinema*, p. 139.
115. Mohammad Malas, 'Between Imaging and Imagining, Women in Film', in Salti, *Insights into Syrian Cinema*, p. 119.
116. El-Ariss, *Trials of Arab Modernity*, p. 52.
117. Avery F. Gordon, *Ghostly Matters: Haunting and the Sociological Imagination* (Minneapolis: University of Minnesota Press, 1997) pp. 179, 183.
118. El-Ariss, *Trials of Arab Modernity*, p. 50.

119. Lev Kuleshov, 'The Origins of Montage', in Luda Schnitzer *et al.* (eds) (trans. David Robinson), *Cinema in Revolution* (London: Secker and Warburg, 1973), p. 68.
120. Malas, 'Between Imaging and Imagining', p. 120.
121. United Nations Relief and Works Agency for Palestine Refugees in the Middle East, *Statistics*, http://www.unrwa.org/etemplate.php?id=253
122. Khatibi, *Maghreb Pluriel*, pp. 17–18 (translation by author).
123. Abdallah Laroui (trans. Diarmid Cammell), *The Crisis of the Arab Intellectual: Traditionalism or Historicism?* (Berkeley: University of California Press, 1976), pp. 45–6.
124. United Nations High Commission for Refugees, *2011 UNHCR Country Operations Profile*.

3 THE ROAD OF MOST RESISTANCE: FILM-MAKING OF THE SECOND PALESTINIAN INTIFADA

1. Cited in Amin Maalouf, *The Crusades Through Arab Eyes* (London: Zed Books, 1984), p. 212.
2. Cited in Nicole Chareyron, *Pilgrims to Jerusalem in the Middle Ages* (New York: Columbia University Press, 2005), p. 81.
3. According to an Israeli general quoted in *Ha'aretz*, cited in Main B. Qumsiyeh, *Popular Resistance in Palestine: A History of Hope and Empowerment* (London: Pluto Press, 2011), pp. 168–9.
4. Rema Hammami and Salim Tamari, 'The Second Uprising: End or New Beginning?', *Journal of Palestine Studies* vol. 30 no. 2 (2001), p. 9.
5. 'Izz al-Din Ibn al-Athir (trans. D. S. Richards), *The Chronicle of Ibn al-Athir for the Crusading Period from al-Kamil fi'l-ta'rikh. Part 1, The Years 491–541/1097–1146, The Coming of the Franks and the Muslim Response* (Farnham: Ashgate, 2010a), p. 22.
6. Ibn al-Qalanisi, *The Perfect History*, translated by and cited (n.p.) in Maalouf, *The Crusades Through Arab Eyes*, pp. 50–1.
7. Nabil I. Matar, 'Renaissance Cartography and the Question of Palestine', in Ibrahim Abu-Lughod *et al.* (eds), *The Landscape of Palestine: Equivocal Poetry* (Birzeit, Palestine: Birzeit University, 1999), p. 150.
8. John Collins, *Global Palestine* (London: Hurst and Co., 2011), p. x.
9. Ibid., p. 10.
10. Palestinian Cinema Group, 'The Palestinian Cinema and the National Question: Manifesto of the Palestinian Cinema Group', *Cinéaste* vol. 9 no. 3 (Spring 1979), p. 35.
11. Box Office Mojo, '*Divine Intervention*', http://www.boxofficemojo.com/movies/?page=main&id=divineintervention.htm
12. Box Office Mojo, '*Paradise Now*', http://www.boxofficemojo.com/movies/?id=paradisenow.htm
13. Fawaz Turki, *Soul in Exile: Lives of a Palestinian Revolutionary* (New York: Monthly Review Press, 1988), p. 57.
14. Ameen Rihani, *Around the Coasts of Arabia* (London: Constable and Co., 1930), p. 4.
15. Nurith Gertz and George Khleifi, *Palestinian Cinema: Landscape, Trauma, and Memory* (Bloomington and Indianapolis: Indiana University Press, 2008), p. 114.
16. Mark Twain, *The Innocents Abroad*, in *The Complete Travel Books of Mark Twain. The Early Works: The Innocents Abroad and Roughing It* (Garden City, NY: Doubleday & Co., Inc., 1966), p. 397.

17. Ibid., p. 405.

18. Mahmoud Darwish (trans. Sarah Maguire and Sabry Hafez), 'State of Siege', *Modern Poetry in Translation* vol. 3 no. 1 (2004), p. 8.

19. Jaś Elsner and Joan-Pau Rubiés, 'Introduction', in Elsner and Rubiés (eds), *Voyages and Visions: Towards a Cultural History of Travel* (London: Reaktion, 1999), pp. 15, 17.

20. Edith Turner, 'Preface to the Paperback Edition', in Victor Turner and Edith Turner (eds), *Image and Pilgrimage in Christian Culture* (New York: Columbia University Press, 1996), p. xiii.

21. Talal Asad, *Formations of the Secular: Christianity, Islam, Modernity* (Stanford, CA: Stanford University Press, 2003).

22. Mahmoud Darwish, uncited quotation in Edward Said, 'Reflections on Exile', in Russell Ferguson *et al.* (eds), *Out There: Marginalization and Contemporary Cultures* (Cambridge, MA: MIT Press, 1990), p. 361.

23. Said, 'Reflections on Exile', pp. 359–60.

24. Moshe Fischer *et al.*, *Roman Roads in Judaea II: The Jaffa–Jerusalem Road* (Oxford: Hadrian Books, 1996), p. 32.

25. Victor Turner and Edith Turner, 'Introduction: Pilgrimage as a Liminoid Phenomenon', in Turner and Turner, *Image and Pilgrimage in Christian Culture*, p. 34.

26. For further details, see Thomas Wright (ed.), *Early Travels in Palestine, Comprising the Narratives of Arculf, Willibald, Bernard, Saewulf, Sigurd, Benjamin of Tudela, Sir John Maundeville, de la Brocquière, and Maundrell* (London: Henry G. Bohn, 1848).

27. Multiplicity are a group of visual and spatial culture activists who, at this point in time, comprised Stefano Boeri, Maddalena Bregani, Marco Gentile, Maki Gherzi, Matteo Ghidoni, Sandi Hilal, Isabella Inti, Francesco Jodice, Anniina Koivu, John Palmesino, Alessandro Petti, Cecilia Pirovano, Salvatore Porcaro, Francesca Recchia, Eduardo Staszowski, Kasia Teodorczuk.

28. For an excellent reading of the blurring of fact and fiction in Palestinian cinema, here with an eye to experiences of trauma, see Kamran Rastegar's *Surviving Images: Cinema, War, and Cultural Memory in the Middle East* (New York: Oxford University Press, 2015).

29. Enas Muthaffar, interview with author, 5 September 2007.

30. Hany Abu-Assad, interviewed in *Cinema Palestine* (2013).

31. Said, 'Reflections on Exile', p. 363.

32. Larissa Sansour, speaking at the 'Unfixed Itineraries' symposium, University of California, Santa Cruz, 26 October 2013.

33. Jayce Salloum, in Jayce Salloum and Molly Hankwitz, 'Occupied Territories: Mapping the Transgressions of Cultural Terrain', *Framework* vol. 43 no. 2 (2002), p. 87.

34. Annemarie Jacir, post-screening Q&A after *Like Twenty Impossibles* (2003), Human Rights Watch International Film Festival, Roxy Cinema, London, 20 March 2004.

35. Sandi Hilal and Alessandro Petti, interview with author, 5 September 2007.

36. Nahed Awwad, interview with author, 4 September 2007.

37. Najwa Najjar, interviewed in *Cinema Palestine*.

38. Twain, *The Innocents Abroad*, p. 338.

39. Michel Khleifi, interviewed in 'Interviews with the Filmmakers' DVD extra in boxed set *Route 181* (2003).

40. Yehoshua Ben-Arieh, *The Rediscovery of the Holy Land in the Nineteenth Century* (Jerusalem/Detroit: Magnes Press/Hebrew University Israel Exploration Society/Wayne State University Press, 1979), p. 88.

41. Although the film *Five Broken Cameras* (2011) falls outside the historical period under consideration here, it perhaps best exemplifies the risk and the safety film hardware prompts: one of the protagonist's cameras literally takes a bullet for him, saving his body from its impact.

42. Isaiah 62: 10.

43. See Office of the Spokesman, *A Performance-Based Roadmap to a Permanent Two-State Solution* (Washington, DC: US Government, 2003); Doug Suisman *et al.*, *The Arc: A Formal Structure for a Palestinian State* (Santa Monica, CA: RAND Corporation, 2007).

44. Saewulf, 'The Travels of Saewulf AD 1102 and 1103', in Wright, *Early Travels in Palestine*, p. 36.

45. Fischer *et al.*, *Roman Roads in Judaea II*, p. 7.

46. Ibid., p. 33.

47. Ibid., p. 26.

48. Hilton Obenzinger, *American Palestine: Melville, Twain, and the Holy Land Mania* (Princeton, NJ: Princeton University Press, 1999), p. xv.

49. Palestinian Central Bureau of Statistics, 'PCBS: Released the Results of the Annual Report on Transportation and Communication Statistics in the Palestinian Territory, 2006', http://www.pcbs.gov.ps/Portals/_pcbs/PressRelease/TRANSPA07E.pdf

50. B'Tselem, *Forbidden Roads: Israel's Discriminatory Road Regime in the West Bank* (Jerusalem: B'Tselem, 2004), pp. 14, 16, 18.

51. Ibid., p. 3, likens the state of play in Palestine to the former South African regime and this phrase is in common parlance among a good number of pro-Palestinian activists (although many others think the conflation of the two very different political and historical situations should be avoided).

52. Yehezkel Lein (trans. Zvi Shulman), *Civilians Under Siege: Restrictions on Freedom of Movement as Collective Punishment* (Jerusalem: B'Tselem – The Israeli Information Center for Human Rights in the Occupied Territories, 2007), n.p.

53. So claims B'Tselem, *Forbidden Roads*, p. 5.

54. Lein, *Civilians Under Siege*, n.p.

55. According to OCHA (the UN Office for the Coordination of Humanitarian Affairs) Report, December 2003, cited in 'Fact Sheets – Health', *Palestine Monitor*, http://www.palestinemonitor.org/spip/health.html (website no longer live).

56. Lein, *Civilians Under Siege*, n.p.

57. Sobhi al-Zobaidi, interviewed in *Cinema Palestine*.

58. Figures derived from Eyal Weizman, *Hollow Land: Israel's Architecture of Occupation* (Verso: London, 2007), p. 147, where he cites statistics from the Union of Palestinian Medical Relief Committees; an uncited reference to the OCHA report, itself cited in Amira Hass, 'Israeli Restrictions Create Isolated Enclaves in West Bank', *Occupation Magazine – Life Under Occupation*, http://www.kibush.co.il/show_file.asp?num=12852 (website no longer live).

59. Rashid Masharawi, interview with author, 10 September 2007.

60. Nahed Awwad, interview with author, 4 September 2007.

61. Enas Muthaffar, interview with author, 5 September 2007.

62. For further explorations of this reading of the road movie, see Steven Cohan and Ina Rae Hark, 'Introduction', in Cohan and Hark (eds), *The Road Movie Book* (London: Routledge, 1997), p. 1.

63. Sandi Hilal, interview with author, 5 September 2007.

64. Turki, *Soul in Exile*, p. 10.

65. Gertz and Khleifi, *Palestinian Cinema*, pp. 6–7.

66. Hany Abu-Assad, interviewed in *Cinema Palestine*.

67. Sobhi Al-Zobaidi, 'Tora Bora Cinema', *Jump Cut* vol. 50 (Spring 2008), http://www.ejumpcut.org/archive/jc50.2008/PalestineFilm/index.html

68. Jean Genet (trans. Barbara Bray), *Prisoner of Love* (New York: New York Review of Books, 2003), p. 258.

69. Herman Melville, letter to James Billson, 10 October 1884, Melville, *Correspondence*, p. 483, quoted in Obenzinger, *American Palestine*, p. ix.

70. Obenzinger, *American Palestine*, p. 67.

71. Rashid Masharawi, interview with author, 10 September 2007.

72. Annemarie Jacir, interviewed in *Cinema Palestine*.

73. Nahed Awwad, interview with author, 4 September 2007.

74. Tawfiq Abu Wael, interviewed in *Cinema Palestine*.

75. Rashid Masharawi, interview with author, 10 September 2007.

76. Al-Zobaidi, 'Tora Bora Cinema'.

77. Some of these sentiments were expressed by Rashid Mashrawi, interview with author, 10 September 2007.

78. Livia Alexander, 'Is There a Palestinian Cinema?: The National and Transnational in Palestinian Film Production', in Rebecca L. Stein and Ted Swedenburg (eds), *Palestine, Israel, and the Politics of Popular Culture* (Durham, NC: Duke University Press, 2005), p. 168.

79. Al-Zobaidi, 'Tora Bora Cinema'.

80. Sandi Hilal, in particular, points to this as one of her motives (Sandi Hilal, interview with author, 5 September 2007).

81. Adam Hanieh, 'The Politics of Curfew in the Occupied Territories', in Joel Beinin and Rebecca L. Stein (eds), *The Struggle for Sovereignty: Palestine and Israel, 1993–2005* (Stanford, CA: Stanford University Press, 2006), p. 329.

82. Emma C. Murphy, 'Buying Poverty: International Aid and the Peace Process', in Beinin and Stein, *The Struggle for Sovereignty*, p. 58

83. Alessandro Petti, interview with author, 5 September 2007.

84. Ibid.

85. Nadia Yaqub, '*Waiting* (Rashid Masharawi): A Scattered People Waiting for a Shared Future', in Gugler, *Film in the Middle East and North Africa*, p. 202.

86. Étienne Balibar, *Politics and the Other Scene* (London: Verso, 2002), p. 84.

87. Rashid Masharawi, interview with author, 10 September 2007.

88. See John Urry, *Sociology Beyond Societies: Mobilities for the Twenty-First Century* (London: Routledge, 2000), p. 59, for a neat synopsis of these categories.

89. Turner and Turner, 'Introduction', p. 31.

90. Amal Jamal, *Media Politics and Democracy in Palestine: Political Culture, Pluralism, and the Palestinian Authority* (Brighton: Sussex Academic Press, 2005a), pp. 42–3, 66.

91. Ibid., p. 61.

92. Rema Hammami, 'NGOs: The Professionalization of Politics', *Race and Class* vol. 2 no. 37 (1995), p. 53.

93. Jamal, *Media Politics and Democracy in Palestine*, p. 51.

94. Al-Zobaidi, 'Tora Bora Cinema'.

95. Mohammad Bakri, post-screening Q&A after *Leila's Birthday* (2008), London Palestine Film Festival, Barbican Centre, London, 24 April 2009.

96. For the rationale behind this boycott, see Palestinian Campaign for the Academic and Cultural Boycott of Israel, 'Palestinian Filmmakers, Artists and Cultural Workers Call for a Cultural Boycott of Israel', http://www.pacbi.org/boycott_news_more.php?id=315_0_1_0_C

97. Al-Zobaidi, 'Tora Bora Cinema'.

98. Gertz and Khleifi, *Palestinian Cinema*, p. 34.

99. Jamal, *Media Politics and Democracy in Palestine*, p. 68.

100. Evens Foundation, 'Mission and Objectives', http://www.evensfoundation.be/en/about-us

101. Rashid Masharawi, interview with author, 10 September 2007.

102. Yaqub, '*Waiting* (Rashid Masharawi)', p. 204.

103. Hammami, 'NGOs', p. 56.

104. For further explorations of this issue, in fact the various impacts of NGOisation on the arts, see Hanan Toukan, 'Art, Aid, Affect: Locating the Political in Post-Civil War Lebanon's Contemporary Cultural Practices' (PhD dissertation, School of Oriental and African Studies, University of London, 2011), which thinks them through in relation to the visual arts in Lebanon.

105. Alexander, 'Is There a Palestinian Cinema', p. 156

106. Ibid.

107. House demolition statistics from Derek Gregory, *The Colonial Present* (Oxford: Blackwell, 2004), p. 131.

108. Mahmoud Darwish, 'We Travel Like Other People', in Abdullah al-Udhari (trans.), *Victims of a Map* (London: Saqi, 1984), p. 31.

109. Eyal Sivan, interviewed in 'Interviews with the Filmmakers' DVD extra in boxed set *Route 181*.

110. Genet, *Prisoner of Love*, pp. 70–1.

111. Hussein, *The Future of Culture in Egypt*, pp. 17, 20.

112. Consider, for example, this comment by Nahed Awwad: 'I'm considered luckier than other Palestinians because I have the chance to travel outside and when you travel outside you can see the difference. You can see normal life and then you can compare and then you can start to say, "No, it should not be like this." People who have only lived within Palestine, especially over the last 15–20 years and haven't left either for economic reasons, or because they've not been permitted to leave … begin to believe that things are normal and this is the way it should be. This becomes a way for them to protect themselves. It's adjustment, I don't think it's the healthy way to do it, but it's protection.' Later on she continues, 'Even when I travel outside, I become more attached to Palestine, it's something inside me' (Nahed Awwad, interview with author, 4 September 2007).

113. For a more detailed account of the road movie's generic characteristics, see David Laderman, *Driving Visions: Exploring the Road Movie* (Austin: University of Texas Press, 2002), pp. 19–23.

114. Obenzinger, *American Palestine*, p. xvii.

115. Hamid Dabashi, 'Paradise Delayed: With Hany Abu-Assad in Palestine', *Third Text* vol. 24 no. 1 (2010), p. 11.

116. Kamran Rastegar, 'Scoring the Checkpoint: Reflections on the Practice of Composing Music for Palestinian Films' (conference paper), 'Music in Middle Eastern Cinema', Senate House, London, 28 May 2011.

117. Twain, *The Innocents Abroad*, pp. 401–2.

118. Raed El Helou, interviewed in Janine Habreich-Euvrard, *Israéliens, Palestiniens que peut le cinema?: Carnet de route* (Paris: Éditions Michalon, 2005), p. 95 (translation by author).

119. Darwish, 'We Travel Like Other People', p. 31.

4 'TRAVEL AND PROFIT FROM IT': DUBAI'S FORAYS INTO FILM

1. Hazbun, *Beaches, Ruins, Resorts*, p. 224.

2. Alia Younis, 'Red Carpet Education: The Persian Gulf Approach to Film Festivals', in Dina Iordanova and Stefanie Van de Peer (eds), *Film Festival Yearbook 6: Film Festivals and The Middle East* (St Andrews: St Andrews Film Studies, 2014), p. 271.

3. Shobhit Seth, 'Dubai: Growth Through Diversification', *Investopedia*, 10 November 2014, http://www.investopedia.com/articles/investing/111014/dubai-growth-through-diversification.asp; Ahmed Kanna, *Dubai: The City as Corporation* (Minneapolis: University of Minnesota Press, 2011), p. 40.

4. Govers and Go, *Place Branding*, p. 92; Melodena Stephens Balakrishnan, 'Dubai: A Star in the East', *The Journal of Place Management and Development* vol. 1 no. 1 (2008), p. 67.

5. Kanna, *Dubai*, p. 144.

6. Dubai does not publish statistics on its migrant worker population so this is an estimate given by Govers and Go, *Place Branding*, p. 81.

7. Marijke De Valck, *Film Festivals From European Geopolitics to Global Cinephilia* (Amsterdam: Amsterdam University Press, 2007), p. 211.

8. Jerry H. Bentley, *Old World Encounters: Cross-Cultural Contacts and Exchanges in Pre-Modern Times* (New York: Oxford University Press, 1993), p. 20.

9. Hourani, *Arab Seafaring in the Indian Ocean in Ancient and Early Medieval Times*, p. 21.

10. Ibid., p. 61.

11. Madawi Al-Rasheed, 'Introduction: Localizing the Transnational and Transnationalizing the Local', in Madawi Al-Rasheed (ed.), *Transnational Connections and the Arab Gulf* (London: Routledge, 2005), p. 6.

12. Alia Younis presents this case: 'The festivals [in the Gulf] were struggling for an identity along with their nations: the UAE and Qatar, less than 40 years old at the time of the festival launches were and are still creating their modern national identity from the top down.' (Younis, 'Red Carpet Education', pp. 271–2.)

13. See, for instance, Marijike De Valck's treatment of Rotterdam in De Valck, *Film Festivals From European Geopolitics to Global Cinephilia*, pp. 171–2, and Patricia Avery's more general discussion of regeneration via the media and cultural industries in Patricia Avery, 'Born Again: From Dock Cities to Cities of Culture', in Melanie K. Smith (ed.), *Tourism, Culture, and Regeneration* (Cambridge, MA: CABI, 2006), pp. 151–62.

14. World Shipping Council, 'About the Industry: World Top 50 Container Ports', http://www.worldshipping.org/about-the-industry/global-trade/top-50-world-container-ports

15. Terry Macalister, 'Heathrow Airport Overtaken By Dubai as World's Busiest', *Guardian*, 31 December 2014, http://www.theguardian.com/uk-news/2014/dec/31/heathrow-airport-dubai-world-busiest

16. Stephen J. Ramos, *Dubai Amplified: The Engineering of a Port Geography* (Farnham: Ashgate, 2010), p. 16.
17. Balakrishnan, 'Dubai', pp. 168–9.
18. Ramos, *Dubai Amplified*, p. 10.
19. DP World, 'Our Business', http://web.dpworld.com/our-business/
20. Oxford Business Group, *The Report: Dubai 2013* (London: Oxford Business Group, 2013b), p. 15; Jim Krane, *City of Gold: Dubai and the Dream of Capitalism* (Basingstoke: Macmillan 2009), pp. 12–13.
21. From the Hadiths of Ibn 'Abbas and Ibn 'Umar, cited in as-Saffar, *Disorienting Encounters*, p. 96.
22. S. D. Goitein (trans. and ed.), *Letters of Medieval Jewish Traders* (Princeton, NJ: Princeton University Press, 1973), p. 305.
23. Joannes Leo (Africanus) (trans. Master Pory), *Observation Taken Out of John Leo His Nine Bookes* [sic] (London: Henrie Fetherstone, 1625), pp. 835–7. Only after these details are delivered do we hear of customs and religions.
24. Buzurg Ibn Shahriyar, 'Shipwreck on the Way to India', in *The Book of Wonders in India*, pp.165-68, cited thus and translated in Hourani, *Arab Seafaring in the Indian Ocean in Ancient and Early Medieval Times*, p. 120.
25. Anonymous, *The Voyages and Travels of Sindbad the Sailor, as Related by Himself* (Devonport: Samuel and John Keys, 1840–5), p. 1.
26. Ibid., p. 12.
27. Goitein, *Letters of Medieval Jewish Traders*, p. 154.
28. Ibid., pp. 234–5.
29. Ziad Yaghi, interview with author, 12 December 2009.
30. Chin-Shan Lu *et al.*, 'Segmenting Manufacturers' Investment Incentive Preferences for International Logistics Zones', *International Journal of Operations and Production Management* vol. 28 no. 2 (2008), p. 106.
31. See Simon Anholt, *Competitive Identity: The New Brand Management for Nations, Cities and Regions* (Basingstoke: Palgrave Macmillan, 2007), pp. 21 and 23, for a fuller analysis of how such characteristics are reinforced through branding.
32. Dubai International Film Festival, *5th Dubai International Film Festival Executive Summary* (Dubai: Government of Dubai/Dubai Technology and Media Free Zone Authority, 2008), p. 4.
33. Anholt, *Competitive Identity*, p. 33.
34. Ibid., p. 25.
35. Goitein, *Letters of Medieval Jewish Traders*, p. 305.
36. Olivia Remie Constable, *Housing the Stranger in the Mediterranean World* (Cambridge: Cambridge University Press, 2003), p. 46.
37. Shivani Pandya, interview with author, 15 December 2009.
38. Ibid.
39. Yuwa Hendrick-Wong and Desmond Choong, *MasterCard Global Destination Cities Index*, MasterCard Worldwide Insights, http://newsroom.mastercard.com/wp-content/uploads/2014/07/Mastercard_GDCI_2014_Letter_Final_70814.pdf, pp. 24, 4, 23, 6 and 5.
40. See Johnny Allen *et al.*, *Festival and Special Event Management,* 3rd edn (Milton, Queensland: John Wiley and Sons, 2005), p. 481, and Sandro Formica, 'The Development of Festivals and Special Events Studies', *Festival Management and Event Tourism* vol. 5 no. 3

(1998), p.135, for empirical data on the rise of these types of tourism. There is even an academic journal entitled *Festival Management and Event Tourism* dedicated to its study.

41. World Tourism Organization, 'Why Tourism?', http://www2.unwto.org/content/why-tourism

42. Carolyn Cartier, 'Introduction', in Cartier and Lew, *Seductions of Place*, p. 2.

43. MacCannell, *Empty Meeting Grounds*, p. 1.

44. Anonymous, *The Voyages and Travels of Sindbad the Sailor*, p. 5.

45. Felix Thompson, 'Journeying in the Third World: From Third Cinema to Tourist Cinema', in David Crouch *et al.* (eds), *The Media and the Tourist Imagination: Converging Cultures* (London: Routledge, 2005), p. 215.

46. Dubai International Film Festival, *On This Earth There is That Which Deserves Life and is Worth Living For ...: Palestine at DIFF 2009*, 2009c, n.p.

47. One such instance took place during the Q&A after the 13 December 2014 screening of *Suspended Time*, a programme of short films by Palestinian directors to mark the twentieth anniversary of the Oslo Accords. Anecdotally, these responses are something of which Palestinian film-makers complain frequently.

48. Smith, 'Tourism Economy', pp. 78–9.

49. A connection forged by Habib Saidi, 'Opposite Balcony, Comb Teeth and the Comprador Class: Ethnography of the Establishment of Tourism in a Mediterranean Resort', conference paper delivered at 'Traditions and Transformations: Tourism, Heritage and Cultural Change in the Middle East and North Africa Region', 7 April 2009, Amman, Jordan.

50. Oxford Business Group, 'Dubai Growth in Regional Trade', 8 May 2013a, http://www.oxfordbusinessgroup.com/news/dubai-growth-regional-trade

51. Ramos, *Dubai Amplified*, p. 141.

52. Antonia Carver, interview with author, 10 December 2009.

53. Kanna, *Dubai*, p. 141.

54. Ibid., p. 149.

55. Ibid., p. 57.

56. Mike Davis, 'Sand, Fear, and Money in Dubai', in Mike Davis and Daniel Bertrand Monk (eds), *Evil Paradises: Dreamworlds of Neoliberalism* (New York: The New Press, 2007), p. 56; Kanna, *Dubai*, p. 23; James Onley, 'Transnational Merchants in the Nineteenth-Century Gulf', in Al-Rasheed, *Transnational Connections and the Arab Gulf*, pp. 72–3.

57. Aihwa Ong, 'Introduction: Worlding Cities, or the Art of Being Global', in Ananya Roy and Aihwa Ong (eds), *Worlding Cities: Asian Experiments and the Art of Being Global* (Chichester: Wiley-Blackwell, 2011), p. 11.

58. Al-Rasheed, 'Introduction', pp. 1–18, and Jeffrey Sampler and Saeb Eigner, *Sand to Silicon: Achieving Rapid Growth Lessons from Dubai* (London: Profile Books, 2003), pp. 1–2.

59. Abdulhamid Juma, 'DIFF 2009 Opening Press Conference Speech of Abdulhamid Juma, Chairman, DIFF', delivered 6 December 2009.

60. De Valck, *Film Festivals From European Geopolitics to Global Cinephilia*, p. 105.

61. Dubai International Film Festival, *5th Dubai International Film Festival Executive Summary*, p. 4.

62. Juma, 'DIFF 2009 Opening Press Conference Speech of Abdulhamid Juma, Chairman, DIFF'; Dubai International Film Festival, *5th Dubai International Film Festival Executive Summary*, p. 4.

63. Dubai International Film Festival, 'Pioneering Initiatives Position DIFF 2009 as "Region's Leading Festival"', Press Release, 10 December 2009d, p. 2.
64. Shivani Pandya, speech, delivered 8 December 2009.
65. 'Dubai 2010', presented by Sheikh Mohammed bin Rashid Al Maktoum at the Dubai Strategy Forum 2001, taken from abstracted presentation provided by the Executive Office, as cited by Sampler and Eigner, *Sand to Silicon*, p. 72; Santosh Hejmadi, 'Best Practices in Public Free Zones: Dubai Technology and Media Free Zone, United Arab Emirates', 2004, http://www.ifc.org/ifcext/fias.nsf/AttachmentsByTitle/BangladeshRT2Topic3Hejmadippt.pdf/$FILE/BangladeshRT2Topic3Hejmadippt.pdf (website no longer live), p. 12.
66. Govers and Go, *Place Branding*, p. 57.
67. Antonia Carver, interview with author, 10 December 2009.
68. For a fuller picture of how this has played out in the Arab world, see Chad Haines, 'Cracks in the Façade: Landscapes of Hope and Desire in Dubai', in Roy and Ong, *Worlding Cities*, p. 162.
69. Alia Younis notes that, 'The UAE made international industry headlines when the government-owned Abu Dhabi Media Company announced the formation of Image Nation … a billion-dollar-funded production company that, since opening in 2008, has co-financed several Hollywood productions with its partners, including Warner Bros and Participant Media, with whom it made *The Help* (Tate Taylor, US, 2011) and several other less successful studio films, such as *Contagion* (Steven Soderbergh, US, 2011), *The Double* (Michael Brandt, US, 2011) and *Shorts* (Roberto Rodriguez, US, 2009).' (Younis, 'Red Carpet Education', p. 272.)
70. Nashen Moodley, Director of AsiaAfrica Programme, speech, delivered 8 December 2009; Dubai International Film Festival, *5th Dubai International Film Festival Executive Summary*, p. 4.
71. Adam Hanieh, 'Egypt and the Gulf: Rethinking the Nature of Counter-Revolution', conference paper delivered at the Historical Materialism Conference 2012, 8 November 2012, SOAS, University of London, London.
72. As noted in Roland Marchal, 'Dubai: Global City and Transnational Hub', in Al-Rasheed, *Transnational Connections and the Arab Gulf*, p. 94.
73. Ziad Yaghi, interview with author, 12 December 2009.
74. Antonia Carver, interview with author, 10 December 2009.
75. Jane Williams, interview with author, 9 December 2009.
76. Shivani Pandya, interview with author, 15 December 2009.
77. Mohamed Hefzy, 'The Arab Film Industry and the Financial Crisis', panel discussion, Dubai International Film Festival, 12 December 2009.
78. Younis, 'Red Carpet Education', pp. 270–1.
79. Khadija Al-Salami, 'How Gulf Filmmakers See their Future in Film', panel discussion, Dubai International Film Festival, 14 December 2014.
80. Jane Williams, interview with author, 9 December 2009.
81. Shivani Pandya, interview with author, 15 December 2009.
82. Ziad Yaghi, interview with author, 12 December 2009.
83. Dubai Film Market, *Focus 2014: World Film Trends* (Cannes: Marché du Film, Festival de Cannes, 2014), p. 59; Ziad Yaghi, interview with author, 12 December 2009; Mario Haddad (Vice President of Empire International) 'What are the Challenges of Distributing Arab Films?', panel discussion, Dubai International Film Festival, 12 December 2014.

84. Jane Williams, interview with author, 9 December 2009; Layali Badr of TV channel ART claims that 60 per cent of the budgets of Arab films come from TV now (Badr, 'The Arab Film Industry and the Financial Crisis', panel discussion, Dubai International Film Festival, 12 December 2009).

85. Dubai Exports, *Dubai Trade Profile, 2006–2011* (Dubai: Government of Dubai, 2012), pp. 15–16.

86. Haseeb Haider, 'Dubai Non-Oil Trade Growth to Cool', *Khaleej Times,* 19 May 2014, http://www.khaleejtimes.com/biz/inside.asp?xfile=/data/uaebusiness/2014/May/uae business_May301.xml&section=uaebusiness

87. Jane Williams, interview with author, 9 December 2009.

88. Michel Khleifi, 'Against the Odds: A Study of Filmmaking in Palestine', panel discussion, Dubai International Film Festival, 11 December 2009.

89. Dubai Studio City, *Soundstages: Turning Vision into Reality* (no other info) n.p.

90. Masoud Amralla Al Ali, cited in Dubai International Film Festival, 'DIFF to Strengthen Outreach of Regional Cinema through Distribution Support', Press Release, 15 December 2009a.

91. Dubai International Film Festival, 'DIFF to Strengthen Outreach of Regional Cinema through Distribution Support'.

92. Shivani Pandya, interview with author, 15 December 2009.

93. B. Ramesh Kumar, 'The UAE's Strategy Trade Partnership With Asia: A Focus on Dubai', *Middle East Institute*, 19 August 2013, http://www.mei.edu/content/uae%E2%80%99s-strategic-trade-partnership-asia-focus-dubai#_ftnref1

94. Here are some of the trade agreements and organisations to which Dubai belongs: the Gulf Cooperation Council (GCC), the Greater Arab Free Trade Agreement (which incorporates eighteen Arab countries and four associate members from the Organisation of Islamic Cooperation), the GCC and Singapore Free Trade Agreement, Bilateral Trade Agreements with Syria, Jordan, Lebanon, Morocco and Iraq, the Arab League, the Organisation of Islamic Cooperation, the World Bank, the World Trade Organization and the United Nations Conference on Trade and Development (Dubai Exports, An Agency of the Department of Economic Development, Government of the UAE, 'Re-export from Dubai Mainland' http://www.dedc.gov.ae/en/ExportWorld/pages/exporterschecklist.aspx).

95. Hourani, *Arab Seafaring in the Indian Ocean in Ancient and Early Medieval Times*, p. 70.

96. Constable, *Housing the Stranger in the Mediterranean World*, p. 73.

97. Dubai Exports, *Dubai Trade Profile, 2006–2011*, pp. 15–16.

98. Ramos, *Dubai Amplified*, p. 111.

99. Ibid., p. 130.

100. Kumar, 'The UAE's Strategy Trade Partnership With Asia: A Focus on Dubai'.

101. Department of Economic Development, Government of Dubai, 'Exporting and Re-exporting from Dubai', http://www.dubaided.gov.ae/en/startbusiness/Pages/ExportingRe_exportingFromDubai.aspx

102. John Mangan *et al.*, 'Port-Centric Logistics', *International Journal of Logistics Management* vol. 19 no. 1 (2008), p. 35.

103. Chin-Shan Lu *et al.*, 'Segmenting Manufacturers' Investment Incentive Preferences for International Logistics Zones', pp. 108, 110.

104. Anonymous, *The Voyages and Travels of Sindbad the Sailor*, p. 3.

105. As-Saffar, *Disorienting Encounters*, pp. 114–18.

106. Mangan *et al.*, 'Port-Centric Logistics', p. 35.
107. Shivani Pandya, interview with author, 15 December 2009.
108. Melodena Stephens Balakrishnan notes how, in the lead up to my fieldwork period, 'average guest nights have not increased significantly (2.5 nights in 1999 to 2.7 nights in 2007)'. (Balakrishnan, 'Dubai', p. 72.)
109. Goitein, *Letters of Medieval Jewish Traders*, pp. 146–7.
110. Ibid., pp. 245–6.
111. Shivani Pandya, interview with author, 15 December 2009.
112. Ibn 'Awkal, cited in Goitein, *Letters of Medieval Jewish Traders*, p. 33.
113. Jane Williams, interview with author, 9 December 2009.
114. Dina Iordanova and Stefanie Van de Peer 'Introduction', in Iordanova and Van de Peer, *Film Festival Yearbook 6*, p. xxxvii.
115. Shivani Pandya, interview with author, 15 December 2009.
116. Ziad Yaghi, interview with author, 12 December 2009.
117. For a readable account of all these technological developments and their social and economic impact, see Marc Levinson, *The Box: How the Shipping Container Made the World Smaller and the World Economy Bigger* (Princeton, NJ: Princeton University Press, 2010).
118. World Port Source, 'Port of Jebel Ali: Port Commerce', http://www.worldportsource.com/ports/commerce/ARE_Port_of_Jebel_Ali_1423.php
119. Ziad Yaghi, interview with author, 12 December 2009.
120. Ibid.
121. Jane Williams, interview with author, 9 December 2009.
122. Goitein, *Letters of Medieval Jewish Traders*, pp. 14–15.
123. Ibid., p. 184.
124. Antonia Carver, interview with author, 10 December 2009.
125. Jasper Bernes, 'Logistics, Counterlogistics and the Communist Prospect', *Endnotes* vol. 3 (September 2013), http://endnotes.org.uk/en/jasper-bernes-logistics-counterlogistics-and-the-communist-prospect
126. Deborah Cowen, *The Deadly Life of Logistics: Mapping Violence in Global Trade* (Minneapolis: University of Minnesota Press, 2014), pp. 8 and 103.
127. Khayr al-Din al-Tunisi (trans. Leon Carol Brown), *The Surest Path: The Political Treatise of a Nineteenth-Century Muslim Statesman* (Cambridge, MA: Harvard University Press, 1967), pp. 77–8.
128. During a panel discussion at DIFF, Irit Neidhardt (Director, MEC Film), Mario Haddad (vice president, Empire International) and Hania Mroue (director, Metropolis Cinema) all concluded that there was currently a surfeit of film production in the Arab world, thanks, in part, to various funds provided by regional festivals. In contrast, there were seen to not be enough traditional exhibition spaces programming this material, while multiplexes concentrated mainly on US blockbusters. ('What are the Challenges of Distributing Arab Films?', panel discussion, Dubai International Film Festival, 12 December 2014.)
129. For an example of this critical response, see Joseph Fahim, 'Dubai's Disappointing Film Festival', *Al Monitor: The Pulse of the Middle East*, January 2015, http://www.al-monitor.com/pulse/originals/2015/01/dubai-film-festival-poor-budgets.html#. For DIFF's own response, see Shivani Pandya's justifications in Alex Ritman, 'Dubai Film Festival Scraps Major Industry Section, Focuses on Distribution', *The Hollywood Reporter*, 30 October 2014, http://www.hollywoodreporter.com/news/dubai-film-festival-scraps-major-745034

130. Dubai Film and TV Commission, *Film Dubai Production Guide 2014* (Dubai: CAD, 2014), p. 24.

131. Bernes, 'Logistics, Counterlogistics and the Communist Prospect'.

132. Levinson, *The Box*, p. 268.

133. Dubai Film and TV Commission, *Film Dubai Production Guide 2014*, p. 25.

134. Dubai Studio City, *Soundstages*, n.p.

135. As summarised by Robert G. Picard, 'Media Clusters: Local Agglomeration in an Industry Developing Networked Virtual Clusters', *Jonkoping International Business School Working Papers Series* vol. 3 (2008), p. 6.

136. Dubai Studio City, *Soundstages*, n.p.

137. Shivani Pandya, interview with author, 15 December 2009.

138. Mohammed Sharif al Baidhaei from Studio City, 'Meet the Arab Film Industry', panel discussion, Dubai International Film Festival, 13 December 2009.

139. Al Tamimi and Co., 'Media Query: Setting Up in Dubai Media City', http://www.tamimi.com/Legal-Brochures.aspx (website no longer live), p. 2; Sampler and Eigner, *Sand to Silicon*, p. 89.

140. Gaëlle Le Pottier, 'The Emergence of a Pan-Arab Market in the Modern Media Industries', in Al-Rasheed, *Transnational Connections and the Arab Gulf*, p. 120.

141. Dubai Technology and Media Free Zone Authority, Government of Dubai, 'Law No. 1 of 2000 of the Emirate of Dubai: The Dubai Technology, Electronic Commerce & Media Free Zone Law', http://www.tecom.ae/law/law_1.htm, Articles 12, 13 and 15; Santosh Hejmadi, 'Best Practices in Public Free Zones: Dubai Technology and Media Free Zone, United Arab Emirates', pp. 6–7; Al Tamimi and Co., 'Media Query: Setting Up in Dubai Media City', pp. 4–8.

142. Dubai Technology and Media Free Zone Authority, 'Law No. 1 of 2000 of the Emirate of Dubai', Article 15.

143. Al Tamimi and Co., 'Media Query: Setting Up in Dubai Media City', p. 8.

144. These statistics derive from Easterling, p. 38, and Hejmadi, 'Best Practices in Public Free Zones', p. 28.

145. Cowen, *The Deadly Life of Logistics*, p. 192.

146. Sampler and Eigner, *Sand to Silicon*, p. 119.

147. Dubai Technology and Media Free Zone Authority, 'Law No. 1 of 2000 of the Emirate of Dubai', Article 5.

148. Al Tamimi and Co., 'Media Query: Setting Up in Dubai Media City', p. 8.

149. Antonia Carver, interview with author, 10 December 2009.

150. Dubai Technology and Media Free Zone Authority, 'Law No. 1 of 2000 of the Emirate of Dubai', Article 17; Christopher M. Davidson, *Dubai: The Vulnerability of Success* (London: Hurst and Co., 2008), pp. 116–17.

151. Shivani Pandya, interview with author, 15 December 2009.

152. See, for example, the arguments laid out by Davidson, *Dubai*, p. 84.

153. Haines, 'Cracks in the Façade', p. 171.

154. Shivani Pandya, interview with author, 15 December 2009.

155. Mohammed Sharif al Baidhaei, 'Meet the Arab Film Industry', panel discussion, Dubai International Film Festival, 13 December 2009.

156. Marchal, 'Dubai', p. 98; Ramos, *Dubai Amplified*, p. 12; Kanna, *Dubai*, p. 145; Al-Rasheed, 'Introduction', p. 3.

157. Shah, 'Arab Migration Patterns in the Gulf', pp. 91–113; Govers and Go, *Place Branding*, p. 81.
158. For an overview of how Dubai imagines itself to offer this in purely facilities terms, see Chris Forrester, 'Content Distribution: Dubai Studio City: "Build It and They Will Come"', *International Broadcast Engineer* (March/April 2006), p. 12.
159. Brigitte Suter, 'Labour Migration in the United Arab Emirates Field Study on Regular and Irregular Migration in Dubai', Master's dissertation, 2005, http://dspace.mah.se/bitstream/handle/2043/3161/?sequence=1, p. 27.
160. Shah, 'Arab Migration Patterns in the Gulf', p. 97.
161. Oxford Business Group, *The Report: Dubai 2007* (London: Oxford Business Group, 2009), pp. 7–8.
162. Shivani Pandya, interview with author, 15 December 2009.
163. Jane Williams, interview with author, 9 December 2009.
164. Forrester, 'Content Distribution', p. 12.
165. Douglas Massey *et al.*, *Worlds in Motion: Understanding International Migration at the End of the Millennium* (Oxford: Clarendon Press, 1998), p. 144.
166. For further details, see Syed Ali, *Dubai: Gilded Cage* (New Haven: Yale University Press, 2010); Suter, 'Labour Migration in the United Arab Emirates Field Study on Regular and Irregular Migration in Dubai', p. 48; Papastergiadis, *The Turbulence of Migration*, p. 30.
167. Ray Jureidini, 'Human Rights and Foreign Contract Labour: Some Implications for Management and Regulation in Arab Countries', in International Organization of Migration, *Arab Migration in a Globalized World*, pp. 201–15.
168. Suter, 'Labour Migration in the United Arab Emirates Field Study on Regular and Irregular Migration in Dubai', pp. 38–9; Jureidini, 'Human Rights and Foreign Contract Labour', pp. 201–15.
169. Al Tamimi and Co., 'Media Query: Setting Up in Dubai Media City', p. 10.
170. Ibid., p. 7.
171. Dubai Technology and Media Free Zone Authority, 'Law No. 1 of 2000 of the Emirate of Dubai', Article 18.
172. Suter, 'Labour Migration in the United Arab Emirates Field Study on Regular and Irregular Migration in Dubai', p. 30.
173. Jane Williams, interview with author, 9 December 2009.
174. Le Pottier, 'The Emergence of a Pan-Arab Market in the Modern Media Industries', p. 111.
175. Haines, 'Cracks in the Façade', p. 163.
176. Ong, 'Introduction', p. 2.
177. Cowen, *The Deadly Life of Logistics*, pp. 68–9, 72, 123, 174, 177.
178. Ramos, *Dubai Amplified*, p. 158.
179. Haines, 'Cracks in the Façade', p. 161.
180. Bentley, *Old World Encounters*, pp. 125, 128–9.
181. Jumeirah Group, 'Future Plans', http://www.jumeirah.com/en/jumeirah-group/development/future-plans
182. Le Pottier, 'The Emergence of a Pan-Arab Market in the Modern Media Industries', pp. 115–16.
183. Mangan *et al.*, 'Port-Centric Logistics', p. 30.
184. DP World, 'Our Business'.
185. Levinson, *The Box*, p. 271.

186. Ramos, *Dubai Amplified*, p. 158.

187. For further elaboration on these developments and the history of finance capitalism in the Gulf Cooperation Council states, please refer to Adam Hanieh, *Capitalism and Class in the Gulf Arab States* (New York: Palgrave Macmillan, 2011) and Hanieh, 'Egypt and the Gulf'.

OUTGOING CARGO

1. Bernes, 'Logistics, Counterlogistics and the Communist Prospect'.

2. Kanafani, *Men in the Sun and Other Palestinian Stories*, p. 37.

Bibliography

'Abd al-Hamid, Bandar, *Sinima'iun Bila Hadud* (*Filmmakers Without Borders*) (Damascus: National Film Organization, 2001).

'Abd al-Wahab al-Hussayni, Muhammad, *Al-Film al-Siyasi fi al-Sinima al-Suriya* (*Political Film in Syrian Cinema*) (Damascus: Union of Arab Writers, 1991).

'Abed al-Jabri, Mohammed (trans. Aziz Abbassi), *Arab-Islamic Philosophy: A Comtemporary Critique* (Austin: University of Texas Press, 1999).

Abourahme, Nasser, 'Camp and Checkpoint', *International Journal of Urban and Regional Research* vol. 35 no. 2 (March 2011), pp. 453–61.

Abu-Lughod, Ibrahim, *Arab Rediscovery of Europe: A Study in Cultural Encounters* (Princeton, NJ: Princeton University Press, 1963).

Abu-Lughod, Ibrahim, Roger Heacock and Khaled Nashef (eds), *The Landscape of Palestine: Equivocal Poetry* (Birzeit, Palestine: Birzeit University, 1999).

Abu-Lughod, Janet L., *Before European Hegemony: The World System AD 1250–1350* (Oxford: Oxford University Press, 1989).

Abu-Rabi', Ibrahim, *Contemporary Arab Thought: Studies in Post-1967 Arab Intellectual History* (London: Pluto Press, 2004).

Abu Remaileh, Refqa, 'Documenting Palestinian Presence: A Study of the Novels of Emile Habibi and the Films of Elia Suleiman' (doctoral thesis, St John's College, University of Oxford, 2010).

Adams, Timothy Dow, *Telling Lies in Modern American Autobiography* (Chapel Hill: University of North Carolina Press, 1990).

Adonis (Ali Ahmed Said) (trans. Samuel Hazo), *The Blood of Adonis: Transpositions of Selected Poems* (Pittsburgh, PA: University of Pittsburgh Press, 1971).

Adonis (trans. Catherine Cobham), *An Introduction to Arab Poetics* (London: Saqi, 1990).

Adonis, *Al-Thabit w al-Mutahawil* (*The Permanent and the Changeable*) (Beirut: Dar al-Saqi, 2006).

Aflaq, Michel, 'Foreign Policy' (series of quotations), http://albaath.online.fr/English/Aflaq-17-Foreign%20Policy.htm

Aflaq, Michel, 'Students and Youth' (series of quotations), http://albaath.online.fr/English/Aflaq-15-Students%20and%20youth.htm

Akoum, Ibrahim F., 'Conducting Business in the UAE: A Brief for International Managers', *Global Business and Organizational Excellence* vol. 27 no. 4 (2008), pp. 51–66.

Alaksan, Jan, *Tarikh al-Sinima al-Suria 1928–1988* (*The History of Syrian Cinema 1928–1988*) (Damascus: Publications of the Ministry of Culture, 1987).

Al-'Awdat, Hussayn, *Al-Sinima w al-Qadaya al-Falastiniya* (*Cinema and the Palestinian Cause*) (Damascus: n.p., 1987).

Al-Hassan, 'Abd al-Karim, 'Al-Sinima al-Suria: al-Bidaya al-Thaniya' ('Syrian Cinema: The Second Beginning') (BA dissertation, Algiers University, 1988).

Al-Jabarti, Abd al Rahman (trans. Shmuel Moreh), *Napoleon in Egypt: Al-Jabarti's Chronicle of the French Occupation, 1798* (Princeton, NJ: Markus Wiener, 2004).

Al-Rasheed, Madawi (ed.), *Transnational Connections and the Arab Gulf* (London: Routledge, 2005).

al-Shidyāq, Faris (ed. and trans. Humphrey Davis), *Leg Over Leg, or The Turtle in the Tree, Concerning the Fariyāq, What Manner of Creature Might He Be* Volumes 1–4 (New York: New York University Press, 2013).

Al-Tahtawi, Rifa'a Rafi' (trans. Daniel L. Newman), *An Imam in Paris: Al-Tahtawi's Visit to France (1826–1831)* (London: Saqi, 2004).

Al Tamimi and Co., 'Labour Law in the UAE', http://www.zu.ac.ae/library/html/UAEInfo/documents/UAELabourLaw.pdf

Al Tamimi and Co., 'Media Query: Setting Up in Dubai Media City', http://www.tamimi.com/Legal-Brochures.aspx (website no longer live).

Al-Tunisi, Khayr al-Din (trans. Leon Carol Brown), *The Surest Path: The Political Treatise of a Nineteenth-Century Muslim Statesman* (Cambridge, MA: Harvard University Press, 1967).

Al-Zobaidi, Sobhi, 'Tora Bora Cinema', *Jump Cut* vol. 50 (Spring 2008), http://www.ejumpcut.org/archive/jc50.2008/PalestineFilm/index.html

Alea, Tomás Gutierrez (trans. Julia Lesage), 'The Viewer's Dialectic', *Jump Cut* vol. 29 (February 1984), pp. 18–21.

Ali, Syed, *Dubai: Gilded Cage* (New Haven: Yale University Press, 2010).

Allen, Johnny, William O'Toole, Ian McDonnell and Robert Harris, *Festival and Special Event Management,* 2nd edn (Milton, Queensland: John Wiley and Sons, 2002).

Allen, Johnny, William O'Toole, Ian McDonnell and Robert Harris, *Festival and Special Event Management,* 3rd edn (Milton, Queensland: John Wiley and Sons, 2005).

Allen, Roger (ed.), *A Period of Time: A Study and Translation of Hadith 'Isa ibn Hisham by Muhammad Al-Muwaylihi* (Reading: Ithaca Press, 1992).

Al-Udhari, Abdullah (trans. and ed.), *Modern Poetry of the Arab World* (London: Penguin, 1986).

Amin, Ahmad (trans. Wolfgang H. Benh), *Orient and Occident: An Egyptian's Quest for National Identity* (Berlin: Adiyok, 1984).

Amin, Samir (trans. Russell Moore), *Eurocentrism* (London: Zed Books, 1989).

Andashev, V. and P. Oglobin, *Soviet–Arab Friendship: What It Means in Practice* (Moscow: Progress, 1972).

Anholt, Simon, *Competitive Identity: The New Brand Management for Nations, Cities and Regions* (Basingstoke: Palgrave Macmillan, 2007).

Anholt, Simon, *Places: Identity, Image and Reputation* (Basingstoke: Palgrave Macmillan, 2010).

Anonymous, 'Fact Sheets – Health', *Palestine Monitor*, http://www.palestinemonitor.org/spip/health.html

Anonymous, 'Law Number One of 2000 of the Emirate of Dubai Establishing the Dubai Technology, Electronic Commerce and Media Free Zone', http://www.tecom.ae/law/law_1.htm

Anonymous, *The Voyages and Travels of Sindbad the Sailor, as Related by Himself* (Devonport: Samuel and John Keys, 1840–5).

Anwar, Syed Aziz and Sadiq Sohail, 'Festival Tourism in the United Arab Emirates: First-Time Versus Repeat Visitor Perceptions', *Journal of Vacation Marketing* vol. 10 no. 2 (2003), pp. 161–70.

Appadurai, Arjun, *Modernity at Large: Cultural Dimensions of Globalization* (Minneapolis: University of Minnesota Press, 1996).

Argo, Nichole, Shamil Idriss and Mahnaz Fancy, *Media and Intergroup Relations: Research on Media and Social Change* (New York: Soliya, 2009).

Asad, Talal, *Formations of the Secular: Christianity, Islam, Modernity* (Stanford, CA: Stanford University Press, 2003).

As-Saffar, Muhammad (trans. and ed. by Susan Gilson Miller), *Disorienting Encounters: Travels of a Moroccan Scholar in France 1845–1846* (Berkeley: University of California Press, 1992).

Avery, Patricia, 'Born Again: From Dock Cities to Cities of Culture', in Melanie K. Smith (ed.), *Tourism, Culture, and Regeneration* (Cambridge, MA: CABI, 2006), pp. 151–62.

Baath Arab Socialist Party National Leadership, *The Constitution of the Baath Arab Socialist Party Approved by the First Congress of the Party in 1947* (1947), www.baath-party.org/eng/constitution.htm (website no longer live).

Balakrishnan, Melodena Stephens, 'Dubai: A Star in the East', *The Journal of Place Management and Development* vol. 1 no. 1 (2008), pp. 62–91.

Balibar, Étienne, *Politics and the Other Scene* (London: Verso, 2002).

Baroud, Ramzy, *The Second Palestinian Intifada: A Chronicle of a People's Struggle* (London: Pluto Press, 2006).

Bashar, Ibrahim, *Alwan al-Sinima al-Suria/The Colours of Syrian Cinema* (Damascus: Publications of the Ministry of Culture, 2003).

Bataille, Georges, *The Accursed Share: An Essay on General Economy, Volume One* (New York: Zone Books, 1991).

BECTU, 'How Many Hours Are You Doing Today?' (2005), http://www.bectu.org.uk/news/gen/ng0217.html (website no longer live).

Beer, Francis A. (ed.), *Alliances: Latent War Communities in the Contemporary World* (Dallas: University of Texas Press, 1970).

Behdad, Ali, *Belated Travelers: Orientalism in the Age of Colonial Dissolution* (Cork: Cork University Press, 1994).

Beinin, Joel and Rebecca L. Stein (eds), *The Struggle for Sovereignty: Palestine and Israel, 1993–2005* (Stanford, CA: Stanford University Press, 2006).

Ben-Arieh, Yehoshua, *The Rediscovery of the Holy Land in the Nineteenth Century* (Jerusalem/Detroit: Magnes Press/Hebrew University Israel Exploration Society/Wayne State University Press, 1979).

Benjamin, Walter (trans. Zohn, Harry), *Illuminations* (New York: Schocken Books, 2007).

Bensmaïa, Réda, *Experimental Nations: Or, The Invention of the Maghreb* (Princeton, NJ: Princeton University Press, 2003).

Bentley, Jerry H., *Old World Encounters: Cross-Cultural Contacts and Exchanges in Pre-Modern Times* (New York: Oxford University Press, 1993).

Bernes, Jasper, 'Logistics, Counterlogistics and the Communist Prospect', *Endnotes* vol. 3 (September 2013), http://endnotes.org.uk/en/jasper-bernes-logistics-counterlogistics-and-the-communist-prospect

Bhabha, Homi, *The Location of Culture* (London: Routledge, 1994).

Boëx, Cécile, 'Autonomous Spaces: Though Funded by the State, Filmmakers in Syria Continue to Find Ways to Make Their Often Critical Voices Heard', *Film Comment* vol. 42 no. 3 (2006), pp. 12–15.

Bolton, A. R. C., *Soviet Middle East Studies: An Analysis and Bibliography, Part VIII Syria and Lebanon* (Oxford: Oxford University Press for the Royal Institute of International Affairs, 1959).

Boniface, Priscilla, *Managing Quality Cultural Tourism* (London: Routledge, 1995).

Bonilla, Frank, Edwin Meléndez, Rebecca Morales and María de los Angeles Torres (eds), *Borderless Borders: US Latinos, Latin Americans, and the Paradox of Interdependence* (Philadelphia: Temple University Press, 1998).

Bookman, Milica Z., *Tourists, Migrants and Refugees: Population Movements in Third World Development* (London: Lynne Reiner, 2006).

Boullata, Issa J., *Trends and Issues in Contemporary Arab Thought* (Albany: State University of New York Press, 1990).

Box Office Mojo, '*Divine Intervention*', http://www.boxofficemojo.com/movies/?page=main&id=divineintervention.htm

Box Office Mojo, '*Paradise Now*', http://www.boxofficemojo.com/movies/?id=paradise now.htm

Brah, Avtar, *Cartographies of Diaspora: Contesting Identities* (London: Routledge, 1996).

B'Tselem, *Forbidden Roads: Israel's Discriminatory Road Regime in the West Bank* (Jerusalem: B'Tselem, 2004).

Bucaille, Laetitia (trans. Anthony Roberts), *Growing Up Palestinian: Israeli Occupation and the Intifada Generation* (Princeton, NJ: Princeton University Press, 2004).

Buheiry, Marwan R. (ed.), *Intellectual Life in the Arab East, 1890–1939* (Beirut: American University of Beirut Press, 1981).

Buss, Robin, *Wary Partners: The Soviet Union and Arab Socialism* (London: Institute for Strategic Studies, 1970).

Cartier, Carolyn and Alan A. Lew (eds), *Seductions of Place: Geographical Perspectives on Globalization and Touristed Landscapes* (London: Routledge, 2005).

Caton, Steven C., *Lawrence of Arabia: A Film's Anthropology* (Berkeley and Los Angeles: University of California Press, 1999).

Chakrabarty, Dipesh, *Provincializing Europe: Postcolonial Thought and Historical Difference* (Princeton, NJ: Princeton University Press, 2000).

Chambers, Iain, *Migrancy, Culture, Identity* (London: Routledge, 1994).

Chareyron, Nicole, *Pilgrims to Jerusalem in the Middle Ages* (New York: Columbia University Press, 2005).

Chejne, Anwar G., 'Travel Books in Modern Arabic Literature', *The Muslim World* vol. 52 (1962), pp. 207–15.

Choueiri, Youssef M., *Modern Arab Historiography: Historical Discourse and the Nation-State* (London: Routledge Curzon, 2003).

Chow, Rey, *Writing Diaspora: Tactics of Intervention in Contemporary Cultural Studies* (Bloomington: Indiana University Press, 1993).

Chow, Rey, *The Age of the World Target: Self-Referentiality in War, Theory, and Comparative Work* (Durham, NC: Duke University Press, 2006).

Clifford, James, 'Notes on Travel and Theory', *Traveling Theories, Traveling Theorists, Inscriptions* vol. 5 (1989), http://www2.ucsc.edu/culturalstudies/PUBS/Inscriptions/vol_5/preface.html (website no longer live).

Clifford, James, *Routes: Travel and Translation in the Late Twentieth Century* (Cambridge: Harvard University Press, 1997).

Clifford, James and Vivek Dhareshwar, 'Preface' to *Traveling Theories, Traveling Theorists*, *Inscriptions* vol. 5 (1989), http://www2.ucsc.edu/culturalstudies/PUBS/Inscriptions/vol_5/preface.html (website no longer live).

Clifford, James and George E. Marcus (eds), *Writing Culture: The Poetics and Politics of Ethnography* (Berkeley: University of California Press, 1986).

Cohan, Steven and Ina Rae Hark (eds), *The Road Movie Book* (London: Routledge, 1997).

Collins, John, *Global Palestine* (London: Hurst and Co., 2011).

Constable, Olivia Remie, *Housing the Stranger in the Mediterranean World* (Cambridge: Cambridge University Press, 2003).

Cooke, Miriam, *Dissident Syria: Making Oppositional Arts Official* (Durham, NC: Duke University Press, 2007).

Cowen, Deborah, *The Deadly Life of Logistics: Mapping Violence in Global Trade* (Minneapolis: University of Minnesota Press, 2014).

Crouch, David and Nina Lübbren (eds), *Visual Culture and Tourism* (Oxford: Berg, 2003).

Crouch, David, Rhona Jackson and Felix Thompson (eds), *The Media and the Tourist Imagination: Converging Cultures* (London: Routledge, 2005).

Czechoslovak State Film, *Guide to Czechoslovak State Cinematography* (Prague: Czechoslovak State Film, 1949).

Dabashi, Hamid (ed.), *Dreams of a Nation: On Palestinian Cinema* (London: Verso, 2006).

Dabashi, Hamid, 'Paradise Delayed: With Hany Abu-Assad in Palestine', *Third Text* vol. 24 no. 1 (2010), pp. 11–23.

Dalrymple, William, 'Home Truths on Abroad', *Guardian* (review section), 19 September 2009, pp. 2–3.

Dann, Graham M. S. (ed.), *The Tourist As a Metaphor of the Social World* (New York: CABI, 2002).

Darwish, Mahmoud, 'We Travel Like Other People', in Abdullah al-Udhari (trans.), *Victims of a Map* (London: Saqi, 1984), p. 31.

Darwish, Mahmoud (trans. Sarah Maguire and Sabry Hafez), 'State of Siege', *Modern Poetry in Translation* vol. 3 no. 1 (2004), pp. 8–33.

Davidson, Christopher M., *Dubai: The Vulnerability of Success* (London: Hurst and Co., 2008).

Davis, Mike and Daniel Bertrand Monk (eds), *Evil Paradises: Dreamworlds of Neoliberalism* (New York: The New Press, 2007).

Department of Economic Development, Government of Dubai, 'Exporting and Re-exporting from Dubai', http://www.dubaided.gov.ae/en/startbusiness/Pages/ExportingRe_exportingFromDubai.aspx

Derrida, Jacques (trans. Patrick Mensah), *Monolingualism of the Other, or The Prosthesis of Origin* (Stanford, CA: Stanford University Press, 1996).

De Valck, Marijke, *Film Festivals From European Geopolitics to Global Cinephilia* (Amsterdam: Amsterdam University Press, 2007).

Dłużewska, A., 'The Influence of Religion on Global and Local Conflict in Tourism: Case Studies in Muslim Countries', in P. Burns and M. Novelli (eds), *Tourism Development: Growths, Myths and Inequalities* (Wallingford: CABI, 2008).

Dorsey, David A., *The Roads and Highways of Ancient Israel* (Baltimore, MD: Johns Hopkins University Press, 1991).

Downing, John D. H. (ed.), *Film and Politics in the Third World* (Brooklyn, NY: Autonomedia, 1987).

DP World, 'Our Business', http://web.dpworld.com/our-business/

Dubai Chamber E-Services, 'Why Dubai?', http://www.dcci.ae/portal/page?_pageid=
53,3350&_dad=portal&_schema=PORTAL

Dubai Exports, An Agency of the Department of Economic Development, Government of Dubai,
'Re-export from Dubai Mainland', http://www.dedc.gov.ae/en/ExportWorld/pages/
exporterschecklist.aspx

Dubai Exports, *Dubai Trade Profile, 2006–2011* (Dubai: Government of Dubai, 2012).

Dubai Film and TV Commission, *Film Dubai Production Guide 2014* (Dubai: CAD, 2014).

Dubai Film Market, *Focus 2014: World Film Trends* (Cannes: Marché du Film, Festival de Cannes,
2014).

Dubai International Film Festival, *5th Dubai International Film Festival Executive Summary*
(Dubai: Government of Dubai/Dubai Technology and Media Free Zone Authority, 2008).

Dubai International Film Festival, 'DIFF to Strengthen Outreach of Regional Cinema through
Distribution Support', Press Release, 15 December 2009a.

Dubai International Film Festival, *Dubai Film Connection Project Dossier 2009*, 2009b.

Dubai International Film Festival, *On This Earth There is That Which Deserves Life and is Worth
Living For ...: Palestine at DIFF 2009*, 2009c.

Dubai International Film Festival, 'Pioneering Initiatives Position DIFF 2009 as "Region's
Leading Festival"', Press Release, 10 December 2009d.

Dubai International Film Festival, 'DIFF Signs Partnership Deal with Beirut DC to Promote
Documentary Film-Making', Press Release, 16 May 2010a.

Dubai International Film Festival, 'Dubai Film Connection Lends Momentum to New Wave in
Arab Cinema', Press Release, 18 May 2010b.

Dubai Statistics Center (Government of Dubai), *Dubai in Figures, First Half of 2009,* http://www.
dsc.gov.ae/En/Pages/Home.aspx

Dubai Studio City, *Soundstages: Turning Vision into Reality* (n.p, n.d.).

Dubai Technology and Media Free Zone Authority, Government of Dubai, 'Law No. 1 of 2000 of
the Emirate of Dubai: The Dubai Technology, Electronic Commerce & Media Free Zone Law',
http://www.tecom.ae/law/law_1.htm

Dubai Technology and Media Free Zone Employment Regulations 2004,
http://www.tecom.ae/law/law_11.htm

Duncan, James and Derek Gregory (eds), *Writes of Passage: Reading Travel Writing* (London:
Routledge, 1999).

Ďurovičová, Nataša and Kathleen Newman (eds), *World Cinemas, Transnational Perspectives*
(London: Routledge, 2010).

Durrant, Sam and Catherine M. Lord (eds), *Essays on Migratory Aesthetics: Cultural Practices
Between Migration and Art-making* (Amsterdam: Rodopi, 2007).

Eade, John and Michael J. Sallnow (eds), *Contesting the Sacred: The Anthropology of Pilgrimage*
(Urbana and Chicago: University of Illinois Press, 2000).

Easterling, Keller, *Extrastatecraft: The Power of Infrastructure Space* (New York: Verso, 2014).

Eickelman, Dale F. and James Piscatori (eds), *Muslim Travellers: Pilgrimage, Migration, and the
Religious Imagination* (London: Routledge, 1990).

El-Ariss, Tarek, *Trials of Arab Modernity: Literary Affects and the New Political* (New York:
Fordham University Press, 2013).

El-Charakawi, Galal, 'History of the UAR Cinema (1896–1962)', in Georges Sadoul (ed.), *The
Cinema in the Arab Countries* (Beirut: Interarab Centre of Cinema and Television, 1966),
pp. 69–97.

Eleftheriotis, Dimitris, *Cinematic Journeys: Film and Movement* (Edinburgh: Edinburgh University Press, 2010).

El-Enany, Rasheed, *Arab Representations of the Occident: East–West Encounters in Arabic Fiction* (London: Routledge, 2006).

El-Hassan, Azza, 'When the Exiled Films Home', *Framework* vol. 43 no. 2 (2002), pp. 64–70.

Elsner, Jaś and Joan-Pau Rubiés (eds), *Voyages and Visions: Towards a Cultural History of Travel* (London: Reaktion, 1999).

Emporiki Bank, 'Country Trading Profiles: Syria – Economic Indicators', 2010a, http://www.emporikitrade.com/uk/countries-trading-profiles/syria/economic-indicators

Emporiki Bank, 'Country Trading Profiles: Syria – Labour Market', 2010b, http://www.emporikitrade.com/uk/countries-trading-profiles/syria/labour-market

Euben, Roxanne, L., *Journeys to the Other Shore: Muslim and Western Travelers in Search of Knowledge* (Princeton, NJ: Princeton University Press, 2006).

Evens Foundation, 'Mission and Objectives', http://www.evensfoundation.be/en/about-us

Fabian, Johannes, *Time and the Other: How Anthropology Makes Its Object* (New York: Columbia University Press, 1983).

Fahim, Joseph, 'Dubai's Disappointing Film Festival', *Al Monitor: The Pulse of the Middle East*, January 2015, http://www.al-monitor.com/pulse/originals/2015/01/dubai-film-festival-poor-budgets.html#

Fanon, Frantz (trans. Constance Farringdon), *Wretched of the Earth* (London: Penguin, 2001).

Faraday, George, *Revolt of the Filmmakers; The Struggle for Artistic Autonomy and the Fall of the Soviet Film Industry* (Pennsylvania: Pennsylvania State Press, 2000).

Featherstone, Mike, *Undoing Culture: Globalization, Postmodernism and Identity* (London: Sage, 1995).

Ferguson, Russell, Martha Gover, Trinh T. Minh-ha and Cornel West (eds), *Out There: Marginalization and Contemporary Cultures* (Cambridge, MA: MIT Press, 1990).

Fieni, David, 'Cinematic Checkpoints and Sovereign Time', *Journal of Postcolonial Writing* vol. 50 no. 1 (2014), pp. 6–18.

Fischer, Moshe, Benjamin Isaac and Israel Roll, *Roman Roads in Judaea II: The Jaffa–Jerusalem Road* (Oxford: Hadrian Books, 1996).

Flamhaft, Ziva, *Israel on the Road to Peace: Accepting the Unacceptable* (Boulder, CO: Westview Press, 1996).

Formica, Sandro, 'The Development of Festivals and Special Events Studies', *Festival Management and Event Tourism* vol. 5 no. 3 (1998), pp. 131–7.

Forrester, Chris, 'Content Distribution: Dubai Studio City: "Build It and They Will Come"', *International Broadcast Engineer* (March/April 2006), pp. 12–13.

Fox, John W., Nada Mourtada-Sabbah and Mohammed al-Mutawa (eds), *Globalization and the Gulf* (London: Routledge, 2006).

Franklin, Adrian and Mike Crang, 'The Trouble with Tourism and Travel Theory', *Tourist Studies* vol. 1 no. 5 (2001), pp. 5–22.

Fussell, Paul, *Abroad: British Literary Traveling Between the Wars* (Oxford: Oxford University Press, 1982).

Gana, Nouri, 'Reel Violence: *Paradise Now* and the Collapse of the Spectacle', *Comparative Studies of South Asia, Africa and the Middle East* vol. 28 no. 1 (2008), pp. 20–37.

Genet, Jean (trans. Barbara Bray), *Prisoner of Love* (New York: New York Review of Books, 2003).

Gertz, Nurith and George Khleifi, *Palestinian Cinema: Landscape, Trauma, and Memory* (Bloomington and Indianapolis: Indiana University Press, 2008).

Ghosh, Amitav, *In an Antique Land: History in the Guise of a Traveler's Tale* (New York: Vintage, 1992).

Girgis, Maurice, 'Would Nationals and Asians Replace Arab Workers in the GCC?', conference paper submitted to fourth Mediterranean Development Forum, Amman, Jordan, 2002.

Goitein, S. D. (trans. and ed.), *Letters of Medieval Jewish Traders* (Princeton, NJ: Princeton University Press, 1973).

Goldman, Marshall I., *Soviet Foreign Aid* (New York: Frederick A. Praeger, 1967).

Golovskoy, Val S. with John Rimberg (trans. Steven Hill), *Behind the Soviet Screen: The Motion Picture Industry in the USSR 1972–1982* (Ann Arbor: Ardis, 1986).

Gordon, Avery F., *Ghostly Matters: Haunting and the Sociological Imagination* (Minneapolis: University of Minnesota Press, 1997).

Govers, Robert and Frank Go, *Place Branding: Glocal, Virtual and Physical Identities, Constructed, Imagined and Experienced* (Basingstoke: Palgrave Macmillan, 2009).

Gregory, Derek, *The Colonial Present* (Oxford: Blackwell, 2004).

Grosfoguel, Ramón and Ana Margarita Cervantes-Rodríguez (eds), *The Modern/Colonial/Capitalist World-System in the Twentieth Century* (Westport, CT: Praeger, 2002).

Gugler, Josef (ed.), *Film in the Middle East and North Africa: Creative Dissidence* (Austin: University of Texas Press, 2011).

Hafez, Sabry, 'The Quest for/Obsession with the National in Arabic Cinema', in Valentina Vitali and Paul Willemen (eds), *Theorising National Cinemas* (London: BFI, 2006), pp. 226–92.

Haider, Haseeb, 'Dubai Non-Oil Trade Growth to Cool', *Khaleej Times,* 19 May 2014, http://www.khaleejtimes.com/biz/inside.asp?xfile=/data/uaebusiness/2014/May/uae business_May301.xml&section=uaebusiness

Halbreich-Euvrard, Janine, *Israéliens, Palestiniens que peut le cinema?: Carnet de route* (Paris: Éditions Michalon, 2005).

Hames, Peter, *The Czechoslovak New Wave*, 2nd edn (London: Wallflower Press, 2005).

Hammami, Rema, 'NGOs: The Professionalization of Politics', *Race and Class* vol. 2 no. 37 (1995), pp. 51–63.

Hammami Rema and Salim Tamari, 'The Second Uprising: End or New Beginning?', *Journal of Palestine Studies* vol. 30 no. 2 (2001), pp. 5–25.

Hamzah, Dyala (ed.), *The Making of the Arab Intellectual: Empire, Public Sphere and the Colonial Coordinates of Selfhood* (London: Routledge, 2013).

Hanieh, Adam, *Capitalism and Class in the Gulf Arab States* (New York: Palgrave Macmillan, 2011).

Hanieh, Adam, 'Egypt and the Gulf: Rethinking the Nature of Counter-Revolution', conference paper delivered at the Historical Materialism Conference 2012, 8 November 2012, SOAS, University of London, London.

Hannerz, Ulf, *Transnational Connections: Culture, People, Places* (London: Routledge, 1996).

Harbord, Janet, *Film Cultures* (London: Sage, 2002).

Harvey, Sylvia (ed.), *Trading Culture: Global Traffic and Local Cultures in Film and Television* (Eastleigh: John Libbey, 2006).

Hass, Amira, 'Israeli Restrictions Create Isolated Enclaves in West Bank', *Occupation Magazine – Life Under Occupation*, http://www.kibush.co.il/show_file.asp?num=12852 (website no longer live).

Haval, Václav (trans. and ed. Paul Wilson), *Open Letters: Selected Writings 1965–90* (New York: Vintage, 1992).

Hazbun, Waleed, *Beaches, Ruins, Resorts: The Politics of Tourism in the Arab World* (Minneapolis: University of Minnesota Press, 2008).

Heikal, Mohamed, *The Sphinx and the Commissar: The Rise and Fall of Soviet Influence in the Arab World* (New York: Harper Row, 1979).

Hejmadi, Santosh, 'Best Practices in Public Free Zones: Dubai Technology and Media Free Zone, United Arab Emirates', 2004, http://www.ifc.org/ifcext/fias.nsf/AttachmentsByTitle/BangladeshRT2Topic3Hejmadippt.pdf/$FILE/BangladeshRT2Topic3Hejmadippt.pdf (website no longer live).

Hendrick-Wong, Yuwa and Desmond Choong, *MasterCard Global Destination Cities Index*, MasterCard Worldwide Insights, http://newsroom.mastercard.com/wp-content/uploads/2014/07/Mastercard_GDCI_2014_Letter_Final_70814.pdf

Hennebelle, Guy and Khemaïs Khayati (ouvrage collectif sous la direction de), *La Palestine et le cinéma* (Paris: E100, 1977).

Hillauer, Rebecca (trans. Allison Brown *et al.*), *Encyclopedia of Arab Women Filmmakers* (Cairo: American University in Cairo Press, 2005).

Holbik, Karel, *The United States, The Soviet Union and the Third World* (Hamburg: Verlag Weltarchiv, 1968).

Holland, Patrick and Graham Huggan, *Tourists with Typewriters: Critical Reflections on Contemporary Travel Writing* (Ann Arbor: University of Michigan Press, 2003).

Hopwood, Derek, *Syria 1945–1986: Politics and Society* (London: Unwin Hyman, 1988).

Hourani, George F., *Arab Seafaring in the Indian Ocean in Ancient and Early Medieval Times* (Princeton, NJ: Princeton University Press, 1995).

Hughes, Howard, *Arts, Entertainment and Tourism* (Oxford: Butterworth Heinemann, 2000).

Hulme, Peter and Tim Youngs (eds), *The Cambridge Companion to Travel Writing* (Cambridge: Cambridge University Press, 2002).

Hussein, Taha (trans. Sidney Glazer), *The Future of Culture in Egypt* (Washington, DC: American Council of Learned Societies, 1954).

Ibn al-Athir, 'Izz al-Din (trans. D. S. Richards), *The Chronicle of Ibn al-Athir for the Crusading Period from al-Kamil fi'l-ta'rikh. Part 1, The Years 491–541/1097–1146, The Coming of the Franks and the Muslim Response* (Farnham: Ashgate, 2010a).

Ibn al-Athir (trans. D. S. Richards), *The Chronicle of Ibn al-Athir for the Crusading Period from al-Kamil fi'l-ta'rikh. Part 2, The Years 541–589/1146–1193: The Age of Nur al-Din and Saladin* (Farnham: Ashgate, 2010b).

Ibn Battutah (ed. Tim Mackintosh-Smith), *The Travels of Ibn Battutah* (Basingstoke: Picador, 2002).

Ibn Fadlan (trans. with commentary Richard N. Frye), *Ibn Fadlan's Journey to Russia* (Princeton, NJ: Markus Wiener, 2006).

Ibn Jubayr (trans. R. J. C. Broadhurst), *The Travels of Ibn Jubayr* (London: Jonathan Cape, 1952).

Ibn Khaldun (trans. N. J. Dawood) in Franz Rosenthal (abridged and ed.), *The Muqaddimah: An Introduction to History* (London: Routledge and Kegan Paul, 1978).

Ibn Khaldun (trans. Charles Issawi), *An Arab Philosophy of History: Selections from the Prolegomena of Ibn Khaldun of Tunis (1332–1406)* (Princeton, NJ: Darwin Press, 1987).

Iordanova, Dina with Ragan Rhyne (eds), *Film Festival Yearbook 1: The Festival Circuit* (St Andrews: St Andrews Film Studies, 2009).

Iordanova, Dina with Ruby Cheung (eds), *Film Festival Yearbook 2: Film Festivals and Imagined Communities* (St Andrews: St Andrews Film Studies, 2010).

Iordanova, Dina and Stefanie Van de Peer (eds), *Film Festival Yearbook 6: Film Festivals and The Middle East* (St Andrews: St Andrews Film Studies, 2014).

International Organization of Migration, *Arab Migration in a Globalized World* (Geneva: International Organization of Migration, 2004).

Ismael, Tareq Y., *The Communist Movement in the Arab World* (London: Routledge, 2005).

Isaac, Benjamin and Israel Roll, *Roman Roads in Judaea I: The Legio-Scythopolis Road* (Oxford: BAR International Series, 1982).

Jamal, Amal, *Media Politics and Democracy in Palestine: Political Culture, Pluralism, and the Palestinian Authority* (Brighton: Sussex Academic Press, 2005a).

Jamal, Amal, *The Palestinian National Movement: Politics of Contention, 1967–2005* (Bloomington: Indiana University Press, 2005b).

Jones, Clive and Ami Pedahzur (eds), *Between Terrorism and Civil War* (London: Routledge, 2005).

Juma, Abdulhamid, 'DIFF 2009 Opening Press Conference Speech of Abdulhamid Juma, Chairman, DIFF', delivered 6 December 2009.

Jumeirah Group, 'Future Plans', http://www.jumeirah.com/en/jumeirah-group/development/future-plans

Kanafani, Aida S., *Aesthetics and Ritual in the United Arab Emirates: The Anthropology of Food and Personal Adornment Among Arabian Women* (Beirut: American University of Beirut Press, 1983).

Kanafani, Ghassan (trans. Hilary Kilpatrick), *Men in the Sun and Other Palestinian Stories* (Boulder, CO: Lynne Rienner, 1999).

Kanna, Ahmed, *Dubai: The City as Corporation* (Minneapolis: University of Minnesota Press, 2011).

Kapiszewski, Andrzej, *Nationals and Expatriates: Population and Labour Dilemmas of the Gulf Cooperation Council States* (Reading: Ithaca Press, 2001).

Kaplan, Caren, *Questions of Travel: Postmodern Discourses of Displacement* (Durham, NC: Duke University Press, 1998).

Karsh, Efraim, *Soviet Policy Towards Syria Since 1970* (London: Macmillan, 1991).

Kass, Ilana, *Soviet Involvement in the Middle East: Policy Formulation, 1966–1973* (Boulder, CO: Westview Press, 1978).

Kaufman, Edy, Walid Salem and Julliette Verhoeven (eds), *Bridging the Divide: Peacebuilding in the Israeli–Palestinian Conflict* (Boulder, CO: Lynne Rienner, 2006).

Kaur, Raminder and John Hutnyk (eds), *Travel Worlds: Journeys in Contemporary Politics* (London: Zed Books, 1999).

Kay, Pandora, 'Cross-Cultural Research Issues in Developing International Tourist Markets for Cultural Events', *Event Management* vol. 8 no. 4 (2004), pp. 191–202.

Kernohan, R. D., *The Road to Zion: Travellers to Palestine and the Land of Israel* (Edinburgh: Handsel Press, 1995).

Khatib, Lina, *Filming the Modern Middle East: Politics in the Cinemas of Hollywood and the Arab World* (London: I.B.Tauris, 2006).

Khatibi, Abdelkebir, *Maghreb Pluriel* (Paris: Denoël, 1983).

Kovner, Milton, 'Soviet Aid to Developing Counties: A Look at the Record', in John W. Strong (ed.), *The Soviet Union Under Brezhnev and Kosygin* (New York: Van Nostrand Reinhold, 1971), pp. 61–74.

Krane, Jim, *City of Gold: Dubai and the Dream of Capitalism* (Basingstoke: Macmillan 2009).

Kumar, B. Ramesh, 'The UAE's Strategy Trade Partnership With Asia: A Focus on Dubai', *Middle East Institute*, 19 August 2013, http://www.mei.edu/content/uae%E2%80%99s-strategic-trade-partnership-asia-focus-dubai#_ftnref1

Laderman, David, *Driving Visions: Exploring the Road Movie* (Austin: University of Texas Press, 2002).

Laïdi, Zaki (ed.), *The Third World and the Soviet Union* (London: Zed Books, 1988).

Laidi-Hanieh, Adila, 'Destination: Jerusalem Servees, Interview with Emily Jacir', *Jerusalem Quarterly* vol. 40 (Winter 2009–10), pp. 59–67.

Laroui, Abdallah (trans. Diarmid Cammell), *The Crisis of the Arab Intellectual: Traditionalism or Historicism?* (Berkeley: University of California Press, 1976).

Leask, Nigel, *Curiosity and the Aesthetics of Travel Writing, 1770–1840: 'From an Antique Land'* (Oxford: Oxford University Press, 2002).

Leeuwen, Richard van, *The Thousand and One Nights: Space, Travel and Transformation* (London: Routledge, 2007).

Lein, Yehezkel (trans. Zvi Shulman), *Civilians Under Siege: Restrictions on Freedom of Movement as Collective Punishment* (Jerusalem: B'Tselem – The Israeli Information Center for Human Rights in the Occupied Territories, 2007).

Leo, Joannes (Africanus) (trans. Master Pory), *Observation Taken Out of John Leo His Nine Bookes* [sic] (London: Henrie Fetherstone, 1625).

Levinson, Marc, *The Box: How the Shipping Container Made the World Smaller and the World Economy Bigger* (Princeton, NJ: Princeton University Press, 2010).

Lewis, Reina, *Rethinking Orientalism: Women, Travel and the Ottoman Harem* (London: I.B.Tauris, 2004).

Leyda, Jay, 'Advanced Training for Film Workers: Russia', *Hollywood Quarterly* vol. 1 no. 3 (April 1946), pp. 279–86.

Lippard, Lucy R., *On the Beaten Track: Tourism, Art and Place* (New York: The New Press, 1999).

Loshitzky, Yosefa, 'Travelling Culture, Travelling Television', *Screen* vol. 37 no. 4 (Winter 1996), pp. 323–35.

Lu, Chin-Shan, Chun-Hsiung Liao and Ching-Chiao Yang, 'Segmenting Manufacturers' Investment Incentive Preferences for International Logistics Zones', *International Journal of Operations and Production Management* vol. 28 no. 2 (2008), pp. 106–29.

Maalouf, Amin, *The Crusades Through Arab Eyes* (London: Zed Books, 1984).

Macalister, Terry, 'Heathrow Airport Overtaken By Dubai as World's Busiest', *Guardian*, 31 December 2014, http://www.theguardian.com/uk-news/2014/dec/31/heathrow-airport-dubai-world-busiest

MacCannell, Dean, *Empty Meeting Grounds* (London: Routledge, 1992).

MacCannell, Dean, *The Tourist: A New Theory of the Leisure Class* (Berkeley: University of California Press, 1999).

Makimoto, Tsugio and David Manners, *Digital Nomad* (Chichester: John Wiley and Sons, 1997).

Malas, Muhammad and Rebecca Porteous, 'The Dream: Extracts from a Film Diary by Muhammad Malas', *Alif* vol. 5 (1995), pp. 208–28.

Mangan, John, Chandra Lalwani and Brian Fynes, 'Port-Centric Logistics', *International Journal of Logistics Management* vol. 19 no. 1 (2008), pp. 29–41.

Marché du Film, *Focus 2009: World Film Market Trends* (Cannes: Festival de Cannes, 2009).

Marx, Karl (trans. Martin Nicolaus), *Grundrisse: Foundations of the Critique of Political Economy* (London: Penguin, 1973).

Massey, Doreen and Pat Jess (eds), *A Place in the World? Places, Cultures and Globalization* (Milton Keynes: Open University Press, 1995).

Massey, Douglas, Joaquín Arango, Graeme Hugo, Ali Kouaouci, Adela Pellegrino and J. Edward Taylor, *Worlds in Motion: Understanding International Migration at the End of the Millennium* (Oxford: Clarendon Press, 1998).

Mauss, Marcel (trans. W. D. Halls), *The Gift: The Form and Reason for Exchange in Archaic Societies* (London: Routledge Classics, 2002).

McGuigan, Jim, *Rethinking Cultural Policy* (Maidenhead: Open University Press, 2004).

McLaurin, R. D., *The Middle East in Soviet Policy* (Lanham, MD: Lexington Books, 1975).

Meethan, Kevin, *Tourism in Global Society* (Basingstoke: Palgrave, 2001).

Mehta, Dalpat Singh, *Mass Media in the USSR* (Moscow: Progress, 1987).

Michaelsen, Scott and David E. Johnson, *Border Theory: The Limits of Cultural Politics* (Minneapolis: Minnesota University Press, 1997).

Mignolo, Walter D., *Local Histories/Global Designs: Coloniality, Subaltern Knowledges, and Border Thinking* (Princeton, NJ: Princeton University Press, 2000).

Miller, Jamie, *Soviet Cinema: Politic and Persuasion under Stalin* (London: I.B.Tauris, 2010).

Mitchell, Timothy, *Colonizing Egypt* (Berkeley: University of California Press, 1988).

Morinis, Alan (ed.), *Sacred Journeys: The Anthropology of Pilgrimage* (Westport, CT: Greenwood, 1992).

Moscardo, Gianna, 'Analyzing the Role of Festivals and Events in Regional Development', *Event Management* vol. 11 no. 1–2 (2007), pp. 23–32.

Naficy, Hamid (ed.), *Home, Exile, Homeland: Film, Media, and the Politics of Place* (London: Routledge, 1999).

Naficy, Hamid, *An Accented Cinema: Exilic and Diasporic Filmmaking* (Princeton, NJ: Princeton University Press, 2001).

Nasser, Jamal R. and Roger Heacock (eds), *Intifada: Palestine at the Crossroads* (New York: Praeger, 1990).

Nelson, Cary and Lawrence Grossberg (eds), *Marxism and the Interpretation of Culture* (Urbana: University of Illinois Press, 1988).

Netton, Ian Richard, *Al-Farabi and His School* (London: Routledge, 1992).

Netton, Ian Richard (ed.), *Golden Roads: Migration, Pilgrimage and Travel in Mediaeval and Modern Islam* (Richmond: Curzon Press, 1993).

Netton, Ian Richard (ed.), *Islamic and Middle Eastern Geographers and Travellers: Volume I, Medieval Geographers and Travellers* (London: Routledge, 2008a).

Netton, Ian Richard (ed.), *Islamic and Middle Eastern Geographers and Travellers: Volume II, The Travels of Ibn Jubayr* (London: Routledge, 2008b).

Netton, Ian Richard (ed.), *Islamic and Middle Eastern Geographers and Travellers: Volume III, The Travels of Ibn Battuta* (London: Routledge, 2008c).

Netton, Ian Richard (ed.), *Islamic and Middle Eastern Geographers and Travellers: Volume IV, The Post-Medieval and Early Modern Period* (London: Routledge, 2008d).

Nir, Amiram, *The Soviet–Syrian Friendship and Cooperation Treaty: Unfulfilled Expectations* (Tel Aviv: Jaffee Center for Strategic Studies, 1983).

Niranjana, Tegaswini, 'Alternative Frames? Questions for Comparative Research in the Third World', *Inter-Asia Cultural Studies* vol. 1 no. 1 (2000), pp. 97–108.

Norman, Julie M., *The Second Palestinian Intifada: Civil Resistance* (London: Routledge, 2010).

Nouryeh, Christopher, *Arab-Muslim Views of the West from the Ninth Century to the Twentieth: The Neglected Bridge Builders* (Lewiston: Edwin Mellen Press, 2005).

Obenzinger, Hilton, *American Palestine: Melville, Twain, and the Holy Land Mania* (Princeton, NJ: Princeton University Press, 1999).

Office of the Spokesman, *A Performance-Based Roadmap to a Permanent Two-State Solution* (Washington, DC: US Government, 2003).

Omri, Mohamed-Salah, *Nationalism, Islam and World Literature: Sites of Confluence in the Writings of Mahmud al-Mas'adi* (London: Routledge, 2010).

Orgeron, Devin, *Road Movies: From Muybridge and Méliès to Lynch and Kiarostami* (Basingstoke: Palgrave Macmillan, 2008).

Øvensen, Geri and Pål Sletten, *The Syrian Labour Market: Findings from the 2003 Unemployment Survey* (Oslo: FAFO, 2007).

Oxford Business Group, *The Report: Dubai 2007* (London: Oxford Business Group, 2009).

Oxford Business Group, 'Dubai Growth in Regional Trade', 8 May 2013a, http://www.oxford-businessgroup.com/news/dubai-growth-regional-trade

Oxford Business Group, *The Report: Dubai 2013* (London: Oxford Business Group, 2013b).

Palestinian Campaign for the Academic and Cultural Boycott of Israel, 'Palestinian Filmmakers, Artists and Cultural Workers Call for a Cultural Boycott of Israel', http://www.pacbi.org/boycott_news_more.php?id=315_0_1_0_C

Palestinian Central Bureau of Statistics, 'PCBS: Released the Results of the Annual Report on Transportation and Communication Statistics in the Palestinian Territory, 2006', http://www.pcbs.gov.ps/Portals/_pcbs/PressRelease/TRANSPA07E.pdf

Palestinian Cinema Group, 'The Palestinian Cinema and the National Question: Manifesto of the Palestinian Cinema Group', *Cinéaste* vol. 9 no. 3 (Spring 1979), p. 35.

Papastergiadis, Nikos, *The Turbulence of Migration: Globalization, Deterritorialization and Hybridity* (Cambridge: Polity Press, 2000).

Pennington-Gray, Lori and Andrew Holdnak, 'Out of the Stands and Into the Community: Using Sports Events to Promote a Destination', *Event Management* vol. 7 no. 3 (2002), pp. 177–86.

Picard, Robert G., 'Media Clusters: Local Agglomeration in an Industry Developing Networked Virtual Clusters', *Jonkoping International Business School Working Papers Series* vol. 3 (2008), pp. 1–16.

Pratt, Mary Louise, *Imperial Eyes: Travel Writing and Transculturation* (London: Routledge, 1992).

Qasim, Mahmud, *al-Film al-Riwa'i al-Suri (Syrian Fiction Films)* (Damascus: Publications of the Ministry of Culture, 2003).

Quinn, Bernadette, 'Arts Festivals and Sustainable Development in Ireland', *Journal of Sustainable Tourism* vol. 14 no. 3 (2006), pp. 288–306.

Qumsiyeh, Main B., *Popular Resistance in Palestine: A History of Hope and Empowerment* (London: Pluto Press, 2011).

Ramet, Pedro, *The Soviet–Syrian Relationship Since 1955* (Boulder, CO: Westview Press, 1990).

Ramos, Stephen J., *Dubai Amplified: The Engineering of a Port Geography* (Farnham: Ashgate, 2010).

Ramzi, Kamal, *Sinima al-Ahlam al-Da'i'a Qadaya w Aflam 'Arabiyya (Cinema of Lost Dreams: Issues in Arab Film)* (Damascus: Publications of the Ministry of Culture, 2003).

Rastegar, Kamran, *Literary Modernity Between the Middle East and Europe: Textual Transactions in Nineteenth Century Arabic, English and Persian Literatures* (London: Routledge, 2007).

Rastegar, Kamran, *Surviving Images: Cinema, War, and Cultural Memory in the Middle East* (New York: Oxford University Press, 2015).

Rihani, Ameen, *The Path of Vision: Pocket Essays of East and West* (New York: James T. White and Co., 1921).

Rihani, Ameen, *Around the Coasts of Arabia* (London: Constable and Co., 1930).

Rihani, Ameen (trans. Naji Oueijan), *Hymns of the Valleys* (Piscataway, NJ: Gorgias Press, 2002).

Ritman, Alex, 'Dubai Film Festival Scraps Major Industry Section, Focuses on Distribution', *The Hollywood Reporter*, 30 October 2014, http://www.hollywoodreporter.com/news/dubai-film-festival-scraps-major-745034

Roberts, David, *The Ba'th and the Creation of Modern Syria* (London: Croom Helm, 1987).

Roberts, Martin, '*Baraka*: World Cinema and the Global Culture Industry', *Cinema Journal* vol. 37 no. 3 (1998), pp. 62–82.

Robertson, George, Melinda Mash, Lisa Tickner, Jon Bird, Barry Curtis and Tim Putnam (eds), *Travellers' Tales: Narratives of Home and Displacement* (London: Routledge, 1994).

Robinson, Mike, David Picard and P. Long, 'Festival Tourism: Producing, Translating, and Consuming Expressions of Culture(s)', *Event Management* vol. 8 (2004), pp. 187–9.

Rojek, Chris and John Urry (eds), *Touring Cultures: Transformation of Travel and Theory* (London: Routledge, 1997).

Roy, Ananya and Aihwa Ong (eds), *Worlding Cities: Asian Experiments and the Art of Being Global* (Chichester: Wiley-Blackwell, 2011).

Rubiés, Joan-Pau, *Travel and Ethnology in the Renaissance: South India through European Eyes, 1250–1645* (Cambridge: Cambridge University Press, 2000).

Rumley, Dennis and Julian V. Minghi (eds), *The Geography of Border Landscapes* (London: Routledge, 1991).

Ruoff, Jeffrey (ed.), *Virtual Voyages: Cinema and Travel* (Durham, NC: Duke University Press, 2006).

Sabry, Tarik, *Cultural Encounters in the Arab World: On Media, the Modern and the Everyday* (London: I.B.Tauris, 2010).

Sabry, Tarik (ed.), *Arab Cultural Studies: Mapping the Field* (London: I.B.Tauris, 2012).

Said, Abdel Moghny, *Arab Socialism* (London: Blandford Press, 1972).

Said, Edward, *The World, the Text and the Critic* (London: Vintage, 1991).

Said, Edward W., *Culture and Imperialism* (New York: Knopf, 1994).

Said, Edward W., *Representations of the Intellectual* (New York: Vintage, 1996).

Said, Edward W., 'Archaeology of the Roadmap', *Al-Ahram Weekly* no. 642, 2003a, http://weekly.ahram.org.eg/2003/642/op10.htm

Said, Edward W., *Orientalism* (London: Penguin, 2003b).

Saidi, Habib, 'Opposite Balcony, Comb Teeth and the Comprador Class: Ethnography of the Establishment of Tourism in a Mediterranean Resort', conference paper delivered at 'Traditions and Transformations: Tourism, Heritage and Cultural Change in the Middle East and North Africa Region', 4–7 April 2009, Amman, Jordan.

Salazkina, Masha, 'Moscow–Rome–Havana: A Film-Theory Road Map', *October* no. 139 (Winter 2011), pp. 97–116.

Salih, Tayeb (trans. Denys Johnson-Davies), *Season of Migration to the North* (London: Penguin Classics, 1969/2003).

Salloum, Jayce and Molly Hankwitz, 'Occupied Territories: Mapping the Transgressions of Cultural Terrain', *Framework* vol. 43 no. 2 (2002), pp. 85–103.

Salti, Rasha, 'Critical Nationals: The Paradoxes of Syrian Cinema', *Kosmorama* vol. 237 (2006), pp. 1–17. Also published in Salti (ed.), *Insights into Syrian Cinema: Essays and Conversations with Contemporary Filmmakers* (New York: AIC Film Editions/Rattapallax Press, 2006).

Salti, Rasha (ed.), *Insights into Syrian Cinema: Essays and Conversations with Contemporary Filmmakers* (New York: AIC Film Editions/Rattapallax Press, 2006).

Sampler, Jeffrey and Saeb Eigner, *Sand to Silicon: Achieving Rapid Growth Lessons from Dubai* (London: Profile Books, 2003).

Sargent-Baur, Barbara N. (ed.), *Journeys Toward God: Pilgrimage and Crusade* (Kalamazoo, MI: Medieval Institute, 1992).

Schmid, Heiko, *Economy of Fascination: Dubai and Las Vegas as Themed Urban Landscapes* (Berlin: Gebrüder Borntraeger, 2009).

Schnitzer, Luda, Jean Schnitzer and Marcel Martin (eds) (trans. David Robinson), *Cinema in Revolution* (London: Secker and Warburg, 1973).

Scott, Walter, *The Talisman* (London: Collins Clear-Type Press, 1825/n.d.).

Seth, Shobhit, 'Dubai: Growth Through Diversification', *Investopedia*, 10 November, 2014, http://www.investopedia.com/articles/investing/111014/dubai-growth-through-diversification.asp

Shafik, Viola, *Arab Cinema: History and Cultural Identity* (Cairo: American University in Cairo Press, 1998).

Shaheen, Jack, *Reel Bad Arabs: How Hollywood Vilifies a People* (New York: Olive Branch Press, 2001).

Shannon, Jonathan Holt, *Among the Jasmine Trees: Music and Modernity in Contemporary Syria* (Middletown, CT: Wesleyan University Press, 2006).

Shapiro, Michael J., *Cinematic Geopolitics* (London: Routledge, 2009).

Sharabi, Hisham (ed.), *Theory, Politics and the Arab World: Critical Responses* (London: Routledge, 1990).

Shields, Rob, *Places on the Margin: Alternative Geographies of Modernity* (London: Routledge, 1991).

Smith, Valene L. (ed.), *Hosts and Guests: The Anthropology of Tourism*, Second Edition (Philadelphia: University of Pennsylvania Press, 1989).

Smolansky, Oles M., *The Soviet Union and the Arab East Under Khrushchev* (Lewisburg, PA: Bucknell University Press, 1974).

Souyad, Azzedine, 'The Soviet Union in Syria's Foreign Policy 1970–1980: Ideology Versus Regime Interest' (PhD thesis, Exeter University, 1999).

Stam, Robert, 'Beyond Third Cinema: The Aesthetics of Hybridity', in Anthony R. Guneratne and Wimal Dissanayake (eds), *Rethinking Third Cinema* (London: Routledge, 2003), pp. 31–48.

Stein, Rebecca L. and Ted Swedenburg (eds), *Palestine, Israel, and the Politics of Popular Culture* (Durham, NC: Duke University Press, 2005).

Strain, Ellen, *Public Places, Private Journeys: Ethnography, Entertainment, and the Tourist Gaze* (New Brunswick: Rutgers University Press, 2003).

Stringer, Julian, 'Global Cities and the International Film Festival Economy', in Mark Shiel and Tony Fitzmaurice (eds), *Cinema and the City: Film and Societies in a Global Context* (Oxford: Blackwell, 2001), pp. 134–44.

Suisman, Doug, Steven Simon, Glenn Robinson, C. Ross Anthony and Michael Schoenbaum, *The Arc: A Formal Structure for a Palestinian State* (Santa Monica, CA: RAND Corporation, 2005/2007).

Suter, Brigitte, 'Labour Migration in the United Arab Emirates Field Study on Regular and Irregular Migration in Dubai', Master's dissertation, 2005, http://dspace.mah.se/bitstream/handle/2043/3161/?sequence=1

Taha, Hesham, 'Tawfiq Saleh (1926–2013)', *Ahram Online*, 29 August 2013, http://english.ahram.org.eg/News/80208.aspx

Tawil-Souri, Helga, 'Coming Into Being and Flowing Into Exile: History and Trends in Palestinian Film-Making', *Nebula* vol. 2 no. 2 (2005), pp. 113–40.

Tawil-Souri, Helga, 'Cinema as the Space to Transgress Palestine's Territorial Map', *Middle East Journal of Culture and Communication* vol. 7 (2014), pp. 169–89.

Taylor, John, *A Dream of England: Landscape, Photography and the Tourist's Imagination* (Manchester: Manchester University Press, 1994).

Taylor, Richard and Ian Christie (eds), *Inside the Film Factory: New Approaches to Russian and Soviet Cinema* (London: Routledge, 1991).

Tickner, F. J., *Technical Cooperation* (London: Hutchinson University Library, 1965).

Tobing Rony, Fatimah, *The Third Eye: Race, Cinema, and Ethnographic Spectacle* (Durham, NC: Duke University Press, 1996).

Toukan, Hanan, 'On Being the Other in Post-Civil War Lebanon: Art in Processes of Contemporary Cultural Production', *Arab Studies Journal* vol. XVIII no. 1 (Spring, 2010), pp. 118–61.

Toukan, Hanan, 'Art, Aid, Affect: Locating the Political in Post-Civil War Lebanon's Contemporary Cultural Practices' (PhD dissertation, School of Oriental and African Studies, University of London, 2011).

Turki, Fawaz, *Soul in Exile: Lives of a Palestinian Revolutionary* (New York: Monthly Review Press, 1988).

Turner, Victor and Edith Turner (eds), *Image and Pilgrimage in Christian Culture* (New York: Columbia University Press, 1996).

Twain, Mark, *The Complete Travel Books of Mark Twain. The Early Works: The Innocents Abroad and Roughing It* (Garden City, NY: Doubleday & Co., Inc., 1966).

United Nations High Commission for Refugees, *UNHCR Syria Fact Sheet*, July 2010, http://www.unhcr.org/4c907abd9.html

United Nations High Commission for Refugees, *2011 UNHCR Country Operations Profile – Syrian Arab Republic*, 2011, http://www.unhcr.org/cgi-bin/texis/vtx/page?page=49e486a76

United Nations Relief and Works Agency, 'Number of Registered Refugees', http://www.un.org/unrwa/refugees/pdf/reg-ref.pdf (website no longer live).

United Nations Relief and Works Agency for Palestine Refugees in the Middle East 'Statistics', http://www.unrwa.org/etemplate.php?id=253

Urry, John, *The Tourist Gaze: Leisure and Travel in Contemporary Studies* (London: Sage, 1990).

Urry, John, *Sociology Beyond Societies: Mobilities for the Twenty-First Century* (London: Routledge, 2000).

Van Den Abbeele, Georges, *Travel as Metaphor: From Montaigne to Rousseau* (Minneapolis: University of Minnesota Press, 1992).

Various, *Cinémas des Pays Arabes* (Paris: Cinémathèque française/Cinémathèque algérienne, n.d).

Vizitei, Maria, 'From Film School to Film Studio: Women and Cinematography in the Era of Perestroika', in Lynne Attwood (ed.), *Red Women on the Silver Screen: Soviet Women and Cinema from the Beginning to the End of the Communist Era* (London: Pandora Press, 1993), pp. 215–24.

Wedeen, Lisa, *Ambiguities of Domination: Politics, Rhetoric, and Symbols in Contemporary Syria* (Chicago: University of Chicago Press, 1999).

Weiner, Annette B., *Inalienable Possessions: The Paradox of Keeping-While-Giving* (Berkeley: University of California Press, 1992).

Weizman, Eyal, *Hollow Land: Israel's Architecture of Occupation* (Verso: London, 2007).

Wilkinson, John, with Joyce Hill and W. F. Ryan, *Jerusalem Pilgrimage 1099–1185* (London: Hakluyt Society, 1988).

Wolff, Janet, 'On the Road Again: Metaphors of Travel in Cultural Criticism', *Cultural Studies* vol. 7 no. 2 (1993), pp. 224–39.

Woll, Josephine, 'The Russian Connection: Soviet Cinema and the Cinema of Francophone Africa', in Francoise Pfaff (ed.), *Focus on African Films* (Bloomington: Indiana University Press, 2004), pp. 223–40.

World Bank, 'Public Data', http://www.google.ca/publicdata/explore?ds=d5bncppjof8f9_&met_y=sp_pop_totl&idim=country:SYR:IRQ:SAU&hl=en&dl=en

World Port Source, 'Port of Jebel Ali: Port Commerce', http://www.worldportsource.com/ports/commerce/ARE_Port_of_Jebel_Ali_1423.php

World Shipping Council, 'About the Industry: World Top 50 Container Ports', http://www.world-shipping.org/about-the-industry/global-trade/top-50-world-container-ports

World Tourism Organization, *UNWTO Tourism Highlights 2014*, http://www.e-unwto.org/doi/pdf/10.18111/9789284416226

World Tourism Organization, 'Why Tourism?', http://www2.unwto.org/content/why-tourism

Wright, Thomas (ed.), *Early Travels in Palestine, Comprising the Narratives of Arculf, Willibald, Bernard, Saewulf, Sigurd, Benjamin of Tudela, Sir John Maundeville, de la Brocquière, and Maundrell* (London: Henry G. Bohn, 1848).

Yared, Nazik Saba, *Arab Travellers and Western Civilization* (London: Saqi, 1996).

Yoshimoto, Mitsuhiro, 'The Difficulty of being Radical: The Discipline of Film Studies and the Postcolonial World Order', *boundary* 2 vol. 18 no. 3 (1991), pp. 242–57.

Zadeh, Travis, 'The Wiles of Creation: Philosophy Fiction, and the '*Ajā'ib* Tradition', *Middle Eastern Literatures* vol. 13 no. 1 (April 2010), pp. 21–48.

Zéki, Ahmed, *Mémoire sur les moyens propres à déterminer en Égypte une renaissance des lettres arabes* (Cairo: Imprimerie M. Roditi, 1910).

Zubaida, Sami and Richard Tapper (eds), *A Taste of Thyme: Culinary Cultures in the Middle East* (London: I.B.Tauris, 2000).

Zuhur, Sherifa, *Asmahan's Secrets: Woman, War and Song* (Austin: Center for Middle Eastern Studies, University of Texas at Austin, 2000).

Index

ART (television channel) 138, 150

Arte 110, 111

Asad, Talal 87

Ascent of Rain, The 59

Asia 26, 27, 122, 123, 135, 136, 138, 140, 141, 144, 148, 159; East Asia 122, 158; South Asia 26, 119, 132, 154, 158, 171; West Asia 26

as-Saffar, Muhammad 71, 126, 142

Atlas, Natacha 89

Audiard, Jacques 157

authenticity 6, 9, 12, 18, 31, 35, 48

autobiography and the autobiographical 14, 15, 20, 21–2

Avatar 134

Awwad, Nahed 90, 92, 94, 97–8, 101, 103

B'Tselem 97

Ba'athism 39, 42, 52, 58–60, 66, 68, 69, 73, 80; Ba'ath Party 42, 49, 58; Ba'ath Party Constitution 39, 52, 59, 62, 73

Bacha, Julia 139

Baghdad 26, 122

Bakri, Mohammad 109

Balata refugee camp 97, *see also* refugee camps

Balibar, Étienne 105

Banana 133

Basra 1, 3, 165

Battle of Algiers, The 53

Bazmee, Anees 125

Be Quiet 94

becoming 'Palestinized' **82–3**, 114

Bedirxan, Wiam Simav 39

Behdad, Ali 21–2

Beirut 1, 37, 70, 128

Ben-Arieh, Yehoshua 91

Benjamin, Walter 77

Bentley, Jerry H. 160

Berlin Wall 42

Bethlehem 94

Bird, Brad 27

Bitar, Salah al-Din 59

Bollywood 125, 135, 154

borders 8–9, 12, 15, 21, 23, 36, 37, 44, 49, 53, 63, 71–4, 79, 80, 87, 88, 91, 105, 110, 111, 122, 123, 140, 146, 148, 150, 159, 161, 163, 164; border gnosis/border thinking 15, 74; Kuwait's borders 1, 164, 166; Iraq's borders 94, 113, 166; Palestine's borders (including those illegally imposed by the state of Israel) 82, 83, 84, 86, 89, 94, 96, 97, 100, 105, 112, 113, 114, 139; Syria's borders 56, **71–8**; the United Arab Emirates' borders 28, 160

Bosra 75

Bourne Legacy, The 150

Brezhnev, Leonid 75

Britain 28, 123, 133, 135, 158; British citizenship 9, 22; British film industry 61, 153; British imperialism 51, 71, 95, 122

brokerage 124, 142, 143, 146

Bucharest 54

Budrus 139

Bulgaria 48, 49

bureaucracy and bureaucratic procedures 9, 42, 43, 48, 49, 56, 123, 132, 142

Burj Al Arab hotel *120*, 160

Burj Khalifa 27, 162

Busan International Film Festival 132

Butros, Raymond 42, 47, 65, 78

bypass roads, *see* roads

Cairo 41, 42, 45, 46, 106, 126

Cameron, James 134

Canaan 82, 94

Cannes International Film Festival 54, 135, 138, 143

capital 6, 8, 25, 44, 62, 72, 83, 111, 131, 133, 139, 146, 148, 150, 151, 152, 154, 155, 158, 159, 161, 164, 165

capitalism 7, 19, 24, 27, 30, 42, 44, 49, 72, 50, 54, 86, 92, 98, 106, 108, 123, 126, 131, 132, 133, 134, 135, 138, 139, 146, 158, 159, 160, 161, *see also* anti-capitalism

cars 1, 89, 92, 93, 97, 99, 103, 104, 106–7, 108, 112, 113, 114, 158

Carthage Film Festival 2, 54

Cartier, Carolyn 130

casualisation 52, 66, *see also* labour

Centre National de la Cinématographie 108, 110

Chahine, Youssef 31

Chakrabarty, Dipesh 20

charity 108, 109, 110, *see also* aid, *see also* humanitarianism, *see also* NGOs and NGOisation

checkpoints 4, 8, 84, 85, 86, 89, 91, 92, 93, 94, 97, *99*, 100, 103–4, 105, 107, 112, 114

chiaroscuro 72, *65*

Fez 21
Film and TV School of the
    Academy of the
    Performing Arts, *see*
    FAMU
*Film Essay on the Euphrates
    Dam* 70
film festivals 2, 3, 6, 8, 35,
    55, 83, 110, 111, 120–1,
    122, 123, 124, 127, 130,
    134, 137, 138, 140, 142,
    144, 146, 157, 158, *see
    also* Busan International
    Film Festival, *see also*
    Cannes International
    Film Festival, *see also*
    Carthage Film Festival,
    see also Damascus Film
    Festival, *see also* Dubai
    International Film
    Festival, *see also* London
    Palestine Film Festival,
    see also Moscow Film
    Festival, *see also* Toronto
    International Film
    Festival
film schools 13, 40, 42, 47,
    50–1, 53, 61, 109, *see also*
    FAMU, *see also* VGIK, *see
    also* university
Film Studies 13, 14, 22, 29,
    40, 82, 128, 130, 140
first-person narration, *see*
    autobiography
Fischer, Moshe 95
Fistful of Dollars, A 113
Fix Me 137
Flamhaft, Ziva 93
Flaubert, Gustave 15
flexible labour, *see* labour, *see*
    casualisation
Flood in Baath Country, A
    70
folk culture 48, 68, 70, 91
Ford Transit 92, 94, 98, 113,
    115

foreign direct investment 28,
    136, 150, 151, 152, 161
Forrester, Chris 154
Foucault, Michel 105
Fourth Room, The 94
France 2, 19, 31, 45, 46, 51,
    55, 57, 70, 71, 74, 76, 81,
    83, 111, 113, 137, 142,
    154; French colonialism
    31, 51, 56, 67, 68, 71
free ports, *see* ports
free trade, *see* trade
free zones 8, 28, 36, 120,
    123, 124, 125, 132, 133,
    142, **147–52**, 154, 155,
    156, 159, 161, 162, *see
    also* Dubai Duty Free
    Zone, *see also* Knowledge
    Village, *see also* Logistics
    City, *see also* Media City,
    see also Studio City, *see
    also* Technology and
    Media Free Zone
    Authority, *see also* Tecom
French New Wave 56
full employment 63, *see also*
    security
funadiq 128–9, 141, 142, *see
    also* hotels
funduq, see funadiq

Gaghan, Stephen 150
gas 36, 53–4, 91, 94, 141, *see
    also* oil, *see also* petrol
gated communities 96, 151,
    159
Gaza 82, 84, 87, 96, 97, 101,
    103, 105, 110, 111, 131
GCC, *see* Gulf Cooperation
    Council
GDR, *see* German Democratic
    Republic
Genet, Jean 101, 113
genre 14, 86, 111, 112, 113,
    115, 116, 117, 162; film
    genres 8, 86, 111, 112,

genre (*cont.*)
    113, 114, 115, 116, 117,
    145; writing genres 14,
    15, 45, 60, 77, 162; *see
    also rihla, see also* road
    (block) movies, *see also*
    road movies
German Democratic Republic
    (East Germany) 47, 49
Gertz, Nurith 85, 97, 100
Get on the Bus 115
Gethsemane 84
Ghosh, Amitav 5
Gilroy, Tony 150
global capital and capitalism,
    see capital and capitalism
global hip hop 116
Global North 13, 17, 19, 25,
    34, 35, 111, 115, 136,
    156, 159
Global Palestine, *see*
    becoming 'Palestinized'
Global South 31, 124, 136,
    138, 141, 159, *see also*
    third world
Going for a Ride? 92, 94, *95,*
    103
Golan Heights 36, 71, 72–3,
    75–7
Golden Voyage of Sinbad, The
    126
Gordon, Avery 87
Gregory, Derek 29, 30
Guinness, Alec 25, *26*
Gulf, the (Arabian/Persian)
    1, 2, 4, 35, 119, 122, 126,
    132, 136, 138, 141, 143,
    153, 155, 157, 158, 160,
    161, 163
Gulf Cooperation Council
    138, 140
Gunning, Tom 6

hajj 13
Hama 42
Hamas 139